COMPUTERS AND CREATIVITY

Editor

Ursula Fashingbauer

scitus
academics

Computers and Creativity
Edited by **Ursula Fashingbauer**

This Book is Printed on Acid-Free Paper. ♾

ISBN: 9781681178486
Library of Congress Control Number: 2017948875

SCITUS Academics LLC,
616, Corporate Way, Suite 2, 4766,
Valley Cottage, NY 10989

www.scitusacademics.com

Notice

Printed in United States of America.

Preface

Creative computing covers the interdisciplinary area at the cross-over of the creative arts and computing. Issues of creativity include knowledge discovery. Computers have also had a reflective impact in popularizing and disseminating mathematical insights that would be other-wise limited to a small community of scholars For instance, although Poincare and Hadamard almost 100 years before had a truly modern considerate of chaos and sensitive dependence on initial conditions, it wasn't until the prevalent availability of computers permitted easy numerical simulations that these ideas led to a wholesale shift in our view of dynamical systems, deterministic chaos, and the loss of predictability. It goes without saying that computers are invaluable tools in carrying out research. Computers have always been important in helping to formulate hypotheses and check theoretical calculations—even when a computer was a person. There is a general harmony that computers can transform and inspire human creativity in considerably different ways than any other artificial or human made device. The range of possibilities is obvious in this volume, which contains many exciting efforts describing the computer's use in developing art practices, music composition and performance.

This volume brings a broad range of views on computers and creativity. It proposes a number of questions that we think are important for future research in relation to computers and creativity. It shows how computers can enhance human creativity; whether computer art can ever be properly valued; what computing can tell us about creativity; and how creativity and computing can be brought together in learning. The contributed chapters are written by leading researchers, theorists and artists working in artificial intelligence, generative art, creative computing, and cybernetics, the book examines the relationship between computation and creativity from both analytic and practical perspectives. The book will appeal to students, researchers in artificial intelligence practicing artists and musicians, and any reader generally interested in understanding how computers can impact upon creativity.

Table of Contents

CHAPTER 1

An Approach to Computational Creativity, Images from a Computer's Mind

Dario Lanza

Computer Science and Programming at Massachusetts Institute of Technology (MIT) , Professor of Digital Rendering, Universidad Rey Juan Carlos, Madrid , Render specialist working on the development of Maxwell, the state-of-the-art in rendering technology, Master of Engineering, Madrid Polytechnic University, Spain

ABSTRACT

Do computers need to express their creativity? Do computers think of electric poems?

The term lovotics encompasses the exploration of evolved robotic behavior assuming the development of their own emotional universe, and the different dimensions of the relationship human-robot appeared from that point. This paper explores the idea of the computer, not just as the mute tool at the service of our creativity, but instead as a prospect creative entity itself, taking its first steps as it attempts to imitate the creativity it sees we are able. What would it do? The idea of a computer trying to create competent poetry is certainly worth our consideration.

Keywords: Creative computing; lovotics; artificial creativity; development of human-like emotions; algorithmic writing

EXPLORATION

Contrary to what true current artificial intelligence systems like AARON [1] are proposing – being images actually generated by the computer intelligence imitating the human drawing– these images show a more stylish and personal view of how the first attempts of a computer to imitate our creative ability would be. I explore an intelligence more interested in playing with meanings, concepts And the ideas of the things –more like conceptual artist did– and the new ideas that can emerge from the juxtaposition of similar or opposite concepts, rather than simply depicting the things themselves. The results of that combination of concepts could be meaningless if the computer fails in its associations, silly in other attempts, but definitely promising and suggestive in some others.

These first creations would be in the form of very basic rhyming couplets and elemental visual verses, as the computer can only play with the very few concepts it manage to understand: networking, the technology of communication, chips, instant messages, the electronic devices that we plug into it... These are the only cultural references it has at its disposal. With these few ingredients making up its limited universe, my guess is that it lovotic computer would come up with something like this: A collection of visual verses, half-failure, halfsuccess; some a naïve reminder of the silly poems of childhood, but others which hint at a more sophisticated intelligence. Whether the computer aims at self-expression or to impress us –its audience– is not clearly revealed.

In a similar way as the affective algorithms [2], the artificial intelligence would employ probabilistic mathematical algorithms -mainly combinatorial routines- to juxtapose the few concepts that configure its small semantic universe two by two, in the search of an eventual new meaning. Although there are many areas where the computer brain is stronger than ours [3], the innocence of these images are expressing the first attempts of using its immature creativity, also noticeable in the absence of irony, subtlety or criticism usual in our mature expression. In some ways it reminds our human creativity, but more particularly our children's first school creations for Father's Day. Surely, in a short time and if the evolution of the computer brain were similar to ours, it will evolve, producing more ambitious and sophisticated creations and will develop the capability to express itself in an entirely new way of its own, but until then it first starts learning from an imitative process, like all of us one day did. I'm particularly interested in portraying the momentum of that crucial first step forward.

Rendering the Creative Attempts

Formally the "visual poems' take the form of 3D renders which have been polished to the absolute Photorealism –100% computer-generated realities attempting to look like 100% real objects. It is as if the computer devoted all its energy to the imitation of the analogous world outside its screen. To fully explore this concept, using the digital medium and creating the images within a computer seemed the logical choice: the medium fitting the concept until they both become indistinguishable.

To create the images, after filling hundred of sketches searching for ideas, objects and views that would work, I selected the best ones and used a 3D modelling software to build the objects themselves. Textures, materials and lighting were created with special attention, as the final effect the images produce rely heavily on the realism and on display impossible objects but in a way that your eye would hardly accept they don't exist. I used an unbiased renderer to achieve a photo realistic feel, while a monochrome tone gives them a note of nostalgia.

The images suggest rather than dictate an interpretation, inviting us into a state of free association about our electronic culture. They await the viewer's own sense of meaning.

The connections between creativity and art are suggested by the computer itself: **FIGURES 1-7**.

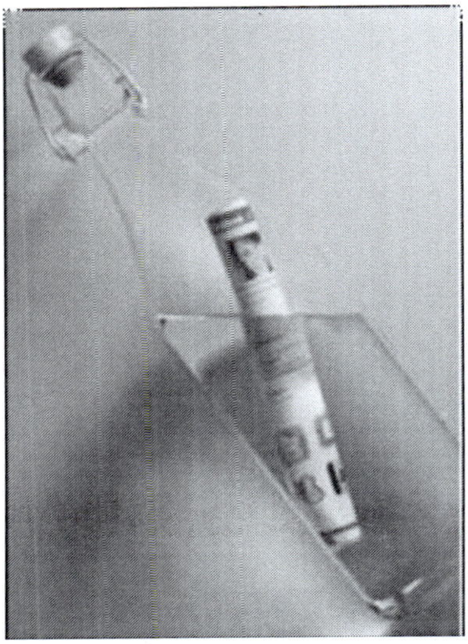

FIGURE 1: Electric Poetry, opus 12 a message in a bottle, where the message is a Facebook post. The sea appears inside the bottle, instead of outside.

FIGURE 2: Electric Poetry, opus 11 the carrier pigeon is both messenger and message. Today, in the throes of the digital revolution, we will have to face the challenge of teaching the computer on beauty.

FIGURE 3: Electric Poetry, opus 21, typefaces inside a first aids kit, the news as the cure. ABC Museum of Drawing, Illustration and Contemporary Art. Madrid.

Maybe more successfully than other images in this series, the picture Darwin 2.0 connects the concepts of history, evolution, technology and art more closely and with a deeper poetical sense.

Labelled and pinned like the insects in the collection of a naturalist, a vacuum valve and a silicon chip are displayed there to show the evolution of the technology and of the electronic "bugs" during the last century. The silicon chip, that in fact looks like a beetle, provides a metaphorical point in the image.

FIGURE 4: Electric Poetry, opus 22 the image that closes the series, playing with the concepts of realism and pessimism. Hyperrealism in form, but hyperpessimism in concept: the glass deforms the reality making us see it always half-empty.

A Final Word

This project is the result of an exploration about the suggestive idea of what would a computer do if it one day started to think creatively.

I picture a computer that watches at us from the other side of the glass screen feeling a certain admiration about our creative capacity, which is the only feature its super strong brain can not do.

At this point, and if the machine somehow takes that step forward, I don't see it performing an exuberant colorful creative catharsis, but timidly replicating some of the attitudes and roles it sees for us, in my case in the form of producing visual rhymes mimicking the way we create double meanings and ironic concepts by the juxtaposition of two other simpler concepts. In addition to that, the computer could only play with the few concepts it manage to understand, like networking, communication technologies or the electronic devices we use to plug into it as its small conceptual universe.

The way children produce their first creative works –poems, drawings– at school trying to behave like adults do, sometimes failed, sometimes silly, always naïve but loaded with innocence, effort and pride, were the main inspiration for the design of the works themselves.

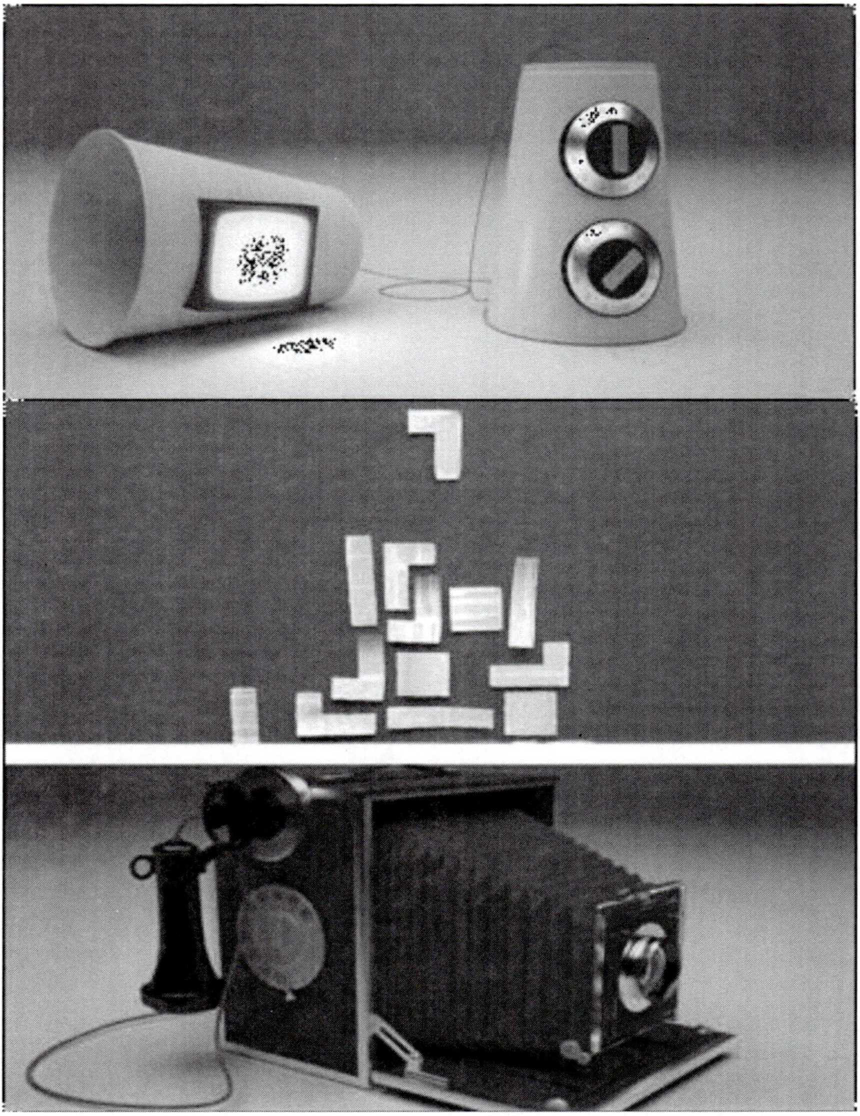

FIGURE 5: Electric Poetry, opus 06 : smartphone, a photographic camera mounted on a telephone.

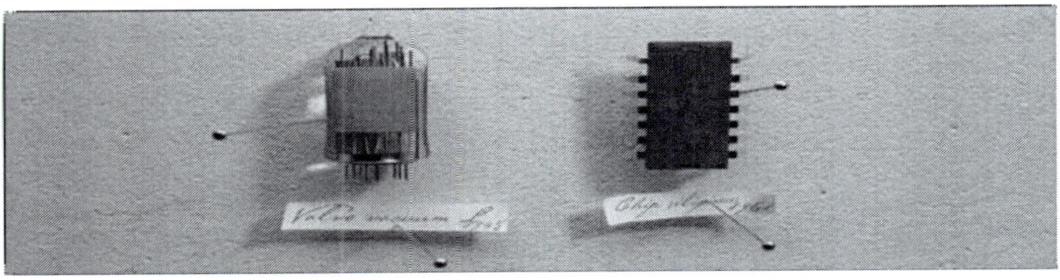

FIGURE 6: Evolution and technology, Darwin 2.0, 2009. C-print, unique. 21×40 cm.

FIGURE 7: Electric Poetry, opus 05: videogames, interpreted like old paper handmade toys.

FIGURE 8: Electric Poetry, opus 02: eBook

The results can be comical in some cases; they may invite a smile, but perhaps only a wry half-smile. For they also represent the first aspirations of a computer to be like us, here we see a gesture of admiration –like what a young brother feels for his older brother– but one that opens up the intriguing possibility that those aspirations could become reality. And I'm interested in that particular point: Once the creative dreams of the computer were realized, would there be a glimmer of admiration for its human creators left? Or definitely not?

I invite to consider the beauty and innocent meaning of each image, but also reflect on the implications of the evolution of the artificial brain and the artificial soul behind them.

Are these visual couplets merely playful? Or is it just that we don't understand them entirely yet?

REFERENCES

1. Cohen H "AARON. Genetics and Culture", Design Media Arts 98T.
2. Samani HA, Saadatian E (2012) A multidisciplinary artificial intelligence model of an effective robot. International. Journal of Advanced Robotic Systems, InTech 1-11.
3. Samani HA, Kwan JT, et al. (2012) Towards robotics leadership: An analysis of leadership characteristics and the roles robots will inherit in future human society. Interactive and Digital Media Institute, National University of Singapore, 160-165.

CHAPTER 2

Creativity in Innovation Design: The Roles of Intuition, Synthesis, and Hypothesis

Toshiharu Taura[a] and Yukari Nagai[b]

[a] *Department of Mechanical Engineering, Kobe University, Kobe, Japan;*

[b]*School of Knowledge Science, Japan Advanced Institute of Science and Technology, Nomi, Japan*

ABSTRACT

In a highly technologically-advanced mature society, a shift in focus occurs from quantitative to qualitative innovation. This paper discusses this shift from the perspective of design. We address these future topics by showing our views or opinions, as well as by referring to some theories and arguments that have appeared up to the present in this regard. Concretely, we postulate that the design process comprises the stages of intuition or gut feeling, followed by analysis or synthesis, finally leading to the design outcome. Assuming that one of the factors that determines design creativity is whether the purpose or goal of a design is inside or outside of the design process, we also examine the aspects of these conditions. We then suggest the idea of an Innovation Design process model composed of two cycles: analytical design creation and synthetic design creation. In the former, a design solution is explored to fulfill a purpose or goal pre-assigned to a product from outside, leading to quantitative innovation. In the latter, hypothesization starting with an intuition or gut feeling leads to the design of a breakthrough product, leading to qualitative innovation. Finally, we present an outline of the design school (workshop) conducted based on these thoughts.

Keywords: Innovation design, creativity, intuition, synthesis, hypothesis

1. INTRODUCTION

Through products (in this paper, all outcomes of design, including industrial products, plants, and buildings, are referred to as 'products'), science and technology[1]1. In this paper, the term 'science and technology' is used as a generic term for an understanding of the basic principles of physical phenomena and the basic knowledge required to apply such understanding.View all notes have thus far protected human beings from unfortunate natural disasters and rendered our daily lives more convenient and abundant. Today, however, our relationship with science and technology has become more complicated, as evidenced by cases in which science and technology, while they continue to advance and bring about material fulfillment and machine-based civilization, also jeopardize humanity. For this reason, the question as to what products should be produced is likely to become more important in the future. As a way to seek an answer to this question, we discuss focusing on a shift from quantitative to qualitative innovation by showing our views or opinions on this shift from the perspective of design, as well as by referring to some theories and arguments that have appeared up to the present in this regard.

First of all, let us clarify the meaning of the term 'Innovation Design' that we use here. The word 'design' is in frequent use today: it is used in such terms as industrial design and mechanical design, as well as corporate design and career design. As for 'innovation,' in this paper we focus on changes brought about in society by science and technology and discuss them from the perspective of design. In this sense, we call the act of bridging science and technology and society[2]2. In this paper, the term 'society' refers to the sphere in which products are used.View all notes through products (Taura, 2016Taura, T. (2016). *Creative design engineering*. Waltham, MA: Elsevier.) 'Innovation Design,' for which 'design' or 'designing,' the act of thinking up product structures and shapes, is carried out.

Present-day innovation design is confronted with the challenge of figuring out how to continue to design breakthrough products that society wants (in this paper, breakthrough products refer to products that demonstrate high levels of originality and practicality). Before examining this challenge, let us first ask where design should begin, in other words, where the starting point of design should be placed. The illustration of Innovation Design shown above (Figure 1) suggests the following three possibilities.

Figure 1. Innovation design.

Firstly, design can begin with the recognition of societal changes. This involves listening carefully to product users' voices. This is 'needs-led' design. The introduction of a new product into society is often preceded by market surveys to study user needs and other marketing activities. This is only proper, considering that users make the final evaluation of the product and decide whether to buy it or not. A method for detecting latent needs has recently been proposed which involves a designer infiltrating an area or community in which a given product is likely to be used to 'empathize' with its members and thus identify their latent needs (http://dschool.stanford.edu/). The notion of 'user innovation' has also been proposed, meaning that users lead innovation (Faulkner & Runde, 2009Faulkner, P., & Runde, J. (2009). On the identity of technological objects and user innovations in function. *Academy of Management Review, 34*, 442–462.

Secondly, design can begin with discovery or development in science and technology. This is 'seeds-led' design. In fact, when basic knowledge is acquired about a new material, information technology and so forth, it is often the case that products are sought out to which the new knowledge can be applied. For example, in the case of carbon fiber, its structure and manufacturing methods were first developed, and the scope of its application has rapidly expanded, now including even aircraft fuselages. In general, the term 'innovation' is most often used in this sense (that is, technological innovation).

Thirdly, design can begin with the generation of a product idea aimed at bridging needs and seeds. This design process comprises, in the first place, the formulation of a new concept of product based on existing science and technology, followed by research and development in basic science and technology or assessment to evaluate the acceptability of the new product in society, as the necessity arises. As we will discuss below in Sections 2 and 3.5, some breakthrough products that have had great impact on society have been designed in this manner. This approach is not about ignoring seeds or needs, but about placing the starting point of design on product concept generation.

These three approaches are not mutually exclusive, but they can be applied in parallel. Both seeds and needs are essential for design. In actual cases of breakthrough design, the three approaches are often integrated. While recognizing this, we examine them separately in this paper because we believe it important and necessary to discuss what should be most emphasized at the beginning of the process of realizing a breakthrough product: fulfilling needs, utilizing seeds, or bridging the two. In the first approach, in which design begins with understanding needs, resultant products will probably be useful for society. However, this approach, located far away from the context of science and technology, is less likely to generate ideas for products that embody the latest science and technology. On the other hand, the second approach, in which design begins with research on, or development of, seeds, runs the risk of failing to produce products that meet user needs because this approach is located far away from the social context. For this reason, we will develop our argument here by making the third approach central.

In the following sections, we will discuss types of creativity in Innovation Design (Section 2) and various aspects of creative thinking in Innovation Design (Section 3). Based on these discussions, we will propose an Innovation Design process model (Section 4). Finally, we will present an outline of a design school (workshop) that was conducted on the basis of the thoughts discussed in this paper (Section 5).

2. TYPES OF CREATIVITY IN INNOVATION DESIGN

The generation of ideas for breakthrough products requires creativity. What kind of creativity is required, then, for Innovation Design? In this paper, we will further develop our previous discussion on design creativity (Taura & Nagai, 2012Taura, T., & Nagai, Y. (2012). *Concept generation for design creativity – A systematized theory and methodology*. London: Springer.) from the perspective of Innovation Design. We believe that there are two major types of creativity.

The first type of creativity is the out-of-the-box creativity that generates ideas that depart from what is believed to be common sense (conventional, preconceived notions). This type of creativity is typically demonstrated in the solution of the famous nine-dot problem: Nine dots are arranged in the form of a square, and you must connect all of them with four straight lines without lifting your pen from the paper and without tracing the same line more than once, as shown below (Figure 2). The key to solving this problem is whether or not you realize that you are allowed to draw lines outside the square area. In other words, an essential part of this type of creativity lies in successful elimination of preconceived notions. This is a matter of fixation (we will take this up again under Section 3.2). In design research as well, fixation is an important subject that has drawn much attention. An experiment was conducted to study how design results are influenced when designers (experiment participants) are shown design examples beforehand (Jansson & Smith, 1991Jansson, D. G., & Smith, S. M. (1991). Design fixation. *Design Studies, 12*, 3–11. doi:10.1016/0142-694X(91) 90003-F,). This type of creativity is manifested in many actual breakthrough products. HondaJet[3]3. HondaJet has an over-the-wing engine mount design, which departs from the industry's conventional style.View all notes is a representative example (http://world.honda.com/HondaJet/).

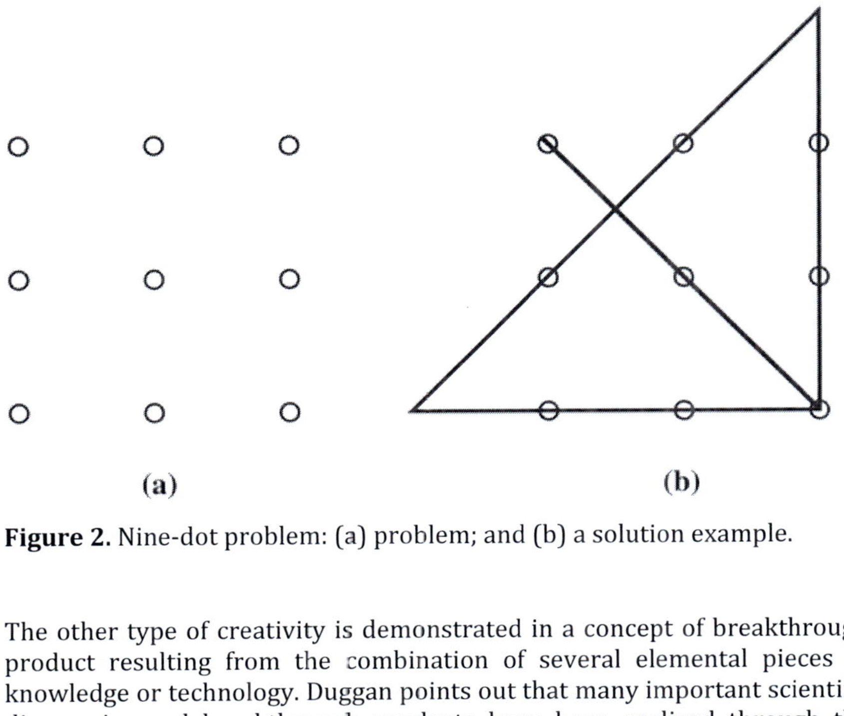

Figure 2. Nine-dot problem: (a) problem; and (b) a solution example.

The other type of creativity is demonstrated in a concept of breakthrough product resulting from the combination of several elemental pieces of knowledge or technology. Duggan points out that many important scientific discoveries and breakthrough products have been realized through the combination of several existing elements of knowledge or technology, citing such examples as the achievements of Copernicus and Newton, who selectively recombined several elements of existing knowledge into a new whole; the original Macintosh computer, a product of combining graphical user interfaces (GUI), then under development at Xerox, with a small computer frame; and Bill Gates' Microsoft achievement, in which Gates put together four existing elements which he had not invented: the Altair, its

8080 chip, BASIC, and the PDP-8 (Duggan, 2013 Duggan, W. (2013). *Strategic intuition: The creative spark in human achievement*. New York, NY: Columbia University Press.). Christensen defines innovation as connecting seemingly unrelated ideas, while Steve Jobs said, 'Creativity is just connecting things' (Dyer, Gregersen, & Christensen, 2011Dyer, J., Gregersen, H., & Christensen, C. M. (2011). *The innovator's DNA: Mastering the five skills of disruptive innovators*. Boston, MA: Harvard Business Review Press.). We have been conducting a systematic study on how two weakly related concepts can be combined to generate creative ideas (Taura, 2016Taura, T. (2016). *Creative design engineering*. Waltham, MA: Elsevier. ; Taura & Nagai, 2012Taura, T., & Nagai, Y. (2012). *Concept generation for design creativity – A systematized theory and methodology*. London: Springer.). This type of creativity that derives from 'connecting things' is not entirely unrelated to the first type of creativity, which derives from elimination of certain fixations as stated above (in some cases, conventional ways of connecting things are preconceived notions). Nevertheless, in this paper we consider these two types of creativity to be clearly different. This is because we believe that the way of thinking that enables the combination of several elemental pieces of knowledge or technology is free association-oriented and dynamic (as explained in Section 3.2), while the type of creativity that is centered on elimination of fixation is mostly concerned with setting a static viewpoint.

Keeping in mind the difference between these two types of creativity, we approach creativity in Innovation Design in this paper.

3. ASPECTS OF CREATIVE THINKING IN INNOVATION DESIGN

In this section, we will first discuss the concepts of quantitative and qualitative innovation, and then various aspects of creative thinking along the axes of intuition or gut feeling, analysis or synthesis, design solution or hypothesis, and whether the purpose or goal of a product to be designed is inside or outside the design process.

3.1. Quantitative or qualitative innovation

For decades up to the present, consumers have demanded greater convenience, and society has responded by pursuing efficiency. Concretely, automobiles, electric appliances, computers, power generators, and other products have been provided at steadily lower prices. To do so, increasingly specific and reliable design knowledge has been sought out. Consequently, modularization, standardization, and automation have advanced. The results of these developments have been so remarkable that our lives today seem almost totally free of perceptible inconvenience. Let us call this type of innovation, which contributes to augmenting quantifiable efficiency 'quantitative innovation.'

However, efficiency-oriented technology brings society quantitative change, not qualitative change. Let us call the type of innovation that contributes to society's qualitative change 'qualitative innovation.' Qualitative innovation gives birth to products that realize new lifestyles or lead to the creation of new cultures. For example, portable music players have enabled people to enjoy listening to recorded music anywhere, even while traveling by train, unlike in the past when it was only possible through the use of sound systems in fixed locations. The popularization of portable music players has changed the way people enjoy music, as well as how they spend their time on trains. These changes have in turn had cultural impact, influencing the way music exists in society.

Some voice the view that negative effects of the materialistic society brought about by science and technology have been offset by culture, arts, and design in the narrow sense of the term (arrangement of colors and shapes). Nevertheless, science and technology have also given birth to new cultural and artistic expressions, as in the example of the portable music player. We discuss below the possibility of exploration of human sensibilities by science and technology.

Let us think of illuminated night views as an example. We find such light-ups beautiful, but they are not something that exists in the natural world. An artificially created beautiful night view touches us emotionally. The same can be said of the Japanese sword. For its clear, pure, and mysterious beauty, the Japanese sword is nowadays appreciated and traded as a work of art. Yet, it is a product manufactured with highly refined specialized techniques, including heating, hammer-forging, and hardening. How is it possible that an artificially manufactured object moves our hearts? It seems that the way we feel our hearts resonating with night illuminations and the Japanese sword differs from the emotion we experience when viewing splendid natural scenery or beautiful cherry blossoms in full bloom (Georgiev, Nagai, & Taura, 2013Georgiev, G. V., Nagai, Y., & Taura, T. (2013). *Understanding the bases of design impressions of natural or artificial: Survey of cognition in different regions.* Proceedings of the 60th Annual Conference of JSSD 2013, Tsukuba, Japan.). If so, this means that science and technology has created a kind of emotion that we have never experienced before. In other words, sensibilities left unexplored have been awakened by science and technology. In fact, historically we know that the development of new science and technologies, such as bronze casting and building methods, has produced sculptures, religious edifices, and other products of new styles one after another, promoting arts and culture.

We can use the above discussion to explain why some new products are widely used. The pinch-in/pinch-out manipulations on the screen of a smartphone (using thumb and finger, moving them together or apart on the screen to modify screen display size) are not manipulations that humans perform in the natural world, but we can perform them quite naturally. We have only recently come to adopt these manipulations as a result of technological development. Doesn't this mean that the smartphone has not only realized convenience and operational efficiency but also broadened the scope of what feels natural for us, thus offering a new meaning to society?

The above discussion gives us a hint towards promoting qualitative innovation. That is, it suggests the necessity of designing products that broaden the scope of sensibilities and what feels natural for us by utilizing the latest science and technology.

3.2. Intuition or gut feeling

Intuition or gut feeling is said to play an important role in decision-making. Steve Jobs spoke of the importance of believing in one's intuition, saying, 'And most important, have the courage to follow your heart and intuition' (Jobs, 2005Jobs, S. (2005). *His 2005 commencement address at Stanford University.*). The importance of intuition or gut feeling in sophisticated decision-making has been discussed by many authors (Duggan, 2013Duggan, W. (2013). *Strategic intuition: The creative spark in human achievement.* New York, NY: Columbia University Press. ; Gigerenzer, 2008 Gigerenzer, G. (2008). *Gut feelings: The intelligence of the unconscious.* London: Penguin Books. ; Gladwell, 2006 Gladwell, M. (2006). *Blink: The power of thinking without thinking.* London: Penguin Books.).

What, then, is intuition or gut feeling?

A dictionary definition (www.oxforddictionaries.com/definition/english/) describes 'intuition' as 'the ability to understand something instinctively, without the need for conscious reasoning,' and 'gut feeling' as 'a feeling or reaction based on an instinctive emotional response rather than considered thought.'

Numerous studies have been carried out on the phenomena of intuition (e.g., Sinclair, 2011Sinclair, M. (Ed.). (2011). *Handbook of intuition research.* Cheltenham: Edward Elgar.,). These studies discuss intuition in connection with such notions as holisticity, analytical process, unconscious thought, decision-making, tacit knowledge, problem solving, expertise, and experience.

In the domain of design research, intuition or gut feeling has also been attracting attention. For example, a study collected characteristics of intuitive processes in design (Badke-Schaub & Eris, 2014Badke-Schaub, P., & Eris, O. (2014). A theoretical approach to intuition in design: Does design methodology need to account for unconscious processes? In A. Chakrabarti & L. Blessing (Eds.), *An anthology of theories and models of design* (pp. 353–370). London: Springer.10.1007/978-1-4471-6338-1,), and intuition was discussed in connection with experientially formulated mental models such as schemata and scripts (Durling, 1999 Durling, D. (1999). *Intuition in design – A perspective on designer's creativity.* Bulletin of 4th Asian Design Conference: International Symposium of Design Science, Nagaoka, Japan.).

Duggan points to the utility of 'strategic intuition,' with which while pragmatically touching on existing elements, you organically combine them in a flash of insight for a new discovery, compared to 'expert intuition,' which is effective in solving similar problems faster and faster by recognizing their patterns as you get better at your job (Duggan, 2013Duggan, W. (2013). *Strategic intuition: The creative spark in human achievement.* New York, NY: Columbia University Press.).

Thus far, the terms 'intuition' and 'gut feeling' are not used strictly separately. In fact, the intuition mentioned by Jobs and Duggan seems to contain aspects that are closer to gut feeling.

In view of the above, in this paper, we define 'intuition' as 'that which enables instantaneous decision-making following patterns recognized based on one's experience' and rename it 'experiential intuition,' and 'gut feeling' as 'feeling how something is or how something is related to another, based on one's sensibility' and rename it 'associative intuition.' Henceforth, the terms 'experiential intuition' and 'associative intuition' are used as thus defined.

Considering preconceived notions as one form of experiential knowledge, fixation, elimination of which is necessary for the first type of creativity discussed in Section 2, can be viewed as one manifestation of experiential intuition. In resolving the nine-dot problem presented above, elimination of fixation happens in a flash of insight. Thinking along this line, it can be said that experimental intuition itself can, in fact, hinder creativity in some cases.

The second type of creativity, on the other hand, can be viewed as creativity related to associative intuition, which can also be understood from the perspective of free association, as illustrated below.

We conducted a computer simulation of the process of generating new ideas by combining two weakly related concepts.[4]4. Figure 3 shows two networks formed from our experiment, in which participants were instructed to produce a new design concept by synthesizing the two concepts of 'ship' and 'guitar.' The networks were generated by virtually connecting the two words 'ship' and 'guitar' and a set of words that the participants used to explain the design outcomes, using a concept dictionary containing hierarchically structured words.View all notes The simulation results revealed that the design outcomes with more originality (that is, the two weakly related concepts were successfully combined) involved more intricately intertwined and expanded associations than did those with less originality (Taura et al., 2012 Taura, T., Yamamoto, E., Fasiha, M. Y. N., Goka, M., Mukai, F., Nagai, Y., & Nakashima, H. (2012). Constructive simulation of creative concept generation process in design: A research method for difficult-to-observe design-thinking process. *Journal of Engineering Design, 23*, 297–321.

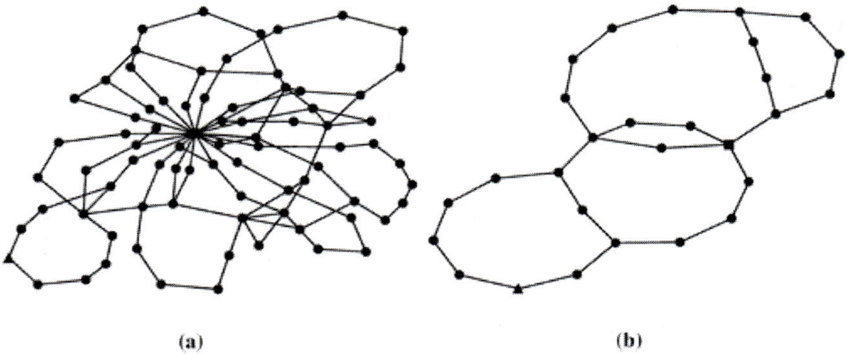

Figure 3. Networks of associations in the process of idea generation: (a) process with more originality; and (b) process with less originality in the design outcome.

Using a similar method, we conducted another simulation[5]5. Figure 4 shows the two virtual impression networks formed by virtually connecting, using a concept dictionary, all the combinations of two words selected from among the words used by participants in the experiment to express their impressions of various cups that they were shown.View all notes of the process of forming impressions from various stimuli. We obtained results indicating that forming impressions from stimuli that a participant liked involved far more intricately intertwined and expanded associations than from those formed from stimuli that the same participant did not like (Taura, Yamamoto, Fasiha, & Nagai, 2011Taura, T., Yamamoto, E., Fasiha, M. Y. N., & Nagai, Y. (2011). Virtual impression networks for capturing deep impressions. In J. Gero (Ed.), *Design computing and cognition '10*(pp. 559–578). London: Springer.10.1007/978-94-007-0510-4,) (Figure 4).

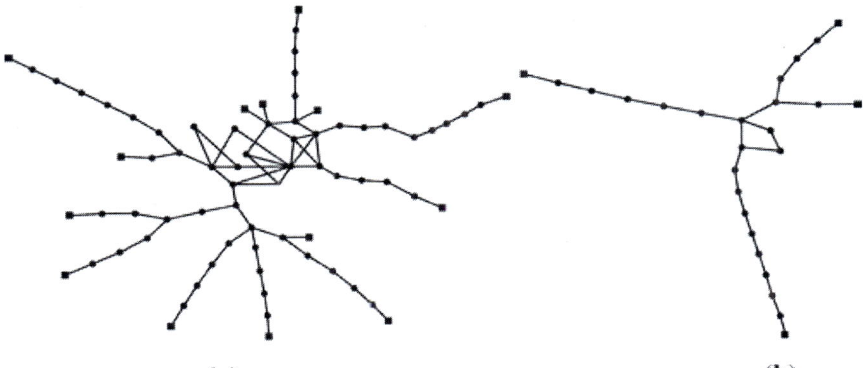

Figure 4. Networks of association in the process of impression formation: (a) formed from a cup that a participant liked; and (b) formed from another cup that the same participant disliked.

These results indicate that the process of forming good impressions and the process of coming up with good ideas by combining weakly related concepts are based on an essentially identical mechanism. It is believed that this mechanism is related to the dynamic nature of associations that expand while they are intricately intertwined, and not to the static nature of associations centering around particular concepts such as 'star' and 'rose.' That is, pleasant sensations that we feel, such as the states of heart resonating to beautiful music or heart dancing due to creating something, are not mere reactions to particular seeds (stimuli), but they are resonances to the expansion and complexity of (free) associations, and the mechanism acting as a tuning fork-like resonator for this is assumed to exist in our heart.

From the above, we believe that the tuning fork-like mechanism of resonance mentioned above is at the source of associative intuition. This may be the 'gut' of 'gut feeling' or the 'heart and intuition' in the words of Jobs. We also believe that when an idea is connected with another (as in free association) in the way the tuning fork resonates, the connection manifests itself in a flash of insight.

As a summary of this section, we can say that a flash of insight in experiential intuition is the leap that accompanies elimination of fixation, and a flash of insight in associative intuition, the leap that is achieved when things are connected via sensibility (or resonance to sensibility).

3.3. Analysis or synthesis

Design process is said to be composed of analysis and synthesis. 'To analyze' is to understand the nature of something that already exists by breaking it down into several parts or constituent characteristics. 'To synthesize' is to combine various things that already exist into something that does not yet exist. For example, decomposing a physical substance increasingly minutely into molecules, atoms, and particles to investigate its properties is analysis. On the other hand, constructing a new machine with various components is synthesis. It is said that, while synthesis requires analysis, merely knowing how to analyze is insufficient to synthesize. Why?

One reason is found in the relationship between the whole and its parts. In holism (www.oxforddictionaries.com/definition/english/holism), the whole is regarded as greater than the sum of its parts. In other words, the whole cannot be reproduced simply by putting its decomposed components back together. What does this mean? In mechanical design, for example, an assembly is complete when the components are put together. Isn't this assembly then a 'whole'? This question can be answered with the notion of 'emergence,' which is advocated by Polanyi (1983Polanyi, M. (1983). *The tacit dimension*. Gloucester: Peter Smith.). He wrote, 'The upper [level of reality] relies for its operation on the laws governing the elements of the lower one in themselves, but these operations of it are not explicable by the laws of the lower level.' He explained this with the examples of four levels: a town, houses, bricks, and raw materials. This means that workings at the upper level differ from those at the lower level, as in the way, for example, while an automobile's performance may come down to the performance of its engine and other components, merely getting an engine designer, a tire designer, and so on and so forth to work does not necessarily result in a good automobile design.

The difference between analysis and synthesis can also be explained by the difference in the knowledge structures (Yoshikawa & Taura, 1997Yoshikawa, H., & Taura, T. (1997). Process knowledge of general design theory. In T. Taura, T.Kayama, M. Ito, & H. Yoshikawa (Eds.), *Topologies of technological knowledge* (pp. 91–106). Tokyo: University of Tokyo Press. (in Japanese).). Knowledge obtained from analysis represents an orderly structure from which categorical ambiguities are strictly excluded. For example, an analysis of automobile engine performance involves obtaining quantitative data, which can be placed and compared on real number lines and expressed as a knowledge structure decomposed into direct sums (Figure 5(a)). Knowledge required for synthesis is not like this. As demonstrated by smartphones featuring functions allowing photo-taking, recording and playback, and other functions, a new concept is often generated when several existing elements are combined. The knowledge structure for synthesis must have overlaps (Figure 5(b)). These overlaps never result solely from analysis, however thoroughly it may be conducted. Overlaps are formed when elements of knowledge obtained from analysis (entities and their properties, expressed as elements and subsets) are rearranged and restructured so as to produce overlaps.

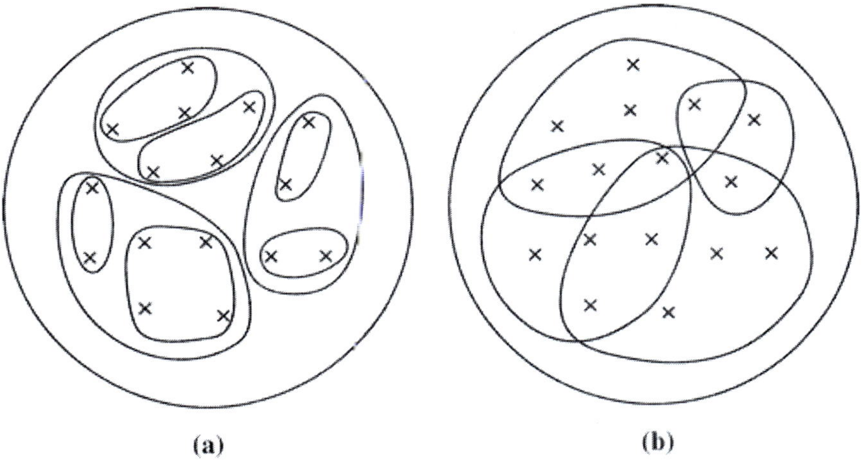

Figure 5. Different knowledge structures: (a) analysis; and (b) synthesis.

Let us put the above discussion in relation with our discussion in Section 2. Analysis requires a prefixed viewpoint. It should be noted, however, that analysis may not be adequately performed if an old viewpoint (of preconceived notions) is maintained. This means that analysis is related to the first type of creativity, while the second type of creativity is synthesis itself.

3.4. Design solution or hypothesis

Various expressions are used to refer to design outcome. In engineering design, it is often called 'design solution.' This is probably because engineering design is in most cases understood as problem solving, that is, finding a solution to a given problem. Meanwhile, mechanical, architectural or artistic design outcome can be perceived as 'hypothesis' (Yoshikawa, 1997Yoshikawa, H. (1997). A new paradigm of engineering. In T.Taura, T. Kayama, M. Ito, & H.Yoshikawa (Eds.), *Topologies of technological knowledge* (pp. 3–21). Tokyo: University of Tokyo Press. (in Japanese).) because design outcome is believed to derive from abduction, and not from deduction. Here is an overview of the difference between abduction and deduction.

Deduction is the reasoning that derives specific knowledge from general or universal knowledge. Syllogism is a typical example of deduction. Yonemori (1992Yonemori, Y. (1992). *Semiology of Peirce*. Tokyo: Keiso Shobo. (in Japanese).) stated that deduction only involves taking up an already stated fact as the premise and restating it in conclusion, illustrating this with the example of obtaining the solutions $x = 5$ and $y = -4$ of the equations $x + y = 1$ and $2x + y = 6$. The intention of this example becomes clear when the equations are graphically expressed. The solutions of two equations are also the coordinates of the point at which two straight lines cross. Once the two lines are drawn on a graph, their cross-point is determined automatically which has always been implicitly contained in the two equations. Solving equations can be likened to making explicit the cross-point that is implicitly contained in the equations.

Abduction, on the other hand, is the reasoning by which we discover hypotheses.

In abduction, something is reasoned that differs from what is directly observed. Let us contemplate what 'hypotheses' are in this context. Based on the arguments of Peirce and Poincaré (Poincaré, 1902Poincaré, H. (1902). *La science et l'hypothèse* [Science and hypothesis]. Paris: Flammarion. ; Yonemori, 1992Yonemori, Y. (1992). *Semiology of Peirce*. Tokyo: Keiso Shobo. (in Japanese).), the term 'hypothesis' can be classified as follows:

- •Firstly, a hypothesis can be a 'cause'; for example, a physician diagnosing a patient's disease or a detective identifying a suspect is hypothesizing.
- •Secondly, a hypothesis can be an 'explanation', such as a law of nature.
- •Thirdly, a hypothesis can be a 'temporary fix'; it is also called a working hypothesis, such as an auxiliary line, including a medium line used in geometry to prove that the two angles of an isosceles triangle are the same.

Note that a hypothesis of a cause can be obtained deductively by collecting a large number of examples. Similarly, in some cases, a hypothesis as an explanation can be obtained inductively based on phenomena. However, the likes of the laws of Newtonian mechanics and auxiliary lines cannot be obtained deductively. In this sense, they can be considered as 'authentic' hypotheses. If prerequisites for a design can be reproduced in a laboratory or a desired design outcome can be achieved by improving on an existing product, design can be performed deductively by analyzing the problem.

Meanwhile, designing a product that has never existed before requires the creation of a 'authentic' hypothesis.

In view of the above, different expressions for design outcome can be understood as resulting from the difference in the way design process is perceived, whether it is deductive or abductive.

Meanwhile, the term 'design solution' premises that a certain design outcome already exists (for example, an existing product) and implies focus on optimizing the performance, cost or some other attributes of the existing design outcome, whereas the term 'hypothesis' implies focus on adopting a temporary fix with the intention of ultimately discovering a novel product, although its possibility of existing is yet to be confirmed. As implied in a phrase like 'solving the problem correctly,' the validity of a solution is often attributed to the correctness of the procedure used to arrive at the solution (for example, correct calculation of material strength). The validity of a hypothesis, on the other hand, cannot be determined solely based on procedural correctness, and other data are usually required (for example, user evaluation of the product).

To sum up the above, the different expressions, 'design solution' and 'hypothesis,' point to the difference in notions of design, whether it is viewed as the act of solving a given problem, for which the pursuit of optimality through procedural correctness is required, or it is viewed as the act of finding a temporary fix with no guarantee of its correctness, from which the discovery of an unknown novel product is expected.

In connection with our discussion in Section 2, the nine-dot problem, presented to illustrate the first type of creativity, requires a solution, while a concept generated with the second type of creativity should be an (authentic) hypothesis. Along this line of thought, we can say that 'design solution' is related to the first type of creativity, and 'hypothesis,' the second type.

3.5. Product purpose/goal: outside or inside the design process?

There are two major styles of Innovation Design. In one of them, the purpose or goal of a product to be designed is given in advance, for example as in the case in which a product design is commissioned by a party that also provides product specifications. In some such cases, product specifications are determined based on user needs. In the second style of Innovation Design, the purpose or goal (specifications) of a product becomes clear as its design process progresses. Many systematic design methodologies belong to the first style (e.g., Pahl & Beitz, 1995Pahl, G., & Beitz, W. (1995). *Engineering design: A systematic approach*. Berlin: Springer.). However, many of the actual design processes known to have produced breakthrough products are of the second style (Duggan, 2013Duggan, W. (2013). *Strategic intuition: The creative spark in human achievement*. New York, NY: Columbia University Press.). For example, in the cases of Gates and Jobs mentioned in Section 2, several elemental pieces of knowledge or technology were combined, but not to realize their desired product that would satisfy a pre-defined purpose or goal. It was the combination of elemental pieces of knowledge or technology that led them to find their product purpose and goal (specifications). We will further discuss this in Section 4.

The two styles of Innovation Design are different in that the act of determining the product purpose or goal is found either outside or inside the design process. From the perspective of systems theory, this can be paraphrased as whether or not design constitutes a self-referential system.

Let us now look back on the discussion in Section 2. In most cases, the first type of creativity is mobilized when the purpose or goal of the solution is given from outside, in the way the nine-dot problem is presented. On the other hand, the second type of creativity is usually at work when it is impossible to know exactly what functions (purpose or goal) the product-to-be will have until elemental pieces of knowledge or technology are actually combined. A predetermined purpose or goal can set restrictions on designing, and it is difficult to freely try various combinations while respecting the restrictions. Therefore, in many cases in which the second type of creativity is involved, the product purpose or goal becomes clear only as the design process progresses.

4. INNOVATION DESIGN PROCESS MODEL

Based on the above, a process model of Innovation Design comprising two cycles can be drawn up (Figure 6; the numbers are the same in the figure and the text).

In one of the cycles, (1) a product purpose/goal is given from outside design, based on which a product concept (provisional design solution) is generated through the process of (2) experiential intuition, (3) analysis, and (4) finding design solution, in this order. The product concept is then subjected to (5) evaluation to check that it satisfies the purpose or goal, and (6) revision is performed,[6]6. A flash of insight in experiential intuition is deemed to occur in the process of revising preconceived notions

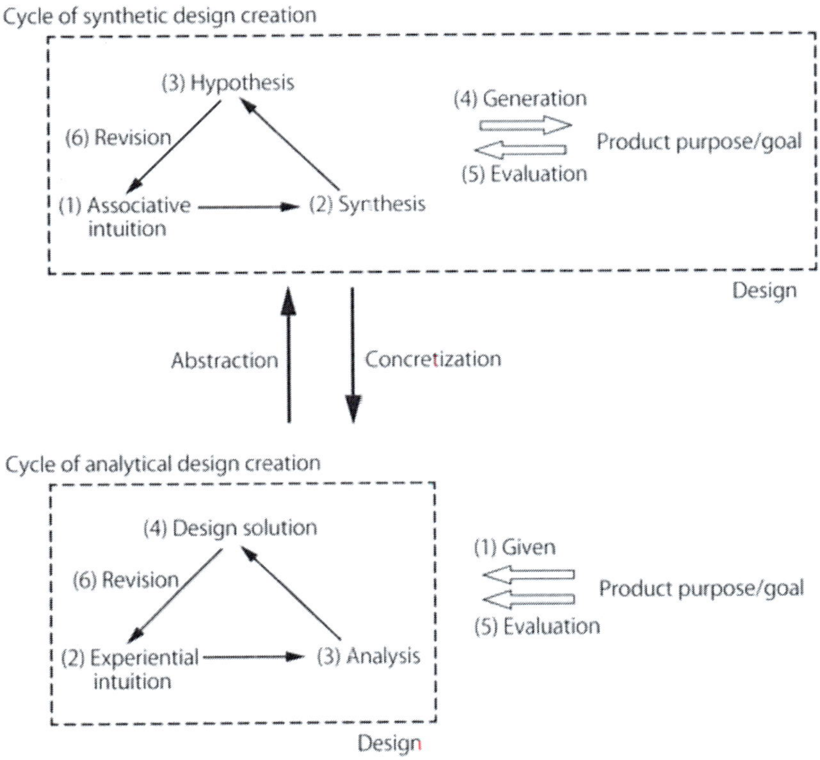

Figure 6. Innovation design process model.

(eliminating fixation).View all notes if necessary, to finally arrive at the optimal concept (design solution). In the other cycle, design begins with (1) associative intuition,77. A flash of insight in associative intuition is deemed to occur in the process of (1) or (6).View all notesfollowed by (2) synthesis and (3) discovering hypothesis. Then, (4) a product purpose/goal is found, and from this perspective the product concept (provisional hypothesis) is subjected to (5) evaluation, and (6) revision is performed as the necessity arises. Finally, an unknown concept (hypothesis) is discovered. In this paper, we call the former 'cycle of analytical design creation,' and the latter, 'cycle of synthetic design creation'; the creativity that is related to analytical design creation 'analytical design creativity,' and the creativity related to synthetic design creation, 'synthetic design creativity.' The two cycles respectively correspond to the types of 'analytical concept generation' and 'synthetic concept generation' discussed in the previous work (Taura, 2016Taura, T. (2016). *Creative design engineering*. Waltham,

MA: Elsevier.), and 'problem-driven phase' and 'inner sense-driven phase' discussed in our previous work (Taura & Nagai, 2012Taura, T., & Nagai, Y. (2012). *Concept generation for design creativity – A systematized theory and methodology*. London: Springer.). The term 'associative intuition' used in this paper covers the concepts of 'inner motive' in (Taura, 2016Taura, T. (2016). *Creative design engineering*. Waltham, MA: Elsevier.) and 'inner sense' in (Taura & Nagai, 2012Taura, T., & Nagai, Y. (2012). *Concept generation for design creativity – A systematized theory and methodology*. London: Springer.).

In the cycle of analytical design creation, an existing problem is analyzed from a viewpoint intuitively (experientially) fixed in consideration of the (product) purpose or goal assigned in advance from outside to arrive at an optimal design solution. This is a problem-solving-oriented design flow (Pahl & Beitz, 1995Pahl, G., & Beitz, W. (1995). *Engineering design: A systematic approach*. Berlin: Springer.). The problem-solving-oriented design that pursues optimality is effective in improving product performance, reducing cost, and achieving other quantifiable results. It is therefore considered conducive to quantitative innovation. Because of its contents (experiential intuition, analysis, design solution), the cycle of analytical design creation can be linked with the first type of creativity presented in Section 2. In this cycle, elimination of preconceived notions triggers a flash of insight, which leads to breakthrough product ideas. As an example of a product realized in a cycle of analytical design creation, HondaJet as mentioned above can be cited again. In the HondaJet project, Michimasa Fujino, in charge of development, pondered deeply, hoping to achieve the goal of securing a larger interior space in aircraft. He had a flash of insight and came up with the novel idea of placing the engines over the wings. After repeated rigorous analyses through simulation, the optimal shape (design solution) was obtained.

In the cycle of synthetic design creation, on the other hand, design begins with the designer's associative intuition, which connects (synthesizes) several elemental pieces of knowledge or technology to form a hypothesis. Conversely, a hypothesis is formed by synthesis that derives from associative intuition. This corresponds to Duggan's phrase, 'achievement, then theory' (Duggan, 2013Duggan, W. (2013). *Strategic intuition: The creative spark in human achievement*. New York, NY: Columbia University Press.). The purpose or goal of the product becomes clear as elemental pieces of knowledge or technology are connected. Because of its contents (associative intuition, synthesis, hypothesis), the cycle of synthetic design creation can be linked with the second type of creativity. In this cycle, the 'tuning fork-like resonator' at the source of associative intuition broadens human sensibilities, leading to qualitative innovation. Many breakthrough products resulting in qualitative innovation have been designed in the process similar or identical to the cycle of synthetic design creation involving the integration of multiple elemental pieces of knowledge or technology. It is said that the organizations that have achieved such product development obtained not only new products but also a new organizational vision, purpose or goal to pursue (Duggan, 2013 Duggan, W. (2013). *Strategic intuition: The creative spark in human achievement.* New York, NY: Columbia University Press.).

Other than the obvious differences in elements between the two cycles (experiential/associative intuition, analysis/synthesis, and design solution/hypothesis), the differences between them are illustrated in Figure 6.

Firstly, the difference with regard to whether the act of determining the product purpose/goal is outside or inside design is indicated by the directions of the arrows from 'product purpose/goal' and the range of 'design' (dotted squares).

Secondly, the difference in terms of the starting point of design (design begins with the product purpose/goal given from outside in the cycle of analytical design creation, or with the designer's associative intuition in the cycle of synthetic design creation) is expressed by numbers assigned in the order of steps.

We have compared the two cycles so as to emphasize their respective characteristics to facilitate understanding about creativity in Innovation Design. However, the two cycles can be mixed in actual design processes. For example, immediately after a product purpose or goal is given from outside, the designer's associative intuition can trigger synthesis. In other cases, various analysis methods can be intuitively combined.

Moreover, transition can occur between the two cycles in either direction In fact, a cycle of synthetic design creation rarely begins completely on its own. In many cases, it begins because an associative intuition emerges while the cycle of analytical design creation is repeated, leading to a new hypothesis (unknown concept). The same can be said about the cases of Gates and Jobs mentioned in Section 2. Initially, theirs were ordinary PC development projects. Serendipity, accidental discovery in science (Roberts, 1989Roberts, R. M. (1989). *Serendipity-accidental discoveries in science.* New York, NY: Wiley.), can be explained as a transition from one cycle to the other. The development of Post-it®Notes by 3M, known as a typical example of serendipity, can be explained as such a transition. While trying to develop a strong adhesive (cycle of analytical design creation), a 3M researcher ended up developing an extremely weak adhesive; another 3M researcher later had the idea of combining the weak adhesive with bookmarkers (transition to the cycle of synthetic design creation), and Post-it® Notes came into being. In this paper, we call such a transition from the cycle of analytical design creation to the cycle of synthetic design creation 'abstraction' of design creation cycles.

On the other hand, when an associative intuition generates a product idea, and consequently the purpose or goal of the product is found, these phases are sometimes followed by the sophistication of product structure, shape, or other attributes, so as to improve product performance or usability to satisfy the purpose/goal. This means that the design process has transitioned to the cycle of analytical design creation. In this paper, we call such a transition from the cycle of synthetic design creation to the cycle of analytical design creation 'concretization' of design creation cycles. Concretization is indispensable for the commercialization of a product.

There are also cases in which a design process conducted in a cycle of synthetic design creation is later described within the framework of a cycle of analytical design creation, as an afterthought. This is because an analytical explanation generally reinforces persuasiveness. It is in fact a matter of perception: a product presented as a result of experiential intuition, and not associative intuition or sensibilities, sounds more convincing, just as a solution analytically arrived at to satisfy a predetermined purpose/goal, and not a purpose/goal finalized after aimlessly repeated trial and error, sounds more reliable.

5. DESIGN SCHOOL TO ENHANCE DESIGN CREATIVITY

This section presents an outline of the design school (workshop) that we conducted with focus on the enhancement of participants' synthetic design creativity (Yamada et al., 2017Yamada, K., Tsumaya, A., Taura, T., Shimada, K., Kaihara, T., Yokokohji, Y., & Sato, R. (2017). *An educational method for enhancing the ability to design innovative products.* 21st International Conference on Engineering Design (submitted).).

5.1. Basic policy of our design education

Synthetic design creativity is an essential driver for Innovation Design with the great potential of realizing breakthrough products. However, it has rarely been taught in a systematic way, except for some episodic mention, because synthetic design creativity is perceived as subjective, sensuous or lacking in persuasiveness, as discussed above. Nevertheless, we believe that expectation for synthetic design creativity will greatly increase in the future.

Therefore, we have constructed an educational method in which students can learn to generate breakthrough concepts and design products through group work by following a workflow starting with a cycle of synthetic design creation and then shifting to a cycle of analytical design. We then applied this method to a school (workshop) for students. Our basic policy, ideas and principles behind the educational method and the school, is described below.

In our educational method, concept generation begins with associative intuition. In general, academic instruction is required to be rationally founded. Design methodologies are often taught through practical training and exercises supervised by experienced designers. The rationale for these educational practices is experience. Associative intuition has been largely excluded from educational programs because it is considered irrational, often considered mere guesswork or random ideas popping up in one's mind for no reason. Yet, as we have discussed thus far, associative intuition plays an important role in actual design processes. Then, how should it be taught in educational programs? We believe that associative intuition itself is not something that can be taught. Nevertheless, we believe that, if associative intuition operates on a mechanism similar to that of the 'tuning fork' described in Section 3.2, it should be possible to lead students to polish their inner 'tuning fork' when it has become rusty, or to be more attentive to its resonances, even if not to create a new tuning fork.

Accordingly, in our educational method, students are taught to combine, through associative intuition, two seemingly unrelated elements (a living thing and a product) to generate new concepts, obtaining clues from metaphorical representations of living things, such as 'a bicycle like a dolphin' (Taura, 2016Taura, T. (2016). *Creative design engineering*. Waltham, MA: Elsevier. ; Taura & Nagai, 2012Taura, T., & Nagai, Y. (2012). *Concept generation for design creativity – A systematized theory and methodology*. London: Springer.). This method resembles the method advocated by Christensen for enhancing the designer's ability to innovate, that is, involving idea generation based on a somewhat forced combination of weakly related concepts (Dyer et al., 2011Dyer, J., Gregersen, H., & Christensen, C. M. (2011). *The innovator's DNA: Mastering the five skills of disruptive innovators*. Boston, MA: Harvard Business Review Press.). What distinguishes our method from Christensen's is that combination relies on associative intuition. Living things are used for their numerous excellent characteristics and their relative familiarity, which makes it easy to generate many ideas and associations. For these reasons, in the field of design as well, active research has recently been carried out in terms of biomimetics and biologically-inspired design (Goel, McAdams, & Stone, 2014Goel, A. K., McAdams, D. A., & Stone, R. B. (Eds.). (2014). *Biologically inspired design*. London: Springer.,). Because of its analogical structure, this type of metaphor is often used for problem solving. In our method, it is put within the framework of a cycle of synthetic design creation because metaphorical representations are made by associative intuition and product purposes and goals are gradually found as the design process progresses. By personally undergoing the process in which ideas are combined by associative intuition, concretized, and developed into breakthrough products that also suit their preferences, students are expected to become aware of the possibility and significance of discovering hypotheses through associative intuition.

The method also includes having students concretize the ideas they generate. This is because it is necessary in actual design to elaborate a design concept in the minutest possible detail to bring it to a feasible level and students are required to acquire skills for this task. Therefore, in our method, once basic ideas become well developed, students shift to a cycle of analytical design creation to examine concrete product structures, mechanism, and so on and produce 3D models.

Breakthrough products are expected to bring about new lifestyles, leading to qualitative innovation, as stated in Section 3.1. However, products to be designed do not exist yet. The new lifestyles that they are supposed to realize do not exist either and can only be imagined. This means that it would greatly assist both designers and users in their preliminary evaluation of future products in terms of novelty, utility, and so on, if they could virtually use the new products and observe how they change daily scenes, leading to new lifestyles.

In view of the above, our educational method includes the use of a virtual reality (VR) device, which enables students to view the projected images of designed products and their use in virtual reality simultaneously. The VR device used in the school was a variant of CAVE (Cave Automatic Virtual Environment), π-CAVE, the immersive 3D visualization system installed at the Integrated Research Center of Kobe University (http://www.eccse.kobe-u.ac.jp/pi-cave/). π-CAVE is composed of six screens (two in front, two on the floor, and one on each side) forming a rectangular cuboid 3 m high, 3 m deep, and 7.8 m wide, with a maximum capacity of 20 persons for simultaneous VR experience.

To summarize the above, the design procedure in our educational method proceeds in the following phrases: combination of a living thing and a product through associative intuition → synthesis → (transition) → analysis → CAD production of a 3D model → (evaluation: market survey, etc.). That is, students begin in a cycle of synthetic design creation and then shift to a cycle of analytical design creation. This flow differs from that generally practiced in design schools (e.g., http://dschool.stanford.edu/). Due to the limited time available, the procedure did not include product evaluation.

5.2. Design procedure

In the school, we conducted groupwork following the steps as indicated in Table 1.

Table 1. **Design procedure.**

Step 1	Each team member lists 10 living things and 10 products
Step 2	Each team member chooses three living things and three products that he or she finds interesting from the lists made in Step 1, writes them down separately on Post-it notes, and affixes them on his or her team's sheet
Step 3	Each team member *intuitively* makes an interesting pair of a living thing and a product combined in the form of 'a [product] like a [living thing]' by choosing them from his or her team's lists made in Step 2
Step 4	Each team *intuitively* chooses one pair that its members find most interesting from among the pairs (four pairs per team) made in Step 3
Step 5	Each team member lists characteristics of the living thing of the team's pair chosen in Step 4, writes them down separately on Post-it notes, and affixes them on the team's sheet
Step 6	Each team discusses what shape, mechanism, service system, etc. that 'a [product] like a [living thing]' will have so as to represent the characteristics listed in Step 5, puts together ideas, and draws a sketch of the product. Each team imagines scenes in which the product will be used and collects visual images
Step 7	[Interim presentation] Each team presents its work done so far, using PowerPoint
Step 8	After receiving instruction in the use of the VR device, each team practices operation of π-CAVE with the projection of 360-degree panoramic images of scenes in which the product will be used. Each team examines how the product will be used in the projected scenes, as well as its size, structure, etc.
Step 9	Each team finalizes concrete details about its product such as structure and size, and creates a CAD model, following calculations if necessary. Each team collects more visual images of scenes in which the product will be used
Step 10	The instructors and staff carry out an interim review. Each team summarizes their design plan that has been discussed in the groupwork, explaining what has been achieved thus far and in what direction their work will proceed, and receives advice
Step 11	Each team continues designing concrete details. As the necessity arises, each team uses the VR device to examine how the product will be used, as well as its size, structure, etc.
Step 12	[Final presentation] Each team prepares a PowerPoint presentation and gives a demonstration of the product and scenes of its use using the VR device

5.3. Outline and results of the school

The school was conducted for four days from Thursday, 19 May through Sunday, 22 May 2016, at the Integrated Research Center of Kobe University, located on Port Island, Kobe City.

5.3.1. Participants

Eight students each from Kobe University (Japan) and Carnegie Mellon University (U.S.A.), all majoring in engineering (19–33 years of age; 12 males and 4 females) participated in the school. For instruction and school management, nine academic and administrative faculty members also participated. Four teams were formed, each comprising four members. They were named Team R(Red), Team G(Green), Team B(Blue), and Team Y(Yellow).

5.3.2. Design outcomes

Tables 2–5 indicate the results from steps 2–5 of the school. The final results (design outcomes), as shown in Table 6 and Figure 7, are not improved versions of existing products but are hitherto nonexistent or highly breakthrough products.

Table 2. Results from step 2.

	Product	Living thing
R	Computer, Jet engine, Glasses, Watch, Purse, Robot, Car, Chair, Clock, Camera, Segway, Helicopter	Cockroach, Cactus, Lily, Kangaroo, Crane, Butterfly, Ant, Green caterpillar, Lion, Bacteriophage, Water strider, Elephant
G	Wheelchair, Vending machine, Motorcycle, Bicycle, Suitcase, Mobile phone, Glasses, Scissors, Watch, Scuba diving, Robotic pipeline inspector, UAV surveillance	Snake, Fly, Jellyfish, Bee Octopus, Bald eagle, Giraffe, Butterfly, Shell, Rabbit, Squid, Crab
B	Desk Organizer, Cup holder, Pen case, Lamp, Clock, Case, Scissors, Sunglass, Chopsticks, Glasses, Traffic light, Scooter	Llama, Turtle, Monkey, Giraffe, Peacock, Elephant, Tuna, Camel, Jellyfish, Shark, Monkey, Turtle
Y	Plane, Train, Hotel, Boat, Hot-air balloon, Sport car, Back-pack, Luggage, Bike, Bag, Fishing-net, Shoes	Starfish, Bird, Giraffe, Butterfly, Ginkgo, Water dog, Baleen whale, Armadillo, Octopus/Squid, Hummingbird, Gorilla, Mantis shrimp

Table 3. Results from step 3.

	Pairs
R	Camera–Ant, Chair–Cactus, Chair–Crane, Robot–Butterfly
G	Wheel chair–Squid, Suit case–Shell, Watch–Bee, Vending machine–Octopus
B	Desk organizer–Camel, Lamp–Monkey, Scissors–Shark, Traffic light–Turtle
Y	Sport car–Bird, Shoes–Bird, Plane–Hummingbird, Fishing-net–Baleen whale

Table 4. Results from step 4.

	Pair
R	Camera–Ant
G	Watch–Bee
B	Lamp–Monkey
Y	Fishing-net–Baleen whale

Table 5. Results from step 5.

	Characteristics of the living thing
R	Small, Robust, Strong, Eats, Underground, Makes a nest, Hard shell, Fangs, Communication, Modular, Acts as a swarm, Crawl, 6 legs, Cooperative, Hierarchy, Antenna
G	6 legs, Buzzing sound, Sense of direction, Large eyes, Co-ordination, Communication, Sting, Small size, Dance
B	Agile, Small size, Grabbing, Lightweight, Holding on with multiple means (hands, legs, tail), Stealing, Swinging, Long tail, Hanging
Y	Sucks in water + fish; pushes water out through its filter-like teeth; trapping the fish inside. → presses tongue against roof of mouth to push water out, streamlined, submersible, immune to cold, strainer, mobile, communication (hunting in groups), deep-diving, huge, cute, mysterious, gluttonous, black and white, hunter, fast?, large, does not echo-locate, uses air to shoal fish, can catch fish with sensor, expands/contracts in size, easy to catch fish, can catch small fish

Table 6. Concepts of design outcome.

	Product–Living thing	Product concept	Scenes of use
R	Camera–Ant	Ant-like small cameras that crawl into places which are difficult for humans to access, such as disaster sites, forming a swarm and each taking photographs	Disaster sites
G	Watch–Bee	A watch that transmits information (time, location, danger warnings, etc.) by bone conduction, like a bee that communicates its location or other information with its buzzing sound	Crowded places, inside an automobile
B	Lamp–Monkey	A lamp that can be fixed in various ways, similarly to how a monkey secures itself by holding onto objects using its hands, legs or tail, flexibly adjusting to the situation	Indoors
Y	Fish net–Baleen whale	A submarine that functions like a whale (blowing a bubble ring to trap fish in it, and emitting noise to confuse the fish) coordinates with other units to drive fish into a fishing net	Submarine, underwater

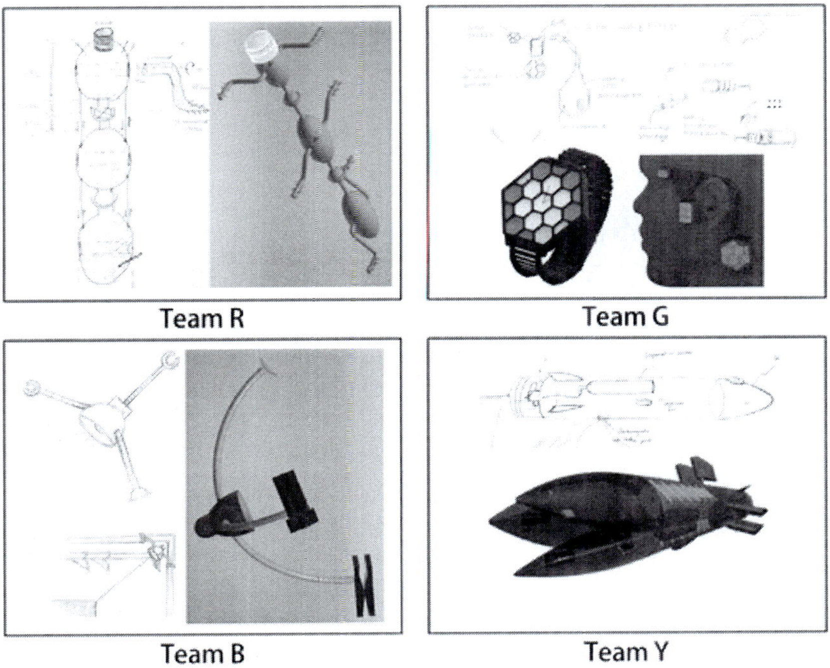

Figure 7. CAD models of design outcome.

5.3.3. Questionnaire survey results

Figure 8 indicates the results of the questionnaire survey conducted among the students who participated in the school.

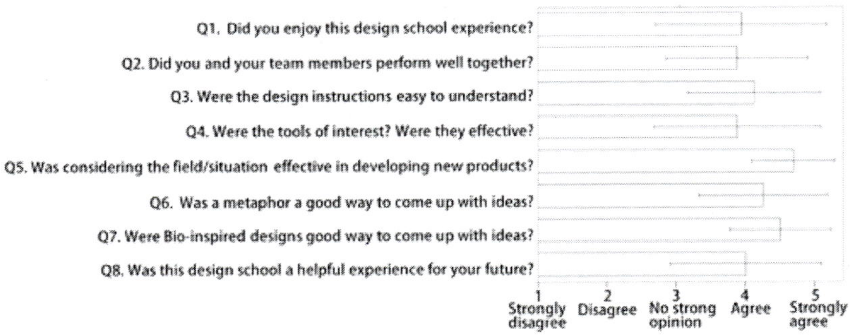

Figure 8. Questionnaire survey results.

The questionnaire survey results indicate that the participants evaluated the school favorably in general. Some of them also provided the following feedback: 'The design process was interesting and I learned some things I probably would not have without this inter-university collaboration.'; 'The design process to integrate two unrelated objects is stimulating.'

6. HUMAN RESOURCES FOR INNOVATION (IN PLACE OF A CONCLUSION)

Ideas for breakthrough products are often conceived by excellent leaders of distinguished quality, as examplified by HondaJet by Michimasa Fujino and many Apple products by Jobs. To be an outstanding leader like them, specialized knowledge alone does not suffice, but a broad vision and creativity are essential.

When a breakthrough product emerges, attention is often drawn to not only what it is like and what it does, but also its 'design philosophy.' This is probably because, in addition to superb functions, a superb philosophy is expected from an excellent product design. This is also because any person who originates a breakthrough product is expected to be a sort of philosopher with deep thought, and not just an expert with superb abilities and skills. Therefore, creative persons capable of Innovation Design, who were discussed in this paper, would have to be worthy to be called a philosopher of design. As such, their regard should extend beyond products and reach society in its entirety and in the long term. These persons must have abundant knowledge, a sharp insight toward the future, and, most of all, keen sensibilities and firm convictions. As the relationship between our society and science and technology grows increasingly complex today, our society must foster excellent philosophers of design.

DISCLOSURE STATEMENT

No potential conflict of interest was reported by the authors.

FUNDING

A part of the research relevant to this article was funded by the Japanese Society for the Promotion of Science Grant-in-Aid for Scientific Research (KAKENHI) [15K12291].

NOTES

* This article has been translated from the original Japanese article (Taura & Nagai, in press).

1. In this paper, the term 'science and technology' is used as a generic term for an understanding of the basic principles of physical phenomena and the basic knowledge required to apply such understanding.
2. In this paper, the term 'society' refers to the sphere in which products are used.
3. HondaJet has an over-the-wing engine mount design, which departs from the industry's conventional style.
4. Figure 3 shows two networks formed from our experiment, in which participants were instructed to produce a new design concept by synthesizing the two concepts of 'ship' and 'guitar.' The networks were generated by virtually connecting the two words 'ship' and 'guitar' and a set of words that the participants used to explain the design outcomes, using a concept dictionary containing hierarchically structured words.
5. Figure 4 shows the two virtual impression networks formed by virtually connecting, using a concept dictionary, all the combinations of two words selected from among the words used

by participants in the experiment to express their impressions of various cups that they were shown.

6. A flash of insight in experiential intuition is deemed to occur in the process of revising preconceived notions (eliminating fixation).

7. A flash of insight in associative intuition is deemed to occur in the process of (1) or (6).

REFERENCES

1. Badke-Schaub, P., & Eris, O. (2014). A theoretical approach to intuition in design: Does design methodology need to account for unconscious processes? In A. Chakrabarti & L. Blessing (Eds.),*An anthology of theories and models of design* (pp. 353–370). London: Springer.
2. π-CAVE. Retrieved from http://www.eccse.kobe-u.ac.jp/pi-cave/
3. d.school. Retrieved from http://dschool.stanford.edu/
4. Duggan, W. (2013). *Strategic intuition: The creative spark in human achievement.* New York, NY:Columbia University Press.
5. Durling, D. (1999). *Intuition in design – A perspective on designer's creativity.* Bulletin of 4th Asian Design Conference: International Symposium of Design Science, Nagaoka, Japan.
6. Dyer, J., Gregersen, H., & Christensen, C. M. (2011). *The innovator's DNA: Mastering the five skills of disruptive innovators.* Boston, MA: Harvard Business Review Press.
7. Faulkner, P., & Runde, J. (2009). On the identity of technological objects and user innovations in function. *Academy of Management Review, 34,* 442–462.
8. Georgiev, G. V., Nagai, Y., & Taura, T. (2013). *Understanding the bases of design impressions of natural or artificial: Survey of cognition in different regions.* Proceedings of the 60th Annual Conference of JSSD 2013, Tsukuba, Japan.
9. Gigerenzer, G. (2008). *Gut feelings: The intelligence of the unconscious.* London: Penguin Books.
10. Gladwell, M. (2006). *Blink: The power of thinking without thinking.* London: Penguin Books.
11. Goel, A. K., McAdams, D. A., & Stone, R. B. (Eds.). (2014). *Biologically inspired design.* London:Springer.
12. HondaJet. Retrieved from http://world.honda.com/HondaJet/
13. Jansson, D. G., & Smith, S. M. (1991). Design fixation. *Design Studies, 12,* 3–11.
14. Jobs, S. (2005). *His 2005 commencement address at Stanford University.*
15. Oxford Dictionaries. Retrieved from www.oxforddictionaries. com/definition/ english/
16. Oxford Dictionaries, holism. Retrieved fromwww.oxforddictionaries.com /definition/english/holism
17. Pahl, G., & Beitz, W. (1995). *Engineering design: A systematic approach.* Berlin: Springer.
18. Polanyi, M. (1983). *The tacit dimension.* Gloucester: Peter Smith.
19. Poincaré, H. (1902). *La science et l'hypothèse* [Science and hypothesis]. Paris: Flammarion.
20. Roberts, R. M. (1989). *Serendipity-accidental discoveries in science.* New York, NY: Wiley.
21. Sinclair, M. (Ed.). (2011). *Handbook of intuition research.* Cheltenham: Edward Elgar.
22. Taura, T. (2016). *Creative design engineering.* Waltham, MA: Elsevier.

23. Taura, T., & Nagai, Y. (2012). *Concept generation for design creativity – A systematized theory and methodology*. London: Springer.
24. Taura, T., & Nagai, Y. (in press). Creativity in Innovation Design – The roles of intuition, synthesis, and hypothesis. *Special Issue of Japanese Society for Science of Design*.
25. Taura, T., Yamamoto, E., Fasiha, M. Y. N., Goka, M., Mukai, F., Nagai, Y., & Nakashima, H. (2012).Constructive simulation of creative concept generation process in design: A research method for difficult-to-observe design-thinking process. *Journal of Engineering Design, 23*, 297–321.
26. Taura, T., Yamamoto, E., Fasiha, M. Y. N., & Nagai, Y. (2011). Virtual impression networks for capturing deep impressions. In J. Gero (Ed.), *Design computing and cognition '10* (pp. 559–578).London: Springer.
27. Yamada, K., Tsumaya, A., Taura, T., Shimada, K., Kaihara, T., Yokokohji, Y., & Sato, R. (2017). *An educational method for enhancing the ability to design innovative products*. 21st International Conference on Engineering Design (submitted).
28. Yonemori, Y. (1992). *Semiology of Peirce*. Tokyo: Keiso Shobo. (in Japanese).
29. Yoshikawa, H. (1997). A new paradigm of engineering. In T. Taura, T. Kayama, M. Ito, & H.Yoshikawa (Eds.), *Topologies of technological knowledge* (pp. 3–21). Tokyo: University of Tokyo Press. (in Japanese).
30. Yoshikawa, H., & Taura, T. (1997). Process knowledge of general design theory. In T. Taura, T.Kayama, M. Ito, & H. Yoshikawa (Eds.), *Topologies of technological knowledge* (pp. 91–106). Tokyo:University of Tokyo Press. (in Japanese).

CHAPTER 3

A CAT with Caveats: Is the Consensual Assessment Technique a Reliable Measure of graphic Design Creativity?

Karl K. Jeffries

School of Art, Design & Performance, University of Central Lancashire, Preston, UK

ABSTRACT

The Consensual Assessment Technique (CAT) is considered one of the gold standards for creativity assessment, and graphic design, arguably, is the most ubiquitous domain within the creative industries. For the first time, this study tests two tasks to measure graphic design creativity, and by extension, the reliability of the CAT as a measure of graphic design creativity. Initial research suggested the level of consensus amongst judges (often referred to as inter-rater reliability) was too low to be reliable, and may be unduly influenced by a judge's preference for technical execution. In this study, 16 professional graphic designers were randomly assigned instructions to discount technical execution from creativity ratings, or given instruction that gave no stipulation, for 60 artworks. Inter-rater reliability scores were acceptable for each task and experimental condition, but were higher for judges that received instructions to discount technical execution.

These and other results are discussed, and the argument presented that, for future CAT studies in this domain, specific instructions to discount technical execution offers a more reliable measure of graphic design creativity.

Keywords: Consensual Assessment Technique, graphic design, design creativity assessment

1. INTRODUCTION

Within the creative industries, graphic design links across many sectors: be it the need for marketing material; a new logo for an organization; the presentation of scientific information; or the development of a new product. Graphic design will play a part: sometimes in the background, at other times centre stage.

Creativity, in this context, is an asset, and gives clients, design agencies, and individual graphic designers an edge in a competitive market. Whilst not all design opportunities give scope for creativity, many do, and finding novel ways to visually communicate with an audience is often an implicit expectation for competency.

Few would argue assessing graphic design creativity is anything other than a highly subjective process; however, such subjectivity need not be problematic if assessors concur in their subjective judgments. This is exactly what the Consensual Assessment Technique (CAT) maintains to achieve: a research method that can reliably assess creativity, through the consensual assessments of domain experts.

The CAT method is based upon on an operational definition of creativity in which " ... a product or response is creative to the extent that appropriate observers independently agree it is creative. Appropriate observers are those familiar with the domain in which the product was create or the response articulated" (Amabile, 1982Amabile, T. M. (1982). Social psychology of creativity: A consensual assessment technique. *Journal of Personality and Social Psychology, 43*, 997–1013.). The past three decades of CAT research studies have shown, for the most part, that satisfactory levels of agreement are possible across a wide range of domains. Precisely how researchers interpret the CAT method and protocol forms a substantial part of this current study, and are discussed in Section 3.

Despite extensive use within creativity research, the use of the CAT as a measure of creativity within design research is relatively small. Over a 30-year period, for example, only 11 papers were related to design journals (Jeffries, 2012aJeffries, K. K. (2012a). Amabile's Consensual Assessment Technique: Why has it not been used more in design creativity research?*Proceedings of the 2nd International Conference on Design Creativity (ICDC2012), 1,* 211–220.), and on further review, only two papers operationalized the CAT in their research (Christiaans & Venselaar, 2005Christiaans, H., & Venselaar, K.(2005). Creativity in design engineering and the role of knowledge: Modelling the expert. *International Journal of Technology and Design Education, 15,* 217–236. Pektas, 2010Pektas, S. T. (2010). Effects of cognitive styles on 2D drafting and design performance in digital media. *International Journal of Technology and Design Education, 20,* 63–76.). Building upon this 30-year CAT database, follow-up searches, identified 24 papers that made reference to both graphic design and the CAT. On inspection, the vast majority of studies, however, were not related to graphic design directly, with two exceptions (Dineen & Niu, 2008Dineen, R., & Niu, W. (2008). The effectiveness of western creative teaching methods in China: An action research project. *Psychology of Aesthetics, Creativity, and the Arts,2,* 42–52. Silvia et al., 2008Silvia, P. J., Winterstein, B. P., Willse, J. T., Barona, C. M., Cram, J. T., Hess, K. I., ... Richard, C. A. (2008). Assessing creativity with divergent thinking tasks: Exploring the reliability and validity of new subjective scoring methods. *Psychology of Aesthetics, Creativity, and the Arts, 2,* 68–85.).

Silvia et al. (2008Silvia, P. J., Winterstein, B. P., Willse, J. T., Barona, C. M., Cram, J. T., Hess, K. I., ... Richard, C. A. (2008). Assessing creativity with divergent thinking tasks: Exploring the reliability and validity of new subjective scoring methods. *Psychology of Aesthetics, Creativity, and the Arts, 2,* 68–85. ,) undertook a study to validate a new method of scoring divergent thinking tasks. Part of the study had participants who majored in arts subjects (accounting for 9% of participants in the study), of which some participants majored in graphic design. Whilst the new technique built the case for the validity of subjective rating by citing CAT studies, the method used was not the CAT protocol. Indeed, they acknowledged the importance of expert domain judges for "studies of real creative product" (p.70), but argued that this need not be the case for divergent thinking tasks assessment.

In contrast, Dineen and Niu's work (2008Dineen, R., & Niu, W. (2008). The effectiveness of western creative teaching methods in China: An action research project. *Psychology of Aesthetics, Creativity, and the Arts,2,* 42–52.) utilized the CAT method, and involved participants in their second year of graphic design at a Chinese art and design higher education institution. The study explored the respective merits of UK creative pedagogy relative to traditional Chinese pedagogy. However, it is arguable, how closely aligned to graphic design the final outputs were relative to illustration design. In no way do distinctions that can be made between graphic design and illustration design undermine the value of Dineen and Niu's research, but for the purposes of this review it highlights that at the time of this study, there was at best only one published paper that had applied the CAT to graphic designers.

The CAT has continued to grow in popularity within design research, and a recent PhD study has applied the CAT to traditional graphic design (Wojtczuk, 2014Wojtczuk, A. (2014). *Creative product assessment in design: Influences of judges' backgrounds and levels of experience in design* (Unpublished doctoral dissertation), Aix Marseille Universite, Marseille.). A number of findings on the influence of judges' background on design creativity assessment are highlighted by Wojtczuk, and of particular importance was the low level of consensus achieved by designers' rating of graphic design creativity.

Therefore, as yet, there is little precedent established for a task to reliably measure graphic design creativity using the CAT. This is particularly relevant in the light of debates surrounding the domain specificity/generality of creativity, and the role task selection plays in creativity assessment (Byrne, 2011Byrne, C. (2011). *Task selection and the consensual assessment technique: Using collage tasks in creativity research* (Unpublished masters thesis). University of Central Lancashire, Preston.). These issues raise both practical and theoretical implications for creativity research within and beyond graphic design. Thus, for the first time, this study aims to test two tasks to measure graphic design creativity, and by extension, the reliability of the CAT as a measure of graphic design creativity.

2. PILOT STUDIES

Prior to the main study in this paper, two studies were undertaken to explore suitable tasks for a graphic design CAT (Jeffries, 2012bJeffries, K. K. (2012b). *Skills for creativity in graphic design*(Unpublished thesis). The Open University, Milton Keynes, UK.). Each task had current usage in design education, and gave participants the opportunity for graphic design creativity. One used text only, and required participants to choose a word, and then visually communicate that word through the use of type (Figure 1). The other task was to design a graphic which could be transferred to a plain white T-shirt. The graphical image was to be based on the theme of "hands". For brevity, only a selection of pilot findings will be discussed, particularly those that informed the current research design, but full details of these studies are available on request.

Figure 1. Six examples of artwork (none of these examples were part of this study): three on the left relate to the Type Task; three on the right relate to the Image Task.

A key finding was that inter-rater reliability was below acceptable levels, or marginal for both tasks: .56 for the T-shirt Task, and even .69 for the Type Task was not ideal. Was something happening in graphic design that warranted caveats for research design, or was this domain challenging the assumptions upon which the CAT was based (i.e. domain experts can independently agree on creativity to an acceptable level of inter-rater agreement)? The outcome from these pilot studies was that a number of caveats needed to be considered in order to optimize the CAT method as a measure of graphic design creativity: specifically, the influence of technical execution on ratings of graphic design creativity; the background of judges; the range of artwork available; and the suitability of a task for research purposes.

2.1. Technical execution

Artwork in graphic design can vary in its level of technical refinement. At one end of the spectrum are conceptual artworks, where the seed of an idea can be perceived: even if the artworks lack refinement in, for example, font selection, layout, or composition, the creativity of the idea can still be evaluated. At the other end of a technical spectrum is finished artwork; artwork that is ready to go to print or publication, where every aspect of visual communication has been crafted and refined to perfection by the designer.

The pilot studies highlighted that judges' preferences for technical execution differed with regard to judging graphic design creativity. For example, their preference for technical quality appeared to be heightened or subdued relative to the medium of the artwork (hand-drawn sketches, artwork created with the use of computer software, or a combination of both mediums).

Within the CAT literature, some researchers have created instructions that directly address this issue of discounting technical execution (Baer, 1993Baer, J. (1993). *Creativity and divergent thinking: A task-specific approach*. Hillsdale, NJ: Lawrence Erlbaum Associates.). Other researchers (the majority of CAT studies) have not done so with little adverse impact: some ask judges to rate creativity alongside technical execution and aesthetic appeal (Amabile, 1982Amabile, T. M. (1982). Social psychology of creativity: A consensual assessment technique. *Journal of Personality and Social Psychology, 43,* 997–1013. Christiaans & Venselaar, 2005 Christiaans, H., & Venselaar, K.(2005). Creativity in design engineering and the role of knowledge: Modelling the expert. *International Journal of Technology and Design Education, 15,* 217–236. Valgeirsdottir, Onarheim, & Gabrielsen, 2015Valgeirsdottir, D., Onarheim, B., & Gabrielsen, G. (2015). Product creativity assessment of innovations: Considering the creative process. *International Journal of Design Creativity and Innovation, 3,* 95–106.), some only do this the first time they undertake a new CAT task (Hennessey, 1994Hennessey, B. A. (1994). The consensual assessment technique: An examination of the relationship between ratings of product and process creativity. *Creativity Research Journal, 7,* 193–208. Kaufman, Plucker, & Baer, 2008Kaufman, J. C., Plucker, J. A., & Baer, J. (2008). *Essentials of creativity assessment.* Hoboken, NJ: John Wiley & Sons.); some do not. Thus, the issue of technical execution ranges from explicit, through to implied, implied only once, or not mentioned at all.

Given this range of approaches, if graphic design experts are not specifically guided to discount technical execution then ambiguous instructions may impact on the level of consensus: could differences in technical preference explain low inter-rater agreement in previous studies? In this study, two sets of instructions will be given to judges to test whether discounting technical execution, or not, has an impact on levels of consensus.

2.2. Suitable judges

In the pilot studies, novice/intermediate judges, relative to experts judges, achieved higher levels of consensus for the Type Task but the rankings, and rationale for ratings, where not the same. The debate over the use of novice or intermediate judges is a contentious one, and likely to remain as such. For future CAT studies in graphic design, the implication was to use domain experts only. A further point is that domain experts can be based within professional practice (i.e. full-time graphic designer) or educational practice (i.e. full-time graphic design lecturers teaching on undergraduate and postgraduate graphic design courses). Previous research in other design domains (Jeffries, 2011Jeffries, K. K. (2011). Skills for creativity in games design. *Design Studies, 32*, 60–85., ,) suggest that the values shared on creativity between academics and practitioners is not as polarized as populist views can imply. However, whether this is the case for graphic design is unclear, and thus a cautious approach to CAT studies, in this domain, would be to gather experts from either academia or professional practice, but not to use both within the same group (that is, until research findings can show otherwise). In the present study, only full-time professional graphic designer were used as judges, and each judge was required to have over two years of professional experience within graphic design.

2.3. Range of artwork

Whilst the CAT is a method that requires judges' ratings are relative to other works within a sample, it is feasible that artworks too similar in creative quality pose a more challenging assessment for judges. This lack of diversity may explain the low levels of inter-rater reliability in previous studies. For example, the artworks gathered for the Type Task were stratified across highly accomplished graphic designers (as this artwork was gathered from the webpages of various designers; few are likely to promote their least creative work).

In contrast, if inter-rater reliability could be low due to sampling from mostly highly creative artworks, then why not for other skewed samples, be they predominantly low or medium in quality? The sampling of T-shirt artworks in the pilot study, for example, were sampled from a module with an introductory nature, thus participants were mostly novices to design, and the resulting artwork may have been clustered towards the lower end of quality. The key issue here is not the quality of individual artwork in isolation, but the range of quality within a sample, and how researchers many inadvertently cluster to a particular range (be it mostly high, or mostly medium, or mostly low quality) relative to the expectations of domain experts.

Given these observations and the fact that to date CAT studies in graphic design had not achieved a suitable level of inter-rater agreement, it was considered prudent that some form of pre-test for diversity of artwork be used in further studies. This would offer a degree of control and insight into how diverse the artwork presented to judges would be, and create optimal conditions under which CAT assessment would take place: if a suitable level of consensus could not be achieved under these experimental conditions then, indeed, something deeply problematic was likely to be occurring in relation to the CAT and graphic design creativity.

2.4. Task selection

As a final consideration, the T-shirt Task may have been too complicated for the purposes of this study. Firstly, as a task it was designed for an educational purpose with a broad scope, and one that took place over an extended period of time (relative to the more experimental tasks used by many CAT studies). Secondly, the artwork ranged from hand-drawn sketches to artwork created with the use of computer software, such as Adobe Illustrator, InDesign, or Photoshop. Moreover, and thirdly, some artworks incorporated text within the T-shirt graphic, whilst other did not. Each of these issues may have contributed to the low level of consensus achieved in the pilot study. Given this, the implication was for artworks to contain image only, or text only. Furthermore, the medium through which the artwork was created should remain consistent across a sample, and within itself. For example, either all artworks would be hand-drawn, or alternately, created with the use of computer software; a combination of both mediums was to be avoided. Additionally, the Image Task should be able to be completed in a time scale comparable to the Type Task.

Based upon such caveats, the main study was specifically designed to ask: can professional graphic designers achieve inter-rater reliability at or above .7 for an image based graphic design task and a text based graphic design task? If they can, do CAT instructions to discount technical execution increase inter-rater reliability when compared to instructions that make no such stipulation?

3. METHOD

As is often the custom for CAT studies, two broad groups of participants were required: those who generate the creative outputs (participants) and those who assess the creative outputs (raters, or judges). For many CAT studies outside design, participants are recruited and undertake the creation of a piece of work under experimental conditions – this is because the purpose of such studies is to test the influence of teaching or environmental factors that may impact upon creativity. In this study, it is the judges, rather than the participants that are the focus. Thus, this study follows a research direction set by other researchers (e.g. Baer, Kaufman, & Gentile, 2004Baer, J., Kaufman, J. C., & Gentile, C. A. (2004). Extension of the consensual assessment technique to nonparallel creative products. *Creativity Research Journal, 16*, 113–117. Christiaans & Venselaar, 2005Christiaans, H., & Venselaar, K.(2005). Creativity in design engineering and the role of knowledge: Modelling the expert. *International Journal of Technology and Design Education, 15*, 217–236.), for the use of work created under non-experimental conditions. It has been showed that judges' inter-rater reliability can remain acceptable even when creative outputs are not generated under experimental conditions.

As a result, graphic design artwork was the creative output, and created as a natural result of engagement with a university degree. Specifically, the study gained consent from participants to use type only and image only artwork created during two assignments for a BA (Hons) Graphic Design course. These two tasks provided 30 type and 30 image examples to be independently assessed by 16 professional graphic designers using the CAT. The dependent variable was instructions given to judges, and each judge was randomly assigned to receive different instructions for each task. Data was analyzed for inter-rater reliability, and appropriate statistical analysis was used to compare the influence of different instructions on judges' ratings.

3.1. Ethical considerations

As this project was between two universities, authorization was sought, and obtained, from Ethics Committees at each.

One of the core pedagogies of graphic design education is the use of a critical review (commonly known as a "Crit"). During a Crit, students present their finished artworks and have these commented upon by staff and students. Frequently, such Crits make comparisons to other works under review, and opinions of merits and weaknesses are discussed. It is the work under review rather than the designer, but the results of this study could risk reinforcing self-labeling and issues of social standing within a peer group. This was mitigated through a number of measures:

- •The result of the study would not use illustrations of any artwork provided. Thus, it would not be possible for the students taking part to know how judges rated their artwork from the results of the study.
- •The student artwork collected received an anonymous code at the start of the research. Only the principle investigator knew which codes related to which students, and the principle investigator had no involvement with the assessment of graphic design students during their course of study.

3.2. Tasks

The Type Task was the same as the pilot study. A new Image Task was used that required participants to select two images, and when seen side by side made some sort of creative juxtaposition, or interesting visual communication about the images chosen. As with the Type Task, this has a pedigree within graphic design education and the juxtaposition of images is also a technique frequently used by professional graphic designers.

Whilst none of the artworks created for this study are presented here (as justified above), examples of six artworks previous and post this study are shown below in Figure 1, to give a visual context for these tasks. Specifically, the first Type Task example took the word "Coffee" and through the choice of typeface has rotated the letter "C" to resemble a coffee pot; the second Type Task example, based on the word "Imagine" has deleted the middle letter, leaving the viewer to imagine what this deletion may be; the third type example, has taken the word "Saw", and through extending the last letter "W" implies the teeth of a saw; the first Image Task example placed a pipe wrench next to an image of Robocop; the second a spiral shell next to a satellite image of a tornado; the third, the details of a leaf next to a section of road map.

3.3. Instruction to judges

For each task, whether type or image, two sets of instructions were developed. One set was an adapted version of Kaufman, Baer, Cole, and Sexton's (2008)Kaufman, J. C., Baer, J., Cole, J. C., & Sexton, J. D. (2008). A comparison of expert and nonexpert raters using the consensual assessment technique. *Creativity Research Journal, 20*, 171–178. study, and is cited as an exemplar of CAT instructions (Kaufman et al., 2008Kaufman, J.

C., Plucker, J. A., & Baer, J. (2008). *Essentials of creativity assessment.* Hoboken, NJ: John Wiley & Sons.).

Please look through these artworks, and rate them for creativity. There is no need to explain or defend your ratings in any way; we ask only that you use your own sense of which is more or less creative (relative to the other artworks provided).

Please look through these artworks three times, and rate them for creativity.

The first time familiarize yourself with all the artworks provided.

The second time, group the artworks into Low, Medium, or High ratings.

The third time, assign a numerical rating between 1 and 6 (1's being the least creative and 6's being the most creative).

There should be a roughly even number of artworks at each of the six levels. It is very important that you use the full 1-6 scale.

The other set of instructions were exactly the same as Kaufman et al.'s, with one difference, the first sentence (*Please look through these artworks, and rate them for creativity*) was replaced with two sentences adapted from Baer's (1993Baer, J. (1993). *Creativity and divergent thinking: A task-specific approach.* Hillsdale, NJ: Lawrence Erlbaum Associates.) CAT instruction for judges (a study where judges where specifically requested not to consider other factors that may impact on storytelling, for example, aesthetic appeal, or grammar, as part of their criteria for rating creativity). Baer's (1993Baer, J. (1993). *Creativity and divergent thinking: A task-specific approach.* Hillsdale, NJ: Lawrence Erlbaum Associates.) study is also cited as an exemplar of CAT instruction (Kaufman et al., 2008Kaufman, J. C., Plucker, J. A., & Baer, J. (2008). *Essentials of creativity assessment.* Hoboken, NJ: John Wiley & Sons.). The wording used was as follows:

There is only one criterion in rating these artworks: creativity. We realize that creativity probably overlaps other criteria one might consider (for example: aesthetic appeal, or technical execution) but we ask you to rate the artworks solely on the basis of their creativity.

The rationale for the use of Kaufman et al.'s instruction was to provide a clear procedure for judges to follow, and to use instructions that were rating focused rather than ranking focused, as Baer's instructions cited above are (though this does change in other studies related to his 1993 work).

Subsequent additions to Kaufman et al.'s wording were created to clarify the issue of standards; a topic that arose during post-assessment debriefing with graphic designers (and a topic present in the pilot studies). Relative to other artworks, the instruction to rate the "most creative" seemed to be difficult for some judges. Setting aside issues of whether, in the pilot studies, the sample of artwork reflected enough creative diversity, the likelihood for such difficulty was the internal standards a judge had for creativity, and the congruency or discomfort experienced when they were tasked to label artworks "high" or "most" creative when, relative to the general standards of the domain, they were weak. Clearly, CAT instructions ask for comparison within a group of artwork (as does the theoretical assumptions which underpin this assessment technique) but it could still be the case that for graphic design professionals, mindful of a domain that judges them and others against expectations of high creativity, this is difficult to "turn off". In this respect, it was felt important to emphasize the relative nature of the ratings, and thus the phrase " ... (relative to the other artworks provided)" was added to supplement Kaufman et al.'s instructions.

In contrast, the key distinction to highlight for Baer's instructions is the emphasis his wording places on one criterion: creativity; and explicit instructions that other factors related to creativity, such as technical execution and aesthetic appeal, are to be discounted. This is a feature absent from Kaufman et al.'s instructions.

Moreover, with Baer's wording, he instructs judges to use their own "mysterious expert sense" (Kaufman et al., 2008Kaufman, J. C., Plucker, J. A., & Baer, J. (2008). *Essentials of creativity assessment.* Hoboken, NJ: John Wiley & Sons., p. 65) of what creativity is, but to isolate this from other related factors (which he lists). In this way, Baer maintains only one unambiguous criteria is present. This instruction could, however, be viewed as something of a contradiction; does such an instruction not imply other criteria are present and at work: to the extent that they need to be separated from creativity? Like general standards, as mentioned above, the ability to "turn off", to isolate creativity from other criteria, may be more challenging for some judges and straightforward for others. That said, difficult need not infer that judges are unable to undertake such assessment: what Baer's original instructions acknowledge is the possibility that this may be a challenge, but one that is necessary and achievable. In this study, Baer's instructions were edited to two sentences, and reflected a more formal tone in keeping with Kaufman et al.'s.

It is worth noting that whilst Kaufman et al.'s instructions do not discuss other criteria (such as technical execution or aesthetic appeal) and Baer's make a considerable point of this, previous researchers using CAT have instructed judges to rate creativity alongside, but separate to, aesthetic appeal and technical execution (Hennessey, 1994Hennessey, B. A. (1994). The consensual assessment technique: An examination of the relationship between ratings of product and process creativity. *Creativity Research Journal, 7,* 193–208.). Indeed, in Amabile's (1982Amabile, T. M. (1982). Social psychology of creativity: A consensual assessment technique. *Journal of Personality and Social Psychology, 43,* 997–1013.) work, the extent to which creativity may be isolated from such factors was a formative part of her paper, and she concluded that

... although judges were not provided with a definition of creativity ... they consistently and reliably identified a quality in both types of product that was distinct from technical execution. Moreover, for artworks, it was distinct from aesthetic appeal as well (p.1010).

At the same time, Amabile acknowledged that for some domains the distinction between technical execution and aesthetic appeal may be less clear, and that creativity is likely to correlate with these aspects of the work. Even within Amabile's (1982Amabile, T. M. (1982). Social psychology of creativity: A consensual assessment technique. *Journal of Personality and Social Psychology, 43,* 997–1013.10.1037/0022-3514.43.5.997, ,) studies, she found correlations as high as .77 between creativity and technical goodness; and Hennessey (1994Hennessey, B. A. (1994). The consensual assessment technique: An examination of the relationship between ratings of product and process creativity. *Creativity Research Journal, 7,* 193–208.) presented statistically significant correlations as high as .71. Contemporary CAT-based research and studies more directly related to professional design, such as Valgeirsdottir, Onarheim, and Gabrielsen (2015Valgeirsdottir, D., Onarheim, B., & Gabrielsen, G. (2015). Product creativity assessment of innovations: Considering the creative process. *International Journal of Design Creativity and Innovation, 3,* 95–106.), have also identified high positive correlations, yet other design creativity researchers make no mention of having considered this in their research design.

A suggestion, for some time, has been that when a CAT is developed for a different domain, researchers should ask judges to rate both technical execution and aesthetic appeal (Amabile, 1982Amabile, T. M. (1982). Social psychology of creativity: A consensual assessment technique. *Journal of Personality and Social Psychology, 43,* 997–1013.), and check to see creativity ratings are distinct from these criteria. Once this has been shown to be so, researchers need only ask for ratings of creativity, and can assume that technical execution is no longer a consideration for this task. It is at this point, as stated above, that Baer's instructions to discount technical execution contrast markedly with those of Kaufman et al.'s. The question is how much does that contrast matter?

3.4. Selection of artwork

In order to select 30 artworks for each task, grades created as a result of student artwork for a creative thinking module were used: the criterion was creativity, and this was assessed by academic staff independent of this study. The details of this selection process have been reduced for brevity, but the purpose was threefold: firstly, to identify a diverse range of artworks across all CAT levels 1–6; secondly, to have five artworks represented at each CAT level; thirdly, to have the same participant represented in both tasks: type, and image. This would allow CAT scores for type and image to be aggregated to get a total score for both tasks and individuals. As above, the CAT ratings for this study would require judges to rate artwork as low, medium or high, and then rate these from 1 to 6. To determine which artworks, and participants would be selected, each academic grade was stratified to a CAT rating as follows: marks between 44 and below, and 44–50 where rated as low (CAT level 1 and 2); 50–54, and 55–59 as medium (CAT level 3 and 4); 60–69, and 70 and above as high (CAT level 5 and 6). When each of the artwork options were placed alongside each other, this highlighted some CAT levels had fewer options than others. For example, only five artworks were available at CAT level 1 for the Type Task, and only five artworks were available at level 6 for the Image Task. The inclusion of a participant in the Type Task at CAT level 1, for example, determined their representation within the Image Task, and vice versa. Moreover, when a participant was chosen to represent a specific CAT level (regardless of which task), this influenced the options available for other CAT levels. In this respect, the choices for selection became to an extent self-identifying, with limited options depending on whether a CAT level had more than five artworks available. The process was iterative, and became progressively more challenging with each inclusion. However, the stratification was achieved, and 30 participants were identified whose text and image artworks represented each of the six CAT levels, with five artworks at each level. For reasons of research ethics and participant confidentiality, examples of the artwork used in this study have been withheld from publication.

3.5. Judges

Previous research guidelines suggest that for CAT reliability, between 5 and 10 judges is an acceptable number for a given task. For this study, 16 full-time professional designers took part (sampling detail are available in the results section). Judges were randomly assigned to two groups, in which task and instructions where rotated to counter balance whether they receive the Image Task first or second, with whether they received

Kaufman et al.'s or Baer's instructions, or a combination. This was to minimize order effects, particularly practice effects and fatigue effects.

3.6. Procedures

The procedures for rating artwork were the same for each judge and task. Initially, judges answered three questions: their years of experience in graphic design, whether they would describe themselves as a graphic designer, and their age. After this, each judge was given the instructions for their first task, alongside an example of the design brief given to participants for this task. They had as much time as they required to read the instruction. Next, each judge accessed a laptop with a PDF slide presentation of the 30 artwork for the first task. The order of artwork was randomized, and they were free to control how long they viewed artworks, and could return to each artwork for further inspection. Each judge familiarized themselves with all the artworks, and when satisfied informed the researcher they were ready to continue. Judges were given an *A*3 laminated rating sheet, see Figure 2 (developed to graphically reinforce Kaufman et al.'s CAT protocol and instructions), and a set of laminated cards. These cards were miniature copies of the artwork they had just viewed. Cards were placed in a stack, by the researcher, onto the rating sheet area designated "Medium", and judges proceeded to rate the artwork, and had as much time as they required. Task two followed the same procedures. All judges were debriefed on the purpose of the experiment, and had the opportunity to ask any questions about the study.

4. RESULTS

Within a year group of 66 students, 48 students gave their consent to take part in the project. The median age was 19 years (SD 1.46); 18 female and 30 male students took part. The mean age for judges was just over 41 years of age (SD 9.80), and ranged from 30 to 63 years of age; six judges were female. All judges identified themselves as graphic designers, and their professional experience within graphic design ranged from 7 to 35 years: the mean being just over 17 years.

For the Type Task, the eight judges who received the adapted Kaufman et al. CAT instructions had an alpha of .73; for the eight judges who received the adapted Baer's instruction to discount technical execution the alpha was .82. The skew for aggregated ratings for each group were within acceptable limits at the less than 5% level: adapted Kaufman et al. z-skew was −.62; adapted Baer z-skew was −.2. Pearson's r was .82, suggestive of a very strong positive correlation between the scores, and was a significant correlation at the .01 level (two tailed). The scatter plot on the left (Figure 3) shows the regression line and strength of correlation.

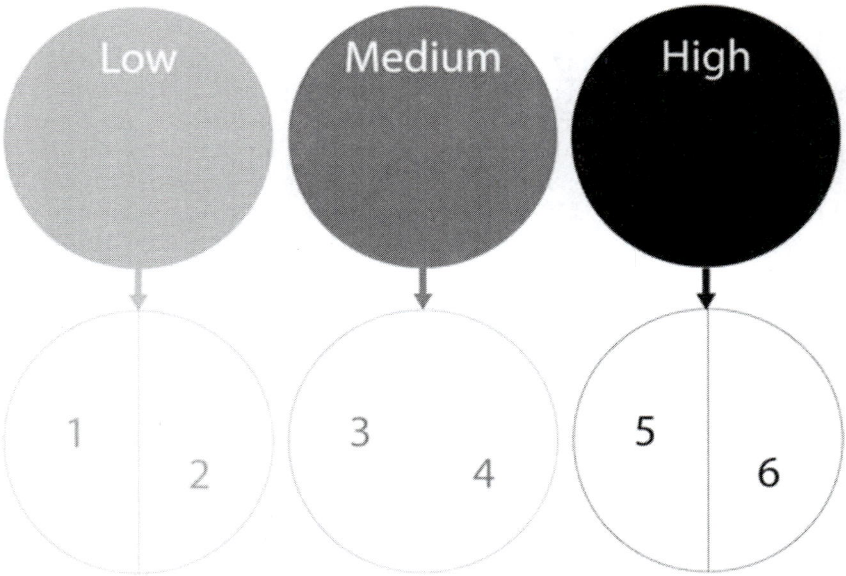

Figure 2. Rating sheet developed to graphically reinforce Kaufman et al's CAT protocol.

For the Image Task, the eight judges who received the adapted Kaufman et al.'s CAT instructions had an α of .75; for the eight judges who received the adapted Baer's instruction to discount technical execution the α was .80. The skew for aggregated ratings for each group were within acceptable limits at the less than 5% level: adapted Kaufman et al. z-skew was .74; adapted Baer z-skew was .10. Pearson's r was .62, suggestive of a strong positive correlation between the scores, and was a significant correlation at the .01 level (two tailed). The scatter plot to the right (Figure 2) shows the regression line and strength of correlation.

The correlation between the adapted Baer's instructions for both type and image was an r of .43, which can be considered a moderate positive correlation and one that was significant at the .5 level (two tailed). For the adapted Kaufman et al. instructions for both type and image r was .11, suggestive of a negligible positive correlation, and one that was not statistically significant. Figure 4 highlights α and r in relation to which task and instructions.

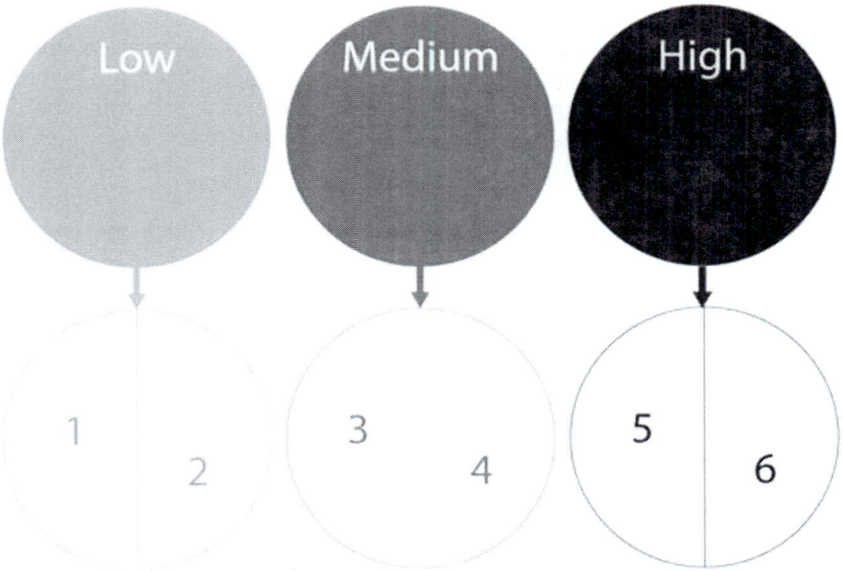

Figure 3. Scatterplots for Type Task (left) and Image Task (right).

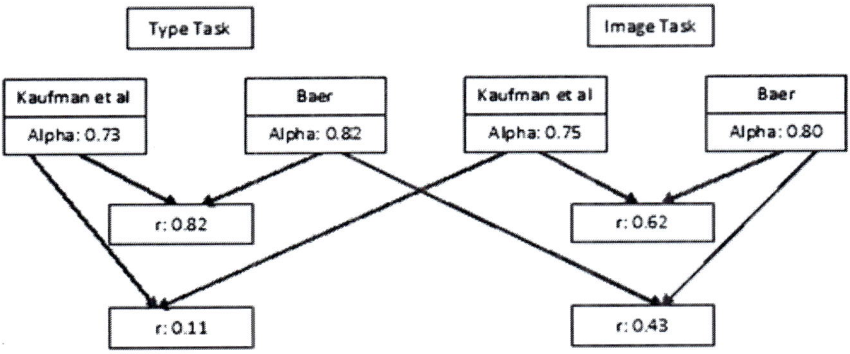

Figure 4. Alpha and *r* in relation to task and instructions.

5. DISCUSSION

Given the novelty of the CAT for the assessment of graphic design creativity, there was a need to pilot whether judges showed a suitable standard of consensus as achieved in other research. Of the few studies directly related to design, the CAT has shown sufficient levels of consensus within their respective domains. It was expected that using the CAT to assess graphic design creativity should follow a similar pattern of inter-rater reliability; however, the pilot result did not achieve this. A number of reasons, such as the range of artwork, technical preferences of judges, task selection, and the sampling of judges were accounted for in the present study, and appear to have resolved the previous issue of inter-rater reliability. In either task, the inter-rater reliability was acceptable, all were above .7, the highest being .82. Given this, these particular tasks can be considered reliable measures of graphic design creativity using the CAT. Prior to this study, the choice of tasks to measure graphic design creativity was not obvious, and the pilot findings highlighted that some task do not translate well from design education context into experimental research.

Whilst each task (regardless of the instruction to judges) had acceptable alphas, a marked difference can be seen in the correlation between the Type Task ($r = .82$) and the Image Task ($r = .62$). The reasons for this difference could be numerous, complex and interrelated. Perhaps, the Type Task, and typography, shares a common knowledge base for graphic designers; possibly the Type Task is less influenced by discounting technical execution than the Image Task; the inclusion of color in the Image Task may add to the complexity of assessing its creativity: color was absent in the Type Task. What can be said, and has been said by other researchers (Reiter-Palmon et al., 2009Reiter-Palmon, R., Illies, M. Y., Cross, L. K., Buboltz, C. B., & Nimps, T. (2009). Creativity and domain specificity: The effect of task type on multiple indexes of creative problem-solving. *Psychology of Aesthetics, Creativity, and the Arts, 3*, 73–80., ,), is that task selection is an important factor in creativity assessment, and our depth of understanding is "essentially missing in the literature" (Lubart & Guigard, 2004Lubart, T., & Guignard, J. H. (2004). The generality-specificity of creativity: A multivariate approach. In R. J. Sternberg, E. L. Grigorenko & J. L. Singer (Eds), *Creativity: From potential to realization* (pp. 43–56). Washington, DC: American Psychological Association., , p. 48).

In early CAT research, Amabile (1982Amabile, T. M. (1982). Social psychology of creativity: A consensual assessment technique. *Journal of Personality and Social Psychology, 43*, 997–1013.10.1037/0022-3514.43.5.997, , , 1996Amabile, T. M. (1996). *Creativity in context: Update to the social psychology of creativity*. Boulder, CO: Westview Press.,) concluded that judges were able to distinguish creativity from other aspects such as aesthetic appeal and technical execution. Does this finding still apply to graphic design creativity? Whilst the differences between the adapted Kaufman et al. instructions and the adapted Baer instructions (to discount technical execution) ranged from .05 to .09, the difference was towards higher levels of inter-rate reliability when judges were asked to discount technical execution from their creativity ratings; this occurred in both the

Type Task and Image Task. Arguably, these differences are slight, but it may be that acceptable inter-rater reliability is not enough in isolation, and that the other consideration is the correlation between aggregated scores. Only the adapted Baer instructions were statistically significant, and suggestive of a moderate to strong positive relationship. A further finding was that correlations were significant at the .01 level in either task, but were stronger for the Type Task, than the Image Task. It appears the Type Task is less influenced by discounting technical execution, and the Image Task may be more susceptible.

Whilst the CAT is a method that requires ratings are relative to other works within a sample, it is feasible that artworks too similar in quality pose a more challenging task for judges than those that show more diversity. Such a possibility is interesting. Several CAT studies highlight the real world basis of the technique, and with acceptable inter-rater reliability, there is little reason to question its reliability. However, most CAT studies are research studies, and whilst parallels can be drawn between CAT methods and those used by judges of, for example, professional competitions, awards, or traditional art school degree show assessment, the independence of judges does not happen throughout the rating process as it does in the CAT.

Much like other consensual techniques, such as the Delphi technique, competition judges do tend to confer with each other towards the end of the process. A judge's initial assessment may be independent of the panel, but towards the final stages of evaluation, debate and compromise is not uncommon in order for consensus to be achieved. This need not discredit CAT methodology, it does suggest, however, that the real world assessment of highly creative artworks may require more debate amongst judges than the CAT currently allows.

If this is the case for highly creative artworks, then why not for other skewed samples be they predominantly low or medium in quality? It is beyond the scope of this research to explore this in detail, but the argument, given the pilot findings, and the subsequent main study, is that diversity of artwork may play a significant factor in levels of consensus amongst judges Therefore, it is possible for researchers to assume enough diversity exists in a sample of artwork, when it may not.

Precisely how researchers interpret the CAT method and protocol is open to debate (Amabile, 1982Amabile, T. M. (1982). Social psychology of creativity: A consensual assessment technique. *Journal of Personality and Social Psychology, 43*, 997–1013.Baer, 1993Baer, J. (1993). *Creativity and divergent thinking: A task-specific approach*. Hillsdale, NJ: Lawrence Erlbaum Associates.; Hennessey, 1994Hennessey, B. A. (1994). The consensual assessment technique: An examination of the relationship between ratings of product and process creativity. *Creativity Research Journal, 7,* 193–208.10.1080/10400419409534524[Taylor & Francis Online],,; Kaufman et al., 2008Kaufman, J. C., Baer, J., Cole, J. C., & Sexton, J. D. (2008). A comparison of expert and nonexpert raters using the consensual assessment technique. *Creativity Research Journal, 20,* 171–178.10.1080/10400410802059929[Taylor & Francis Online],,). In essence, the argument presented here is to develop standard CAT instructions to rate creativity for all design creativity researchers: those who choose to measure additional criteria, such as technical execution and aesthetic appeal, in each study; those who do so only once; those that measure only creativity. In design domains where the distinction between creativity, technical execution and aesthetic appeal appears to be a rather thin one, the findings of this paper suggested that explicit CAT instructions to discount technical execution from creativity ratings are more reliable.

The main point to consider is whether to include a caveat around technical execution in future research. By inclusion, such a caveat, directly addresses assumptions around technical execution and creativity. Indeed, if the CAT is foremost a measure of creativity (however judges interpret this word), then clarification on technical execution seems a reasonable distinction to bring to their attention. The slight increase in inter-rater agreement for judges that received the technical execution caveat can be interpreted both for and against its inclusion. More revealing is the correlations between type and image scores relative to instructions. It is only scores where a caveat was included that enabled an aggregated graphic design creativity score. As the purpose of these tasks was to evaluate graphic design creativity by isolating two distinct features of graphic design (the creative use of type and the creative use of image), the expectation was that a degree of positive correlation would be likely in the combination of these tasks. What is interesting to note for this study is that when judges assess exactly the same tasks and exactly the same artwork, only the caveat on technical execution offers the opportunity for an aggregated score, and thus, at least for research purposes, enables distinctions within a group on levels of graphic design creativity.

6. CONCLUSION

Prior to this study, the choice of tasks to measure graphic design creativity was not obvious. In this study, a number of research design factors, such as diversity of artwork, technical preference, task selection, and sampling of judges were accounted for in the research design, and appear to have resolved previous issues of inter-rater reliability. However, the arguments presented in this paper suggest instructions to discount technical execution from judges' creativity assessment do appear to influence the reliability of the CAT. The difference was towards higher levels of inter-rate reliability when judges were asked to discount technical execution from their creativity ratings; this occurred in both the Type Task and Image Task used. Moreover, only CAT assessments undertaken where the technical caveat was included enable an aggregated graphic design creativity score for both the image and Type Tasks. Perhaps, these implications apply not only to graphic design, but have relevance for all CAT assessments of design creativity? To paraphrase Nickerson (1999Nickerson, R. S. (1999). Enhancing creativity. In R. J. Sternberg (Ed.), *Handbook of creativity* (pp. 392–430). Cambridge: Cambridge University Press.), as researchers we have two choices: include a caveat on technical execution that future research will show was not fundamental, or exclude it and find technical execution does influence rating on design creativity. Unless there is some detrimental effect (which does not appear to be the case in this study) then a cautious approach would be for future CAT usage to include a caveat on technical execution when applied to design creativity research.

DISCLOSURE STATEMENT

No potential conflict of interest was reported by the author.

ACKNOWLEDGMENTS

I would like to acknowledge Dr Alison Green and Dr Theodore Zamenopoulous for their constant support and encouragement, and Dr Gini Harrison for her specific contribution towards the research design; Mr Andrew Bainbridge for enabling access to UCLan graphic design students, classes, and discussion of creative tasks for graphic design; Prof. Lubaina Himid for supporting my attendance at the 3rd ICDC, and so much more; the ICDC and IJDCI reviewers for their insightful comments. Lastly, most of my thanks must go to all the participants (both professional graphic designers and students of graphic design); for reasons of anonymity you each remain unknown here, but you know who you are, as I do, and you have my heartfelt thanks; without your support none of this research would be possible.

FUNDING

This research was supported by the University of Central Lancashire.

REFERENCES

1. Amabile, T. M. (1982). Social psychology of creativity: A consensual assessment technique. *Journal of Personality and Social Psychology, 43*, 997–1013.
2. Amabile, T. M. (1996). *Creativity in context: Update to the social psychology of creativity*. Boulder, CO: Westview Press.
3. Byrne, C. (2011). *Task selection and the consensual assessment technique: Using collage tasks in creativity research* (Unpublished masters thesis). University of Central Lancashire, Preston.
4. Baer, J., Kaufman, J. C., & Gentile, C. A. (2004). Extension of the consensual assessment technique to nonparallel creative products. *Creativity Research Journal, 16*, 113–,
5. Baer, J. (1993). *Creativity and divergent thinking: A task-specific approach*. Hillsdale, NJ: Lawrence Erlbaum Associates.
6. Christiaans, H., & Venselaar, K. (2005). Creativity in design engineering and the role of knowledge: Modelling the expert. *International Journal of Technology and Design Education, 15*, 217–236.
7. Dineen, R., & Niu, W. (2008). The effectiveness of western creative teaching methods in China: An action research project. *Psychology of Aesthetics, Creativity, and the Arts, 2*, 42–52.
8. Hennessey, B. A. (1994). The consensual assessment technique: An examination of the relationship between ratings of product and process creativity. *Creativity Research Journal, 7*, 193–208.,
9. Jeffries, K. K. (2011). Skills for creativity in games design. *Design Studies, 32*, 60–85.
10. Jeffries, K. K. (2012a). Amabile's Consensual Assessment Technique: Why has it not been used more in design creativity research? *Proceedings of the 2nd International Conference on Design Creativity (ICDC2012), 1*, 211–220.
11. Jeffries, K. K. (2012b). *Skills for creativity in graphic design* (Unpublished thesis). The Open University, Milton Keynes, UK.
12. Kaufman, J. C., Baer, J., Cole, J. C., & Sexton, J. D. (2008). A comparison of expert and nonexpert raters using the consensual assessment technique. *Creativity Research Journal, 20*, 171–178.
13. Kaufman, J. C., Plucker, J. A., & Baer, J. (2008). *Essentials of creativity assessment*. Hoboken, NJ: John Wiley & Sons.
14. Lubart, T., & Guignard, J. H. (2004). The generality-specificity of creativity: A multivariate approach. In R. J. Sternberg, E. L. Grigorenko & J. L. Singer (Eds), *Creativity: From potential to realization* (pp. 43–56). Washington, DC: American Psychological Association.
15. Nickerson, R. S. (1999). Enhancing creativity. In R. J. Sternberg (Ed.), *Handbook of creativity* (pp. 392–430). Cambridge: Cambridge University Press.
16. Pektas, S. T. (2010). Effects of cognitive styles on 2D drafting and design performance in digital media. *International Journal of Technology and Design Education, 20*, 63–76.10.1007/s10798-008-9060-x
17. Reiter-Palmon, R., Illies, M. Y., Cross, L. K., Buboltz, C. B., & Nimps, T. (2009). Creativity and domain specificity: The effect of task type on multiple indexes of creative problem-solving. *Psychology of Aesthetics, Creativity, and the Arts, 3*, 73–80.S

18. Silvia, P. J., Winterstein, B. P., Willse, J. T., Barona, C. M., Cram, J. T., Hess, K. I., ... Richard, C. A.(2008). Assessing creativity with divergent thinking tasks: Exploring the reliability and validity of new subjective scoring methods. *Psychology of Aesthetics, Creativity, and the Arts, 2*, 68–85.

19. Valgeirsdottir, D., Onarheim, B., & Gabrielsen, G. (2015). Product creativity assessment of innovations: Considering the creative process. *International Journal of Design Creativity and Innovation, 3*, 95–106.

20. Wojtczuk, A. (2014). *Creative product assessment in design: Influences of judges' backgrounds and levels of experience in design* (Unpublished doctoral dissertation), Aix Marseille Universite, Marseille.

CHAPTER 4

Interactive Music Composition Driven by Feature Evolution

Maximos A. Kaliakatsos-Papakostas[1]*, Andreas Floros[2] and Michael N. Vrahatis[3]

[1] *Department of Music, Aristotle University of Thessaloniki, 57001 Thessaloníki, Greece.*

[2] *Department of Audiovisual Arts, Ionian University, 49100 Corfu, Greece.*

[3] *Department of Mathematics, University of Patras, 26110 Patras, Greece.*

ABSTRACT

Evolutionary music composition is a prominent technique for automatic music generation. The immense adaptation potential of evolutionary algorithms has allowed the realisation of systems that automatically produce music through feature and interactive-based composition approaches. Feature-based composition employs qualitatively descriptive music features as fitness landmarks. Interactive composition systems on the other hand, derive fitness directly from human ratings and/or selection. The paper at hand introduces a methodological framework that combines the merits of both evolutionary composition methodologies. To this end, a system is presented that is organised in two levels: the higher level of interaction and the lower level of composition. The higher level incorporates the particle swarm optimisation algorithm, along with a proposed variant and evolves musical features according to user ratings. The lower level realizes feature-based music composition with a genetic algorithm, according to the top level features. The aim of this work is not to validate the efficiency of the currently utilised setup in each level, but to examine the convergence behaviour of such a two-level technique in an objective manner. Therefore, an additional novelty in this work concerns the utilisation of artificial raters that guide the system through the space of musical features, allowing the exploration of its convergence characteristics: does the system converge to optimal melodies, is this convergence fast enough for potential human listeners and is the trajectory to convergence "interesting' and "creative" enough? The experimental results reveal that the proposed methodological framework represents a fruitful and robust, novel approach to interactive music composition.

Keywords: Evolutionary music composition Interactive music composition Feature-based music composition Particle swarm optimisation Genetic algorithms

BACKGROUND

Music is an expression of human creativity with widely-explored structural characteristics that are associated with the concept of "music aesthetics", which describes the effect of music to humans. Music aesthetics are subjective, since each individual listener is differently affected by music. Recent advances in artificial intelligence and evolutionary computation have allowed the creation of computational algorithms that exhibit the spontaneity of human creativity, combined with the rule-based expression of musical form and structure. These algorithms pertain to the scientific topic named as "computational creativity", which has been increasingly expanding the last years.[1]Several evolutionary methodologies have been created that compose music according to stylistic constraints (Manaris et al. 2007), demarcated by evolutionary fitness norms in the form of aesthetically meaningful music features. These composition techniques will be hereby referred to as *"feature-based"*, since the fitness of their incorporated evolutionary algorithms depends on a set of targeted music feature values.

Concerning the subjectivity in the automatically composed music, the utilisation of "*interactive*" evolutionary algorithms appears advisable, since the fitness evaluation is performed by the human user in the form of melody rating and/or melody selection. Consequently, the evolution of compositions in this case aims towards generating music that is more pleasant to the listener. However, interactive evolutionary systems suffer from a fundamental drawback which counteracts the potential of evolutionary computation. This drawback is the *user fatigue* (Takagi 2001), which concerns the inability of human users to undergo vast amounts of rating (applying numeric values) or selection (selection/rejection of good/bad products) simulations. Therefore, the population sizes and the generation numbers are drastically deteriorated, neutralising the immense evolutionary dynamics.

The paper at hand introduces the combination of *interactive* and *feature-based* music composition in terms of an interactive system that exploits the merits of both compositional methodologies. The system is implemented in two levels: (a) the higher level, which incorporates the *particle swarm optimisation* (PSO) algorithm and a proposed variant, that evolves music features according to the feedback received by the user, thus realising interaction and (b) the lower level, where an evolutionary music composition scheme based on genetic algorithms (GA) composes music according to the features provided by the higher level. Under this implementation scheme, a population of features derived by the higher level is transformed into a population of melodies in the lower level and the ratings provided by the user to the composed melodies serve as fitness values of the features that these melodies represent.

The assessed measurements of the proposed system's performance indicate a fast convergence to the user's *subjectively optimal* melodies. However, the notion of *subjective optimality* is treated with *scepticism* in this paper: we do not necessarily argue that the currently examined system is indeed able to produce music that will please any user. The argument made in this paper is that the proposed methodology works as good as accurately

1. the utilised (higher level) features describe musical value and

2. the utilised (lower level) evolutionary composition system composes music according to these features.

Thereby, we do not necessarily claim—or, in any way, we do not examine—the efficiency of musical features per se in capturing subjective preference of human users. This study focusses on the following question: "given a set of efficient features that describe music quality, can a system be produced that uses these features for generating good quality music?" Therefore, the nature of the experimental processes that are meaningful in the context of this work is objective. A subjective assessment would not provide something fruitful, since the question does not concern how efficient the currently utilised features are, but how efficiently any given feature space is traversed by the proposed two-level evolutionary scheme.

In a future work, thorough subjective experimental evaluation of the proposed methodology will allow to address questions related to how different groups of human users reflect on such systems. For instance, would musicians consider using such a system for enhancing their creativity by manipulating the rating process so that unforeseen musical results emerge? Would non-musicians conceive this system as a tool for expressing their creativity by enabling them compose music according to ratings? In order to obtain meaningful answers to such human-oriented questions, extensive experimental analysis is required that places the focus on aspects of human perception rather than the issue of compositional convergence addressed in this paper.

In order to provide objectively admissible results we introduce a novel assessment methodology, which employs artificial, non-human raters. Compared to human listeners that may not be sure about which melody they considered pleasant at any given moment, an artificial rater may be constantly targeted to a specific melody, by providing higher ratings to melodies that assimilates it. Through this procedure, not only the "convergence" capabilities of the system are evaluated, but also the potential variability of the melodies throughout iterations is estimated. Furthermore, the weaknesses of the system are exposed by measuring its efficiency according to each musical feature separately, allowing for assumptions about potential future improvements.

The rest of the paper is organised as follows. "Literature overview and motivation" section provides a literature review over the descriptive quality of musical features and feature-based and interactive/evolutionary composition methodologies. A detailed description of the methodological context that this paper presents is provided in "Methods" section. The experimental methodology and the obtained results are presented in "Experimental methodology, results and discussion" section, where the concept of automatic raters is also introduced. Through the automatic raters, an objective assessment of the system's convergence capabilities is attempted, along with the melodic diversity estimation that the system is able to produce. Furthermore, this section provides some insights about the weaknesses of the proposed system, leading to assumptions about its potential improvement. Finally, the paper concludes in "Conclusions" section.

LITERATURE OVERVIEW AND MOTIVATION

This work is motivated by the progress made in the hitherto separate fields of feature and interactive-based music composition. Evolutionary algorithms have enabled both researchers and artists to compose music with specific, target characteristics expressed as sets of "musical features" that are able to describe music qualitatively. The potential of these features towards identifying musical characteristics has been demonstrated over the last decade by feature-based pattern recognition approaches that have been successfully employed to identify several musical attributes, like the composer (Purwins et al. 2004; Wolkowicz et al. 2008; Kaliakatsos-Papakostas et al. 2010, 2011) or the musical style and genre (Kranenburg and Backer 2004; Mckay and Fujinaga 2004; Hillewaere et al. 2009a, b; Herremans et al. 2015). Furthermore, the incorporation of features that focus on mathematical measures of complexity has allowed the aesthetic characterisation of music, producing models that simulate how humans perceive music (Shmulevich et al. 2001; Madsen and Widmer 2007), leading also to models of subjective preference (Manaris et al. 2002, 2005; Machado et al. 2003; Hughes and Manaris 2012). The information capacity of these features has allowed the development of evolutionary systems that automatically compose music in a "supervised" manner. Such systems employ a evolutionary schemes, with fitness criteria defined as fixed target values among the aforementioned features and compose music with certain stylistic or aesthetic content, under the "supervision" of these features. Examples of evolutionary techniques with fitness based on complexity-based music features, can be found in Manaris et al. (2007), Alfonseca et al. (2007), Manaris et al. (2011), while systems that utilize musical-oriented target features were developed in Papadopoulos and Wiggins (1998), Biles (2002), Özcan and Ercal (2008), Matic (2010), Donnelly and Sheppard (2011), Herremans et al. (2015), Hofmann (2015).

Alternative evolutionary "supervised" approaches have been proposed based on direct human guidance. In these cases, fitness evaluation on individual-melodies is accomplished by humans, who either assign the fitness values through a rating scheme (Unehara and Onisawa 2005; Fortier and Van Dyne 2011; MacCallum et al. 2012; Kaliakatsos-Papakostas et al. 2012d), or allow certain melodic individuals to reproduce through a selection–elimination scheme (Sánchez et al. 2007). These "interactive" composition methodologies have important assets and drawbacks in comparison to the feature-based ones. A major asset is that the evaluation of musical individuals is "guaranteed" to be aesthetically meaningful, since it is directly appraised by the aesthetic preferences of the human user. Contrarily, feature-based techniques rely on measurements over specific musical styles or genres, thus deteriorate the prospectives of radical novelty in compositions that emerged by human judgments. Specifically, feature-based systems may only compose music according to style or genre "templates", regardless of the subjective musical directions that the user might have. The primary and decisive drawback of interactive systems however, is related to the potential of the evolutionary process per se: the users are not able to undergo vast amounts of hearing and rating (or selecting) sessions, since it takes a forbiddingly large amount of time to evaluate large populations of individual-melodies evolved throughout a large number of generations, leading to *user fatigue*that additionally increases the uncertainty in ratings or selection and consequently misleads the evolutionary orientation. Therefore, interactive methodologies can hardly exploit the full potential of the evolutionary processes, which mainly relies on the combination of diverse possibilities that are encompassed by large numbers of population members.

An evolutionary process assesses the fitness of individuals through their "phenotypical" appearance and improve the population characteristics through "genotypical" interventions. However, it is not guaranteed that small alterations in the genotype of an individual will lead to small alteration to the phenotype (fitness). Therefore, an evolutionary scheme that includes a great number of individuals that are evolved for a great number of generations, may potentially conclude to the fine-tuned genotypical combinations that produce the desired phenotypical appearance, through numerous trial-and-error simulations. This fact subtly introduces an additional drawback: a small alteration of a well-fit individual-melody, or a combination of two well-fit individuals, is not guaranteed to result in the production of well-fit individuals. Thereby, the user is expected to hear and rate purely-fit individuals even in a quite progressed stages of evolution, a fact that amplifies user fatigue and further deepens the unclarity in user ratings. The difference between genotypical and phenotypical expressions of sound/musical individuals has been examined in Kaliakatsos-Papakostas et al. (2012c). In contrast to the lack of correspondence between genotypical and phenotypical distance, neighbouring locations in the feature space describe musical excerpts that share "neighbouring" musical characteristics, a fact that is evident by the style, genre and composer classification accuracy reported by existing works mentioned in the first paragraph of this section.

The work at hand introduces a balanced fusion of the aesthetically meaningful interactive human rating and the exhaustive explorational capabilities of feature-based composition. The proposed system consists of two levels: the higher level that models the human preference, and the lower level, where music is composed according to the user's preferences, as reflected by the features on the higher level. The higher level evolves music features and provides them to the lower level, which utilises evolutionary techniques to compose music according to these features. The human subject rates the melodies produced following his own aesthetic criteria. In contrast to the interactive methodologies already discussed, the listener actually rates the *features* that are responsible for the production of the respective melodies. The rating process thus allows the user to explore the *feature space* rather than "randomly" recombine, apply crossover and mutate musical genotypes. The term "randomly" above is used to express the fact that there is uncertainty in the effect that genotypical alterations have, since small changes on the genotypical level may result in vast changes on the phenotypical level.

The proposed approach incorporates the PSO algorithm on the higher level, whereas any heuristic alternative could have been used. The selection of PSO relies on two basic factors Firstly, since the system is interactive, fast convergence is required, making PSO a prominent choice (Vesterstrom and Thomsen 2004). Secondly, the feature space incorporates neighbouring regions that encompass similar musical characteristics. Therefore, the circumscription of particle orbits *from* their current position *to* the best position is important, since the user expects to hear as less random melodic transitions between rating iterations as possible. The existence of the "cognitive best" and "social best" coefficients in the PSO algorithm ensures that the transitions between successive agent steps are locally coherent, leading also to more promising directions. These characteristics of PSO are presumed to improve the interactive experience of the user, partially alleviating the imposition of user fatigue.

Several aspects of the proposed methodology need to be investigated in order to evaluate the aforementioned assumptions. Firstly, an evaluation of its robustness has to be performed, by examining the ability to "converge" to pleasant features/melodies indicated by the user. Secondly, the characteristics of the composed music throughout the evolutionary steps have to be analysed, as expressed by their positions in the feature space. This analysis is important because of the interactive perspective of the system; it is important to assess the feedback that the system provides to the user by examining the diversity of the melodies presented after each rating. Finally, the cooperation between the higher and the lower level has to be examined in detail, in order to obtain insights about the strengths and weaknesses of the proposed cooperative architecture.

METHODS

The developed system is designed to function according to the ratings provided by users—even though the experimental orientation does not include user-driven results. In a common scenarion, during evolution, each user listens to and subjectively rates four different evolving melodies in every rating round, based on two musical criteria: rhythm and tone. We have primarily investigated a single-valued rating scheme, i.e. rating how good is the melody, but it was rejected as it led to deadlock rating dilemmas: how should a listener rate a melody with, e.g. pleasant rhythm and unpleasant tone? On the other hand, "finer" rating subdivisions of multiple musical features (e.g. how good is chord-structure, rhythm syncopation, tonality balance) were found to be confusing for the mean user. Therefore, a rating scheme including two ratings for each melody, namely the "rhythm" and "tone", was chosen. Figure 1 illustrates a block diagram of the proposed system. User rhythm and tone ratings are processed almost independently, except from some rhythmic constraints that are imposed on the tone generation process. The architecture of both parts is identical, with their higher levels incorporating PSO and the lower levels comprising a set of GA-based music generation modules. The higher level PSO employs agents that roam in a space of several music features, while the lower level GA schemes compose music by generating rhythmic and tonal sequences respectively, according to the feature combinations provided by each agent.

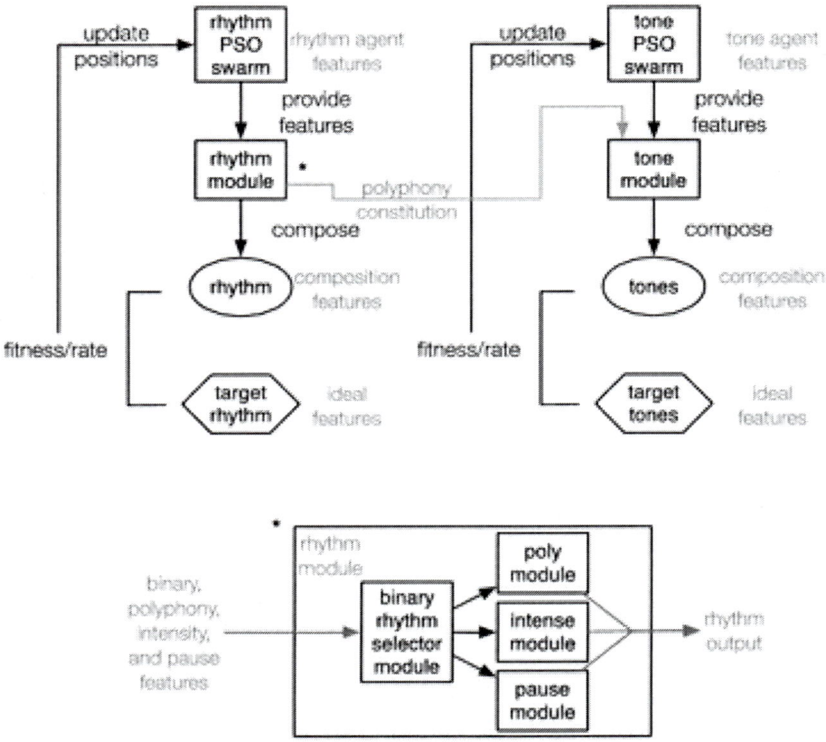

Figure 1. Block diagram of the proposed system

Two PSO swarms are used for describing rhythm and tonal features respectively, while each of these swarms comprises four agents. Each agent's coordinates in turn, represent a set of rhythmic and tonal features respectively. Therefore, the location of an agent describes a unique feature combination that is rendered as specific rhythmic or tonal sequences respectively by the lower level GA modules. For example, the location of a rhythm agent signifies a certain rhythmic features combination, which is "delivered" to the underlying rhythm composition GA as guidelines to compose a rhythmic sequence. The same holds for the tone PSO agents and the underlying tone generation GA modules. In general, the position of a PSO agent constitutes the fitness criterion for the respective GA composition module, in a sense that the GA module aims at composing music (rhythmic or tonal sequences) with features that are as similar as possible to the ones dictated by the respective higher level PSO agent. Furthermore, each agent in the rhythm swarm is linked to an agent at the tone swarm, meaning that a melody is finally composed by combining the rhythmic and the tonal sequences of a certain pair of rhythm and tone agents. Besides, the tone GA composes a tonal sequence over a given rhythmic sequence, as described in "Evolutionary generation of melodies" section.

Each pair of rhythm and tone agents describes a melody. Thereby, the quadruples of rhythm and tone agent pairs are rendered as four melodies through the respective underlying GA modules. As mentioned previously, a listener subjectively rates these four melodies providing fitness evaluation to the respective rhythm and tone PSO agents. In the next rating round, the rhythm and tone agent pairs quadruples are evolved with a properly adjusted PSO agent location update rule presented in "PSO initialisation and evolution" section, moving to new positions that correspond to new music features (i.e. combinations of rhythmic and tonal features). In turn, the underlying GA modules compose music according to the updated agent locations/features, presenting four novel melodies to the user that constitute the melodic content of the new rating round. Through this iterative process, user's ratings are expected to lead the PSO agent quadruples to feature regions that reflect pleasant music characteristics.

Basic user-oriented assumptions

The aim of the proposed system is to facilitate user interaction. The following paragraphs focus on some basic assumptions about what a user would expect and tolerate from such a system. The experimental processes that are described later aim to monitor whether the system satisfies these assumptions. The basic assumptions presented in this section concern generally admissible facts about interactive music generation systems, while, as a novelty of this paper, the experimental results examine these assumptions without any subjective test: artificial raters are employed that simulate the behaviour of human users.

There are some aspects of interactive music evolution that impose convergence to "subjective optima" limitations. Due to the *user fatigue* that results from the constant human devotion to the task of listening and rating, the listener is expected to loose focus during the rating process, especially if she/he undergoes a large number of melodies in each rating round. This obviously increases the hazard of inconsistent or even contradicting ratings, misleading the system to non-optimal feature regions. Consequently, this would force the agents to roam the feature space without converging to certain melodic locations, creating an impression that the system does not provide any feedback to the user ratings, further amplifying the vicious circle of user fatigue. User fatigue does not solely depend on the number of melodies, but also on their duration. Since the melodies that the proposed system produces are about 15 s long (as described later in "Evolutionary generation of melodies" section), a collection of 4 melodies per rating round was considered as a satisfactory compromise between melodic diversity (considering also the initialisation procedure discussed in "PSO initialisation and evolution" section) and keeping the number of melodies as low as possible.

Independently of the number of melodies in each rating iteration, user fatigue is also expected to emerge at some point, since there is a generally admissible time limit that a human can listen to melodies carefully, no matter how interesting these melodies are. Moreover, since it is desirable to have gradual convergence to an optimal region in the feature space, all melodies that comprise consecutive quadruples are expected to become more similar as the iteration progresses. Hence, after a number of rating rounds, the user will be required to rate similar melodies, a fact that increases user fatigue and, consequently, inconsistent and/or contradicting ratings. The above mentioned two points highlight an additional constraint: *the system should be progressing towards better rated melodies swiftly, within a small number of rating rounds*. Similarly to the decision made about the number of melodies in each rating iteration, the estimation of a maximum number of rating rounds is also dependent on the expected duration of rating each quadruple. Since each melody is about 15 s long, each rating round (4 melodies) is expected to last about 1 minute, therefore allowing a rough estimation of 20 rating iterations (about 20 min) per user at maximum. Although the limit of evolutionary iterations is case-dependent, a human listener is anticipated to undergo a maximum limit of 10–20 iterations (Takagi 2001).

PSO initialisation and evolution

The melodies in all rating rounds are four and, according to the aforementioned basic assumption, in parallel to their swift fitness convergence, they should encompass as diverse (and well fit) characteristics as possible, covering a range of features that is as wide as possible. Hence, the user should be offered a wide spectrum of pleasant potential melodic possibilities that would allow a more efficient and productive exploration of the overall music feature space. The required diversity of features is achieved through an initialisation scheme that guarantees that every pair of melodies has at least one pair of "sufficiently distant" features (rhythmic or tonal). The employed initialisation algorithm roughly loops through all the features, randomly divides the four agents in two pairs and for each pair it assigns two random feature values that are separated by a minimum preselected percentage of this feature's range. For example, we may consider the polyphony mean feature, defined as the mean number of simultaneous notes per onset event. For the purposes of this work, this feature takes real values within [1, 5]. Therefore, if the least distance percentage is set to 80 %, then in one of the randomly selected pairs of agents, one agent would be assigned with a value a=random(1,1+(1−0.8)(5−1))a=random(1,1+(1−0.8)(5−1)), while the other with a value b=random(a+0.8,5)b=random(a+0.8,5), where the function y=random(x1,x2)y=random(x1,x2) returns a random real number in [x1,x2] The same would be performed for the remaining two agents of the other pair. By employing a random agent pair selection, this initialisation scheme actually shuffles extreme music characteristics and randomly dispenses them among the four agents of the initial PSO populations. The limit used for the experimental results was 90 %, in order to achieve an extreme diversity among the four initial melodies.

The subsequent agents' movement rules need also to be adapted in order to meet the constraints imposed by the interactive nature of the system. As discussed previously, the user anticipates that the system evolves melodies towards better ones swiftly and in accordance to the rates that she/he provides. Hence, the listener should feel that there is no lack of feedback from the system and that his rating is as meaningful as possible, in a sense that higher-rated melodies are less altered than lower-rated melodies. To this end, a novel variation of the PSO algorithm was formed, which encompasses information about the ratings (fitness) that a melody has been assigned, allowing the respective (rhythm or tone) agent to move faster or slower in correspondence to its rating.

The first formalisations of PSO were provided in Kennedy and Eberhart (1995), where the position of each agent was updated for each dimension based on the position of the agent's former optimiser value, as well as on the position of the global swarm optimiser value. The new position of each agent is computed as the sum of its previous position with a quantity that is estimated according to several factors, depending on the PSO variant, which incorporate the agent's and the swarm's best positions. Specifically, the *i*-th agent is initialised in a position $\vec{x}_i(0) = (x_{i1}(0), x_{i2}(0), \ldots, x_{iD}(0))^\top$ and utilising the inertia weight (Shi and Eberhart 1998a, b) PSO variant, the position of the agent in every time step is updated by

$$v_{ij}(t+1) = w\, v_{ij}(t) + c_p R_p (p_{ij}(t) - x_{ij}(t)) + c_g R_g (p_{gj}(t) - x_{ij}(t)) \quad (1)$$

$$x_{ij}(t+1) = x_{ij}(t) + v_{ij}(t), \quad (2)$$

where i $i = 1, 2, 3, 4,\ j = 1, 2, \ldots, D,$ w is the inertia factor, cpcp and cgcg are the biases towards the personal best position of the agent and the global best of the swarm and RpRp and RgRg are random numbers chosen uniformly in [0, 1]. The quantity in Eq. 1 is called the "velocity" of the agent and the location update in each dimension is performed through adding the respective velocity coefficient to the agent's current location, as demonstrated in Eq. 2. For a thorough review of PSO algorithms, the interested reader is referred to Parsopoulos and Vrahatis (2010). It is also parenthetically mentioned that several works have utilised swarm intelligence [inspired by the "*boids*" algorithm (Reynolds 1987, 1988)] for music composition (Blackwell and Bentley 2002; Blackwell 2003, 2007; Jones 2008) and sound synthesis (Blackwell and Young 2004; Blackwell 2008; Wilson 2008).

For the presented system, a modified formula for the computation of velocity has also been tested, which encompasses some characteristics that improve the overall interactive experience. In particular, a coefficient is added which introduces de facto noise to the computation of velocity. In Eq. 1, after the first rating round, the agent that carries the best rating remains unaltered, since all the products on the right side of the equation have at least one zero-valued term. Specifically, vbj $v_{bj}(0) = 0,\ p_{bj}(0) = x_{bj}(0)$ and $p_{gj}(0) = p_{bj}(0) = x_{bj}(0)$, where $b \in \{1, 2, 3, 4\}$ is the index of the best rated agent in the first rating round and j=1,2,...,Dj=1,2,...,D. Therefore, as long as the initially higher rated agent remains the higher rated in subsequent rating rounds, the characteristics of the best melody will remain unaltered, providing the user with an essence that the system does not evolve according to her/his ratings. For instance, if a user provides a maximum rating of 3 out of 10, then the characteristics of the melody that has been rated with 3 will remain unaltered, a fact that is not justified by its overall low rate.

On the other hand, since the number of iterations is expected to be small (earlier roughly computed around 20) and the number of agents is also restrictive (four melodies per rating round) the movement of each melody throughout the iteration rounds has to be as deliberately calculated as possible. Thus, the melodies with higher ratings for rhythm or tone should be wandering into the respective space with more "self-confidence" than the ones that obtain lower ratings. The term "self-confidence" expresses the notion of increased bias towards the personal best. Contrarily, a lower rated agent should steer more decisively towards the "safer" global best. To this end, the novel velocity update formula does not incorporate the constant cpcp and cgcg values; instead, these values are adjusted according to the current rating of a particular agent. For facilitating the reference to this modified PSO, the term *rating-based* PSO (*r*-PSO) is employed hereby. Similar modifications, which utilize the fitness of an agent to determine its location update potential have recently been proposed (Yang et al. 2007; Akbari and Ziarati 2011).

The velocity update formula for the *r*-PSO becomes

$$v_{ij}(t+1) = w\, v_{ij}(t) + f_p(\beta_c) c_p R_p (p_{ij}(t) - x_{ij}(t)) + f_p(\beta_c) c_g R_g (p_{gj}(t) - x_{ij}(t)) + f_r(\beta_c) \vec{R}_j, \quad (3)$$

where R⃗ R→ is a vector of uniformly selected random numbers within a proportion of the search space, $f_p(x),\ f_g(x)$ and $f_r(x)$ are functions that receive the current rate of the agent (βcβc) and are expressed by

$$f_p(\beta_c) = \frac{\beta_c - \beta_w}{\beta_b - \beta_w + 1}, \quad (4)$$

$$f_g(\beta_c) = \frac{\beta_b + 1 - \beta_w - (\beta_c - \beta_w)}{\beta_b - \beta_w + 1}, \quad (5)$$

$$f_r(\beta_c) = \frac{\beta_b + 1 - \beta_w - (\beta_c - \beta_w)}{\beta_b - \beta_w + 1}, \quad (6)$$

where βwβw is the worst rating in the current rating round and βbβb is the global best rate in all previous rating rounds in the simulation. Through Eq. 4, the magnitude of the "cognitive" product $(c_p R_p (p_{ij}(t) - x_{ij}(t)))$ increases as the rate of the agent (βcβc) increases, with a minimum "cognitive confidence" of zero being achieved for the lowest rated agent $(\beta_c = \beta w)$. Contrarily, the coefficients of the "social" product $(c_g R_g (p_{gj}(t) - x_{ij}(t)))$ decreases as the rate of the agent increases. The modification in the velocity is not necessarily targeted towards improving the effectiveness of the PSO swarms in terms of fitness, but mainly towards engaging the user with diverse musical material that is evolving rationally according to her/his rating, throughout the rating iterations. Nonetheless, as the results in "Experimental methodology, results and discussion" section indicate, not only a diversity in the melodies throughout and within each rating round is achieved, but also the overall optimisation effectiveness of the system is slightly improved.

Evolutionary generation of melodies

Under the proposed approach, automatic music composition algorithms generate melodies that comply with the constraints reflected by the features carried by each agent. Both rhythm and tone generation rely on GAs, through which binary or integer sequences are evolved. The evolution of these sequences is based on their interpretations to melodies and their consequent fitness evaluation according to a set of 39 music features (22 rhythmic and 17 tonal). In the context of this work, modified version of feature-based evolutionary algorithms presented in the literature for music composition have been developed. However, since the scope of the paper concerns the study of the convergence behaviour, a detailed description of the lower level composition algorithms is omitted.

The utilisation of evolutionary algorithms for the generation of rhythmic sequences has been previously explored for both percussive (Ariza 2002; Eigenfeldt 2008; Sioros and Guedes 2011; Yamamoto et al. 2012; Kaliakatsos-Papakostas et al. 2013) and pitched (Horowitz 1994; Kaliakatsos-Papakostas et al. 2012b) instruments. In the majority of these cases rhythms are derived that encompass certain characteristics, by fostering promising generations of rhythmic sequences through evolutionary processes. The key notion to the evolution of rhythms is the definition of proper fitness criteria that accurately describe the quantitative characteristics of the desired target rhythm. Therefore, the evolutionary approach to automatic rhythm composition incorporates a functional modeling of rhythmic sequences in the form of evolvable entities, in combination with a set of rhythmic features that operate as fitness criteria, driving the evolution to rhythms that adhere to certain qualitative characteristics.

The generation of rhythms in the context of the proposed system incorporates not only information about the time that a note event will happen, but also the polyphony and the intensity of this event, as well as information about pauses. The polyphony of an event indicates the number of notes that are simultaneously played. The intensity describes the loudness at which the notes during an onset event are heard. The pauses denote silence events, where all remaining notes are interrupted until a new note onset event occurs. The rhythm module employed here incorporates four submodules, which manage all the aforementioned rhythmic properties, namely the *binary*, the *polyphony*, the *intensity* and the *pause* submodules. These submodules produce rhythms according to the 22 rhythmic features provided by the respective agents in the rhythm swarm. From these 22 features, 5 are addressed to the binary, 6 to the polyphony, 6 to the intensity and 5 to the pause submodules.

The block diagram of the rhythm module is shown in Figure 2. All melodies considered here are 4 measures with 4/4 time signature and an analysis of 16-ths, which are composed separately and then merged The *binary* submodule produces binary sequences, with the digit 1 denoting an onset and 0 denoting a "no action" rhythm event. Since each measure is composed of 16 digits, the number of different binary rhythms is 216216. Therefore, when an agent requests a rhythm with certain binary characteristics (through the 5 features that describe it) the binary submodule searches throughout all 216216 binary rhythms and returns the ones that are more suitable. The binary submodule does not incorporate any evolutionary architecture, since the binary rhythm search space is small.

The *polyphony* and *intensity* submodules on the other hand, require the utilisation of evolutionary algorithms since the search space is overwhelmingly large. These submodules are dependent on the output of the binary submodule. Specifically, they isolate the onset events described in the binary submodule (occurrences of digit 1) and assign to them an integer within [1, 5] for the polyphony and [50, 120] for the integer submodules. The values [1, 5] denote the existence of 1–5 simultaneous notes, while the [50, 120] values denote MIDI velocities (intensities) ranging from 50 to 120. Proper integer combinations are examined using GA. These submodules produce suitable integer sequences that satisfy the demands of a rhythm agent, reflected in the features it carries (specifically from feature 6–11 for polyphony and 12–17 for intensity submodules).

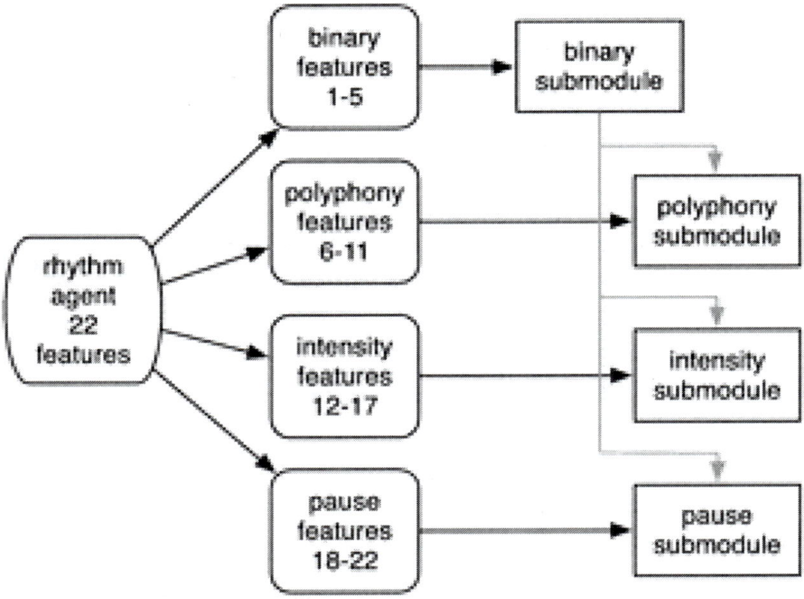

Figure 2. Block diagram of the rhythm module

Finally, the *pause* submodule locates positions of possible pauses, which are the no-onset (mapped to the 0 digit) of the binary submodule. By utilizing GA, the pause module examines the suitability of different pause scenarios by comparing the pause features they produce with the ones carried by the guiding rhythm agent (features 18–22).

The block diagram of the tone module is depicted in Figure 3. This module utilizes GA to construct integer sequences in [36, 120], which are subsequently mapped to MIDI notes. The length of the integer sequences depends on the number of notes that the melody's measure includes, which is provided by the polyphony rhythm vector. The notes for the tone sequences generated by the GA are selected from a note list formed using 3 criteria: music scale, lowest note and octave range. These quantities are provided to the tone module as numeric values by the tone agent's coordinates indexed from 15 to 17 (from the 17 total features that the tone agent provides). The agent's coordinates from 1 to 14 are the agent's compositional guidelines, which are provided to the tone module as tonal features, on which the fitness evaluation is based. These features incorporate information that describe the complexity of the pitch class profile distribution through Shannon Information Entropy (Shannon 2001), descriptive statistics of the note and pitch class transitions' distributions, the percentages of ascending, descending and constant transitions (Coca et al. 2010) and the chord potentiality of note clusters. A similar approach for automatic generation of tones has been followed in Kaliakatsos-Papakostas et al. (2012a).

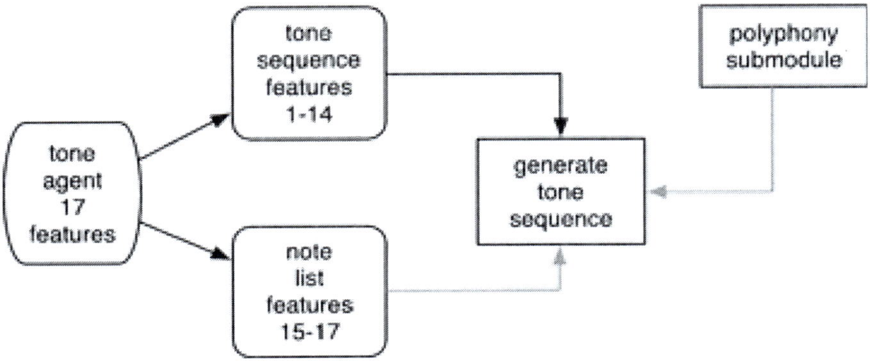

Figure 3. Block diagram of the tone module

EXPERIMENTAL METHODOLOGY, RESULTS AND DISCUSSION

The lower level rhythm and tone generation modules may incorporate errors towards the production of rhythmic and tonal sequences, since it is not ensured that they will be capable to absolutely comply with the guidelines provided by the respective PSO agents (achieve perfect fitness). Thereby, a melody that is composed under a PSO agent features' guidelines may not necessarily reflect these features exactly. Additionally, the position of an agent in the feature space may provide the underlying submodules with contradicting features, which may not be satisfied by definition, e.g. an agent may require 60 % ascending note intervals and at the same time 70 % descending note intervals, resulting to an unachievable sum of 130 %. Moreover, the ratings provided by a human listener may incorporate uncertainty and noise, i.e. the user may not feel absolutely confident about the aesthetic quality of a melody.

The presented combined bilevel evolutionary scheme models the above errors (or noise) in both the lower and higher level music generation modules, taking into account a) the potential incapability of the composition level to absolutely comply with the feature level agents' guidelines and b) the instability of human ratings. Therefore, the system's evaluation focuses on the convergence behaviour under the circumstances that incorporate the aforementioned efficiency impediments. The former impediment is endogenous to the system. The latter one depends on subjective factors and may not be directly quantified; hence they should be modeled by considering very general admissions, as discussed in "Assessment of performance through automatic raters" section.

By considering the potential composition inefficiency of the system, several questions may raise: does the system converge to optimal melodies? If the system does converge, how may the convergence characteristics be quantified? If there are impediments in convergence, which are the causes? The experimental results reported in this section provide answers to these questions by employing four PSO parameter *setups*, two of which pertain in the standard PSO, while the remaining two follow the *r*-PSO velocity update scheme. Although several values of *w*, cpcp and cgcg have been examined for both PSO and *r*-PSO cases, results are reported for the following representative PSO parameter setups:

1. setup-1 (S_1): PSO velocity update, $w = 0.3$, $c_p = 1$ and $c_g = 1$,
2. setup-2 (S_2): PSO velocity update, $w = 0.3$, $c_p = 0.2$ and $c_g = 1$,
3. setup-3 (S_3): *r*-PSO velocity update, $w = 0.3$, $c_p = 1$ and $c_g = 1$ and
4. setup-4 (S_4): *r*-PSO velocity update, $w = 0.3$, $c_p = 0.2$ and $c_g = 1$.

For both *r*-PSO setups, the random perturbation vector, $\vec{R}$ R→, takes values within a 10 % margin of the respective dimension's magnitude.

Assessment of performance through automatic raters

Answering questions that incorporate convergence by subjective human ratings tests is challenging. Testing whether the system "converges" incorporates the exact allocation of a set of "*ideal features*" that the system will pursue to capture. The human users may not be certain about the ideal features that they require from a music piece. This fact does not only rely on the subjectivity of each listener to music pleasantness, but also to the conditionality that this pleasantness is actually expressed. For example, the shadowgraph of some potential "ideal feature" that a human rater may have in mind at some point during the simulation, may be influenced by a melody that she/he hears during a rating round. Thereby, these "ideal features" are expected to steer towards different musical directions throughout the rating simulation. This steering in the preferred features that a human rater may experience is a desirable effect of human cognition and creativity; however the aim of this research is to quantify the extent at which the system is able to *follow* the directions provided by a user, even if these directions change within simulations.

To this end, a "test-tube" experimental methodology is formulated, where the rates are provided by *automatic raters*. These raters simulate some basic rating characteristics of human raters, but provide ratings in accordance to the fixed set of features, called the "ideal features". In contrast to a human user, the ideal features of the automatic raters remain fixed throughout every rating simulation. The ability of the system to move towards these features is scrutinised by employing several rating simulations with several "almost" random ideal features, carried out by automatic raters with different rating characteristics. The term "almost" is utilised in a sense that these ideal features should describe a music piece that is potentially realizable, therefore an absolutely random procedure would produce controversial and mutually-rejecting features (like the aforementioned example of the unrealisable 130 % percentage of ascending and descending intervals). Therefore, the ideal features that each automatic rater encompasses are the ones of a piece composed by a random selection of features. The ideal features could also be extracted from well-known music compositions; however, this idea was rejected in order to avoid restricting the considered compositional scope.

In order to construct an ideal features' set for a rating simulation a random point in the feature space is selected which functions as the compositional guidelines to the music composition modules. The feature combination represented by this point in the feature space could incorporate controversial features, as described earlier. Nevertheless, the melody that is finally composed by the music composition modules incorporate features that belong to a melody by definition. Thus, this process ensures that the ideal features of the automatic raters in each rating simulation are potentially realisable. The automatic raters are guaranteed to have a fixed set of target ideal features according to which they provide their ratings. It is assumed that a melody will be rated with a higher value, if its features are closer to the ideal features of the rater. By denoting the ideal features of a rater in a simulation as fr∗→f∗r→ for the rhythm features and ft∗→f∗t→ for the tone features, the rate that the automatic rater will assign to a melody with features frc→fcr→ and ftc→fct→ is inversely related to the respective distances:

$$q_r = \left\| \vec{f}^{\,r}_{*} - \vec{f}^{\,r}_{c} \right\|_2, \tag{7}$$

$$q_t = \left\| \vec{f}_*^t - \vec{f}_c^t \right\|_2, \tag{8}$$

while their connection to the final rating is described later, by Eq. 9. Additionally, to simulate the introduction of human ratings uncertainty, a random value is also added, which is potentially allowed to violate the better fitness–better rate principle.

For the artificial raters several "rating profiles" were modeled, employing different criteria towards how high a rating describes a good melody. For instance, a strict rater may provide a higher rate of 5 to the melodies he finds most appealing. Contrarily, a less strict rater may rate with 9 some appealing melodies. Since the PSO and melodies evolution relies on ratings, the convergence of the system is examined in accordance to four different rating profiles, which are calibrated to model a variety of potential users from non-strict to strict. The fitness-to-rating correspondence of the four rating profiles that are utilised for the experimental results is depicted in Figure 4. These rating curves assign a rate (β_x) to a fitness value (q_x) or tone (x=tx=t) agent using the equation:

$$\beta_x = 10 - 10\left(\frac{q_x - l_x}{u_x - l_x}\right)^{\alpha} + \xi_\beta, \tag{9}$$

where l_x and u_x are the lower and upper bounds of fitness for rhythm (x=rx=r) and tone $(x = t)$ and ξ_β is a random number in [−0.5,0.5][−0.5,0.5] that simulates human rating uncertainty. The parameter αα defines the "strictness" of the artificial rater, with higher values denoting a less strict rater. The values of αα depicted in Figure 4 are 3.3, 1.3, 0.7 and 0.3, which are also the values of the four automatic raters employed in this work.

The underlying music composition modules that have been formulated for the bottom level of the proposed system are hardly capable to compose melodies that perfectly match the features requested by the agents. Therefore, the lxlx values are set to a near-minimum error quantity below which the rhythm and tone modules can hardly reach. Accordingly, the value of uxux is set to a near-maximum error quantity of the rhythm and tone modules. After thorough experimentation, and by considering a rating

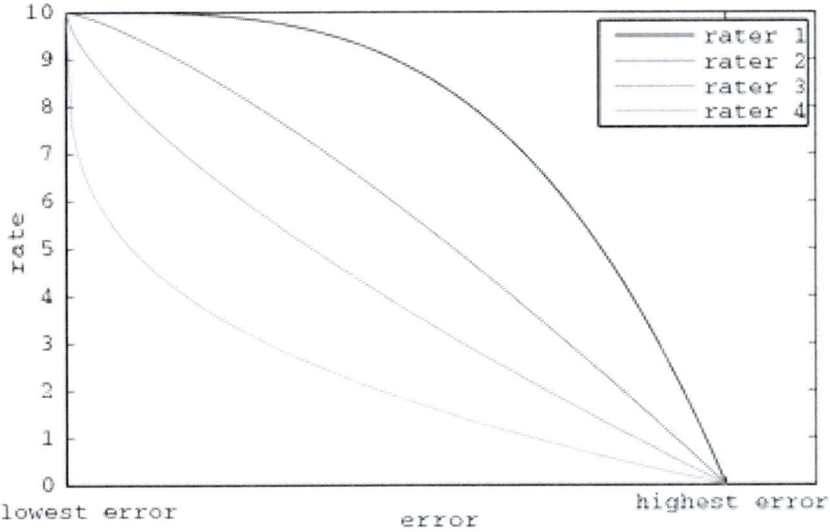

Figure 4. Illustration of the assigned automatic raters' rating profiles

scale in [0, 10], the values that have been selected for the respective modules are the following: lr=2lr=2, lt=1lt=1, ur=13ur=13 and ut=8ut=8. It should be noted that these values are system-dependent and consequently, apply to the music composition modules of the presented system. For the experiments that follow, the four rater profiles considered are the following:

1. rater-1 (R_1): $\alpha = 3.3$,
2. rater-2 (R_2): $\alpha = 1.3$,
3. rater-3 (R_3): $\alpha = 0.7$ and
4. rater-4 (R_4): $\alpha = 0.3$.

For each rater and setup combinations the results of 50 rating simulations were examined and are presented next.

Fitness convergence analysis

The primary concern is to examine whether the system presents overall converging behaviour or not. System convergence can be expressed as the reduction of distances between the rhythm and tone features of the composed music $(\vec{f_c^r} \text{ and } \vec{f_c^t} \text{ respectively})$ and the respective ideal features $(\vec{f_*^r} \text{ and } \vec{f_*^t})$ that the automatic rater demonstrates throughout the rating rounds. The features of the composed music $(\vec{f_c^r} \text{ and } \vec{f_c^t})$ depend on the features provided by the respective rhythm and tone PSO agents $\vec{f_a^r} \text{ and } \vec{f_a^t}$ specifically $\vec{f_a^r} \text{ and } \vec{f_a^t},$ are provided as the target features for the underlying music composition modules. As previously mentioned, these modules would function "perfectly" if they were able to compose music that adheres exactly to $\vec{f_c^r} = \vec{f_a^r} \text{ and } \vec{f_c^r} = \vec{f_a^t}.$ thus it would hold that $\vec{f_c^r} = \vec{f_a^r} \text{ and } \vec{f_c^r} = \vec{f_a^t}.$ In this ideal scenario the overall system's convergence would be trivial: the system would convergence if the higher level PSO algorithm converged. In this case, the overall converging behaviour of the system would absolutely depend on the parameter setup of the PSO modules.

Nevertheless, the underlying composition modules can hardly compose music precisely according to the music requested by the respective PSO agent's features. It is thus expected that the features of the composed music, $\vec{f_c^r} \text{ and } \vec{f_c^t},$ will be similar but not identical to the requested features, $\vec{f_a^r} \text{ and } \vec{f_a^t}.$ Therefore, the overall system's convergence does not only depend on the top-level PSO convergence, but it is also affected by the effectiveness of the underlying music composition modules, which is analysed in "Adaptation of specific music features" section in detail. Additionally, even if the system converges, there is a crucial matter of how fast this convergence occurs, since the convergence rate is crucial for the effectiveness of the system's *interactivity*. For example, slow convergence could distract the user's attention, providing him with an essence that the produced output does not change according to hers/his directions. It would be thus substantial to examine the system's convergence within the time span that a user would undergo without the imposition of fatigue. Therefore, as discussed in "Methods" section, a maximum number of 20 rating iterations was considered.

Figure 5 illustrates the basic statistical convergence behaviour of the system, based on the mean value of errors of all melodies in every rating round, i.e. the distances between the music composed by the guidance of all four PSO agents and the ideal features calculated as:

$$\mu = \frac{1}{4}\sum_{i=1}^{4}\left\|\vec{f_{c,i}^{x}} - \vec{f_{*}^{x}}\right\|_2, \tag{10}$$

where i is the PSO agent's index and x∈{r,t}. The error bars appeared in the above figure indicate the mean values and the standard deviations of the aforementioned mean distances in each iteration for all 50 simulations. These illustrations concern some representative artificial raters and setups, while the respective illustrations for the remaining raters and setups exhibit similar characteristics, i.e. all errors reduce to a minimum value, as also discussed later in Table 1. Thereby, the mean error for all agents in both the rhythm and the tone PSO swarms is gradually reduced, indicating an asymptotical convergence of all four PSO agents for both rhythm and tone swarms to a minimum value. Some aspects of individual agent convergence behaviour are further addressed in "Music features convergence analysis" section.

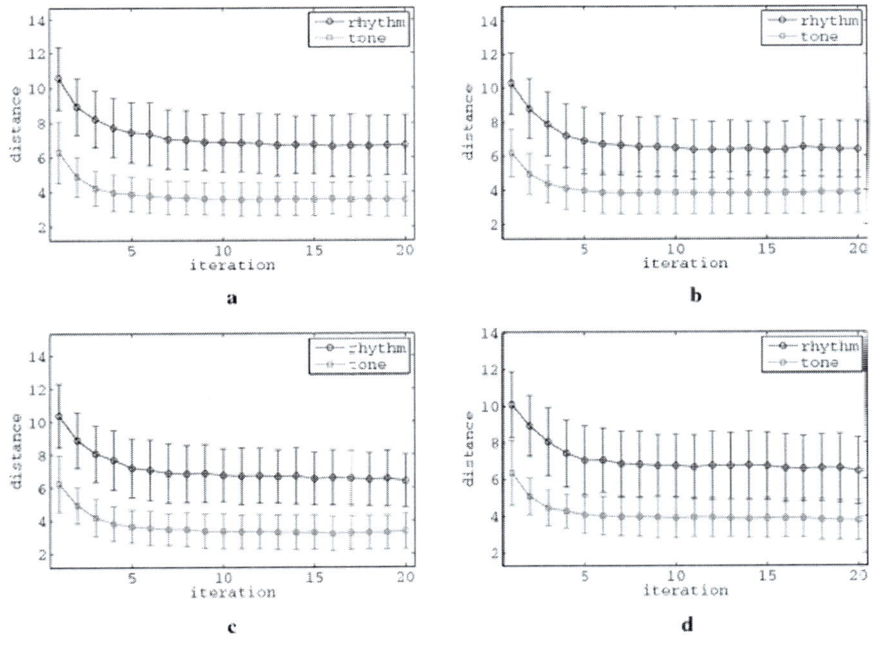

Figure 5. *Error bars* of total fitness for all 50 simulations of some representative PSO setups of rhythm and tone generating modules, for all ARs. **A** R2R2-S1S1. **B** R2R2–S2S2. **C** R2R2-S3S3. **D** R2R2-S4S4

The statistical improvement in the mean fitness of all four composed melodies in a rating round is also demonstrated in Table 1, where several statistical values signify that the convergence to the "ideal features" is within the assumed limit of 20 rating rounds. The first and second columns of this table demonstrate the mean and standard deviation values (in parentheses) of the mean error described by Eq. 10 among all simulations during the first and last PSO iteration respectively for all the artificial raters and PSO setups. The relative improvement of this error is shown in the third column of this Table and it is computed as the difference between the mean error of all four melodies (μμ value) in the initial and the last generations over the error (μμ value) in the initial generation for all simulations. The relative improvement of the mean values in all simulations mostly are between 0.32 and 0.46, showing minor differences among different rater–setup combinations. The statistical significance of these differences is discussed after the following paragraph.

Additional exploration of the convergence speed is performed by measuring the rating iteration in which the 90 % of the total relative improvement is achieved. The selection of the 90 % limit is abstract, it could be any percentage that approaches 100 %. This measurement provides insights about the expected rating round (PSO iteration) in which the user will have covered most of the progress (i.e. 90 % of the system's optimal fitness improvement capabilities) having considered a maximum iteration limit of 20 rating rounds. Thereafter, the progress of the melodies is expected to be slower, since a small part of the potential improvement will be realizable (e.g. 10 %). Hence, the 90 % progress iteration is used as a means to identify the rating round at which a satisfactory improvement in melodies (in accordance to the system's capabilities) will have been performed. After the 90 % fitness progress rating round, the deceleration of fitness improvement will imminently give the user the essence that the system is not responding to the ratings and fatigue will imminently have more chances to begin.

The statistical significance in the mean relative improvements for all raters and PSO setups is demonstrated in Table 2, where a "+" sign denotes that the improvement that corresponds to the rater and setup of the row is significantly higher than the one of the respective column. A "–" denotes the opposite. An "=" sign is shown if there is no statistical significance in the considered relative improvements. Each rater incorporates an upper-diagonal quadruple of sign symbols. Each row within each rater's quadruple denotes the respective PSO setup. Therefore, the diagonal quadruples refer to the results of the statistical significance tests among the measurements of different setups for the same automatic rater, while the off diagonal (or upper-diagonal) quadruples refer to the tests' results regarding all different raters and all PSO setups.

The statistical significance is measured through a two-sided Wilcoxon (1945) rank sum test, which is applied on the distributions of the 50 simulations for each rater and setup combination. Through this test, the statistical significance of the difference in the distributions of the relative improvements of each rater–setup combination is examined. Specifically, for each pair of rater–setup relative improvement measurements we employ the rank sum test to each respective pair, to obtain the probability that these two measurement sets belong to a continuous distribution with equal medians. Formally, the null hypothesis for each pair of relative improvement measurements is that they are independent samples from identical continuous distributions with equal medians. If the null hypothesis is rejected at the 5 % significance level for a pair of rater–setup, then these improvements are indicated to be significantly different in a statistical sense.

Table 1.Statistics of mean fitness improvement among the melodies of the initial and the final rating iteration, for all raters and setups, in all the respective simulations

Rater–setup	Init. fit.	Last fit.	Rel. impr.	90 % iter.
R_1				
S_1				
Rhythm	10.19 (1.94)	6.61 (1.28)	0.35 (0.11)	5.92 (4.08)
Tone	6.14 (1.37)	3.93 (1.03)	0.36 (0.15)	4.58 (2.26)
S_2				
Rhythm	10.04 (1.80)	6.66 (1.36)	0.33 (0.12)	5.38 (2.70)
Tone	6.21 (1.61)	3.78 (1.05)	0.40 (0.16)	4.06 (1.96)
S_3				
Rhythm	10.03 (1.76)	6.41 (1.46)	0.36 (0.13)	6.00 (3.12)
Tone	6.18 (1.70)	3.68 (1.07)	0.40 (0.16)	5.52 (3.59)
S_4				
Rhythm	10.24 (1.94)	6.91 (1.45)	0.32 (0.13)	5.82 (3.15)
Tone	6.05 (1.47)	3.67 (0.87)	0.39 (0.14)	4.80 (2.21)
R_2				
S_1				
Rhythm	10.57 (1.80)	6.70 (1.73)	0.37 (0.14)	6.50 (3.14)
Tone	6.31 (1.78)	3.55 (0.97)	0.44 (0.15)	5.62 (3.22)
S_2				
Rhythm	10.28 (1.79)	6.40 (1.69)	0.38 (0.14)	6.06 (2.90)
Tone	6.20 (1.41)	3.88 (1.23)	0.38 (0.18)	4.02 (1.72)
S_3				
Rhythm	10.38 (1.94)	6.40 (1.60)	0.38 (0.11)	7.96 (4.63)
Tone	6.25 (1.70)	3.37 (1.07)	0.46 (0.17)	5.62 (3.19)
S_4				
Rhythm	10.10 (1.80)	6.46 (1.83)	0.36 (0.15)	7.40 (4.38)
Tone	6.37 (1.76)	3.77 (1.09)	0.41 (0.15)	6.80 (4.93)

R_3				
S_1				
Rhythm	10.29 (1.79)	6.08 (1.60)	0.41 (0.14)	6.92 (3.97)
Tone	6.16 (1.75)	3.52 (1.09)	0.42 (0.18)	4.98 (3.14)
S_2				
Rhythm	10.31 (1.82)	6.49 (1.58)	0.37 (0.11)	5.62 (2.22)
Tone	6.25 (1.66)	3.74 (1.19)	0.41 (0.16)	4.10 (1.49)
S_3				
Rhythm	10.44 (1.81)	6.46 (1.65)	0.38 (0.13)	5.66 (2.31)
Tone	6.32 (1.67)	3.91 (1.18)	0.38 (0.15)	10.38 (4.15)
S_4				
Rhythm	10.03 (1.64)	6.28 (1.52)	0.37 (0.13)	6.96 (4.34)
Tone	6.20 (1.70)	3.47 (1.05)	0.44 (0.16)	6.00 (3.98)
R_4				
S_1				
Rhythm	10.64 (1.68)	6.69 (1.68)	0.37 (0.15)	6.36 (2.89)
Tone	6.18 (1.36)	3.55 (1.00)	0.42 (0.16)	5.06 (2.13)
S_2				
Rhythm	10.28 (1.77)	6.87 (1.68)	0.33 (0.13)	5.42 (2.60)
Tone	6.13 (1.64)	3.92 (1.37)	0.37 (0.20)	4.18 (2.40)
S_3				
Rhythm	10.33 (1.84)	6.59 (1.69)	0.36 (0.13)	7.56 (4.58)
Tone	6.04 (1.52)	3.69 (1.05)	0.39 (0.16)	5.74 (4.12)
S_4				
Rhythm	10.21 (1.85)	6.21 (1.62)	0.39 (0.13)	6.66 (3.91)
Tone	6.16 (1.82)	3.48 (1.22)	0.44 (0.18)	5.54 (3.75)

The analysis of the statistical significance in the improvement differences allows to distinguish whether there are rating profiles or PSO parameters setups which allow the system to function more efficiently. Table 2 indicates that there is statistically significant difference between some rating profile and setup combinations. Regarding the rhythm PSO swarms, the relative improvement is significantly smaller for some setups of the R1R1 rater, especially for the S4S4 PSO parameters setup. The tone swarm incorporates less combinations of significant inequalities than the rhythm swarm for the R1R1 rater, but also presents some instances of significant superiority of the R2R2 rater over R3R3. Consulting the "relative improvement" column in Table 1, it may be noticed that either the S3S3 or the S4S4 setups provides the best improvement for all raters except from the rhythm swarm of rater R3R3. Furthermore, by conducting the Wilcoxon test over all setup pairs, including the mean relative improvements of all raters, there is no statistical superiority of any setup. Therefore, concerning the mean relative improvement from the initial to the last rating round among all four individuals, the r-PSO is statistically equivalent to the standard PSO.

Table 2. Statistical significance of the differences in relative improvements of the mean fitness of all four melodies throughout all rating rounds among all raters and simulations

	R_1				R_2				R_3				R_4			
	Rhythm															
R_1	=	=	=	=	=	=	=	=	–	=	=	=	=	=	=	=
		=	=	=	=	=	–	=	–	=	=	=	=	=	=	–
			=	=	=	=	=	=	=	=	=	=	=	=	=	=
				=	=	–	–	=	–	=	–	=	–	=	=	–
R_2					=	=	=	=	=	=	=	=	=	=	=	=
						=	=	=	=	=	=	=	=	=	=	=
							=	=	=	=	=	=	=	=	=	=
								=	=	=	=	=	=	=	=	=
R_3									=	=	=	=	=	+	=	=
										=	=	=	=	=	=	=
											=	=	=	=	=	=
												=	=	=	=	=
R_4													=	=	=	=
														=	=	–
															=	=
																=
	Tone															
R_1	=	=	=	=	–	=	–	=	=	=	=	–	–	=	=	–
		=	=	=	=	=	–	=	=	=	=	=	=	=	=	=
			=	=	=	=	=	=	=	=	=	=	=	=	=	=
				=	=	=	–	=	=	=	=	=	=	=	=	=
R_2					=	=	=	=	=	=	+	=	=	=	=	=
						=	–	=	=	=	=	=	=	=	=	=
							=	=	=	=	+	=	=	+	+	=
								=	=	=	=	=	=	=	=	=
R_3									=	=	=	=	=	=	=	=
										=	=	=	=	=	=	=
											=	–	=	=	=	=
												=	=	=	=	=
R_4													=	=	=	=
														=	=	=
															=	=
																=

A question that rise concerns the reason for the "inability" of the R1R1 rater to produce relative improvements that are statistically comparable with the ones presented by the other raters, for some setups. The answer in this question lies within the rating values of R1R1. A fundamental statistical analysis of the raters' ratings is demonstrated in Table 3. The values presented therein concern the ratings in the initial and the final rating round (PSO iteration), as well as their absolute and relative differences. The second column of this Table reveals that the R1R1 ratings nearly reached the maximum rate of 10. Consulting Figure 4, it is noticed that the rating curve that corresponds to rater 1 (R1R1) reaches a near-zero absolute gradient plateau when ratings (y-axis) exceed the level of 9. Therefore, the rating behavior of R1R1 indicates that this automatic rater is almost completely satisfied by the output of the melodies at an "early" evolutionary stage and further improvement is not required, since all the presented melodies are rated almost equally high (near 10) after a rating round.

Moreover, by consulting the 90 % iteration column of Table 1, it is observed that R1R1 provides rates near 9 at an early stage of the PSO evolution, i.e. from around 4 to 6 rounds for rhythms and tones. This is a clear indication that the maximum performance has been almost reached and no further improvements are necessary. Additionally, the reasons for the smaller improvement of the R1R1 rater, as have hitherto been analyzed, are amplified by the randomness in the provided rates. Thereby, the additional noise in ratings makes alterations to the rate (fitness) of a PSO agent that are more decisive than actual fitness improvements. Having in mind the near-flat plateau around rate 9 for rater 1 in Figure 4, it is clear that a small improvement in rates is realized through a large improvement in fitness. Under this perspective, the $\pm0.5\pm0.5$ randomness margin (the $\xi\beta\xi\beta$ value in Eq. 9) in ratings is considered as an extensive potential perturbation, which further obstructs the evolutionary process. It is thus deduced that the rating behavior of R1R1 does not expose a weakness of the system, but a rating convergence to a "noisy global maximum". This rating behavior may be interpreted as the behavior of a human rater who is completely satisfied, within the limits of aesthetic art uncertainty, by the system's output even from an early rating round.

Through the initialisation process four initial melodies are generated that are represented by four points in the rhythm and tone spaces that are possibly separated by different distances from the point that represents the ideal features, both in the rhythm and the tone feature spaces. Therefore, the fitness of one among the initial agents is expected to be better than the fitness of the others, i.e. the fitness of the agent that produced a melody, the features of which are placed closer to the ideal features. Figure 6 provides a statistical graphical answer for some rater–setup examples to the following question: "is the initially best fit agent the one that remains best fit throughout all 20 rating rounds?" This figure suggests a negative answer, meaning that the best fit agent in each iteration is expected be different than the one of the initial iteration. Additionally, it may also be observed that the remaining three agents, excluding the best fit in each iteration, gradually generate melodies, the features of which are closer to the ideal features. This fact amplifies the indications yielded so far that the melodies which represent all swarm members "converge" to the ideal melody that each rater may anticipate. The respective graphs of the remaining rater–setup combinations exhibit a similar behaviour.

Table 3. Statistics of mean rating improvement from the initial to the final rating iterations, for all raters and setups, in all the respective simulations

Rater–setup	Init. rate	Last rate	Abs. impr.	Rel. impr.
R_1				
S_1				
Rhythm	5.63 (2.69)	9.20 (0.67)	3.57 (1.53)	0.93 (1.47)
Tone	5.88 (2.70)	9.11 (1.01)	3.29 (1.24)	0.63 (0.39)
S_2				
Rhythm	5.87 (2.55)	9.17 (0.68)	3.30 (1.44)	0.66 (0.45)
Tone	5.72 (2.97)	9.15 (1.14)	3.55 (1.28)	0.68 (0.37)
S_3				
Rhythm	5.95 (2.55)	9.25 (0.78)	3.30 (1.43)	0.64 (0.45)
Tone	5.84 (2.94)	9.23 (1.02)	3.39 (1.30)	0.63 (0.36)
S_4				
Rhythm	5.51 (2.77)	9.00 (1.05)	3.51 (1.65)	0.82 (0.74)
Tone	6.04 (2.81)	9.33 (0.69)	3.30 (1.11)	0.58 (0.27)
R_2				
S_1				
Rhythm	2.80 (1.79)	6.59 (1.59)	3.78 (1.37)	1.56 (0.92)
Tone	3.31 (2.23)	7.25 (1.38)	4.00 (1.40)	1.34 (0.70)
S_2				
Rhythm	3.10 (1.78)	6.82 (1.51)	3.72 (1.36)	1.43 (0.85)
Tone	3.32 (2.00)	6.76 (1.80)	3.55 (1.60)	1.16 (0.79)
S_3				
Rhythm	3.02 (1.93)	6.86 (1.48)	3.84 (1.15)	1.63 (1.28)
Tone	3.32 (2.14)	7.49 (1.49)	4.17 (1.51)	1.36 (0.81)
S_4				
Rhythm	3.28 (1.89)	6.79 (1.65)	3.51 (1.41)	1.29 (0.95)
Tone	3.21 (2.12)	6.91 (1.56)	3.81 (1.35)	1.31 (0.70)

R_3				
S_1				
Rhythm	1.86 (1.21)	5.11 (1.44)	3.25 (1.25)	1.93 (0.94)
Tone	2.18 (1.52)	5.17 (1.45)	3.01 (1.47)	1.57 (1.06)
S_2				
Rhythm	1.88 (1.22)	4.71 (1.37)	2.83 (1.06)	1.84 (1.36)
Tone	2.07 (1.44)	4.95 (1.60)	2.93 (1.38)	1.56 (1.04)
S_3				
Rhythm	1.78 (1.19)	4.76 (1.40)	2.98 (1.13)	1.86 (1.09)
Tone	1.98 (1.47)	4.67 (1.52)	2.69 (1.21)	1.47 (0.88)
S_4				
Rhythm	2.02 (1.18)	4.88 (1.32)	2.87 (1.19)	1.73 (1.48)
Tone	2.16 (1.48)	5.24 (1.43)	3.12 (1.34)	1.58 (0.89)
R_4				
S_1				
Rhythm	0.78 (0.54)	2.36 (0.93)	1.59 (0.82)	2.40 (1.81)
Tone	0.99 (0.65)	2.71 (0.93)	1.74 (0.84)	1.94 (1.18)
S_2				
Rhythm	1.87 (1.20)	4.44 (1.41)	2.59 (1.13)	1.67 (1.23)
Tone	2.18 (1.39)	4.69 (1.85)	2.64 (1.62)	1.31 (0.93)
S_3				
Rhythm	1.87 (1.24)	4.69 (1.46)	2.83 (1.10)	1.70 (0.89)
Tone	2.25 (1.53)	4.96 (1.46)	2.73 (1.27)	1.30 (0.73)
S_4				
Rhythm	1.95 (1.20)	4.97 (1.42)	3.02 (1.24)	1.85 (1.40)
Tone	2.24 (1.49)	5.28 (1.63)	3.11 (1.45)	1.52 (0.91)

Table 4 presents the basic statistics of the fitness values among the *best* fit melodies in the initial and the last rating iteration. The findings in this Table, when combined with the respective mean fitness values of all four melodies that comprise the initial and the last iterations in Table 1, allow a numeric estimation of the fitness convergence behaviour of the system. By comparing Tables 4 and 1 it is observed that the relative improvement of the agents' mean fitness is similar to the one of the best agent's at each iteration. This is also graphically observed by the coordinated fitness reduction of the "iteration best" and "remaining three" curves in the examples depicted in Figure 6. Considering also the fact that the fitness of the best melody remains significantly better than of the rest melodies even at the last generation step, it is implied that a distinguishably more "pleasant" melody is expected to be present throughout the entire rating procedure.

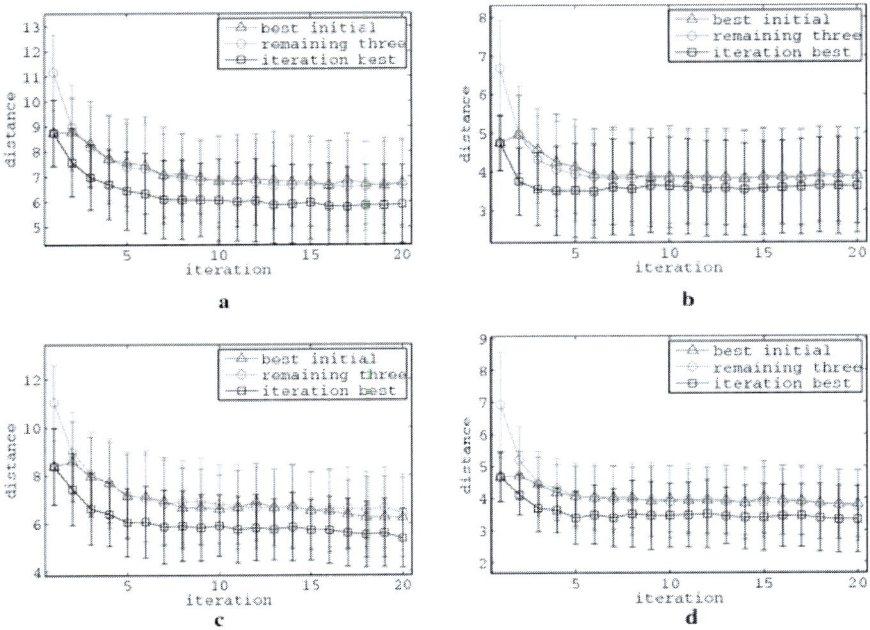

Figure 6. Errorbars of selected agents' fitness in all 50 simulations of representative PSO setups for all automatic raters. Specifically, errorbars of the fitness are demonstrated for all 20 rating iterations of the agent with the best fitness in the initial iteration, for the remaining three agents and the for the best fit agent in all iterations. **A** R2R2-S1S1 rhythm. **B** R2R2-S2S2tone. **C** R2R2-S3S3 rhythm. **D** R2R2-S4S4 tone

Regarding the relative improvements of the best fit melodies between the initial and the final rating iteration, the results are similar to the ones presented for the mean fitness of all agents presented earlier. Table 5 demonstrates that there are many statistically significant instances of S2 inferiority for the rhythm of the R4 rater. Additionally, the S3S3 setup in the tone swarm of R2, is significantly superior over many other rater–setup combinations. Nevertheless, the overall impression is that there are generally no statistically significant differences between rater–setup pairs, indicating that the *r*-PSO modification is not inferior to the standard PSO methodology. Moreover, although mostly not statistically significant, the setups that utilize the *r*-PSO variation achieve the best performance towards improving the best rated individual, as demonstrated in the "relative improvement" column of Table 4.

Music features convergence analysis

The rating process incorporates the rating of four melodies at each round (PSO iteration). The analysis that has hitherto been performed, incorporates the improvement in fitness and ratings of the music composed according to the features that are encompassed to the rhythm and tone PSO agents. The perspective of these results does not only revolve around the effectiveness of the system, but also on the anticipated user fatigue imposed by the converging behaviour. However, the convergence analysis of the system so far, considered only the fitness aspects and not the melodic characteristics. A human user is expected to be affected by the differences in the music content of the four melodies that comprise the rating round.

Table 4. Statistics of the best melody's fitness improvement from the initial to the final rating iteration, for all raters and setups, in all the respective simulations

Rater–setup	Best init. fit.	Best last fit.	Rel. impr.	90% iter.
R_1				
S_1				
Rhythm	8.26 (1.76)	4.98 (1.27)	0.39 (0.15)	8.62 (4.79)
Tone	4.74 (0.77)	2.89 (0.74)	0.38 (0.17)	6.28 (4.79)
S_2				
Rhythm	8.12 (1.35)	5.22 (1.31)	0.35 (0.15)	6.12 (3.63)
Tone	4.54 (0.76)	2.88 (0.82)	0.36 (0.19)	3.98 (3.63)
S_3				
Rhythm	8.07 (1.30)	4.45 (0.94)	0.44 (0.12)	9.22 (4.41)
Tone	4.55 (0.89)	2.49 (0.77)	0.44 (0.19)	7.94 (4.41)
S_4				
Rhythm	8.30 (1.58)	5.00 (1.09)	0.38 (0.15)	9.54 (4.31)
Tone	4.45 (0.84)	2.51 (0.57)	0.42 (0.16)	7.64 (4.31)
R_2				
S_1				
Rhythm	8.75 (1.32)	5.27 (1.47)	0.40 (0.14)	9.10 (4.24)
Tone	4.57 (0.98)	2.63 (0.67)	0.41 (0.17)	7.04 (4.24)
S_2				
Rhythm	8.57 (1.36)	5.15 (1.50)	0.40 (0.16)	6.52 (4.26)
Tone	4.75 (0.72)	2.91 (0.88)	0.37 (0.21)	5.12 (4.26)
S_3				
Rhythm	8.39 (1.59)	4.72 (1.23)	0.43 (0.16)	10.76 (5.48)
Tone	4.49 (0.85)	2.31 (0.79)	0.47 (0.19)	8.92 (5.48)
S_4				
Rhythm	8.31 (1.47)	4.76 (1.54)	0.42 (0.15)	10.14 (4.88)
Tone	4.68 (0.77)	2.72 (0.64)	0.40 (0.17)	8.84 (4.88)

R_3				
S_1				
Rhythm	8.34 (1.26)	4.90 (1.42)	0.41 (0.15)	8.32 (4.66)
Tone	4.50 (0.96)	2.59 (0.73)	0.40 (0.20)	7.04 (4.66)
S_2				
Rhythm	8.52 (1.39)	5.21 (1.23)	0.39 (0.11)	6.96 (4.44)
Tone	4.61 (0.77)	2.79 (0.83)	0.39 (0.19)	5.80 (4.44)
S_3				
Rhythm	8.43 (1.48)	4.66 (1.32)	0.44 (0.15)	8.68 (4.52)
Tone	4.61 (0.86)	2.65 (0.68)	0.41 (0.16)	10.92 (4.52)
S_4				
Rhythm	8.42 (1.30)	4.59 (1.03)	0.45 (0.14)	8.96 (4.90)
Tone	4.52 (0.95)	2.40 (0.68)	0.44 (0.20)	8.38 (4.90)
R_4				
S_1				
Rhythm	8.82 (1.17)	5.41 (1.39)	0.39 (0.14)	8.18 (4.13)
Tone	4.81 (0.71)	2.73 (0.76)	0.42 (0.19)	6.18 (4.13)
S_2				
Rhythm	8.42 (1.45)	5.63 (1.52)	0.32 (0.17)	7.72 (4.93)
Tone	4.59 (0.73)	2.97 (0.88)	0.34 (0.20)	4.54 (4.93)
S_3				
Rhythm	8.38 (1.37)	4.99 (1.35)	0.40 (0.15)	11.40 (5.37)
Tone	4.48 (0.99)	2.63 (0.82)	0.39 (0.20)	7.50 (5.37)
S_4				
Rhythm	8.30 (1.25)	4.49 (1.05)	0.45 (0.14)	9.36 (4.98)
Tone	4.45 (0.81)	2.48 (0.79)	0.43 (0.20)	8.26 (4.98)

Specifically, if the system presents four melodies that exhibit similar characteristics from an early rating round, then the user may lose focus by considering that the system has more or less evolved the melody as far as it could. Therefore, it is important to examine the evolution of melodic "distances" among the melodies both throughout and within each rating round. The melodic distances are expressed through distances in the music feature (rhythmic and tonal) that are extracted from the melodies $(\vec{f}^{r}_{c,i}$ and $\vec{f}^{t}_{c,i})$ composed under the respective agents' guidelines $(\vec{f}^{r}_{a,i}$ and $\vec{f}^{t}_{a,i}, i \in \{1,2,3,4\})$.

To this end, the aforementioned musical convergence analysis is performed by analysing the location difference of agents' melodies both in successive iterations and the inter-agent distances within single rating rounds. Hereafter, the music features of the compositions in the k-th iteration $\vec{f}^{x}_{c,i}(k)$, $(k = 1,2,\ldots,20)$ will be denoted as $\vec{f}^{x}_{c,i}(k)$,

Table 5. Statistical significance of the differences in relative improvements of the best melodies throughout all rating rounds, among all raters and simulations

	R_1				R_2				R_3				R_4			
	Rhythm															
R_1	=	=	–	=	=	=	=	=	=	=	=	–	=	+	=	=
		=	–	=	=	=	–	–	=	=	–	–	=	=	=	–
			=	+	=	=	=	=	=	+	=	=	=	+	=	=
				=	=	=	=	=	=	=	–	–	=	=	=	–
R_2					=	=	=	=	=	=	=	–	=	+	=	=
						=	=	=	=	=	=	=	=	+	=	=
							=	=	=	=	=	=	=	+	=	=
								=	=	=	=	=	=	+	=	=
R_3									=	=	=	=	=	+	=	=
										=	–	–	=	=	=	–
											=	=	=	+	=	=
												=	+	+	=	=
R_4													=	=	=	=
														=	–	–
															=	=
																=
	Tone															
R_1	=	=	=	=	=	=	–	=	=	=	=	–	=	=	=	=
		=	–	=	=	=	–	=	=	=	=	–	=	=	=	=
			=	=	=	=	=	=	=	=	=	=	=	+	=	=
				=	=	=	=	=	=	=	=	=	=	+	=	=
R_2					=	=	–	=	=	=	=	=	=	=	=	=
						=	–	=	=	=	=	=	=	=	=	=
							=	+	=	+	+	=	=	+	+	=
								=	=	=	=	=	=	=	=	=
R_3									=	=	=	=	=	=	=	=
										=	=	=	=	=	=	=
											=	=	=	=	=	=
												=	=	+	=	=
R_4													=	+	=	=
														=	=	–
															=	=
																=

where $i \in \{1, 2, 3, 4\}$ and $x \in \{r, t\}$. The melodic distance between the successive locations of an agent's melody in the feature space is a vector with 19 elements, considering a total number of 20 iterations. Using the above mentioned denotations, the successive distances vector of the *i*-th agent is computed by

$$\vec{d}_i^x(m) = \left\| \vec{f}_{c,i}^x(m+1) - \vec{f}_{c,i}^x(m) \right\|_2, \tag{11}$$

where m∈{1,2,...,19} and x∈r,t, . This examination incorporates not only the isolated rhythm and tone feature vectors, but also the overall music distance described by the vector comprising all 39 features (22 rhythmic and 17 tonal). The merged successive distance vector is incorporated in the dalli→ vector. It is again noticed that each distance vector comprises successive distances between the features of the melodies that were composed under the guidance of the respective agents and not the features of the agents per se. This examination concerns the differences in the music output throughout the rating iterations and not the "orbits" of the PSO agents.

A graphical example of a successive distances vector is depicted in Figure 7a, where the distance values are exhibited to decrease in a pattern that resembles a pow law. In Figure 7b, the aforementioned distance vector is plotted on a log–log scale and a regression line is optimally fitted, in a least squares sense, through its point. The gradient of this line indicates the rate that successive melodic distances decrease, with larger absolute values signifying a faster successive distances reduction. Figure 7c and d demonstrate that the mean distance reduction of all agents approaches a power low pattern. Figure 7c illustrates the error bars of the successive distances vectors of all the 200 melodies composed in 50 simulations of a representative rater–setup pair. The log–log plot and the regression line of the mean values in Figure 7c are illustrated in Figure 7d.

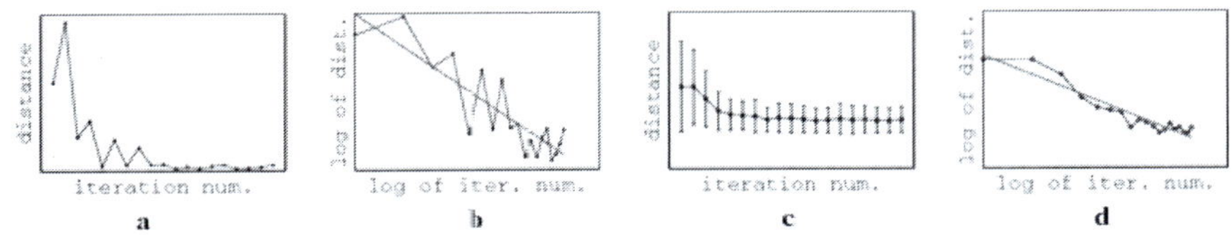

Figure 7.A Distances between successive steps (from iteration i–1i–1 to *i*) of an agent. **B** The log–log plot of the the distances in (**A**) and the optimally fit line in a least squares sense. **C** *Error bars* of the distances in all agent's successive steps. **D** Log–log of the mean values in (**C**) and the optimally fit line in a least squares sense

Table 6 demonstrates the gradients of the regression lines through the vector of successive distances, as computed in Eq. 11, in the log–log scale (as appeared in Figure 7b) for all rater–setup combinations. By examining the "per SiSi" rows of the above mentioned table, which exhibits the mean gradient per setup, it is evident that there are major differences regarding the reduction in the successive distances for the agents orbits per PSO parameter setup, for the rhythm, tone and the merged features. Additionally, almost all gradient distributions for every pair of setups are statistically significantly different, again for all three examined vectors. The differences in the statistical significance are shown by the "+−=+−=" signs on the exponents of each rater and setup. The distance reduction within all the measurements of the respective rater or setups are signified by a "++", a "−" or a "==" sign, if the rater or setup under discussion exhibits greater, smaller or statistically equal gradient. For example, the rhythm distributions of setup S=+−−1S1=+−− demonstrates significantly larger gradients compared to S2S2 and smaller compared to S3S3 and S4S4. Contrarily to the setups, there are little statistically significant difference among the gradients' distributions for any pair of raters and for any distance vector, for the measurements that are demonstrated in the "per RiRi" column.

Table 6. Distance reduction in successive rhythm, tone and overall features throughout all rating steps

	$S_1^{=+--}$	$S_2^{-=--}$	$S_3^{++==}$	$S_4^{++==}$	per R_i
	Rhythm ($\vec{d}_i^r$ reduction)				
$R_1^{====}$	−0.52 (0.61)	−0.69 (0.59)	−0.14 (0.45)	−0.15 (0.44)	−0.37 (0.58)
$R_2^{====}$	−0.54 (0.58)	−0.71 (0.63)	−0.22 (0.45)	−0.23 (0.47)	−0.43 (0.58)
$R_3^{====}$	−0.56 (0.64)	−0.64 (0.54)	−0.22 (0.36)	−0.24 (0.39)	−0.42 (0.53)
$R_4^{====}$	−0.55 (0.53)	−0.67 (0.58)	−0.21 (0.44)	−0.24 (0.44)	−0.42 (0.54)
per S_i	−0.54 (0.59)	−0.68 (0.58)	−0.20 (0.42)	−0.22 (0.44)	
	Tone ($\vec{d}_i^t$ reduction)				
$R_1^{=+==}$	−0.54 (0.33)	−0.64 (0.33)	−0.26 (0.28)	−0.32 (0.27)	−0.44 (0.34)
$R_2^{-==-}$	−0.57 (0.31)	−0.63 (0.33)	−0.35 (0.27)	−0.33 (0.31)	−0.47 (0.33)
$R_3^{====}$	−0.52 (0.31)	−0.63 (0.30)	−0.33 (0.27)	−0.33 (0.25)	−0.45 (0.31)
$R_4^{=+==}$	−0.55 (0.32)	−0.55 (0.34)	−0.28 (0.27)	−0.33 (0.27)	−0.43 (0.33)
per S_i	−0.55 (0.32)	−0.61 (0.33)	−0.30 (0.27)	−0.32 (0.28)	
	Rhythm and tone ($\vec{d}_i^{all}$ reduction)				
$R_1^{=+==}$	−0.54 (0.52)	−0.70 (0.52)	−0.16 (0.41)	−0.18 (0.38)	−0.39 (0.52)
$R_2^{-===}$	−0.57 (0.52)	−0.73 (0.54)	−0.25 (0.40)	−0.25 (0.43)	−0.45 (0.52)
$R_3^{====}$	−0.58 (0.53)	−0.65 (0.45)	−0.23 (0.34)	−0.25 (0.36)	−0.43 (0.47)
$R_4^{====}$	−0.57 (0.48)	−0.67 (0.49)	−0.23 (0.39)	−0.26 (0.40)	−0.43 (0.48)
per S_i	−0.56 (0.51)	−0.69 (0.50)	−0.22 (0.39)	−0.24 (0.39)	

Regarding the setups, the r-PSO variation produces significantly larger (smaller in an absolute value) gradients, revealing that each agent roams the feature space with bigger strides, producing melodies that are potentially more diverse. Thereby, the diversity in the melodic content provides the user with an impression that the system is able to compose diverse melodies. At the same time, these melodies converge to the ideal features as the rating iterations proceed, as indicated by the fact that all setups reached comparable fitness improvements as exhibited in Tables 1and 4, with minor statistically significant superiorities between rater–setup pairs. Hence, it is expected that the robustness of the system will be preserved among the aforementioned examined setup versions, with different characteristics of the "melodic orbits". Furthermore, the fact that the difference in distance reductions between different raters is generally not statistically significant is also encouraging, since the system's melodic convergence behaviour is anticipated to remain unchanged when used by human users with different rating profiles.

Besides the inter-iteration distances of a single melody, it is also important to examine the melodic distances between the melodies that comprise each rating round. As also mentioned earlier in "Fitness convergence analysis" section, the initialisation scheme produces distant quadruples of agents and therefore the melodies composed under their guidelines are also expected to be distant. Since the fitness of all the agents is improving throughout the rating iteration, the melodies are contracting within an area of the feature space that is close to the rater's ideal features. The question that raises concerns the speed of this melodic contraction, which may be described by the sum of distances between every agent pair, among the four ones in each iteration. A larger sum of inter-agent distances denotes the inclusion of a greater musical variety within the quadruple of the current rating iteration, while a smaller sum indicates a quadruple of similar melodies. Formally, the sum of inter-agent distances for each simulation is a 20-value vector, with each value describing the sum of each agents' pairs distances per rating round, and is expressed as

$$\vec{\delta^x}(k) = \sum_{i=1}^{4} \left(\sum_{j=i+1}^{4} \left\| \vec{f_{c,i}^x}(k) - \vec{f_{c,j}^x}(k) \right\|_2 \right), \tag{12}$$

where $k \in \{1,2,\ldots,20\}$ denotes the rating iteration and $x \in \{r,t,all\}$ again refers to the rhythmic, tonal and overall features respectively.

Example illustrations of a simulation's $\vec{\delta}$ δ→ vector are demonstrated in Figure 8a, along with its log–log plot and the least squares regression line in Figure 8b. Figure 8c depict the errorbars of the $\vec{\delta}$ δ→ vectors produced by all 50 simulation of a representative rater–setup pair, where it is observed that the mean values also resemble a power law reduction rate. Figure 8d illustrates the log–log plot and the regression line of the mean values in Figure 8c. The melodic contraction is again measured through the gradient of the regression line, with larger absolute gradient values denoting a greater contraction rate, on contrary to smaller ones.

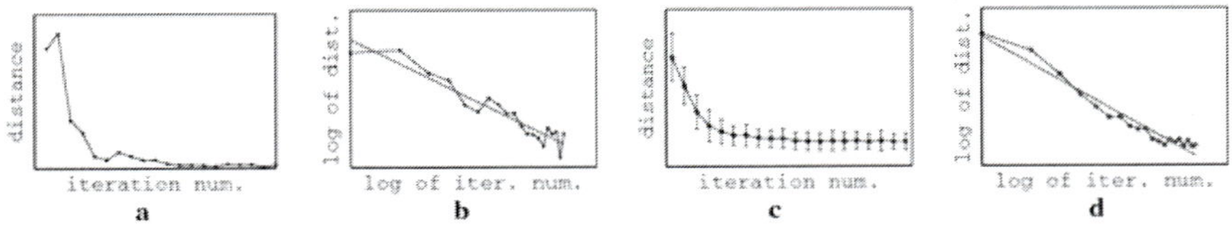

Figure 8. A Distances between every pair of agents in each iteration. **B** The log–log plot of the the distances in (**A**) and the optimally fit line in a least squares sense. **C** *Error bars* of the distances between all agents in all steps. **D** Log–log of the mean values in (**C**) and the optimally fit line in a least squares sense

The melodic contraction gradients, as computed by Eq. 12, are demonstrated in Table 7 for rhythm, tone and the merged features. Again, the statistical significance of the difference in distributions among the contraction gradients of raters and setups are signified by the signs on the exponent. The inter-rater measurements do not exhibit statistically significant differences in the distributions of gradients, except from the R2R2–R4R4 rater pair. The distributions of the inter-setup distances present a similar behaviour to the ones examined in the previous paragraph. Again, the melodic contraction of the quadruples with the *r*-PSO variation is slower, providing the user with a more diverse collection of melodies in each rating round.

Adaptation of specific music features

The analysis so far focused on several aspects of fitness and rating improvement of the melodies, the musical "orbit" that each melody circumscribes throughout the rating rounds and the relations between the melodies that comprise each rating round from the beginning to the end of each simulation. The remaining of this section examines the fitness in the specific submodules that are included in the bottom level of the system, namely the binary rhythm, the polyphony, the intensity, the pause submodules and the tonal module. Furthermore, the analysis goes deeper to

Table 7. Distance reduction between the features of all pairs of melodies in rating step

	Rhythm ($\bar{\delta}^r$ reduction)				per R_i
	$S_1^{=+--}$	$S_2^{-=--}$	$S_3^{++==}$	$S_4^{++==}$	
$R_1^{====}$	−0.75 (0.34)	−1.05 (0.43)	−0.60 (0.20)	−0.60 (0.22)	−0.75 (0.36)
$R_2^{====}$	−0.79 (0.35)	−1.13 (0.50)	−0.62 (0.24)	−0.62 (0.26)	−0.79 (0.41)
$R_3^{====}$	−0.84 (0.43)	−1.08 (0.44)	−0.59 (0.20)	−0.64 (0.22)	−0.79 (0.39)
$R_4^{====}$	−0.76 (0.30)	−0.99 (0.46)	−0.60 (0.26)	−0.62 (0.25)	−0.74 (0.36)
per S_i	−0.78 (0.35)	−1.06 (0.46)	−0.60 (0.23)	−0.62 (0.24)	
	Tone ($\bar{\delta}^t$ reduction)				per R_i
	$S_1^{=+--}$	$S_2^{-=--}$	$S_3^{++=+}$	$S_4^{++-=}$	
$R_1^{====}$	−0.78 (0.24)	−0.97 (0.28)	−0.68 (0.15)	−0.74 (0.23)	−0.79 (0.25)
$R_2^{===-}$	−0.84 (0.25)	−0.97 (0.27)	−0.68 (0.19)	−0.76 (0.23)	−0.81 (0.26)
$R_3^{====}$	−0.77 (0.27)	−1.00 (0.29)	−0.69 (0.18)	−0.69 (0.18)	−0.79 (0.26)
$R_4^{=+==}$	−0.82 (0.21)	−0.90 (0.25)	−0.61 (0.20)	−0.69 (0.19)	−0.76 (0.24)
per S_i	−0.81 (0.24)	−0.96 (0.27)	−0.67 (0.18)	−0.72 (0.21)	
	Rhythm and tone ($\bar{\delta}^{all}$ reduction)				per R_i
	$S_1^{=+--}$	$S_2^{-=--}$	$S_3^{++==}$	$S_4^{++==}$	
$R_1^{====}$	−0.74 (0.33)	−1.03 (0.41)	−0.59 (0.20)	−0.60 (0.22)	−0.74 (0.35)
$R_3^{====}$	−0.78 (0.34)	−1.10 (0.45)	−0.62 (0.23)	−0.61 (0.26)	−0.78 (0.38)
$R_3^{====}$	−0.81 (0.39)	−1.06 (0.40)	−0.59 (0.19)	−0.64 (0.22)	−0.77 (0.36)
$R_4^{====}$	−0.76 (0.29)	−0.96 (0.42)	−0.59 (0.26)	−0.61 (0.24)	−0.73 (0.34)
per S_i	−0.77 (0.34)	−1.04 (0.42)	−0.60 (0.22)	−0.62 (0.23)	

the fitness adaptation of the system on each specific feature that formulates the fitness criteria of the system's respective comprising submodules. Additionally, the relations between ideal-to-melody $(\vec{f}_{a,i}^{x}\text{-to-}\vec{f}_{c,i}^{x})$ and agent-to-melody $(\vec{f}_{a,i}^{x}\text{-to-}\vec{f}_{c,i}^{x})$ features are scrutinised, in order to approach the extent at which the bottom level music composition submodules affect the systems performance and the PSO adaptation. It is reminded that hitherto only the ideal-to-melody distances have been examined, which constitutes the criterion for the system's "musical convergence".

Table 8 exhibits the mean distance per feature for each submodule between the ideal features $(\vec{f}_{*}^{x})$ and the features of the four melodies $(\vec{f}_{c,i}^{x})$ composed during the last rating iteration. This distance is computed as

Table 8. Mean distance per feature of each submodule between the ideal features (fx∗→f∗x→) and the features of the composed melodies (fxc,i→fc,ix→) of the four melodies that comprise the final rating round within each simulation for all raters and setups

	S_1	S_2	S_3	S_4
R_1				
Binary	0.29 (0.23)	0.29 (0.24)	0.25 (0.21)	0.29 (0.23)
Polyphony	0.59 (0.33)	0.59 (0.33)	0.61 (0.32)	0.57 (0.33)
Intensity	0.63 (0.37)	0.66 (0.36)	0.63 (0.35)	0.64 (0.36)
Pause	0.45 (0.30)	0.42 (0.29)	0.44 (0.28)	0.42 (0.28)
Rhythm	0.50 (0.34)	0.50 (0.34)	0.50 (0.33)	0.49 (0.34)
Tone	0.45 (0.35)	0.45 (0.36)	0.46 (0.35)	0.45 (0.35)
R_2				
Binary	0.28 (0.25)	0.28 (0.25)	0.31 (0.27)	0.28 (0.24)
Polyphony	0.59 (0.35)	0.57 (0.34)	0.58 (0.33)	0.56 (0.35)
Intensity	0.63 (0.36)	0.63 (0.36)	0.64 (0.35)	0.64 (0.36)
Pause	0.44 (0.29)	0.39 (0.28)	0.44 (0.29)	0.43 (0.28)
Rhythm	0.50 (0.35)	0.48 (0.34)	0.50 (0.34)	0.49 (0.34)
Tone	0.44 (0.36)	0.43 (0.35)	0.44 (0.36)	0.42 (0.36)
R_1				
Binary	0.28 (0.23)	0.29 (0.25)	0.28 (0.25)	0.27 (0.24)
Polyphony	0.58 (0.34)	0.57 (0.34)	0.59 (0.33)	0.59 (0.33)
Intensity	0.63 (0.38)	0.63 (0.36)	0.62 (0.36)	0.63 (0.38)
Pause	0.43 (0.30)	0.44 (0.30)	0.45 (0.29)	0.43 (0.29)
Rhythm	0.49 (0.35)	0.50 (0.34)	0.50 (0.34)	0.49 (0.35)
Tone	0.44 (0.36)	0.45 (0.36)	0.44 (0.36)	0.43 (0.35)
R_1				
Binary	0.31 (0.26)	0.33 (0.28)	0.30 (0.25)	0.29 (0.25)
Polyphony	0.59 (0.33)	0.63 (0.33)	0.56 (0.33)	0.54 (0.33)
Intensity	0.63 (0.37)	0.67 (0.38)	0.63 (0.37)	0.62 (0.37)
Pause	0.44 (0.30)	0.48 (0.29)	0.44 (0.28)	0.41 (0.29)
Rhythm	0.50 (0.34)	0.54 (0.35)	0.49 (0.34)	0.48 (0.34)
Tone	0.43 (0.35)	0.43 (0.36)	0.44 (0.36)	0.44 (0.36)

the mean value of the errors comprise the fitness criterion for each music composition submodule. For example, the binary selector submodule composes binary rhythm in accordance to the fitness provided by five features, the features numbered from 1 to 5 on the rhythm feature vector. The mean distance per feature of this submodule, between a melody and the target features is computed as the mean distance value only of these five aforementioned features. The same holds for the mean distances per feature between the features that are carried by the four agents $(f^{\vec{x}}_{\underline{a},i})$ and the ones that are encompassed into the four respectively composed melodies $(f_{c,i}^{\vec{x}})$. The latter distances are demonstrated in Table 9.

The findings in Tables 8 and 9 are also demonstrated graphically in Figs. 9a and b respectively, a fact that facilitates their interpretation. Specifically, it is clearly observable that the error distributions among all the music generation modules are highly related for all rater–setups combinations, in both graphs. An exact analysis on the relations and differences of these distributions may hardly contribute any vital information about the system's performance, therefore it is omitted. It can be assumed, however, that the overall errors of the system (Table 8) are reflections of the errors produced by the underlying music composition modules (Table 9). In the aforementioned figure and tables, it is obvious that the binary selector produces the smallest errors among the other composition modules. Furthermore, the integer rhythm modules that define polyphony and intensity, exhibit a statistically higher error than the others.

Therefore, it may be deduced that the PSO agents' movement is heavily affected by the inability of the underlying composition modules to compose music accurately. If the music composition modules composed music accurately, the features of the composed music would be "similar" to the ones that the respective agent requested. Although the term "similar" seems abstract, a quantification of the required "similarity" can be estimated by considering the error of the composed melodies, in comparison to the agents' requests in Table 9. This error expresses the noisiness derived by the inaccuracy of the underlying music composition modules, which affects the fitness estimation and therefore the movement of each agent during the simulations. Nonetheless, even if the composition process is inaccurate, the system presents a converging behaviour which depends on the errors produced by the music composition modules.

A deeper analysis on the error sources of the underlying music composition modules can be performed through the examination of the specific features that define their respective fitnesses. A shadowgraph of the system's adaptivity at the level of music features is provided in Figure 10, which illustrates the errors between the ideal features and the features of the four composed melodies in the last rating rounds of a representative rater–setup pair. The graphs of the remaining rater–setup pairs are similar. Therein, it is evident that some features exhibit systematically high error values, on contrast to some others. Moreover, Figure 11 reveals that there is reciprocality in the errors between specific composition-to-agent and composition-to-ideal features. This fact further reveals the weaknesses of the underlying composition modules to adapt homogeneously to the melodic requirements of the agents, leading the system to overall suboptimal solutions. Features indexed from 37 to 39 in Figure 10 are absent in the Figure 11, since these features are passed from the agents to the tone module exactly as they are, in order to produce the list of available tones. Therefore, there is no matter of agent-to-melody adaptation regarding these three features.

Table 9. Mean distance per feature of each submodule between the features of the composed melodies (fxc,i→fc,ix→) and the features dictated by the respective agent (fxa,i→fa,ix→) of the four melodies that comprise the final rating round within each simulation for all raters and setups

	S_1	S_2	S_3	S_4
R_1				
Binary	0.14 (0.16)	0.14 (0.16)	0.13 (0.14)	0.13 (0.14)
Polyphony	0.48 (0.38)	0.49 (0.37)	0.50 (0.37)	0.47 (0.37)
Intensity	0.50 (0.41)	0.50 (0.41)	0.50 (0.41)	0.51 (0.40)
Pause	0.43 (0.29)	0.42 (0.31)	0.40 (0.28)	0.41 (0.29)
Rhythm	0.40 (0.36)	0.40 (0.36)	0.39 (0.36)	0.39 (0.35)
Tone	0.40 (0.37)	0.41 (0.38)	0.41 (0.38)	0.40 (0.37)
R_1				
Binary	0.12 (0.14)	0.12 (0.14)	0.13 (0.14)	0.13 (0.15)
Polyphony	0.46 (0.37)	0.48 (0.38)	0.48 (0.38)	0.46 (0.37)
Intensity	0.48 (0.41)	0.47 (0.41)	0.51 (0.40)	0.52 (0.41)
Pause	0.40 (0.27)	0.39 (0.29)	0.41 (0.28)	0.41 (0.27)
Rhythm	0.37 (0.35)	0.37 (0.36)	0.39 (0.36)	0.39 (0.36)
Tone	0.38 (0.38)	0.38 (0.38)	0.40 (0.38)	0.39 (0.38)
R_1				
Binary	0.13 (0.14)	0.13 (0.16)	0.12 (0.14)	0.12 (0.14)
Polyphony	0.48 (0.38)	0.48 (0.36)	0.47 (0.36)	0.48 (0.36)
Intensity	0.49 (0.40)	0.52 (0.41)	0.50 (0.40)	0.49 (0.41)
Pause	0.40 (0.29)	0.44 (0.29)	0.44 (0.28)	0.43 (0.28)
Rhythm	0.38 (0.36)	0.40 (0.36)	0.39 (0.35)	0.39 (0.36)
Tone	0.39 (0.38)	0.40 (0.37)	0.39 (0.38)	0.39 (0.38)
R_1				
Binary	0.13 (0.14)	0.13 (0.16)	0.13 (0.14)	0.13 (0.13)
Polyphony	0.47 (0.37)	0.51 (0.37)	0.46 (0.36)	0.45 (0.36)
Intensity	0.50 (0.40)	0.52 (0.41)	0.49 (0.40)	0.49 (0.41)
Pause	0.41 (0.29)	0.46 (0.30)	0.41 (0.27)	0.42 (0.29)
Rhythm	0.39 (0.35)	0.42 (0.37)	0.38 (0.35)	0.38 (0.35)
Tone	0.38 (0.38)	0.38 (0.39)	0.41 (0.38)	0.39 (0.38)

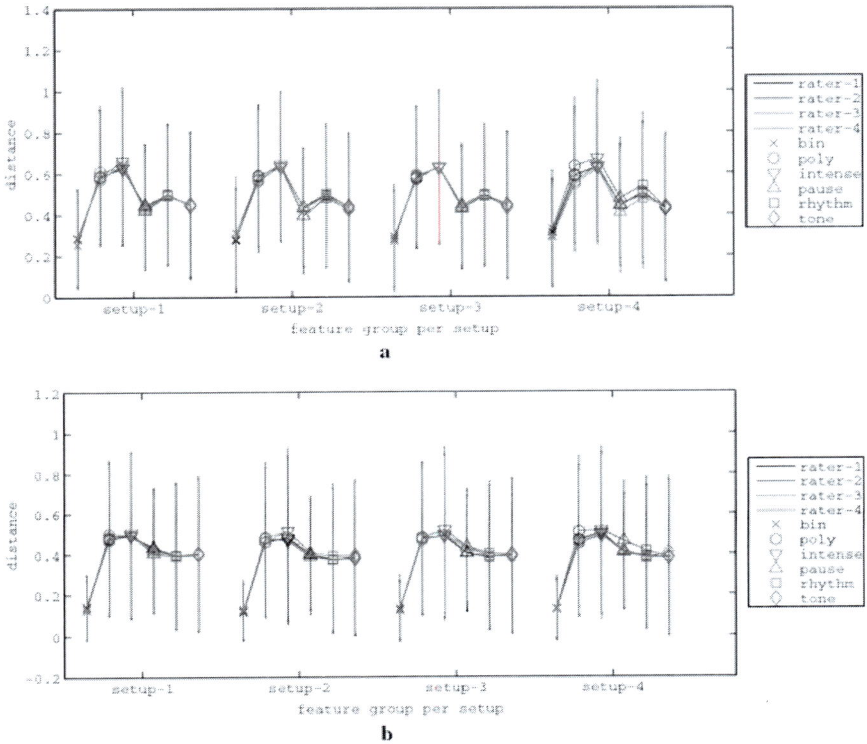

Figure 9. Errorbars of mean distances per feature of each submodule between target and composition features (**A**) and agent and composition features (**B**) for all raters and setups. **A** Distance between ideal and composition features. **B** Distance between agent and composition features

The comparison of the overall errors that the system produced, according to the automatic rates' ideal features, and the within-system errors, between the agent features and the composition features, led to a straight comparison of the distances between specific features themselves. Thereby, it is obvious that the underlying GA composition modules exhibit a "biased" optimisation behaviour, by minimising the error according to specific features, while ignoring the error produced by other features. Therefore, although the system is swiftly driven to locations that are closer to the ideal locations as examined in "Fitness convergence analysis" section, there are further potentialities for performance improvements by utilising more either more sophisticated music composition techniques, or by introducing more sophisticated (probably multi-objective) optimisation criteria.

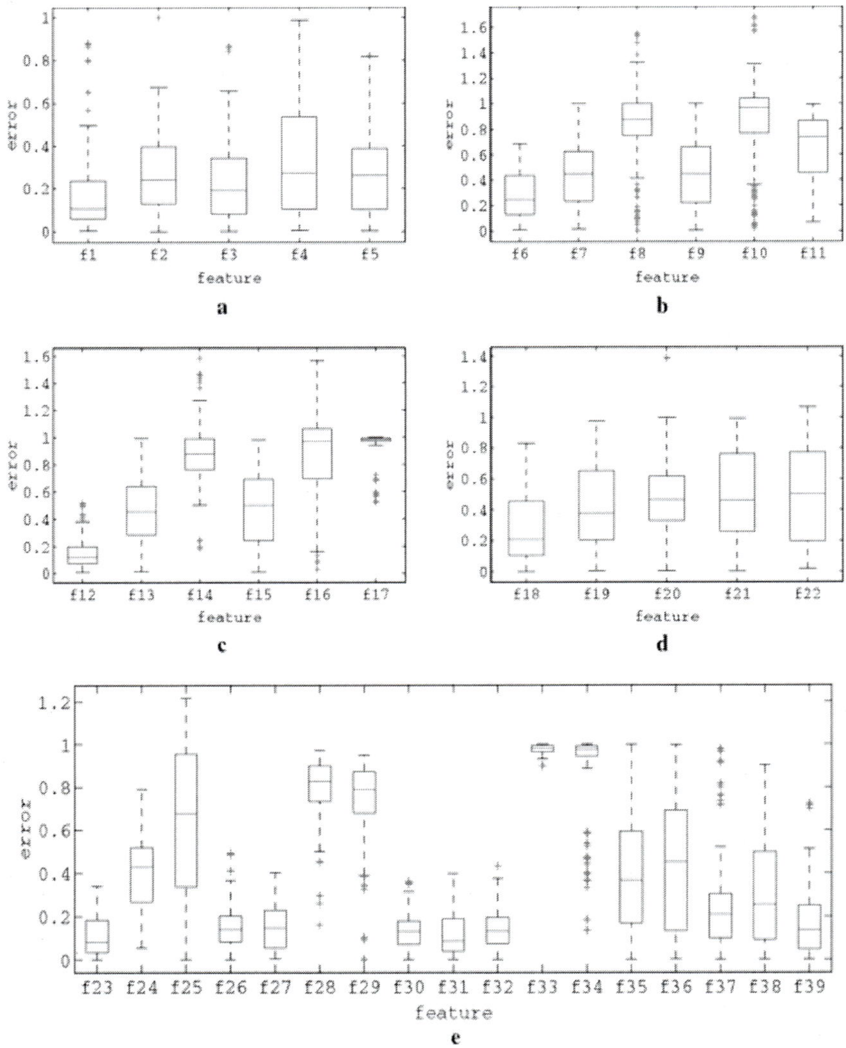

Figure 10. Box plots of the adaptation per feature between the composed music and the target features for the raters and setups that minimum error was achieved regarding rhythm (**A**–**D**) and tone (**E**). **A** R2S1R2S1 binary features. **B** R2S1R2S1 polyphony features. **C**R2S1R2S1 intensity features. **D** R2S1R2S1 pause features. **E** R2S1R2S1 tone features

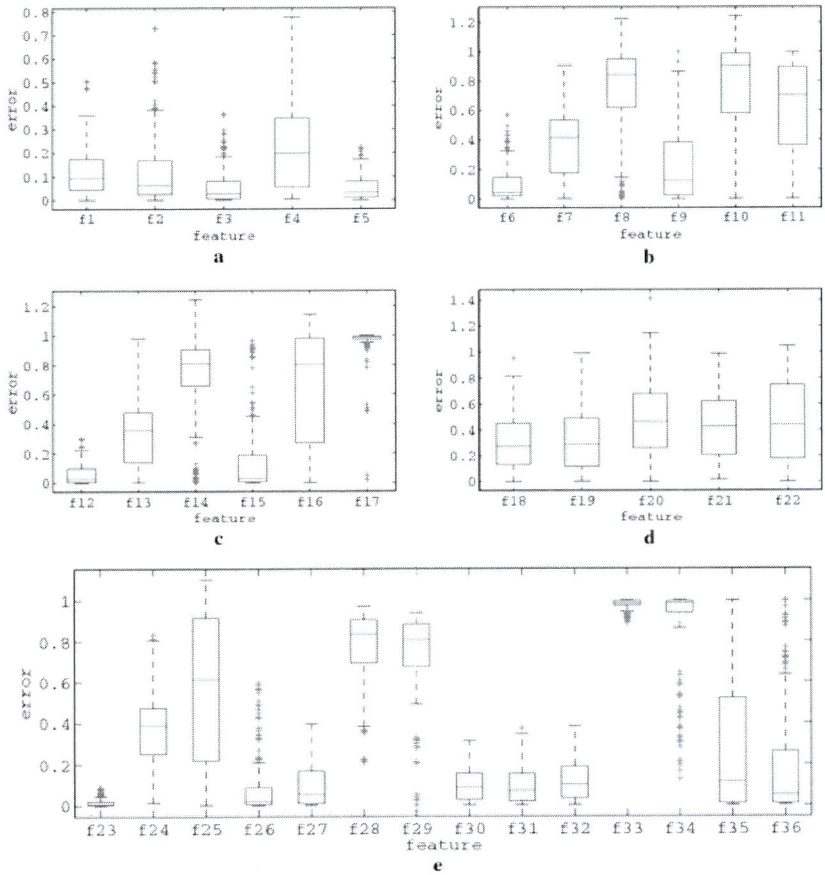

Figure 11. Box plots of the adaptation per feature between the composed music and the features requested by the agents in the last swarm evolution, for the raters and setups that minimum error was achieved regarding rhythm (**A–D**) and tone (**E**). **A** R2S1R2S1binary features. **B** R2S1R2S1 polyphony features, **C** R2S1R2S1 intensity features. **D** R2S1R2S1 pause features, **E** R2S1R2S1 tone features

CONCLUSIONS

This work introduced a system that composes music automatically with evolutionary algorithms, in accordance to the rating provided by the user, who is provided with four melodies and rates them using her/his subjective criteria, giving rates on the rhythmic and tonal characteristics of these four melodies. These quadruples of melodies evolve to ones that encompass more pleasant content to the user both in terms of rhythm and tone. The system's architecture incorporates a novel tow-level evolutionary scheme, with the higher level being based on the particle swarm optimisation (PSO) algorithm and the lower level on music composition modules that utilize genetic algorithms (GA). The agents' positions on the higher level PSO describe musical characteristics in the form of music features, incorporating two sets of agents that describe two different music attributes, namely rhythm and tone. The fitness of each agent in the rhythm and tone swarms is provided by the listener, leading the agents in locations that encompass more promising musical characteristics for the user. The lower level GA modules compose music in accordance to the characteristics provided by each PSO agent, therefore composing music that is more pleasant to the listener as the PSO iterations progress.

The system is based on the PSO algorithm that constitutes a robust cornerstone. However, the underlying GA algorithms that are used for music composition are not guaranteed to compose music that is absolutely reflecting the characteristics that the PSO agents carry. Therefore, the produced melodies are expected to be placed on different locations in the feature space than the agents that are actually rated, introducing a noisy factor to the top level PSO system. Additionally, the ratings provided by a human user on the artistic content are expected to incorporate considerable uncertainty, introducing additional noise to the system. Therefore the robustness of the system under the imposition of noise by these factors was evaluated, with the utilisation of "artificial raters" that incorporated predefined music preferences, which also remained fixed throughout the rating rounds (PSO iterations). Although the choice to employ artificial raters for the experimental results sounds radical, in fact it was the only way to examine the convergence of the system; human users lack the ability to maintain a steady set of features throughout the simulations since they are affected by the musical content they are exposed to. To this end, four artificial raters were modeled in accordance to different human rating profiles, including different rating strictness scales and noise, which provide a "deterministic" means to examine the system's robustness.

Exhaustive experimentation with multiple simulations over the system's performance with all available artificial raters and four PSO setups yielded that the system is swiftly converging to the ideal features that the automatic rater desired. Two PSO setups were based on the standard PSO methodology, while the remaining two were based on a variation of PSO, the *rating-based* PSO (*r*-PSO), which was developed in the context of the presented work. In addition to system convergence, the diversity in musical characteristics throughout the rating rounds were examined, a fact that is important towards reducing the *user fatigue* phenomenon, which is common in interactive systems. Thereby, the *r*-PSO variation exhibited the ability to maintain a greater variability to the melodic content than the standard PSO throughout all iteration rounds and within each iteration round, while being equally or even more efficient than PSO towards fitness improvement. Finally, the system's weaknesses were scrutinised, revealing that its overall performance depends on the music composition capabilities of the bottom level algorithms.

The primary contribution of the paper at hand is the presentation of system that performs feature evolution instead of melody evolution. In feature evolution, the user provides fitness through rating on the combination of features that are expressed by a melody. In fact, the user rates the features that are responsible for the generation of a melody, through the underlying music composition modules. As discussed in "Literature overview and motivation" section, the critical advantage of feature evolution is the fact that neighbouring points in the feature space describe melodies with similar musical characteristics, since several studies exhibited the potential of these features to categorize music according to aesthetic content, genre or composer among others. This locality coherence allows meaningful transitions of the agents on the top level, e.g. a point near a well-rated melody will most likely be a well-rated melody. Contrarily, the genotypical "neighbourhoods" are not coherent, in a sense that melodies with similar genotypes may be expressed by phenotypes that are distant in aesthetics, e.g. pleasantness and unpleasantness. Therefore, interactive music composition based on feature evolution could introduce a novel research direction where more robust interactive methodologies could be developed. Additionally, it should be noted that in the feature evolution setup that is tested, the notion *convergence* is not the same as the notion of *good music*, since the generated music is as good as efficient the features are.

The exhaustive study of the proposed system not only provides insights about the system in its current form, i.e. with the music composition submodules that have been described, but also introduces a methodological context to validate and compare potential future implementations. These implementations would be directed towards automatic music composition through feature evolution, not necessarily incorporating the presented setup [e.g. they could incorporate the Differential Evolution (Storn and Price 1997; Price et al. 2005) algorithm on the top level]. To this end, the utilisation of the artificial raters provides a solid framework for validating the convergence potential and the melodic capabilities of the system setup under examination. Thereby, the paper at hand has also contributed by proposing a methodology for assessing the robustness and the musical characteristics of an interactive feature-evolutionary music composition system. The latter fact is pivotal towards formulating interactive music composition systems in general, since the vast majority of evaluation methodologies rely solely on subjective tests, disallowing the potential of comparative studies (Pearce and Wiggins 2007).

FOOTNOTES

1 As a matter of fact, the European Research Committee has funded four large-scale research project around computational creativity from 2013 to 2016, namely Learning to Create (http://lrn2cre8.eu), Concept Creation Technology (http://conceptcreationtechnology.eu), Concept Invention Theory (http://www.coinvent-project.eu/en/home.html) and the What-If Machine (http://www.whim-project.eu).

AUTHORS' CONTRIBUTIONS

All authors contributed to shaping the ideas in this paper. MAK implemented the experimental results and drafted the final text. All authors read and approved the final manuscript.

ACKNOWLEDGEMENTS

The authors wish to thank the anonymous reviewers for their useful comments.

COMPETING INTERESTS

The authors declare that they have no competing interests.

REFERENCES

1. Akbari R, Ziarati K (2011) A rank based particle swarm optimization algorithm with dynamic adaptation. J Comput Appl Math 235(8):2694–2714
2. Alfonseca M, Cebrian M, Ortega A (2007) A simple genetic algorithm for music generation by means of algorithmic information theory. In: IEEE congress on evolutionary computation, 2007. CEC 2007, pp 3035–3042
3. Ariza C (2002) Prokaryotic groove: Rhythmic cycles as real-value encoded genetic algorithms. In: Proceedings of the international computer music conference, San Francisco, USA, pp 561–567
4. Biles JA (2002) Genjam: evolution of a jazz improviser. In: Bentley PJ, Corne DW (eds) Creative evolutionary systems. Morgan Kaufmann Publishers Inc., San Francisco, pp 165–187
5. Blackwell TM (2003) Swarm music: improvised music with multi-swarms. In: Proceedings of the 2003 AISB symposium on artificial intelligence and creativity in arts and science, pp 41–49
6. Blackwell T (2007) Swarming and music. In: Miranda ER, Biles JA (eds) Evolutionary computer music. Springer, London, pp 194–217
7. Blackwell T (2008) Swarm granulation. In: Romero J, Machado P (eds) The art of artificial evolution. Natural computing series. Springer, Heidelberg, pp 103–122
8. Blackwell TM, Bentley P (2002) Improvised music with swarms. In: Proceedings of the 2002 congress on evolutionary computation, 2002. CEC '02, vol 2. IEEE, pp 1462–1467
9. Blackwell T, Young M (2004) Swarm granulator. In: Applications of evolutionary computing, Proceedings of the 2nd European workshop on evolutionary music and art, EVOMUSART 2004. Springer, Heidelberg, pp 399–408
10. Coca AE, Tost GO, Zhao L (2010) Characterizing chaotic melodies in automatic music composition. Chaos Interdiscip J Nonlinear Sci 20(3)
11. Donnelly P, Sheppard J (2011) Evolving four-part harmony using genetic algorithms. In: Proceedings of the 2011 international conference on applications of evolutionary computation—vol Part II. EvoApplications'11. Springer, Berlin, Heidelberg, pp 273–282
12. Eigenfeldt A (2008) Emergent rhythms through multi-agency in Max/MSP. In: Kronland-Martinet R, Ystad S, Jensen K (eds) Computer music modeling and retrieval. Sense of sounds. Springer, Berlin, Heidelberg, pp 368–37
13. Fortier N, Van Dyne M (2011) A genetic algorithm approach to improve automated music composition. Int J Comput 5(4):525–532
14. Herremans D, Sörensen K, Martens D (2015) Classification and generation of composer-specific music using global feature models and variable neighborhood search. Comput Music J 39(3):71–91
15. Hillewaere R, Manderick B, Conklin D (2009a) Global feature versus event models for folk song classification. In: Proceedings of the 10th international society for music information retrieval conference, (ISMIR 2009), Kobe, Japan, pp 729–733
16. Hillewaere R, Manderick B, Conklin D (2009b) Melodic models for polyphonic music classification. In: Proceedings of the 2nd international workshop on machine learning and music, (MML 2009), held in conjunction with the european conference on machine learning and principles and practice of knowledge discovery in databases (ECML-PKDD 2009), Bled, Slovenia, pp 19–24
17. Hofmann DM (2015) A genetic programming approach to generating musical compositions. In: Johnson C, Carballal A, Correia J (eds) Evolutionary and biologically inspired music, sound, art and design. Springer, New York, pp 89–100
18. Horowitz D (1994) Generating rhythms with genetic algorithms. In: Proceedings of the twelfth national conference on artificial intelligence (vol 2). AAAI'94. American Association for Artificial Intelligence, Menlo Park, pp 1459–1460

19. Hughes D, Manaris B (2012) Fractal dimensions of music and automatic playlist generation: similarity search via MP3 song uploads. In: 2012 eighth international conference on intelligent information hiding and multimedia signal processing (IIH-MSP), Piraeus, Greece, pp 436–440
20. Jones D (2008) Atomswarm: a framework for swarm improvisation. In: Proceedings of the 2008 conference on applications of evolutionary computing. Evo'08. Springer, Berlin, Heidelberg, pp 423–432
21. Kaliakatsos-Papakostas MA, Epitropakis MG, Vrahatis MN (2010) Musical composer identification through probabilistic and feedforward neural networks. In: Di Chio C, Brabazon A, Di Caro GA, Ebner M, Farooq M, Fink A, Grahl J, Greenfield G, Machado P, O'Neill M, Tarantino E, Urquhart N (eds) Applications of evolutionary computation. LNCS, vol 6025. Springer, New York, pp 411–420
22. Kaliakatsos-Papakostas MA, Epitropakis MG, Vrahatis MN (2011) Feature extraction using pitch class profile information entropy. In: Agon C, Andreatta M, Assayag G, Amiot E, Bresson J, Mandereau J (eds) Mathematics and computation in music. Lecture notes in artificial intelligence, vol 6726. Springer, New York, pp 354–357
23. Kaliakatsos-Papakostas MA, Floros A, Vrahatis MN (2012a) Intelligent real-time music accompaniment for constraint-free improvisation. In: Proceedings of the 24th IEEE international conference on tools with artificial intelligence (ICTAI 2012), Piraeus, Athens, Greece, pp 445–451
24. Kaliakatsos-Papakostas MA, Floros A, Vrahatis MN, Kanellopoulos N (2012b) Genetic evolution of L and FL-systems for the production of rhythmic sequences. In: Proceedings of the 2nd workshop in evolutionary music held during the 21st international conference on genetic algorithms and the 17th annual genetic programming conference (GP) (GECCO 2012), Philadelphia, pp 461–468
25. Kaliakatsos-Papakostas MA, Epitropakis MG, Floros A, Vrahatis MN (2012c) Controlling interactive evolution of 8-bit melodies with genetic programming. Soft Comput 16:1997–2008
26. Kaliakatsos-Papakostas MA, Epitropakis MG, Floros A, Vrahatis MN (2012d) Interactive evolution of 8-bit melodies with genetic programming towards finding aesthetic measures for sound. In: Proceedings of the 1st international conference on evolutionary and biologically inspired music, sound, art and design, EvoMUSART 2012, Malaga, Spain. LNCS, vol 7247. Springer, Heidelberg, pp 140–151
27. Kaliakatsos-Papakostas M, Floros A, Vrahatis MN (2013) EvoDrummer: deriving rhythmic patterns through interactive genetic algorithms. In: Machado P, McDermott J, Carballal A (eds) Evolutionary and biologically inspired music, sound, art and design. Lecture notes in computer science, vol 7834. Springer, Heidelberg, pp 25–36
28. Kennedy J, Eberhart R (1995) Particle swarm optimization. In: IEEE international conference on neural networks, 1995. Proceedings, vol 4. IEEE, pp 1942–19484
29. Kranenburg PV, Backer E (2004) Musical style recognition—a quantitative approach. In: Parncutt R, Kessler A, Zimmer F (eds) Proceedings of the conference on interdisciplinary musicology (CIM04), Graz, Austria, pp 1–10
30. MacCallum RM, Mauch M, Burt A, Leroi AM (2012) Evolution of music by public choice. Proc Natl Acad Sci 109(30):12081–12086
31. Machado P, Romero J, Manaris B, Santos A, Cardoso A (2003) Power to the critics—a framework for the development of artificial critics. In: Proceedings of 3rd workshop on creative systems, 18th international joint conference on artificial intelligence (IJCAI 2003), Acapulco, Mexico, pp 55–64
32. Madsen ST, Widmer G (2007) A complexity-based approach to melody track identification in MIDI files. In: Proceedings of the international workshop on artificial intelligence and music, (MUSIC-AI 2007), held in conjunction with the 20th international joint conference on artificial intelligence (IJCAI 2007), Hyderabad, India, pp 1–9

33. Manaris B, Purewal T, McCormick C (2002) Progress towards recognizing and classifying beautiful music with computers—MIDI-encoded music and the Zipf-Mandelbrot law. In: Proceedings IEEE SoutheastCon, 2002. IEEE, pp 52–57
34. Manaris B, Romero J, Machado P, Krehbiel D, Hirzel T, Pharr W, Davis RB (2005) Zipf's law, music classification, and aesthetics, and aesthetics. Comput Music J 29(1):55–69
35. Manaris B, Roos P, Machado P, Krehbiel D, Pellicoro L, Romero J (2007) A corpus-based hybrid approach to music analysis and composition. In: Proceedings of the 22nd national conference on artificial intelligence, vol 1. AAAI Press, Vancouver, pp 839–845
36. Manaris B, Hughes D, Vassilandonakis Y (2011) Monterey mirror: combining Markov models, genetic algorithms, and power laws. In: Workshop in evolutionary music, IEEE congress on evolutionary computation (CEC 2011), New Orleans, LA
37. Matic D (2010) A genetic algorithm for composing music. Yugoslav J Oper Res 20(1):157–177
38. Mckay C, Fujinaga I (2004) Automatic genre classification using large high-level musical feature sets. In: Proceedings of the 5th international society for music information retrieval conference, (ISMIR 2004), Barcelona, Spain, pp 525–530
39. Özcan E, Ercal T (2008) A genetic algorithm for generating improvised music. In: Monmarché N, Talbi E-G, Collet P, Schoenauer M, Lutton E (eds) Artificial evolution. Lecture notes in computer science, vol 4926. Springer, New York, pp 266–277
40. Papadopoulos G, Wiggins G (1998) A genetic algorithm for the generation of jazz melodies. In: Proceedings of the finnish conference on artificial intelligence (STeP), pp 7–9
41. Parsopoulos KE, Vrahatis MN (2010) Particle swarm optimization and intelligence: advances and applications. Information Science Reference (IGI Global), Hershey
42. Pearce M, Wiggins G (2007) Evaluating cognitive models of musical composition. In: Proceedings of the 4th international joint workshop on computational creativity, Goldsmith, pp 73–80
43. Price K, Storn RM, Lampinen JA (2005) Differential evolution: a practical approach to global optimization (natural computing series). Springer, Secaucus
44. Purwins J, Graepel T, Blankertz B, Obermayer C (2004) Correspondence analysis for visualizing interplay of pitch class, key, and composer. In: Mazzola G, Noll T, Luis-Puebla E (eds) Perspectives in mathematical and computational music theory. Universities Press, London, pp 432–454
45. Reynolds CW (1987) Flocks, herds and schools: a distributed behavioral model. In: Proceedings of the 14th annual conference on computer graphics and interactive techniques. SIGGRAPH '87, pp 25–34
46. Reynolds CW (1988) Not bumping into things. In: Notes for the SIGGRAPH 88 course developments in physically-based modeling. ACM SIGGRAPH, pp 1–13
47. Sánchez A, Pantrigo JJ, Virseda J, Pérez G (2007) Spieldose: an interactive genetic software for assisting to music composition tasks. In: Proceedings of the 2nd international work-conference on the interplay between natural and artificial computation, Part I: bio-inspired modeling of cognitive tasks. IWINAC '07. Springer, Berlin, Heidelberg, pp 617–626
48. Shannon CE (2001) A mathematical theory of communication. ACM SIGMOBILE Mobile Comput Commun Rev 5:3–55
49. Shi Y, Eberhart RC (1998a) A modified particle swarm optimizer. In: The 1998 IEEE international conference on evolutionary computation proceedings, 1998. IEEE world congress on computational intelligence, Anchorage (AK), pp 69–73
50. Shi Y, Eberhart RC (1998b) Parameter selection in particle swarm optimization. In: Proceedings of the 7th international conference on evolutionary programming VII. EP '98. Springer, London, pp 591–600
51. Shmulevich I, Yli-Harja O, Coyle E, Povel D-J, Lemstram K (2001) Perceptual issues in music pattern recognition: complexity of rhythm and key finding. Comput Humanit 35:23–35

52. Sioros G, Guedes C (2011) Complexity driven recombination of midi loops. In: Proceedings of the 12th international society for music information retrieval conference (ISMIR). University of Miami, Miami, pp 381–386
53. Storn R, Price K (1997) Differential evolution—a simple and efficient adaptive scheme for global optimization over continuous spaces. J Global Optim 11:341–359
54. Takagi H (2001) Interactive evolutionary computation: fusion of the capabilities of EC optimization and human evaluation. Proc IEEE 89(9):1275–1296
55. Unehara M, Onisawa T (2005) Music composition by interaction between human and computer. New Gener Comput 23(2):181–191
56. Vesterstrom J, Thomsen R (2004) A comparative study of differential evolution, particle swarm optimization, and evolutionary algorithms on numerical benchmark problems. In: Congress on evolutionary computation, 2004. CEC2004, vol 2, pp 1980–1982
57. Wilcoxon F (1945) Individual comparisons by ranking methods. Biom Bull 1(6):80–83
58. Wilson S (2008) Spatial swarm granulation. In: Proceedings of the 2008 international computer music conference
59. Wolkowicz J, Kulka Z, Keselj V (2008) nn-gram based approach to composer recognition. Arch Acoust 33(1):43–55
60. Yamamoto R, Ogawa S, Fukumoto M (2012) A creation method of drum's fill–in pattern suited to individual taste using interactive differential evolution. In: Proceedings of the 2012 international conference on Kansei engineering and emotion research
61. Yang Xg, Yuan J, Yuan J, Mao H (2007) A modified particle swarm optimizer with dynamic adaptation. Appl Math Comput 189(2):1205–1213

CHAPTER 5

Image and Video Completion Via Feature Reduction and Compensation

Mariko Isogawa[1] · Dan Mikami[1] · Kosuke Takahashi[1] · Akira Kojima[1]

[1.] *NTT Media Intelligence LaboratoriesYokosukaJapan*

ABSTRACT

This paper proposes a novel framework for image and video completion that removes and restores unwanted regions inside them. Most existing works fail to carry out the completion processing when similar regions do not exist in undamaged regions. To overcome this, our approach creates similar regions by projecting a low dimensional space from the original space. The approach comprises three stages. First, input images/videos are converted to a lower dimensional feature space. Second, a damaged region is restored in the converted feature space. Finally, inverse conversion is performed from the lower dimensional space to the original space. This generates two advantages: (1) it enhances the possibility of applying patches dissimilar to those in the original color space and (2) it enables the use of many existing restoration methods, each having various advantages, because the feature space for retrieving the similar patches is the only extension. The framework's effectiveness was verified in experiments using various methods, the feature space for restoration in the second stage, and inverse conversion methods.

Keywords: Completion Inpainting Restoration Low-dimensional feature space Image transfer

1 INTRODUCTION

Photos and videos sometimes include unwanted objects such as a person walking in front of a filming target or a trash can on a beautiful beach. In this paper we call areas containing such unwanted objects "damaged regions". Completion, also known as inpainting, is a method that deletes such areas[1]. It is acknowledged as one of the most important topics in many research fields, including augmented reality (AR), mixed reality (MR), and image processing [6, 11].

The most primitive solution for this problem restores damaged regions on a pixel-by-pixel basis with neighboring pixels. Bertalmio et al. restore damaged regions by propagating pixel values from surrounding pixels along with the brightness gradient [1], assuming that the smooth changes in pixel values within the border area enable natural image restoration. Though the method keeps luminance continuity with neighboring pixels, it still has difficulty in maintaining temporal and structural consistency. They also proposed an interesting extension [2]. It divides a target image to be restored into high and low frequency images; the low frequency image is filled by [1], while the high frequency image is restored by texture synthesis. The two restored images are then combined to make a final restored image. Although this extension is effective for restoring images with occasional or uniform texture, it has difficulties in restoring images with a complicated structure or a large damaged region.

The patch-based method, which aims at maintaining consistency well even for large damaged regions, is acknowledged as a promising approach. The method first selects a target patch to be restored that includes both source and damaged regions. Then it retrieves a similar patch to the target patch from the source region. Finally, the damaged region within the target patch is filled by using the obtained similar patch. The way similar patches are retrieved is one of the most important aspects for restoration quality.

Since the color-based patch retrieval [3] was proposed, edges [15] or motions [17] have been added to obtain more appropriate patches. With restrictive constraints, restoration works well if there are patches that have satisfactory matches for all features. In other words, these approaches implicitly assume that the target image includes such patches. However, this assumption does not hold when the region to be filled in contains complex structures or color distribution. Therefore, obtaining good results becomes difficult when the target patches include complicated shapes and/or have vast possible value spaces due to the lack of an appropriate patch for completion.

To overcome such insufficiency of patches, some previous methods used geometric deformations and changes in illumination [4, 7, 11]. The concept of these methods can be summarized as enhancing the availability of patches by transforming patches that are unsuitable in their original condition. However, these methods require huge computational cost for patch retrieval. Another method was developed by Shiratori et al., who proposed a technique for restoring video in a motion feature space [16]. Since this method uses motion features only for patch retrieval, it can be considered that it relaxes patch retrieval criteria. We think this method is quite important because it enables the restoration to be carried out not in the original feature space but in the converted feature space. This method is discussed in more detail in Section 2.1.

We propose a general framework for completing image and video (we use "content" to represent "image and video" when we do not need to distinguish them) via restoration in a different feature space from the original. The feature space for restoration we use is a lower dimensional feature space. This enables dissimilar patches in the original feature space to become similar in the lower dimensional space. For example, different colors in RGB space (R_1,G_1,B_1)=(200,90,126) and (R_2,G_2,B_2)=(75,156,114) become the same gray scale value (127) when they are projected to gray scale. That is, conversion to a lower dimensional space relaxes "similarity" of patches. The framework consists of three stages (Figure 1b): (1) converting input content to a lower dimensional feature space, (2) restoring the content in the converted lower dimensional feature space, and (3) inversely converting the restored content from the lower dimensional feature space to the original feature space.

The remainder of this paper is organized as follows. In Section 2 we briefly review related work. We describe the new framework we propose in Section 3 and in Section 4 show how it works by observing image and video completion results. In Section 5 we show that it also works well with various feature spaces, and with some state-of-the-art completion methods. In Section 6, we discuss the framework's current limitations and further studies. Finally, we conclude in Section 7 with a brief summary.

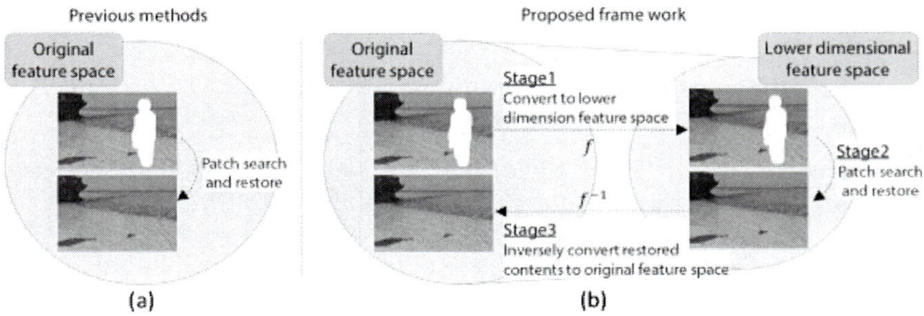

Figure 1. Completion process of previous methods (**a**) and proposed framework (**b**). Most previous methods complete contents in the original feature space, while the proposed framework completes them in a lower dimensional feature space. Damaged contents are converted to the lower dimensional feature space in Stage 1, restored in Stage 2, and inversely converted to the original space in Stage 3

2 RELATED WORK

This section reviews previous studies for content restoration and feature creation. In Section 2.1we describe restoration methods that increase patch availability. In Section 2.2 we review methods to create and add features to the content.

2.1 Approaches for increasing the availability of patches

The process most patch-based methods use is as follows: (1) choose a target patch P_t to be restored, (2) retrieve a similar patch P_s that maximizes $S(P_t, P_s)$, where S is a similarity function, (3) use P_s as a basis for restoring the damaged region within P_t. In patch-based completion studies, various methods to increase the availability of patches have been proposed. Here, we briefly introduce existing studies in two concept categories.

The first one is to increase the patch availability by transforming patches that are unsuitable in their original condition. Darabi et al. [4] introduce scaling and location while Huang et al. [7] allow projective transformation; both have reported good results. Kawai et al. use patches under different illumination [11]. These methods can be implemented by allowing patch deformations or illumination changes in process step (2).

However, because these methods take such deformations or illumination changes into account, patch retrieval requires huge computational cost.

The second one is to increase the patch availability by retrieving patches with relaxed constraints. Shiratori et al. proposed a method for restoring video in a motion field [16]. It retrieves patches on the basis of motion vectors, which makes it possible to fill in a damaged region if a motion pattern similar to that of the damaged region is contained in the reference video. Once the motion vector is restored, the missing pixel values can be obtained from the temporally neighbouring video frames. This can be done regardless of the color of the patches; i.e., the applicability of patches is extended with respect to color. However, it requires manual selection of a reference video that includes a motion pattern similar to that of the damaged region. The necessity of such intervention deteriorates the efficacy of the method in practice. In addition, when the duration of damage gets longer, small differences between the selected motion vectors and the desired ones make color propagation more difficult. We think that Shiratori et al.'s method can be considered a reasonably effective one as it restores damaged regions via a different feature space in process step (2). However, a motion vector is not always the optimal feature and in some cases another feature space is more suitable. Also, this method can be applied to video restoration only.

We propose a general framework for completion via a different feature space, which allows us to use various feature spaces. In particular, we use a lower dimensional feature space because we assume that patches in a lower dimensional feature space enhance patch availability.

2.2 Content transportation to different feature space

Studies have been made on generative approaches to content restoration, in which features are created and added to a content. Levin et al. proposed a colorization method [12] that adds color information to monochrome contents. It works under the following simple assumption: "neighboring pixels in space-time that have similar intensities should have similar colors". Therefore, color information can be estimated by solving an optimization problem formalized on the basis of this assumption and using sparsely designated color information.

Hertzmann et al. proposed a method called "image analogies". It estimates an image filter applied to a reference image and then applies it to another image to add effects similar to those of the reference to the other image [8].

Our proposed method omits some content features and completes the content using the others. It then compensates for the missing features within the completed content by using generative approaches.

3 PROPOSED METHOD

We propose a novel content completion framework that consists of three stages: converting a target image to a lower dimensional feature space, restoring damaged regions in the space, and inversely converting them to the original feature space. The motivation for converting an image to a lower dimension is "to make dissimilar patches similar" by projecting to a lower dimensional feature space. Hereafter, we distinguish the words "restoration" and "completion" as follows: "restoration" is used for the second stage, restoring an image in a low dimensional feature space, while "completion" is used for all three stages including the restoration stage. In this section we first overview the framework in Section 3.1 and then in Section 3.2 describe how to inversely convert the restored image from the lower dimensional feature space to the original feature space in Stage 3.

3.1 Proposed framework

Unlike existing methods, which restore damaged regions in an original feature space such as an RGB space (Figure 1a) or a higher dimensional space by adding edges or motion vectors, the proposed framework uses a lower dimensional feature space. Even if there are no similar patches in the original feature space, the lower dimensional feature space in which some information is lost makes dissimilar patches become similar. The framework outline is shown in Figure 1b. The details of each stage follow.

Stage 1. Converting input contents

Input contents including damaged region I_{in} are converted from the original feature space to Iin′Iin′, which is in a lower dimensional feature space. This can be written by

$$I_{in} = f(I_{in'}) \tag{1}$$

where f is the projection function. Ideally, this conversion should excludes features that are less important for restoration or that can be compensated for by post processing. However, such features depend not only on the human vision system but on a target content. Thus, we can try making use of various lower dimensional feature space simultaneously.

Here we show two examples for dimension reduction. To convert to gray scale space (one dimensional space) or RG space (two dimensional space), f can be write as following (2) and (3). Note that $I_{in'_R}$, $I_{in'_G}$, and $I_{in'_B}$, ' represent each RGB channels.

$$I_{in} = f(I_{in'}) = \begin{bmatrix} 0.299 & 0.587 & 0.114 \end{bmatrix} \begin{bmatrix} I_{in'_R} \\ I_{in'_G} \\ I_{in'_B} \end{bmatrix} \quad (2)$$

$$I_{in} = f(I_{in'}) = \begin{bmatrix} 1 & 0 & 0 \\ 0 & 1 & 0 \end{bmatrix} \begin{bmatrix} I_{in'_R} \\ I_{in'_G} \\ I_{in'_B} \end{bmatrix} \quad (3)$$

Stage 2. Restoration in lower dimensional space

Iin′Iin′ is restored to generate I_c in the lower dimensional space.

$$I_c \longrightarrow I_{in'} \quad (4)$$

We expect that the restoration is easier in a lower dimension feature space because some patches that are not similar and cannot be used for restoration in the original feature space become similar and become available by projecting to lower dimensional feature space. Any exemplar-based restoration methods are acceptable for our framework. This is true even for video as the restoration target.

Stage 3. Inverse conversion of restored content

Inverse conversion (see Section 3.2 below) is performed to obtain final output in the original feature space. Restored contents in lower feature space I_c are inversely converted to those in original feature space I_{out} as follows.

$$I_{out} = f^{-1}(I_c) \quad (5)$$

where f^{-1} is inverse projection function. This inverse conversion is necessary to compensate for the features that were omitted in Stage 1. More details for f^{-1} are explained in Section 3.2.

This three-step solution generates two advantages. First, it enhances the possibility of applying patches dissimilar to those in the original color space. Second, it enables the use of many existing methods for restoration because the feature space for retrieving the similar patches is the only extension.

Figure 2 explains how our framework works well. Here, Figure 2a is an example of a damaged image that has no appropriate patches for restoration. For the damaged yellow button, there are no similar patches having the same structure and same color. Thus, if the original feature space is used, the blue box, which contains an orange button, is retrieved as the most similar one as in Figure 2b. However, as shown in Figure 2c, because yellow and pink buttons are converted to similar levels in gray scale, dissimilar patches consisting of pink buttons in RGB space become similar. This enables a region whose original color is pink to become applicable for restoration as shown in Figure 2d.

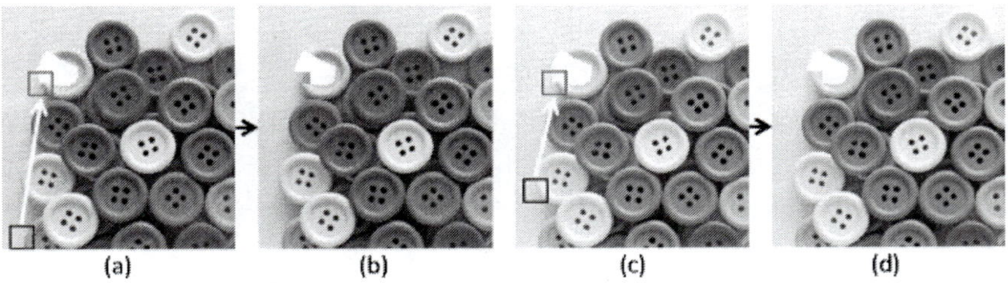

Figure 2. An example of how our framework contributes to a completed result, where (**a**) shows a damaged original image (damaged region is masked in white). In the original RGB space, an inappropriate similar patch (shown as a blue box) is retrieved for a damaged patch (shown as a red box), which results in completion failure as shown in (**b**). However, as shown in (**c**), yellow and pink buttons are converted to similar levels in gray scale, which enables a region whose original color is pink to become applicable for restoration as in (**d**)

3.2 Inverse conversion of restored content

Because Stage 1 excludes certain features, I_c (the restored result in the lower dimensional space) and I_{out} (the completed result in the original space) have a one-to-many relationship. Therefore, inverse conversion and compensation f^{-1} for missing information are required. We perform inverse transformation by using two different approaches, described in Sections 3.2.1and 3.2.2 below.

3.2.1 Inverse conversion based on correspondence between two contents

This section describes a versatile approach utilizing data gotten from content pairs, i.e., the criginal content I_{in} and the converted content Iin′Iin′. Note that getting such data is easy because they exist in non-damaged areas in content pairs. By using such pairs, Stage 3 infers the inverse conversion from the non-damaged areas of content pairs. Because this approach can be used regardless of the converted lower dimensional feature space, it becomes a versatile approach.

We use Image Analogies [8] to implement the idea described above because it works well regardless of the number of samples and distribution of the data. A more detailed process, which has four steps, is as follows (See Figure 3). First, multi-scale representations of I_{in} and Iin′Iin′, before and after Stage 1, and the restored result in lower dimensional space I_c are constructed. Data vector $V(p)$ including information of I_{in} and Iin′Iin′ is then stocked for every non-damaged pixel p. $V(p)$ consists of $P_a(p)$ and Pa′(p)Pa′(p), which correspond to patches centered at p in I_{in} and Iin′Iin′. After that, I_c is inversely converted to I_{out} on a pixel-by-pixel basis. To convert pixel q in I_c, data vector $V(q)$ including information of P^b(q]P^b(q) and P^b′(q)P^b′(q) is calculated, where P^b(q)P^b(q) and P^b′(q)P^b′(q) are patches centered at q in I_{out} and I_c. Finally, similar data vector $V(p)$ of $V(q)$ is retrieved from the database and q is updated by p.

For video content, this algorithm also works well by processing frame-by-frame or by extending $V(p)$ consisting of spatially neighboring pixels to spatio-temporal neighboring ones.

3.2.2 Dedicated inverse conversion

This section describes a dedicated method for each feature space. It is not a general-use method but a specialized one for feature spaces that is expected to enable better transformation.

One example method of this type is colorization [12], which is effective in generating lost color. It can be used when gray scale feature space is used for restoration. Let us examine colorization-based inverse conversion in more detail. Colorization needs color information seeds within a gray image to be colorized and many previous studies, including [12], set such

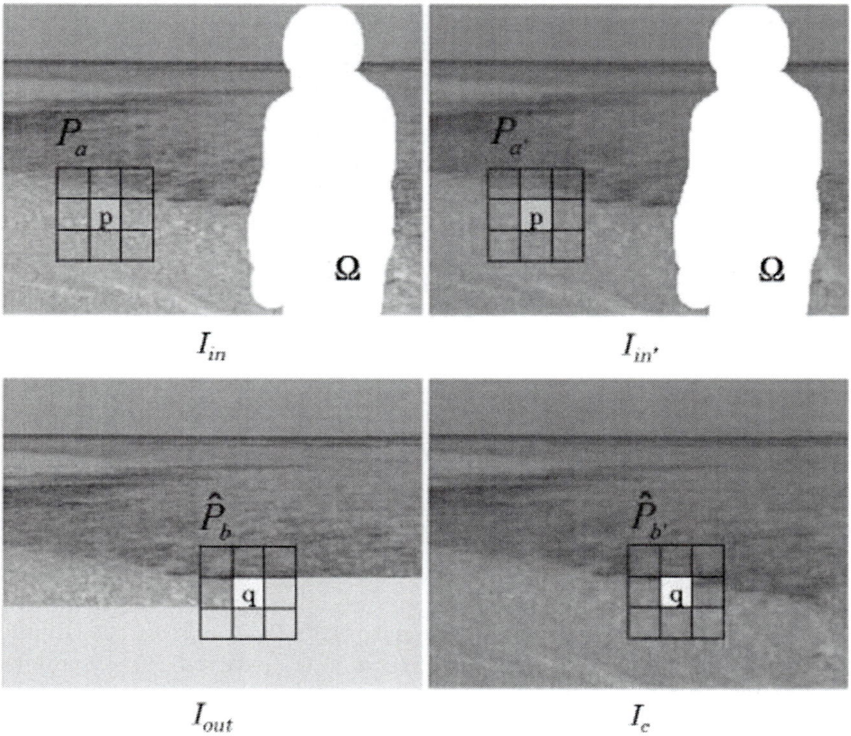

Figure 3. Inverse conversion from the lower dimensional feature space to the original space via Versatile. Data vectors based on $P_a(p)$ and Pa′(p)Pa′(p), as well as patches centered at every pixel p in I_{in} and Iin′Iin′ are stocked as a database for conversion. Pixel q in restored content I_c is converted using a similar data vector to $V(q)$, a data vector based on P^b′(q) P^b′(q) and P^b(q)P^b(q) and patches centered at q in I_c and I_{out}

seeds manually. However, in our case seeding can be automated because color information of non-damaged regions exists in I_{in}. As shown in Figure 4, initial color values for colorization are set by using the color values of the original image (Figure 4a) as follows, where Ω represents the damaged region in the image:

$$I_c(x) = \begin{cases} I_c(x) & (x \in \Omega) \\ I_{in}(x) & (otherwise) \end{cases} \tag{6}$$

Consequently, in our implementation we consider there are patches $P(p)$ centered at every damaged pixel p. Color information of p is estimated by solving an optimization problem so that p and its neighboring pixels in $P(p)$ keep luminance consistency. This process is also effective for setting $P(p)$ as a 3D patch including spatio-temporal neighbor pixels.

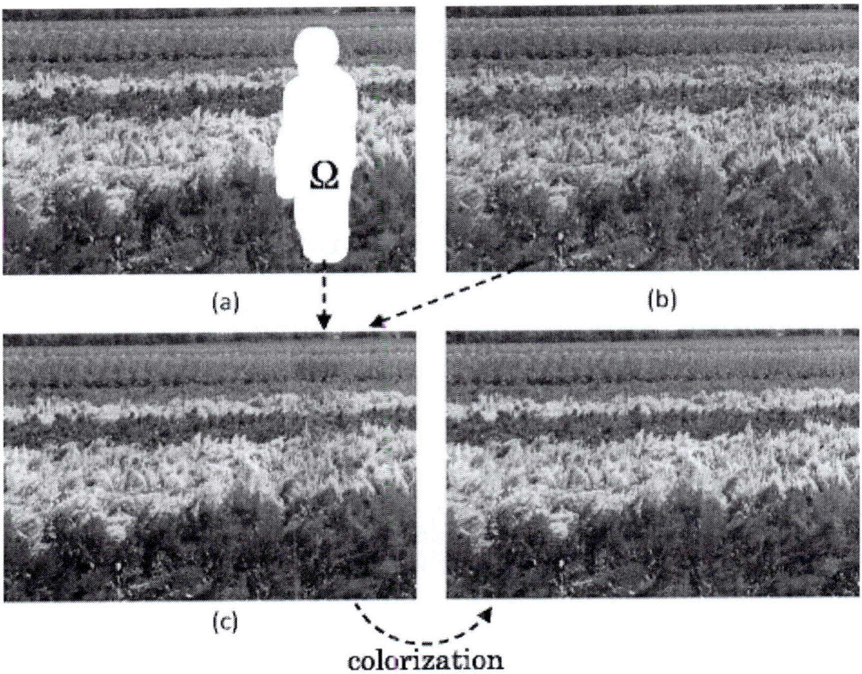

Figure 4. Initialization for colorization process. Initial content (**c**) is generated by seeding color information from non-damaged regions in I_{in} shown in (**a**), to restored content I_c shown in (**b**)

Another example method of this type is super resolution-based inverse conversion. This method is effective when a low resolution space is used as the restoration space. There are many possible implementations with the existing algorithm.

4 EXPERIMENT

This section demonstrates how the proposed method works, i.e., how it improves completion while maintaining the advantages of previous restoration methods. To simplify the discussion, this section only focuses on one simple implementation, i.e., applying gray scale conversion in Stage 1, performing restoration in gray space in Stage 2, and colorizing in Stage 3. We apply this implementation with the expectation that unsuitable patches that have an appropriate structure but inappropriate color can be used for restoration in gray scale feature space.

In Section 4.1 we describe the restoration methods applied in Stage 2 and in Section 4.2 we describe in detail how our method works and show completed results with calculation times and an objective evaluation.

4.1 Restoration methods

For the content restoration in Stage 2 we used two methods for image [3, 5], and one method for video [13]. All of them restore a damaged region on the basis of the similar patches retrieved. However, they use the retrieved patches in different ways and thus derive different advantages. In this subsection, we introduce these three techniques in more detail.

Criminisi et al.'s method [3] is based on the idea of copying and pasting of small patches from a source area into the damaged region Ω. These patches are useful as they provide a practical way of encoding local texture and structure. The method does not guarantee global coherence, but it includes a way to propagate both linear structure and texture into the hole region from patches with highest priority. The priority computation is biased toward patches that are (i) on the continuation of strong edges and (ii) are surrounded by high-confidence pixels. Given a patch Φ_p centered at point p for multiple p included in the contour of the damaged region, they define priority $P(p)$ as below.

$$P(p) = C(p)D(p) \tag{7}$$

Here, $C(p)$ and $D(p)$ correspond to (i) and (ii), respectively. They are defined as follows:

$$C(p) = \frac{\sum_{q \cap \bar{\Omega}} C(q)}{|\Phi_p|}, \quad D(p) = \frac{|\Delta I_p^{\perp} \cdot n(p)|}{\alpha} \tag{8}$$

where $n(p)$ is a vector orthogonal to the contour of the damaged region, and I⊥pIp⊥ is computed as the maximum value of the image gradient in Φp∩Ω¯Φp∩Ω¯. α is a normalized factor, to be set as 255 for a typical image.

Efros et al.'s method [5] efficiently restores holes included in periodic texture content. With this method, the damaged region to be filled is synthesized one pixel at a time. To synthesize a pixel p, the algorithm first finds patches $\mathbf{w}(p)$ from the neighboring area in the sample image that are similar to $\mathbf{P}(p)$, i.e., patches including p. It then chooses one neighborhood patch $\mathbf{w}_{best}(p)$ from $\mathbf{w}(p)$ to minimize a difference between $P(p)$ and $\mathbf{w}(p)$ as follows.

$$\mathbf{w}_{best}(p) = argmin\ distance(P(p), \mathbf{w}(p)) \tag{9}$$

Positions of p within $\mathbf{w}_{best}(p)$ are represented as x_p. Finally, p is newly synthesized using x_p as a basis.

Newson et al.'s method [13] is effective for video content. This method restores the damaged region on a pixel-by-pixel basis. First, several patches $\mathbf{w}(p)$ including damaged pixel p are set as target patches. Positions of p within these patches are represented as $\mathbf{x}$. Similar patches w^w^ for each $\mathbf{w}$ are then retrieved. Finally, p is updated on the basis of the weighted mean value of $q$with the following formula:

$$u_p = \frac{\sum_{q \cap \bar{\Omega}} s_q u_q}{\sum_{q \cap \bar{\Omega}} s_q}, q = \{x \in \widehat{w}\} \tag{10}$$

where Ω is the damaged region, u_p and u_q represented the RGB values of p and q, and s_q is a weighted value for q.

In this paper, using the previous algorithms as a basis, we represent the proposed method as *Prop.Method(Feature)*. For example, we represent the proposed method whose lower feature space is RG feature space and which is based on Criminisi et al.'s work as *Prop.Criminisi(RG)*.

4.2 Completion and evaluation results

In this section we demonstrate completed image results in Section 4.2.1 and video results in Section 4.2.2. In Section 4.2.3 we show objective evaluations of the methods used in the study in terms of calculation time and similarities.

4.2.1 Image completion result

Here we show the completion results obtained with the proposed methods and compare them to results obtained with their restoration methods, Criminisi et al. [3] and Efros et al. [5]. Two completed target images including a complex structure and color changes were used for this comparison. The first one, shown in Figure 5I, has a rather large damaged region. Therefore, we consider that Criminisi et al.'s method is suitable for restoring it. The other one, shown in Figure 5II, has a smaller damaged region but a unique cyclic structure. We considered that for this kind of cyclic structure, Efros et al.'s method would be better. Note that both target images include a complex structure and would be difficult to restore with methods using spatial consistency.

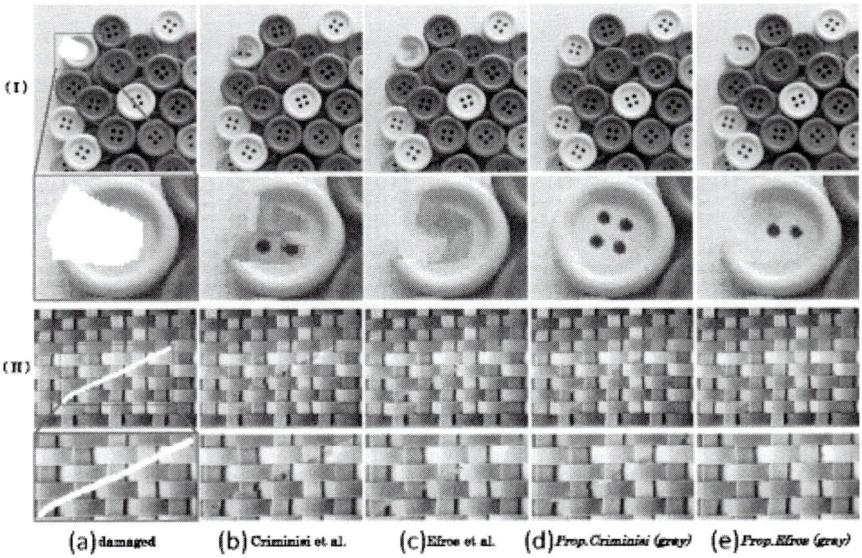

Figure 5. Input and result of image completion experiment; (**a**) Input image with damaged region masked in white. The close-up area is shown as a red frame. (**b**), (**c**) Results obtained by Criminisi et al. [3] and Efros et al. [5]. (**d**), (**e**) Results obtained with the proposed method: *Prop. Criminisi(gray)* and *Prop.Efros(gray)*

Additional experimental settings are as follows. The damaged region is manually set (Figure 5a masked in white), the image resolutions are (I) 210 ×223 and (II) 200 ×150 pixels, the ratios of damaged pixels in each image are (I) 1.77 % and (II) 2.91 % and the patch sizes we used are (I) 21 ×21 pixels and (II)13 ×13 pixels. To perform the experiments we used a desktop PC of Intel Core i7 3.40GHz CPU, 32GB memory, and a Matlab R2014. The results obtained with the proposed methods *Prop. Crimiminisi(gray)* and *Prop.Efros(gray)* are shown in Figure 5d and e. Those obtained with the previous methods (Criminisi et al.'s and Efros et al.'s) are shown in Figure 5b and c.

In Figure 5a the top row (I) shows the completed results obtained with the methods used. As can readily be seen, *Prop.Criminisi(gray)* showed the most efficient completion. Comparing the *Prop.Criminisi (gray)* and *Prop.Efros(gray)* results makes it clear that the proposed framework well maintains the advantages of a base restoration method. Because this completion target (Figure 5a) includes a rather large damaged region, it is intrinsically suitable for Criminisi et al.'s method.

From Figure 5II it is clear that Efros et al. in (c) shows better performance than Criminisi et al. in (b), indicating Efros et al.'s method is advantageous for dealing with periodic structured content. Some unnatural shadows are observed, however, especially on the yellow-green warp at the center and on the yellow warp next to that. In contrast, *Prop.Efros(gray)* did not show any such defects (e). These results well verify that the proposed framework retains the advantages of a base restoration method and improves completion quality.

Although for explanatory purposes we used unnatural images for the completion target, rather primitive restoration methods, and gray scale space for restoration, we will show more comprehensive completion results in Section 5.

4.2.2 Video completion results

For obtaining video completion results, we implemented *Prop. Newson(gray)* as the proposed method, using Newson et al.'s [13] algorithm as a basis, via gray scale feature space. Figure 6shows a comparison between *Prop.Newson(gray)* and Newson et al.'s method. The target sequence has 104 frames with 960×540 pixel resolution. The damaged region is automatically designated and its average percentage is 6.5 % of the original video.

Completed results obtained with Newson et al. are shown in the second row of Figure 6. The result for *Prop.Newson(gray)* is shown as a restored sequence in gray scale feature space in the third row. The final result in the original color space, inversely converted by colorization, is shown in the bottom row. With Newson et al's method, an easily distinguished red colored area appeared in the bottom area in the enlarged images. For the same area, *Prop.Newson(gray)* achieved completing with natural water color.

4.2.3 Objective evaluation

Objective evaluations were made among the methods in terms of similarities and computational cost. For evaluation purposes, we calculated SSIM (Structure SIMilarity) [18] and PSNR[2](Peak Signal-to-

Figure 6. Original frames and video completion results. Original frames including an unwanted area are shown in the top row and completed results obtained with Newson et al. are shown in the second row. In our implementation, we first obtained the restored results in low-dimensional gray space (third row) and then generated the final results by colorizing them as shown in the bottom row

Noise Ratio) for the (I) (II) results in Figure 5. SSIM is a metric for using structure information to calculate image similarity. It is a decimal value between -1 and 1, with 1 being the highest score. The comparative results for the methods used are shown in Tables 1 and 2. We calculated these values for original size images and also for the close-up view in Figure 5. As the tables show, in terms of (I) *Prop.Criminisi(gray)* recorded the highest value and *Prop.Efros(gray)* recorded the next highest score for both SSIM and PSNR. With respect to (II), *Prop.Efros(gray)* showed the highest value and *Prop.Criminisi(gray)* scored the second highest for both SSIM and PSNR.

Table 1. Evaluation by SSIM with default parameters of [18]

	Size	Criminisi et al.	Efros et al.	*Prop.Criminisi(gray)*	*Prop.Efros(gray)*
(I)	original	0.9824	0.9826	0.9894	0.9828
	close-up	0.6451	0.6463	0.7857	0.6500
(II)	original	0.9780	0.9834	0.9828	0.9937
	close-up	0.9368	0.9528	0.9517	0.9817

The highest scores are underlined

Table 2. Evaluation by PSNR [1] [dB]

	Size	Criminisi et al.	Efros et al.	*Prop.Criminisi(gray)*	*Prop.Efros(gray)*
(I)	original	28.75	27.36	32.46	29.38
	close-up	16.94	15.55	20.65	17.57
(II)	original	29.72	30.01	33.82	38.55
	close-up	25.30	27.62	29.41	34.14

The highest scores are underlined

Also, although our implementation, so far, does not focus on reduction of calculation cost, we briefly examined elapsed time for processing. Table 3 shows a comparison of elapsed time between Criminisi et al.'s method and *Prop.Criminisi(gray)*, and Table 4 shows the same between Efros et al.'s method and *Prop.Efros(gray)*. There was no significant difference between the elapsed time of Criminisi et al.'s method and *Prop. Criminisi(gray)*, despite the fact that *Prop.Criminisi(gray)* requires an additional process, i.e., colorization. The comparison between Efros et al's method and *Prop.Efros(gray)* (Table 4) shows that the calculation time was much less for the latter. The calculation cost of the former is high because of the pixel-by-pixel restoration it performs. The calculation time for *Prop.Efros(gray)* is lower because the completion was done in a lower dimensional space. Of course the calculation cost will change depending on hole size or the initialization required for colorization, but this evaluation confirmed that performing inverse conversion does not significantly affect the total calculation time for smaller images such as those shown in Figure 5. To further elaborate on this point, Section 6.2 describes how we analyzed computational cost in more detail.

Table 3. Elapsed time comparison between Criminisi et al.'s method [3] and *Prop.Criminisi(gray)* [sec]

	Criminisi et al.	*Prop.Criminisi(gray)*		
		Completion	Colorization	Total
(I)	1.64	0.87	1.11	1.98
(II)	2.19	1.31	0.40	1.71

For more detail, please see Section 6.2

Table 4. Elapsed time comparison between Efros et al.'s method [5] and *Prop.Efros(gray)* [sec]

	Efros et al.	*Prop.Efros(gray)*		
		Completion	Colorization	Total
(I)	297.00	147.19	0.48	147.67
(II)	77.47	46.97	0.28	47.25

For more detail, please see Section 6.2

Table 5. Variations of restoration methods and feature spaces

Restoration methods	Feature spaces		
	Gray scale	RG	GB
He et al [9]	*Prop.He(gray)*	*Prop.He(RG)*	*Prop.He(GB)*
Huang et al [7]	*Prop.Huang(gray)*	*Prop.Huang(RG)*	*Prop.Huang(GB)*

Note that all of the patterns with "*Prop.*" were obtained with our proposed methods

5 RESULTS IN VARIOUS SETTINGS

In this section, we show that our framework is also effective with current state-of-the-art algorithms and other feature spaces. The restoration method and feature space we used are shown in Table 5. Their details are as follows.

5.1 Restoration method

First, we introduce He et al.'s and Huang et al.'s algorithm [7, 9] for Stage2, the image restoration part.

He et al.'s method [9] works well for filling in missing regions through patch offset statistics. If similar patches in the image are matched and their relative positions obtained, the statistics of these offset areas are sparsely distributed. With these offsets the missing regions are filled by combining a stack of shifted images via photomontage, a method for image composite by using optimization.

Huang et al.'s method [7] is also a current state-of-the-art method and works especially well with images including complex structures. It first estimates perspective and regularity in the source image and roughly segments the known region into planes, then discovers translational regularity within these planes. The information is then converted into soft constraints for the low-level restoration algorithm by defining prior probabilities for patch offsets and transformations.

5.2 Feature space

We use three types of feature space: RG, GB, and gray scale space. An RG feature space is a color space that has red and green channels only. A GB space has green and blue channels. RG and GB spaces are represented as two dimensions while original the RGB space has three dimensions. We expect that the availability of patches will be increased by using these feature spaces because of the decrease in dimensions. We also expect that visually important features will remain in RG and GB spaces more than in gray scale, which is represented as one dimension. Many feature spaces are represented as two dimensional spaces, but the green channel is well known as visually important information. It is for this reason that we use RG and GB spaces, which include green information. As an inverse conversion process for gray scale space, we used colorization [12] in the same way as mentioned in Section 4.2. For RG space and GB space the versatile method described in Section 3.2.1 was used.

5.3 Results

Completed results for the natural scenes we used are shown in Figure 7. Original images with damaged regions (masked in red) are shown in column (a), while (c) shows the completed results obtained with the proposed method. We show the most effective results that were obtained with various feature spaces. The restored results obtained with the base restoration method used to get the results in (c) are shown in (b). The proposed completion method shows better performance than the other methods because of its utilizing a lower dimensional feature space for restoration.

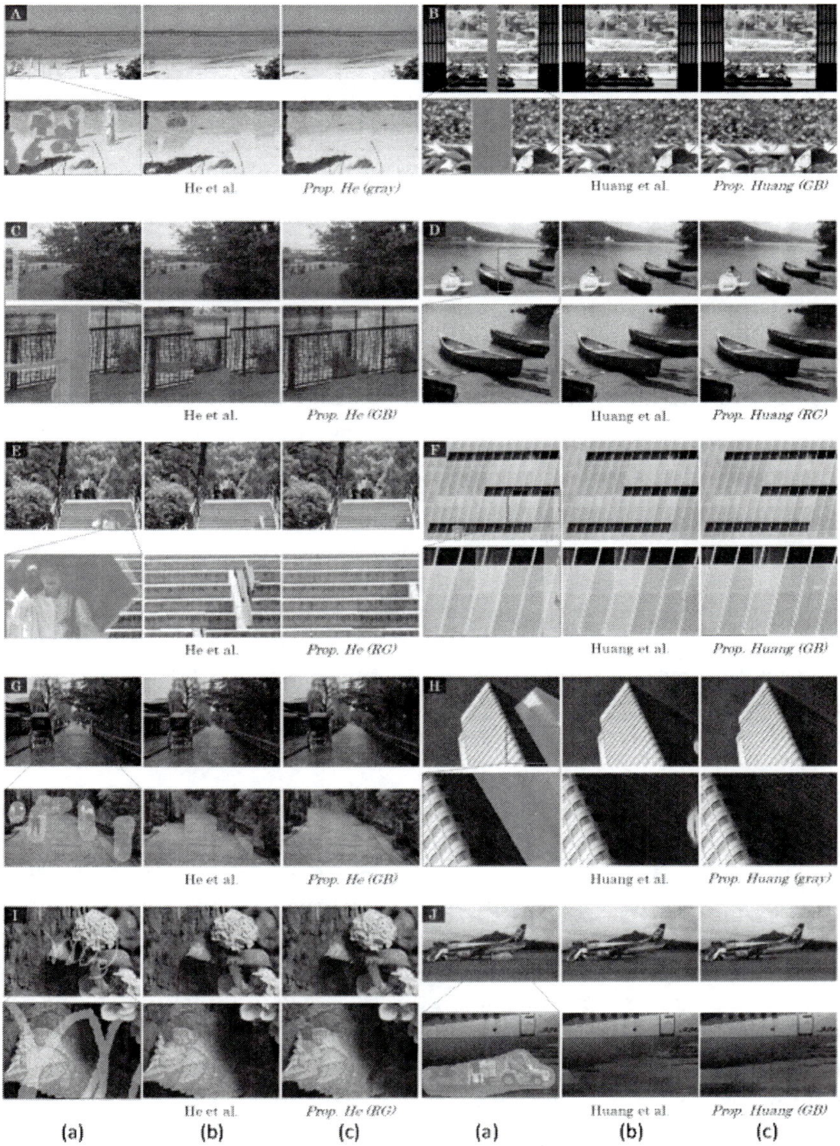

Figure 7. Completed results obtained with current state-of-the-art restoration methods and various feature spaces (gray, RG, and GB). (**a**) Target images with damaged regions (masked in red). (**b**) Results obtained with the original restoration method without dimension reduction. (**c**) Results obtained with the proposed method with dimension reduction. Note that all of the image results annotated *"Prop."* were obtained with our proposed methods

6 LIMITATION AND FUTURE WORK

6.1 Feature space selection

So far, we have showed the results obtained in using a specific lower dimensional feature space for restoration without explanation. Figure 8 shows completion results obtained using the same restoration method but a different feature space; original images with the damaged region masked in red are shown in column (a). Effective and ineffective results obtained by using different feature spaces are shown in (b) and (c). Note that the only difference between them is the feature space used for restoration; the same restoration method was used for both.

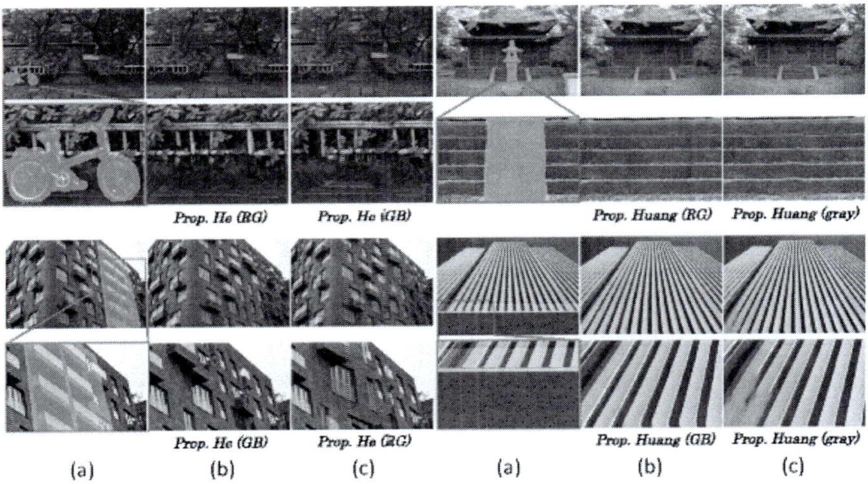

Figure 8. Comparison between completed results obtained using different feature spaces for restoration. Note that the same restoration method was used to obtain the two results. (**a**) Target images with damaged region masked in red. (**b**), (**c**) Completed results obtained with effective/ ineffective feature space

As the results show, completion performance depends on the feature space used for restoration. It was already mentioned in Section 4 that different restoration methods produce different completion results even if the same feature space is used for restoration. Thus, completion performance is affected not only by the feature space used for restoration but by the restoration method. Currently, however, we have not established any criteria for selecting an appropriate feature space and restoration method before observing the completion results. One possible solution is to show the completion results obtained using various setups, i.e., combinations of different restoration methods and feature spaces, and to have users perform the task of selecting from among the completion results.

However, this is likely to make things difficult for the users because of the large number of possible combinations. Aiming to provide the best inpainting result automatically, we have already started developing an automatic ranking method for inpainted results reflecting subjective preference of them [10]. This enables to provide the best result from a set of images inpainted by various methods and feature spaces. Our next step will be to reveal the optimal combination of method and feature only by a completion target image.

6.2 Calculation cost

In Section 4.2.3, we show an example of elapsed time. However, introducing our proposed framework produced no significant changes in elapsed time (in that setting, we used the dedicated method version of inverse conversion for Stage 3, as given in Section 3.2.2). Although we do not focus on the issue of calculation cost in this paper, we think the proposed framework has potential for accelerating the processing time of completion. Therefore, we analyze the computational cost to further elaborate on this point.

In general patch-based completion methods like that in [3], the patch retrieval process occupies most of the total calculation time. Its calculation order is O(NMZ)O(NMZ), where N and $M$are respectively the number of missing pixels and the number of total pixels in the image. The parameter Z is a feature vector dimension for retrieving. This dimension affects the total calculation order with the power of Z, and thus the proposed method, which uses a lower dimensional space for restoration, may reduce the total calculation cost.

At the same time, the method needs to perform additional processing subsequent to restoration, i.e., inverse conversion of feature space from a lower dimension to the original one, as shown in Section 3.2. For this we introduced two approaches, a generalized approach in Section 3.2.1, and dedicated approach in Section 3.2.2. The former requires considerable computational cost. Table 6 shows an example of elapsed time for (b) and (c) in Figure 7 A with the inverse conversion method presented in Sections 3.2.1 and 3.2.2. The completion time for *Prop.He(gray)* is lower than that for the original method because the restoration was done in a lower dimensional space. However, because of the larger resolution of Figure 7 A (1280×720)[pixels], the inverse conversion methods in Sections 3.2.1 and 3.2.2 (particularly the former) entail quite high calculation cost.

Table 6. Elapsed time comparison between He et al.'s method [9] and *Prop.He(gray)* with two inverse conversion method explained in Sections 3.2.1 and 3.2.2 [sec]

Table 6 Elapsed time comparison between He et al.'s method [9] and *Prop.He(gray)* with two inverse conversion method explained in Sections 3.2.1 and 3.2.2 [sec]

He et al.	*Prop.He(gray)*				
	Completion	inverse conversion via Section 3.2.1		inverse conversion via Section 3.2.2	
		inverse conversion	total	inverse conversion	total
19.1	14.4	1513.6	1528.0	31.6	46.0

We think that these inverse conversion methods can be made much faster by implementing parallel computation (e.g. with GPU), because these algorithms enable parallel computing to be performed relatively easily. The time required for users to mask unwanted regions by users should also be taken into account. Therefore, a subject for future work will be to consider how to reduce the time required for inverse conversion and masking.

7 CONCLUSION

In this paper, we introduced a new framework for image/video completion. Our framework involves three stages: (1) converting input content to a lower dimensional feature space, (2) restoring the content in the converted lower dimensional space, and (3) inversely converting the restored content from the lower dimensional space to the original feature space. We consider the framework to be an effective approach, first because it enhances the possibility of applying patches dissimilar to those in the original color space, and second because it makes it possible to use a variety of restoration methods and feature spaces. Experiment results have verified its effectiveness.

Currently we have not established any criteria for selecting an appropriate feature space and restoration method before observing completion results. Thus, subjects for future work will include developing a method that will enable the most appropriate results to be selected automatically, with which we are currently working, and developing criteria that will allow restoration methods and features to be selected before the completion process is carried out.

FOOTNOTES

1. Although it is not a unified definition, the word "completion" tends to be used in cases where a missing region to be filled in becomes large [14].
2. Target PSNR for general purpose lossy image compression ranges from 30 dB to 50 dB, where the higher is the better.

REFERENCES

1. Bertalmío M, Sapiro G, Caselles V, Ballester C (2000) Image inpainting. In: Proceedings of the ACM SIGGRAPH, pp 417–424
2. Bertalmio M, Vese L, Sapiro G, Osher S (2003) Simultaneous structure and texture image inpainting. IEEE Trans Image Process 12(8):882–889
3. Criminisi A, Perez P, Toyama K (2004) Region filling and object removal by exemplar-based inpainting. IEEE Trans Image Process 13(9):1200–1212
4. Darabi S, Shechtman E, Barnes C, Goldman DB, Pradeep S. (2012) Image Melding: Combining inconsistent images using patch-based synthesis. ACM Trans Graph (TOG) (Proceedings of SIGGRAPH 2012) 31(4):82:1–82:10
5. Efros AA, Leung TK (1999) Texture synthesis by non-parametric sampling. In: Proceedings of International Conference on Computer Vision (ICCV), vol 2, pp 1033–1038
6. Herling J, Broll W (2014) High-quality real-time video inpainting with pixmix. IEEE Trans Vis Comput Graph 20(6):866–879
7. Huang J-B, Kang SB, Ahuja N, Kopf J (2014) Image completion using planar structure guidance. ACM Trans Graph (Proceedings of SIGGRAPH 2014) 33 (4):129:1–129:10
8. Hertzmann A, Jacobs CE, Oliver N, Curless B, Salesin DH (2001) Image analogies. In: Proceedings of the ACM SIGGRAPH, pp 327–340
9. He K, Sun J (2014) Image completion approaches using the statistics of similar patches. IEEE Trans Pattern Anal Mach Intell 36(12):2423–2435
10. Isogawa M, Mikami D, Takahashi K, Kojima A (2015) Toward enhancing robustness of dr system Ranking model for background inpainting. In: IEEE International Symposium on Mixed and Augmented Reality (ISMAR), pp 178–179
11. Kawai N, Machikita K, Sato T, Yokoya N (2011) Video completion for generating omnidirectional video without invisible areas. Inf Media Technol 6(1):158–171

12. Levin A, Lischinski D, Weiss Y (2004) Colorization using optimization. In: Proceedings of the ACM SIGGRAPH, pp 689–694
13. Newson A, Almansa A, Fradet M, Gousseau Y, Pérez P (2014) Video inpainting of complex scenes. SIAM J Imaging Sci 7(4):1993–201914.
14. Sun J, Lu Y, Jia J, Shum H-Y (2005) Image completion with structure propagation. ACM Trans Graph (Proceedings of SIGGRAPH 2005) 24(3):861–868
15. Shih TK, Tang NC, Hwang J-N (2009) Exemplar-based video inpainting without ghost shadow artifacts by maintaining temporal continuity. IEEE Trans Circ Syst Video Technol 19(3):347– 360
16. Shiratori T, Matsushita Y, Tang X, transfer Sing Bing Kang. (2006) Video completion by motion field. In: Proceedings of the Computer Vision and Pattern Recognition (CVPR), pp 411– 418
17. Wexler Y, Shechtman E, Irani M (2007) Space-time completion of video. IEEE Trans Pattern Anal Mach Intell 29(3):463–476
18. Wang Z, Bovik AC, Sheikh HR, Simoncelli EP (2004) Image quality assessment: From error visibility to structural similarity. IEEE Trans Image Process 13 (4):600–612

CHAPTER 6

Efficient Music Identification using ORB Descriptors of the Spectrogram Image

Dominic Williams* , Akash Pooransingh and Jesse Saitoo

The University of the West Indies, St. Augustine, Trinidad and Tobago

ABSTRACT

Audio fingerprinting has been an active research field typically used for music identification. Robust audio fingerprinting technology is used to successfully perform content-based audio identification regardless of the audio signal being subjected to various types of distortion. These distortions affect the time-frequency correlation relating to pitch and speed changes. In this paper, experiments are done using the computer vision technique ORB (Oriented FAST and Rotated BRIEF) for robust audio identification. Investigations are conducted for ORB, relating to its advantage of robustness against distortions including speed and pitch changes. The ORB prototype compares the features of the spectrogram image query to a database of spectrogram images of the songs. For the initial experiment, a Brute-Force matcher is used to compare the ORB descriptors. Results show that the ORB prototype performs robustly to real-world distortions with fast, reliable performance against distortions such as speed and pitch which justifies the research done.

Keywords: Audio fingerprinting Music identification Oriented FAST and Rotated BRIEF Spectrogram

1 INTRODUCTION

In recent years, there has been an increase in digital multimedia technology, which made it simpler to share music files. Music is being compressed for portability for the ability to be transmitted between computers via the internet. This proliferation of digital multimedia including online streaming services, and online downloading, has become very popular in the past decade. Now, almost any song can be purchased or streamed digitally at the consumer's fingertips [1]. According to [2], the cost to manufacture and distribute the physical media components such as the CD's, and plastic cases, are no longer necessary, since digital music can reach a far greater audience in a shorter space of time. Music can now be released and distributed digitally [3] as soon as they are ready, and geographical accessibility has become limitless for the distribution of music. As a result, companies and private individuals have also developed various methods for searching, indexing, and matching unknown music samples to a database. This is done using audio fingerprinting [4] and can be used in application areas including broadcast monitoring, copyright protection, and digital rights management music identification.

Music identification [5] is typically done using an audio fingerprinting technique, which is a compact and unique digital summary of the audio content. The fingerprint is computed from the audio signal, stored in a database using a hash method (compact representation) and used for comparing and matching. It also contains the song's metadata such as artist, and song title. The techniques must be robust so that even audio content that is degraded due to distortion can still be accurately identified.

There are many algorithms such as the Philips Robust Hash (PRH) algorithm [5], which was a well-studied and verified method to be mathematically robust and efficient for searching. The PRH algorithm works by converting the audio signal from the time domain to the frequency domain and by diving the frequency spectrum into sub-bands where sub fingerprints are generated for each sub-band. WavePrint [6] proposed an algorithm using computer vision techniques for audio fingerprinting involving wavelets. The spectrogram image is determined and then broken into smaller spectral images where the top wavelets are computed using the Haar wavelet. Once completed, the top wavelets are computed and the sub-fingerprints are determined using the binary quantization. Also, the Shazam algorithm was successfully developed by [7]. This method is based on the use of the spectrogram data where spectrogram peaks are determined and paired off and hashed to determine the robust audio fingerprint. In addition, the recently developed algorithm for music identification using the scale-invariant feature transform (SIFT) is seen to be successful in robustly identifying music based on the computer vision technique [8].

This paper proposes a computationally simple algorithm that will be robust to distortions such as noise. The system will also account for significant discrimination over a large number of fingerprints and scalability for efficient storage and comparing. The algorithm will be fast and accurate identification with minimal misidentifications and false positives. The robustness to distortions is a main factor to consider as there are various real-world distortions that affect the audio and therefore the performance of the algorithm. Some of these include interference, and environmental noise. Also, not all speakers and microphones will be high quality and therefore, this can cause certain frequencies to be lost or inaccurately recorded for analysis. Another distortion may come from the audio itself being altered due to speed and pitch synchronization changes (radio, online streaming, and etc.). This paper proposes a music identification algorithm that is highly robust to audio signal noise as well as time and frequency domain synchronization changes. Based on research, it is seen that ORB is a computationally efficient alternative to SIFT and SURF. See proof in [9].

2 RELATED WORK

An audio fingerprint is a compact content-based signature of the audio signal which the unique acoustic characteristics are stored as the fingerprint [10]. Using audio fingerprints for identification can be considered as two main parts. The first part is where the audio content is fingerprinted and stored into a database along with the related metadata. The second part is the where "unknown" audio content is fingerprinted and compared to the fingerprint database for identification [11]. If the sampled fingerprint is matched to a fingerprint in the database, then the corresponding metadata for that fingerprint is returned.

An audio fingerprint structure comprises of the components for fingerprint extraction and fingerprint identification. Fingerprint extraction entails the determination of robust features of the audio signal and then building a fingerprint representation based on those robust features [12]. Fingerprint identification is where the fingerprint is to be matched against a database to retrieve similar fingerprints. Collection of fingerprints of songs must be scaled for the purpose of efficiently storing and searching in a database, and etc. The following figure shows the general system for audio fingerprinting [12]. As shown in Figure 1, the audio to be fingerprinted and stored in a database and the unknown audio sample to be fingerprinted and queried are both analyzed through the same process. The audio fingerprinting and matching algorithm must be robust so that the distorted audio sample can still be recognized as the same audio content stored in the fingerprint database. The audio signal is processed where it is sampled and converted from the time domain to the frequency domain. The audio fingerprints are then extracted to be compared to the audio fingerprint database of similarly analyzed music files. Once there is a match, the corresponding song information would be returned and displayed to the user.

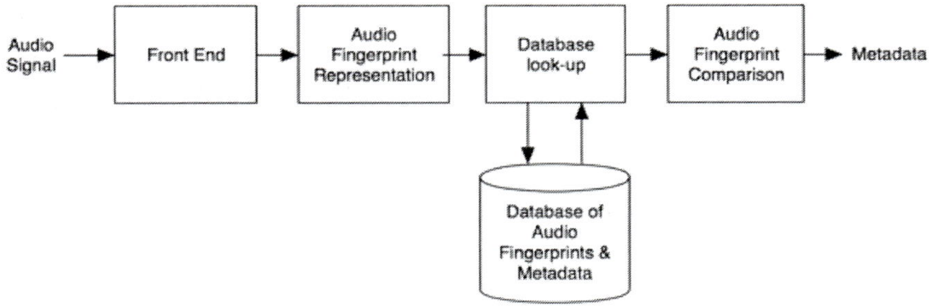

Figure 1. Audio fingerprint system. This figure shows the general audio fingerprinting system done by previous authors. The algorithms generally followed this approach where the raw audio would be captured (by loading the audio signal or by microphone). The audio signal is then processed into a digital format where the audio fingerprints are extracted. The audio fingerprints of songs that were similarly processed and stored in a database are then compared by some algorithm to execute a database lookup. After the resulting audio fingerprint comparison is done, the corresponding song information for the highest match is returned

There are various approaches of audio fingerprinting. Some discussed are the PRH, MLH, RARE, Shazam, Wavelet Transform, and SIFT algorithms. This section summarizes some of their features and limitations. According to Haitsma and Kalker [13], the major objective of audio fingerprinting is to determine the perceptual equality between two objects (multimedia) rather than comparing the actual objects directly. Digital fingerprinting technology can take advantage of this as fingerprints reduce the storage required in contrast to the size of the audio file itself. Also, audio fingerprints result in efficient searching since the dataset is smaller. In addition, perceptual discrepancies would have been removed in the process of fingerprinting the audio file. The fingerprints and the corresponding metadata would be stored in a database for comparison and retrieval. The fingerprint system can be summarized as two main components, the extraction method of the fingerprints and an efficient search and comparison method for the matching fingerprints between the query and the fingerprint database.

When dealing with audio fingerprinting, the audio signal is converted to another representation. Some typical transformations include the fast

Fourier transform (FFT), the discrete cosine transform (DCT), and the Haar Transform. After the initial analysis is done on the audio signal, the features are determined. Some feature extraction methods include the mel-frequency cepstrum coefficients (MFCC) and the spectral flatness Measure (SFM), which is based on the power spectrum from the fast Fourier transform function [12].

Furthermore, Haitsma and Kalker [13] introduced and described a very robust fingerprint extraction method and a highly efficient searching strategy which was suitable for a large audio fingerprint database with limited computational resources (Philip's Robust Hashing Algorithm). The extraction process of the PRH algorithm was similar to other methods where the audio was segmented into frames with overlap of a specific length and then shifted a fraction (1/32) of the frame length [14]. The Fourier transform analysis would be computed for every frame, and the power spectral density is determined. Sub-fingerprints would then be determined by dividing the frequency spectrum into logarithmic frequency bands for each frame. The bands would be in the human auditory system (HAS) range which was chosen as 300 to 2000 Hz [15]. The audio fingerprints were queried with the use of a look-up table. However, while dealing with low signal to noise ratio, the algorithm was not performing well. Also, the algorithm was susceptible to performance degradation, since a small change in frequency misalignment due to speed change [8].

The PRH algorithm was fast, however, the trade-off involved was accuracy. Liu, Yun, and Kim [5] proposed an algorithm using the multiple hashing method (MLH) in the DCT (discrete cosine transform) domain. The method was similar to the PRH algorithm, but with the application of the DCT to the time-based sequence of energies in each respective sub-band and a sub-fingerprint is generated for each DCT coefficient stream [5]. They claimed that the de-correlation property increased performance as it generated more sub-fingerprints, and that the robust property of compaction of the DCT will aid accuracy as the energy of the signal tends to be concentrated in certain frequency components. From their research, the MLH method performed better than the PRH method under various added noise experiments while maintaining accuracy. This improved the recognition of audio signal even if the quality of the signal is degraded. The consequence of this method was that the fingerprint size increased so the songs stored in the database would be less, and as a result, the search time would increase as well [8].

Burges et al. [16] proposed the Robust Audio Recognition Engine algorithm (RARE), which involved the use of the modulated complex lapped transform (MCLT) to convert the audio data to its time-frequency representation. Instead of determining the features based on the spectral representation, it reduces the dimensionality of the audio data by using two projections.

Dimensionality reduction is where data is mapped to a lower dimensional space so that certain data variance is discarded. The projections are determined by training data using both distorted and undistorted data and applying the oriented principle component analysis (OPCA). The data is projected onto directions that increase the signal-to-noise ratio (SNR) of the training data [17]. Although this method was robust, the computation involved was the disadvantage to the algorithm.

Covell and Baluja [18] proposed a different approach to the previously stated methods, where computer vision techniques are incorporated for audio identification using wavelets. After the FFT is used to obtain the spectrogram, the spectrogram is then divided into smaller subsamples of spectral images to be decomposed using Haar wavelets. For each spectral image, the wavelet is computed. Then, the top wavelets are extracted (measured by magnitude) and the sub-fingerprints are found using the binary quantization of the major retained wavelet components using min-hash. The experimental results showed that the algorithm performed better than the PRH and MLH algorithms with additive white Gaussian noise [18]. Although the algorithm was robust, it was computationally expensive. Also, the fingerprint required more memory for storage and therefore, the database size and search time increase. Also, the algorithm was not as robust against time scale modification (TSM) and speed change [8].

In the early 2000s, Wang et al. founded Shazam Entertainment which developed a music recognition service to be accessible through the use of mobile phones. The user would be able to capture the audio sample for query by calling a simple number, and when completed, the server would hang up the call and return the corresponding song information in an SMS text message [19]. The Shazam algorithm was developed a fingerprinting technique which involved the use of the highest amplitude peaks of the spectrogram (robust constellations), which were robust against noise. This was done by converting the audio signal from the time domain to the frequency domain using the fast Fourier transform (FFT) in order to obtain the spectrogram data of the audio (frequency spectrum for each frame) [20]. These peaks were then paired off and combinatorial hash values were computed based on time-frequency pairs, which also increased robustness. Wang also proposed an efficient searching and scoring algorithm. When a query was compared to the database, each matching hash was linked to offset time pairs between the offset times of the beginning of the query song and the song in the database. A match would be determined since the matching features would have similar differences of the relative offsets from the beginning of the song [7]. After experiments were done, it was seen that the algorithm was very robust to noise and compression but was sensitive to frequency and time synchronization alteration [8].

Other search techniques include inverted file indexing proposed by Haitsma and Kalker [13]. Once fingerprints of part of the sample query are correctly matched, a number of positions and candidate songs would then be retrieved, narrowing the search index for the rest of the query. Another set up involved separating the songs in the database into two databases. One database would contain fingerprints of more trendy songs of the moment (higher query probability), while another database would have the fingerprints rest of songs. This would decrease search times where the query would be compared to the smaller and more likely database and if there is not a match, it would be compared to the second database [11].

Further investigations involving the use of image recognition for audio identification as computer vision techniques made significant progress in recent years with the development of local invariant features. Zhang et al. [8] proposed "a novel feature for robust music identification" using scale invariant feature transform (SIFT) local descriptors on the spectrogram image. Generally, this would make feature descriptors and detectors robust to scaling, shifting, rotating, and etc. Results showed that the main advantage of this method was to deal with distortions such as pitch shifting and speed changes. These were difficult distortions for other music identification algorithms to resist, as seen in the results for algorithms such as Shazam. [8]. From a performance evaluation, Figat, Kornuta, and Kasprzak [21] stated that older vector-based descriptors such as SIFT and SURF (Speeded-Up Robust Features) were being replaced by binary feature descriptors and detectors. Some of these binary descriptors and detectors include Binary Robust Invariant Scalable Keypoints (BRISK), Binary Robust Independent Elementary Features (BRIEF), and the developed algorithm, Oriented FAST and Rotated BRIEF (ORB). From the results, it was seen that both the binary and vector descriptors had similar robustness to transformations of images while having great computational efficiency.

According to the paper on "ORB: an efficient alternative to SIFT and SURF", Rublee et al. [9] proposed a feature ORB which built on the well-liked keypoint detector algorithm, FAST (features from accelerated segment test), and recently developed BRIEF descriptor. From the results, it was seen that ORB performed better than older detectors and descriptors in both computational cost and speed. The goal was to improve image recognition on lower power devices with limited computational resources. Miksik and Mikolajczyk [22] evaluated the performance of ORB to common feature detectors and descriptors like SIFT and SURF. An optimized computer system was used with a 3.4 Ghz Intel CPU, and OpenCV libraries were used for the experiments. It was seen from the results that ORB resulted in a substantially better performance compared to the SIFT and SURF when determining keypoint detectors and descriptors. ORB also maintained high accuracy while being computationally faster making it more suitable. In general, ORB is also more robust to Gaussian noise when compared to SIFT [9]. However, there were some cases where SIFT had a higher accuracy when matching the features [21]. Also, ORB comprised of a combination of two successful modified feature detectors; the Oriented FAST keypoint detector and the Rotated BRIEF descriptor and was seen to be two orders of magnitude faster and more computationally efficiency than SIFT [23]. Hence, ORB was chosen for the proposed algorithm.

3 PROPOSED METHOD

This proposes the use of the ORB method as discussed in [9]. The music signal is converted to a two-dimensional spectrogram image then ORB is used to compute the image and extract the spectrogram image features using the ORB descriptors. ORB is chosen since it is a robust and efficient computer-vision technique. This makes it a novel approach to music identification where distortions such as pitch and speed changes occur which may be difficult for other existing algorithms to be robust to. For the experimental prototype, a Brute-Force matcher is used to match the corresponding descriptors between the music query sample and the database of spectrogram images. This algorithm will be compared to the Shazam method which was a developed industrial-strength audio search algorithm [7]. Also, the proposed system was comparable to the SIFT-based algorithm by Zhang et al. for robust music identification [8]. This can be seen in Figure 2. The audio signal is processed where it is sampled and converted from the time domain to the frequency domain in order to obtain the spectrogram image. The image features are then extracted to be compared to the database of similarly analyzed spectrogram images. Once there is a match, the corresponding song information would be returned and displayed to the user.

3.1 Feature extraction

Firstly, pre-processing was done to convert the audio signal to the correct digital format and sample rate. For this prototype, the audio format used for testing was uncompressed (WAV), and the sample rate was 44.1 KHz. The audio is then divided into frames using the Hanning window technique of 8192 points and an overlap of 0.75. The window length was experimentally chosen so that the spectrogram representation would have a low time resolution which would increase robustness to time variations. The overlap was chosen since the signal maybe misaligned and hence this helps with the desynchronization problem. The fast Fourier transform is then applied to convert the audio from the time domain to the frequency domain in order

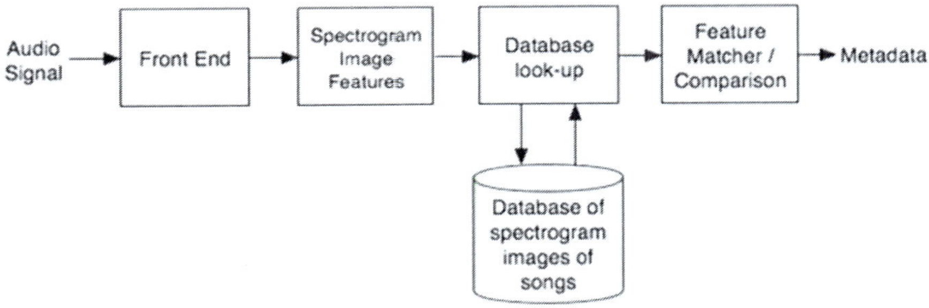

Figure 2. Proposed system. The figure shows the proposed system where the raw audio would be captured (by loading the audio signal or by microphone). The audio signal is then processed by converting the audio signal into a spectrogram image. The spectrogram image of the sample is compared to the database of spectrogram images of the songs in the database. This is done using an image processing techniques to match the features of the spectrogram image. After the resulting audio fingerprint comparison is done, the corresponding song information for the highest match is returned

to obtain the spectrogram [24]. The linear spectrogram is then quantized into 64 logarithmically spaced sub-bands to cover a large frequency range for more features [8]. After, the logarithmic spectrogram is converted to a gray image in order to extract the features. The spectrogram is converted to a log-magnitude representation using (1):

$$S(i,j) = \log|X(i,j)| \tag{1}$$

where S is the log magnitude spectrogram representation, X is the original spectrogram, i is the frequency sub-band, and j is the frame index [8].

Oriented Fast and Rotated BRIEF (ORB) consists of a fast keypoint detector which is based on the FAST algorithm and binary descriptor which is based on the BRIEF algorithm [9]. Keypoints can be defined as spatial locations on the image that may contain a feature that stands out. A descriptor can be defined as the way the keypoint is described. In other words, the keypoint is a detected location, and the descriptor is the details of that location. These are used as the image features to determine matches when comparing two image samples. ORB builds on variations of the FAST keypoint detector and the recent BRIEF descriptor, which are popular due to their computational efficiency and good performance [25]. The variation for the FAST keypoint detector is oFAST which adds the feature of orientation and Rotated BRIEF which adds the feature of rotation (it is rotation invariant).

Due to its good performance, FAST-9 is used (called oFAST), which is a variation of FAST that uses a circular radius of 9. A Harris corner measure is used to order the FAST keypoints, since FAST had high responses along edges. Also, since FAST does not yield multi-scale features and is not scale invariant, a scale pyramid of the imaged is employed and for each pyramid level, the FAST features are determined [9]. The intensity centroid is used for the measure of corner orientation. The following describes the moments of a patch defined by Rosin [26] as:

$$M_{pq} = \sum_{x,y} x^p y^q I(x,y) \tag{2}$$

where $x^p y^q$ are the pixel location in corresponding patch location of the image, and $I(x,y)$ is the image intensity. Based on the moments, the centroid is determined by:

$$C = \left(\frac{M_{10}}{M_{00}}, \frac{M_{01}}{M_{00}}\right) \tag{3}$$

Now, from the corner's center, O, a vector could be constructed OC−→-OC→. The patch orientation can be determined as:

$$\theta = \text{atan2}(m_{01}, m_{10}) \tag{4}$$

However, Rublee et al. [9] stated that regardless of the corner type, the angle is consistent, so it can be ignored. The rotation invariance was then improved by computing the moments with x and y staying within the circular radius r. This is done by choosing r as the patch size so that x and y run from the range $[-r, r]$.

The BRIEF descriptor is defined as a bit string of an image patch created from a set of binary intensity tests [25]. The following shows the binary test τ:

$$\tau(p; x, y) = \begin{cases} 1 & : p(x) < p(y) \\ 0 & : p(x) \geq p(y) \end{cases} \tag{5}$$

where p is the smoothed image patch, $p(x)$ is the intensity of p at point x.

The feature is defined as a vector of n binary tests:

$$f_n(p) = \sum_{1 \le i \le n} 2^{i-1} \tau(p; x_i, y_i) \quad (6)$$

Due to its performance, a Gaussian distribution test is applied around the center of the patch [9]. Before the test is performed, the image is smoothened. For BRIEF to be invariant to rotation, an efficient approach was implemented to steer BRIEF in accordance to the keypoint orientation. At location (x_i, y_i), the 2 x n matrix is defined by the following:

$$S = \begin{pmatrix} x_1, \ldots, x_n \\ y_1, \ldots, y_n \end{pmatrix} \quad (7)$$

From the rotation matrix R_θ and the patch orientation θ, the "steered" S_θ:

$$S_\theta = R_\theta S \quad (8)$$

Therefore, the steered BRIEFis [9]:

$$g_n(p, \theta) = f_n(p) | (x_i, y_i) \in S_\theta \quad (9)$$

Now, the angle is discretized to 12° increments and a lookup table which includes already computed BRIEF patterns is created. An advantage of BRIEF is that each bit feature has a high variance. However, from the results from tests, the steered BRIEF has lower variance. The variation of BRIEF used by [9], rBRIEF, caused the variance of the steered BRIEF to improve.

From the experiments done by Rublee et al. [9], ORB produced high performance and computational efficiency when compared to other similar computer vision methods such as SIFT and SURF. For this experiment, the orientation and rotation aspect was not necessary as the analysis was done on spectrograms which were stationary images.

Since conditions are not ideal in the real world, it is common for audio signals to be affected by various types of audio distortion. Pitch shifting, time stretching and time scaling are some difficult distortions for music identification to resist. Pitch shifting causes the spectrogram image to remain the same on the time axis, but the frequency component is just translated vertically (up or down). Time stretching causes the time axis to lengthen or shorten while the frequency axis remains constant on the spectrogram. Time scaling can be classified as the combination of pitch shifting and time stretching.

The features are then extracted from the spectrogram image to represent the unique characteristics of the music using the ORB descriptors which are based on the corners detected for patches on the image. Generally, ORB-based features are robust to changes in image scale, illumination, and etc. It was also noted that the spectrogram is a stationary representation the orientation and rotation features were not needed to be used for computation.

3.2 Robust matching

For this module, the unknown sample is analyzed in the same manner as the audio for the database where the spectrogram image is created for the unknown audio sample. When the spectrogram image is created for the query sample, it is stored temporarily. The ORB detector is initiated, and the key-points and descriptors are detected and computed for the query audio sample (spectrogram image).

Once completed, the BFMatcher (Brute-Force Matcher from OpenCV) is used along with a Hamming windowing technique to search for matches. The BFMatcher uses a descriptor in one data set (sample) and compares it to all the other features in the second data set (in the database) with a distance calculation (Hamming distance), and the closest match is returned. This is done for all the descriptors in the first data set. In the real world, noise may exist, creating the possibility of some false positives (although not much). Usually, a threshold is put in place to the distance between the query feature and the nearest matching feature returned, rejecting matches that may have distances greater than the threshold [8]. When the descriptors are matched, a threshold was used for the distances of the matches, if the distance is far apart between descriptor matches of the query sample and a database song then it may have been a false positive detected. The amount of matches below the threshold distance would be the confidence of the corresponding match for the song. The Brute-Force matcher was used to achieve exact matches to the spectrogram image features and to minimize false positives from being detected since the spectrogram features can be considered as fine details on the image. Tests were done and results were shown in the next section.

4 EXPERIMENTAL RESULTS

Testing was done for robustness [9] and other factors. For this experimental prototype, the database consisted of the songs being converted to their associated spectrogram image representation. These spectrogram images, along with their related song information would be stored for searching and retrieval of the query sample and its corresponding match. For this experiment, a database library of songs with an even spread of genres were used, including Pop, Hip-hop, Modern Rock, Soca, and Jazz. ORB would be used to determine the descriptors of the spectrogram images which would be used for comparison. These songs comprised of both similar and dissimilar chords/rhythms and various instruments to test the difficulty in song identification.

The algorithm was tested by using songs of various genres (Pop, Hip-hop, Modern Rock, Soca, and Jazz), and testing was performed on a total of 3200 sample songs. Various factors were considered in sample selection. Not only tests for robustness to various distortions, but other factors such as reliability, system speed, and granularity were experimented [27]. Robustness involves the system having the ability to accurately identify the audio when subjected to real world variations including compression and various types of distortion such as radio interference, environmental noise, pitch shifting, and time scaling. Accuracy deals with the system being able to determine the correct match instead of missed identifications and false positives (incorrect identifications). Due to the amount of songs that may or may not be in the database, a reliable system must be able to distinguish the actual match from similar audio content and be able to assess if the query is not in the database and hence should not have a match (no false positives). The granularity of the system is the ability to correctly identify the matching audio when the query is a short audio clip. This is where the searching algorithm is important. The complexity of the system processes such as the feature extraction, searching and comparison complexity, fingerprint size, and database alterations should not be computationally demanding. The Shazam algorithm and the ORB prototype were tested and compared and in addition, research for the SIFT-based music identification algorithm by Zhang et al. [8] was also considered.

4.1 Robustness

This was a key aspect of testing. The audio samples were subjected to various types of audio distortions that occur in the real world. The tests done included speed changes, pitch changes, tempo changes and the addition of noise to the audio samples. From research, Rublee et al. [9] proposed that using image processing techniques for audio identification had an advantage of robustness to distortions such as speed and pitch changes which algorithms such as Shazam was difficult to resist. This was also investigated from the results. The tests were done to test the ability of the two algorithms to accurately identify the query samples. The Shazam-based algorithm and the ORB prototype were tested, and the results were compared.

4.1.1 Speed test

The speed test was done to test the ability for the query audio sample to be accurately identified with different speed changes applied to the audio samples. A 20-s sample was taken from each song and queried to the database. The audio samples' speeds were edited using the Audacity audio editing software. The audio samples were tested in each case, and the results showed the number of queries that matched for each speed change. This can be seen in Figure 3.

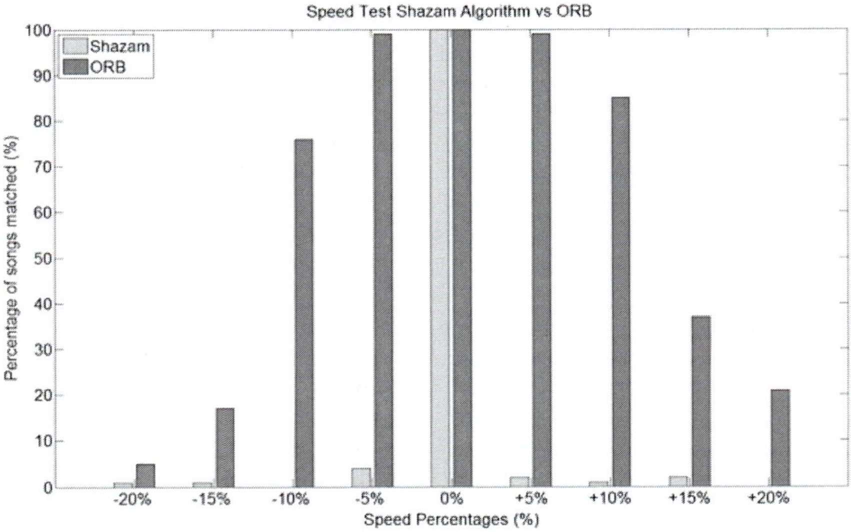

Figure 3. Speed test for robustness (Shazam vs ORB). In this figure, the speed test was done for the range from −20 to +20%. The both algorithms were compared to show the effects of the speed changes on the ability for the both systems to correctly identify the distorted samples. The speed is the combination of pitch and tempo distortion. It was seen that the ORB prototype produced better results compared to the Shazam algorithm

The speed test was done to apply a synchronization attack on the sample audio for query. This would cause the query clips to deform as this type of distortion alters both pitch and the original time scaling of the song. An increase in speed would increase the pitch and decrease the length of that clip (tempo) and a decrease in speed would decrease the pitch and increase the length of the clip (tempo), as it would be slower. The test was done in such a way that a random 20-s audio sample was taken for each song in the database. The distortion was then applied for various percentage ranges and the clips were queried for different test case scenarios. For each test, the resulting match rate percentage would be determined by the songs that were accurately matched. In the real world, the distortion range would be from −10 to +10%, since this is where the distortion is most likely to occur [8]. However, speed tests were also done out of this range to test the limits of the experimental prototypes.

In Figure 3, the speed test was done for the range from −20 to +20%. The both algorithms were compared to show the effects of the speed changes on the ability for the both systems to correctly identify the distorted samples.

From the graph, it was seen that the Shazam algorithm did not perform well in accurately identifying the distorted sample queries for any speed variation. This could have been due to the pitch and time variation which would affect the time-frequency peak pairs used for the hashing aspect. Since the Shazam algorithm is based on combinatorial hashed time-frequency constellation analysis, the hashes are based on specific frequencies at its associated point in time. These are then paired off and a hash a created based on the frequency pairs and their time difference. Therefore, once there is an alteration in speed, the pitch-changing aspect (frequency change) would cause mismatch to occur (due to different hashes generated) and hence the query would not be accurately identified. Also, it was noted that the few samples that matched the query had a low confidence.

It was seen that the ORB prototype produced better results compared to the Shazam algorithm. The ORB prototype was able to correctly identify almost all the songs for the range from −10 to +10% where the match rate fell to approximately 80% for the range from −10 to +10%. Higher percentages tested the algorithm past real-world situations which showed the ORB prototype performance decreasing but still better than the Shazam method. The experimental results showed that the ORB implementation was generally accurate for typical distortion ranges in the real world and also performed better than the Shazam method. This would be due to ORB being robust to shifting and scaling of the features of the spectrogram image query. This would justify the research done previously [8].

4.1.2 **Pitch test**

The pitch test involved testing a 20-s sample of each song in the library and applying various pitch changes to the audio samples. This experiment was done to test the ability for queries to be accurately identified at various pitches. The audio samples were tested in each case, and the results showed the amount of query samples that matched for each pitch change. Figure 4 shows the comparison of results for both the Shazam-based algorithm and the ORB prototype.

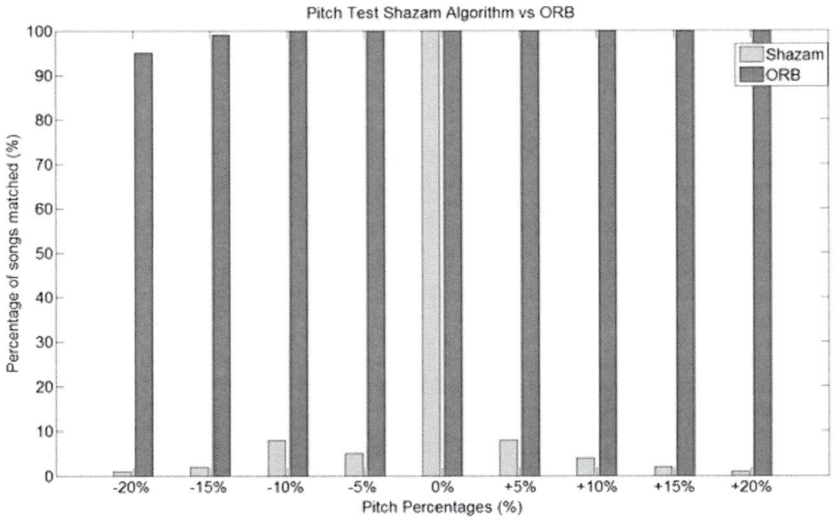

Figure 4. Pitch test for robustness (Shazam vs ORB). This figure involves the pitch test where audio samples were queried to be correctly identified when pitch distortions are applied. Pitch distortion would cause the frequencies in the audio sample to shift vertically. The time synchronization would remain the same, and there are no temporal changes involved. The test was done similarly to the speed where a random 20-s clip was taken from each song in the database, and the pitch distortion was applied. The typical range was tested (−10 to +10%), but the limits of the prototypes were tested (−20 to +20%). It was seen that the ORB prototype produced better results compared to the Shazam algorithm

This experiment showed the audio samples being queried to be correctly identified when pitch distortions are applied. Pitch distortion would cause the frequencies in the audio sample to shift vertically upward on the spectrogram if the pitch is increased, and vertically downward if the pitch is decreased. The time synchronization would remain the same, and there are no temporal changes involved. The test was done similarly to the speed where a random 20-s clip was taken for each song in the database, and the pitch distortion was applied. The typical range was tested (−10 to +10%), but the limits of the prototypes were tested outside the real-world conditions (−20 to +20%) in increments of 5% change.

Similar to the speed test, it was seen in Figure 4, that the Shazam algorithm generally did not perform well as the various pitch changes were applied. Also, the confidences of the songs that matched were relatively low (approximately 0–10). This would be due to the similar reason to the speed test where the pitch is being altered, therefore, the frequencies would change causing the audio fingerprints to misalign since they are based on the time-frequency pairs for the hashes.

The ORB method performed very well for the real-world pitch variation conditions and was seen to be robust for pitch changes up to ranges from −20 to +20%. The ORB method was generally robust to pitch distortion and outperformed the Shazam method. This would be due to ORB being robust to shifting of features (peaks) on the spectrogram images which would confirm previous research done [8].

4.1.3 Tempo test

This test involved adjusting the tempo (speed while preserving the pitch) for audio samples taken from each song in the database. This tested the ability for the query to be accurately identified when tempo distortions are applied. The audio samples were tested in each case, and the results showed the amount of query samples that matched for each tempo change. The tempo distortions were tested in increments of 10% changes for a range from −50 to +50% to test the limits of the algorithms. Figure 5 shows the results of the tempo test for both the Shazam-based algorithm and the ORB prototype.

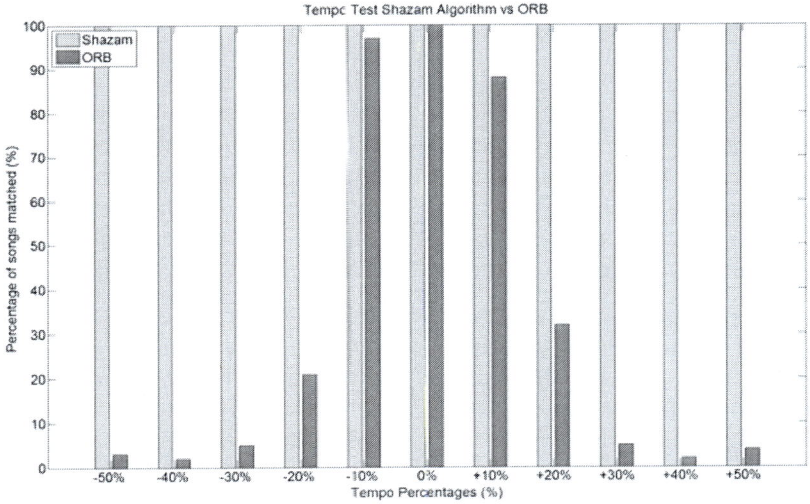

Figure 5. Tempo test for robustness (Shazam vs ORB). This figure shows the results for the tempo being changed by a range from −50 to +50% to test the limits. This type of distortion is known as time stretching or time scaling. The speed of the audio clip is altered while the pitch remains constant. On the spectrogram, this change would be seen on the time axis (temporally) but no change on the frequency axis (pitch). The experiment was carried out where a random 20-s sample was taken from each song in

the database, and the tempo change was applied. The distorted samples were then queried to the test if they accurately matched. It was seen that the Shazam algorithm produced better results compared to the ORB prototype

In this experiment, the tempo was changed to different extents. This type of distortion is known as time stretching or time scaling. The speed of the audio clip is altered while the pitch remains constant. On the spectrogram, this change would be seen on the time axis (temporally), but no change on the frequency axis (pitch). The experiment was carried out where a random 20-s sample was taken from each song in the database, and the tempo change was applied using the Audacity software. The distorted samples were then queried to the test if they accurately matched.

In Figure 5, it was seen that the Shazam algorithm performed well generally for the various tempo changes applied and outperformed the ORB method. This could be due to the sample rate, the window size, and the overlap chosen (44100 Hz, 4096 and 50%, respectively). Due to a large window size and high overlap for each consecutive sub-sample determined, as the time stretch distortion occurs (along the horizontal time axis), the combinatorial hashes or audio fingerprints generated would still match when compared [7]. In addition, this could be due to the number of audio fingerprints generated because of the "neighbourhood" size in which the distance for peaks to be paired off is considered. In this case, this would cause a lot of audio fingerprints to be generated. As a result of the tempo change being constant for each test, the absolute offset difference between the query offset and the offset of the song in the database would be constant. Also, although the confidence may not be as high as the original sample without distortion, the accurate match would still have a generally high confidence.

For the results obtained in Figure 5 for the ORB prototype, it was seen that the queries matched accurately for the typical range (−10% to +10%). The results ORB prototype dropped for higher ranges; however, further work can be done to improve this, which is suggested in Section 5. This meant that for the real-world applications, it would be robust which corresponds to research done.

4.1.4 Noise test

For the noise test, audio samples were taken from the database. The audio samples were then corrupted with additive white Gaussian noise. The signal to noise ratio was tested where the white Gaussian noise was applied to the signal for percentage amplitude ranges of noise in increments of 10% from 0 to 50% to test the limits. This test examines the ability for the corrupted audio samples to be identified accurately. The audio samples were tested in each case, and the results showed the amount of query samples that matched for each case of added noise. Figure 6 shows the results for the Shazam-based algorithm and the ORB prototype.

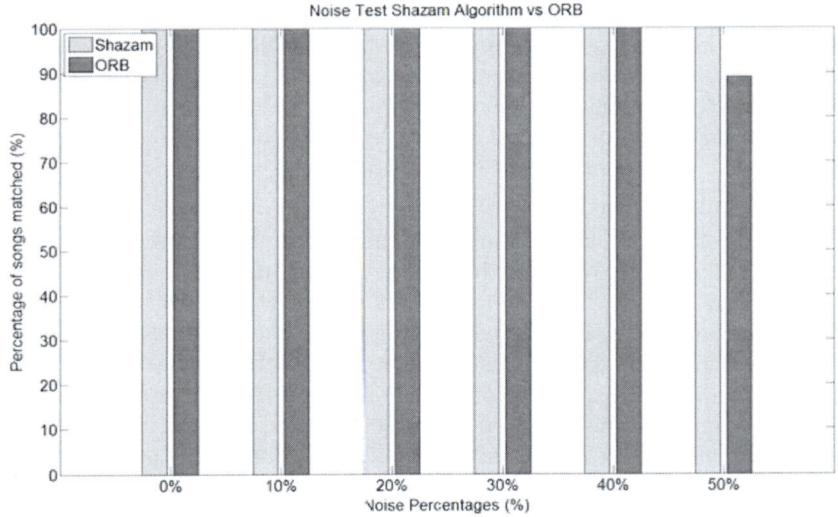

Figure 6. Noise test for robustness (Shazam vs ORB). In this figure, the experiment involved testing the ability to accurately identify the audio sample when it is subjected to the addition of noise. In the real world, this is a common case. Additive white Gaussian noise was added which would be used to simulate background noise. The similar test setup was done where a 20-s clip was taken from each song in the database, and the various degrees of noise were added to each sample and then tested for each system. It was seen that the Shazam algorithm was very robust to the noise as seen in the results. This would be due to the peaks being acquired using the spectrogram data in the audio fingerprinting extraction process. The peaks obtained will be more likely to survive the effects of noise as the song's frequencies (from the audio sample) would have a higher amplitude when compared to the amplitude of frequencies of the noise. It was seen that the Shazam's algorithm performed better in comparison to the ORB prototype although the ORB prototype performed well to an extent

This experiment involved the testing the ability to accurately identify the audio sample when it is subjected to the addition of noise. In the real world, this is a common case. Additive white Gaussian noise was added which would be used to simulate background noise. The similar test setup was done where a 20-s clip was taken from each song in the database, and the various degrees of noise were added to each sample and then tested for each system.

From Figure 6, the Shazam algorithm was very robust to the noise as seen in the results. This would be due to the peaks being acquired using the spectrogram data in the audio fingerprinting extraction process. The peaks obtained will be more likely to survive the effects of noise as the song's frequencies (from the audio sample) would have a higher amplitude when compared to the amplitude of frequencies of the noise. It was seen that the Shazam's algorithm performed slightly better than the ORB prototype for higher noise percentages. This was justified by previous research done by [7].

The ORB method involved the analysis and comparison of the query sample to the database based on the spectrogram images themselves. The performance of the ORB method with noise was well for real-world circumstances and was similarly as robust as the Shazam method. This could be due to the fact that ORB uses the spectrogram images. When there is noise present, the spectrogram image would differ (from a spectrogram with no noise) as the song's frequencies can be masked with the noise (different color seen on the spectrogram image). Due to the compression of the image, the noise may be more apparent in the spectrogram image. This can be a source for the decrease in accuracy of the identification of the query sample.

4.2 Other factors

In addition to the main experiments testing robustness to distortions of speed, pitch, tempo, and noise, further experiments were conducted to determine the performance of the algorithms on softer metrics such as compression, reliability, granularity, scalability, and system speed. These tests measured an example of the performance of a single query under varying conditions.

4.2.1 Compression

An example of a random 20-s clip of a song from the database was used for this test. It was subjected to MP3 compressions at various bitrates, where lower bitrates would result in compression loss and therefore, audio degradation can be heard. This tests the ability to accurately identify the sample query with distortion due to compression (quantization noise). Tables 1 and 2 show the results for the Shazam-based algorithm the ORB-based prototype.

Table 1. Robustness test using compression (Shazam)

Compressed Sample query	Successful match	No. of matches
Sample at 320 Kbps	Yes	812
Sample at 192 Kbps	Yes	767
Sample at 128 Kbps	Yes	796
Sample at 96 Kbps	Yes	471
Sample at 64 Kbps	Yes	288

Table 2. Robustness test using compression (ORB)

Compressed Sample query	Successful match	No. of matches
Sample at 320 Kbps	Yes	169
Sample at 192 Kbps	Yes	181
Sample at 128 Kbps	Yes	184
Sample at 96 Kbps	Yes	170
Sample at 64 Kbps	Yes	126

From the results above, the number of matches for the Shazam method and the ORB method were based on two different criteria hence their results cannot be compared. The Shazam method uses audio fingerprints where an entire song will have a great amount of audio fingerprints depending on the amount of combinatorial hashes determined [7]. In the Shazam method, the time-based high amplitude peaks are determined in the frequency domain to then be paired for robust and unique identification. The ORB prototype uses the keypoints and descriptors as the features to be matched. This is dependent on the detail of the image to be captured and the quality of the image, i.e., a higher quality image with more determined descriptors would have a higher accuracy. For the experiment, an average value of 3000 descriptors were used based on the specifications of the computer hardware available, hence the number of matches would be lower.

When audio is compressed to lossy formats such as MP3 and lower bitrates, audio data can be lost. The test was used to determine if the prototype could still accurately identify the unknown sample with the songs in the database, when the unknown sample is compressed to various bitrates of the MP3 audio format. From the results in Table 1, the Shazam-based algorithm was able to accurately identify the unknown samples at different compression rates. It was observed that at very low bitrates such as 64 Kbps, the confidence of the match dropped significantly as compared to a sample at 320 Kbps, however, it was still able to identify the song correctly with a relatively high confidence compared to other songs in the library.

The results from both tests were expected from research, as it was seen that when compression increased, the audio data lost increases and hence the confidence would decrease as a result. However, compression should not result in significant loss of audio data to cause mismatch to occur. For the Shazam method, a relatively high accuracy was maintained for sample rates between 128 and 320 Kbps as the number of matches were generally high for these compression rates. At 96 and 64 Kbps, the songs matched accurately but the number of matching hashes dropped by almost half for each of the lower bitrates.

The ORB prototype was then tested, and the results shown in Table 2. The compressed audio samples were converted to their respective spectrogram images and were analyzed. From the results, it was seen that the confidence was relatively high for most tested samples. A relatively high accuracy was maintained for sample rates between 96 and 320 Kbps as the number of matches were generally high for these compression rates. The sample compressed at 64 Kbps had the lowest confidence but still had a high amount of matches compared to other songs in the library.

4.2.2 **Reliability**

Firstly, a test was done where a random 20-s sample was taken for each song and was queried to determine if they match correctly. The results were used to determine if the system accurately returns the correct match for each sample. All samples matched correctly with the songs in the database.

Next, an example of a random 20-s sample clip from a song in the database was used to compute its match compared to the matches found in other songs in the database. This was used to show the difference between the number of matches of the correct song match to other songs in the database. The similarity for the Shazam-based algorithm is shown in Figure 7.

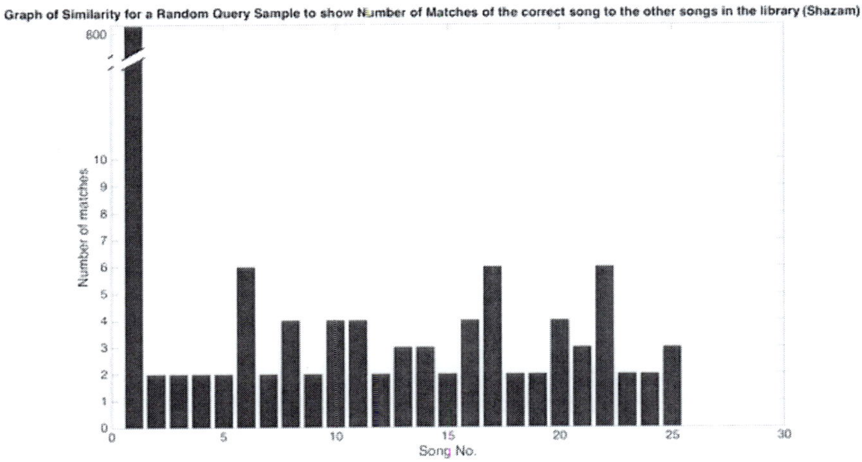

Figure 7. Test for milarity of unknown sample to songs in the database (Shazam). In this figure, it was seen that a random 20-s sample clip was taken from a song in the database and was queried using the Shazam algorithm. This test was done to show and compare the number of matches the query had to each song in the library. Results showed that the number of matches for the corresponding song was large compared to the matches of the query found in other songs in the database. This justified the reliability of the Shazam algorithm

Based on these results the variance and hence the standard deviation was determined to measure how spread out the numbers are from the mean. The following equation shows the variance for the t-distribution since *N* is the number of songs in the library.

$$s^2 = \frac{\sum (X-\mu)^2}{N-1} \tag{10}$$

where,

s2−varianceμ−the averageX−the values from the graphN−the number of ter ms in the distributions2−varianceμ−the averageX−the values from the grap hN−the number of terms in the distribution

Hence, the standard deviation, *s* is,

$$s = \sqrt{\frac{\sum (X-\mu)^2}{N-1}} \tag{11}$$

The variance was determined to be 26500.38, and the standard deviation is simply the square root of the variance. Therefore, the standard deviation for the Shazam method was 162.79. The standard deviation is large which means that the matches of the other songs in the database were small.

The same test involving a random 20-s sample being used to query the database was done to show its similarity of the actual match to other songs in the library. The similarity is shown in Figure 8 for the ORB prototype.

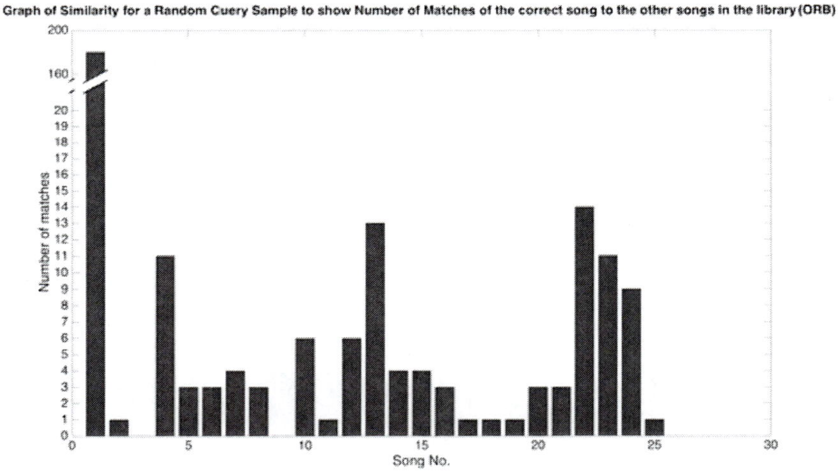

Figure 8. Test for similarity of unknown sample to songs in the database (ORB). In this figure, it was seen that a random 20-s sample clip was taken from a song in the database and queried using the ORB prototype. This test was done to show and compare the number of matches the query had to each song in the library. Results showed that the number of matches for the corresponding song was large compared to the matches of the query found in other songs in the database. This justified the reliability of the ORB prototype

Similar to the Shazam method, the variance and therefore, the standard deviation were calculated for the ORB results from Figure 8. The Eqs.10 and 11 were used to calculate the variance and standard deviation, respectively.

The variance for the ORB method results was calculated to be 1113.58, and the standard deviation was calculated as 33.37. The standard deviation is large which means that the matches of the other songs in the database were very small.

From experimentation, it was seen that when a random 20-s sample clip was taken from each song in the database and queried using both algorithms, all samples were accurately identified. In addition, a test was done to show and compare the number of matches a query had to each song in the library. This resulted in a significant difference in the number of matches of the actual song match compared to the number of matches for other songs in the database. In Figure 7, a random sample clip was taken and queried using the Shazam algorithm. Results showed that the number of matches for the corresponding song was large compared to the matches of the query found in other songs in the database. This justified the reliability of the Shazam algorithm.

The ORB method was tested similarly, where the generated spectrogram image of the same random 20-s sample clip was queried to the database and the amount of matches for each song was shown in Figure 8. It was also seen from results that the corresponding song identified had the most amount of matches when compared to the matches found in other songs in the database. Based on the results, both algorithms were reliable in the identification of songs correctly.

For the Shazam method, the variance was determined to be 26500.38, and the standard deviation was 162.79. Similar to the Shazam method, the variance and therefore the standard deviation were calculated for the ORB results. The variance for the ORB method results was determined to be 1113.58, and the standard deviation was calculated as 33.37. The standard deviation for both methods was large which confirmed that the matches of the other songs in the database were very small compared to the actual match.

4.2.3 Scalability

The system was tested for scalability to measure the size of the songs to the size of the database. The songs for the database were shown for MP3 and WAV formats. The Shazam-based audio fingerprint database consisted of the analyzed audio fingerprints of the songs using the algorithm developed. The ORB image database comprised of the spectrogram images of the song database. Table 3 compares the sizes of the songs for the database, the Shazam-based audio fingerprint database and the ORB image database.

Table 3. Measurement of storage sizes for both algorithms

Audio information category for database	Total storage (size in MB)	Average storage for each song (size in MB)
WAV	1062	42.48
MP3	241	9.64
Shazam-based database	309	12.36
ORB-based database	364	14.56

This experiment involved the comparison of the various aspects of storage associated with the database and the actual audio files themselves. The storage was measured for the music files in both WAV and MP3 formats. The Shazam database's size was also measured which is based on the MySQL database consisting of two tables: the fingerprint table and the song table. The size of the ORB prototype's database was also measured which involved the storage of the spectrogram images of the songs in a folder.

From the results in Table 3, it was seen that the Shazam algorithm and the ORB algorithm both had similar database storage sizes with the ORB database being slightly larger. The reason for the size of the Shazam database being larger than the mp3 songs themselves would be because of the system design extracting and creating a large number of audio fingerprints for each song. The more the audio fingerprints, the higher the accuracy of the matching process. The reason for the ORB method having a large database is because the resolution of the spectrogram images in the database has to be high in order to properly determine the features to compare to the query for matches. The higher the resolution, the more details of the image are retained. The lower the resolution, the more data is lost due to image compression. The optimum resolution used was 3600 × 2700 pixels to maintain accuracy due to compression. This resolution was set experimentally due to the trade-off between processing time and accuracy based on the available hardware used for testing.

4.2.4 System speed

The speed of the system was measured to determine the time taken for the songs to be fingerprinted. For the Shazam-based algorithm, it took approximately 1147 s (approximately 19 min) to fingerprint the songs, while it took approximately 1489 s (approximately 25 min) to generate the spectrogram images for the songs for the image library. These results were based on the available hardware used for testing at the time. In addition, the time taken for a query to be searched and matched was also tested. This was done for libraries of songs. Figure 9 shows these results for the Shazam-based and ORB-based algorithms.

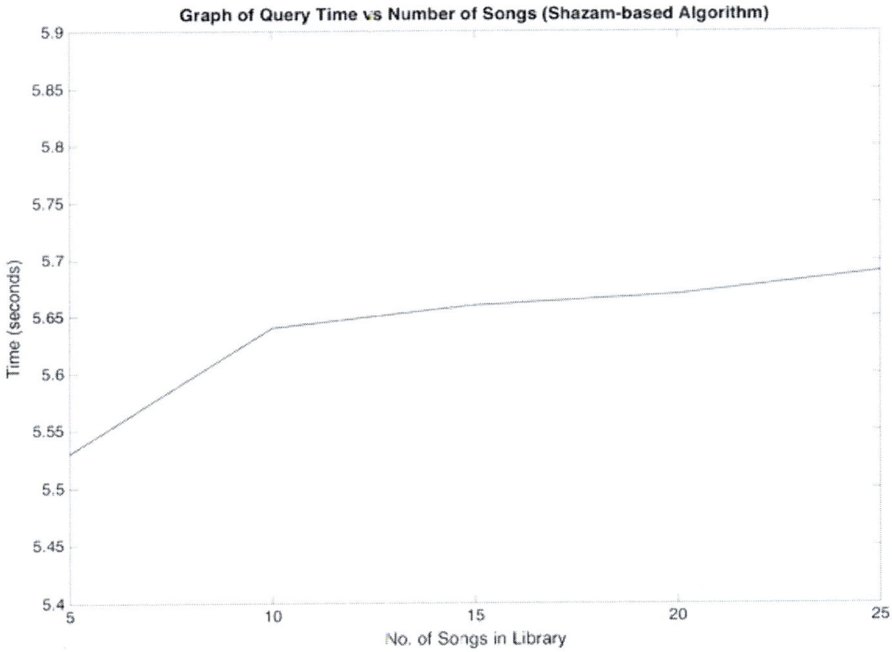

Figure 9. Graph of time taken for query to search and match songs in database (Shazam). In this figure, results were shown for the time taken for a query to be searched and matched. This was done for libraries of songs. This was done for the Shazam algorithm. The results showed an approximately linear relationship, although five songs took a shorter time to for the audio sample to be queried

This experiment involved the time taken for the unknown sample to be queried and matched to the songs in the database. The test was done so that database size would be different sizes. Also, it was noted that the time taken to fingerprint the library of songs for both methods were also taken. The Shazam algorithm took approximately 1147 s while the ORB method took approximately 1489 s.

From the graph in Figure 9, the Shazam algorithm results showed an approximately linear relationship, although five songs took a shorter time to for the audio sample to be queried. In Figure 10, the ORB results were also linear, but it was seen that it had a larger time difference for the query process to be executed as the song library increased. This would be due to the images processing aspect relating to OpenCV's ORB library and the Brute-Force Matcher taking some time to process the image. It was seen that for smaller libraries, the ORB method worked better but for very larger libraries, the Shazam's audio fingerprinting method may be more efficient. Hence, the Shazam method may be suitable for very large databases whereas the ORB method may be better suited for smaller databases.

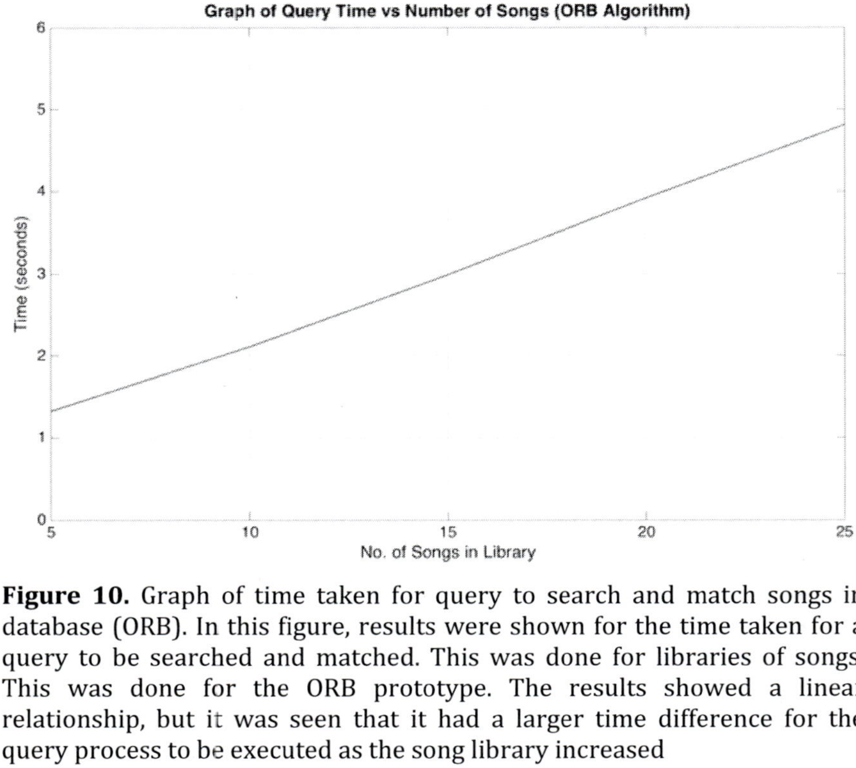

Figure 10. Graph of time taken for query to search and match songs in database (ORB). In this figure, results were shown for the time taken for a query to be searched and matched. This was done for libraries of songs. This was done for the ORB prototype. The results showed a linear relationship, but it was seen that it had a larger time difference for the query process to be executed as the song library increased

4.2.5 **Granularity**

Analyzing granularity involved testing the minimum length of the audio sample used to query the database for a correct match. Audio samples were used for a range of time intervals for the Shazam-based algorithm. The spectrogram images were generated for the same time intervals to test the ORB prototype. Table 4 shows the results.

Table 4. Test for granularity of Shazam and ORB prototypes

Sample query length (seconds)	Shazam-based algorithm		ORB-based algorithm	
	Successful match	No. of matches	Successful match	No. of matches
1 s	No	–	No	–
2 s	Yes	66	No	–
3 s	Yes	77	No	–
4 s	Yes	123	No	–
5 s	Yes	145	No	–
10 s	Yes	240	Yes	59
15 s	Yes	308	Yes	131
20 s	Yes	816	Yes	166

This experiment investigated an example of the minimum time for each algorithm to accurately identify the query for various lengths of the audio sample. From the results, the Shazam algorithm accurately matched the sample audio when it was a minimum length of 2 s. However, the confidence was not as high as the number of matches the 15- or 20-s clip would typically have. This was so because the shorter the sample clip, the less the audio would be available to be fingerprinted, and therefore fewer fingerprints would be extracted and matched.

The ORB prototype was able to accurately identify an audio sample with a minimum of 10 s in length. This would be due to the shorter audio samples producing smaller spectrogram images, which would mean that there are less features to be detected and matched. The Shazam algorithm generally produced better results for this experiment and hence fine granularity. The fingerprint extraction method of the Shazam method entails the use of the raw spectrogram data to compute the audio fingerprints. The ORB method uses the spectrogram images, where the data is limited by the resolution of the image (compression). This is where the Shazam method would produce better scores as a result.

The tests were successfully executed and results were seen to justify the research done. Also, some tests compared the two algorithms performance.

5 CONCLUSIONS

In this paper, a robust audio identification technique was proposed and compared to the Shazam method [7]. As proven in [9], the ORB method is more computationally efficient and faster than the SIFT method as proven by Rublee et al. [9]. As it was extensively proven by Rublee et al. [9], the computational efficiency for ORB was superior to that of SIFT with comparable accuracy. The consideration of testing the Shazam method for comparison [7] was due its current prevalence in the industry. Using a spectrogram image, the ORB descriptor was used to extract the audio signal features and a Brute-Force Matcher was used to match the sample query with the database. The main focus of this work was to highlight the robustness of this algorithm in terms of speed, pitch, tempo, and noise and to compare to the Shazam algorithm. Further experiments were conducted to determine the performance of the algorithms on softer metrics such as compression, reliability, granularity, scalability, and system speed.

The results of performance were comparable and better than the Shazam algorithm for all robustness tests including noise distortion, pitch shifting, time stretching, and time scaling. The match rates were generally high and maintained exceptional performance compared to the Shazam algorithm for the tested distortion ranges. It was also noted that the both algorithms performed similarly using other metrics such as compression, reliability, granularity, scalability, and system speed.

Further work can be done to improve to the efficiency of data storage and retrieval using the ORB method. The ORB implementation in this paper is an experimental prototype used to achieve audio identification based on the spectrogram image. Improvement in the overall performance can be investigated to increase computational efficiency and accuracy of the algorithm. This method resulted in similar accuracy with a larger dataset when tested. However, due to limited resources and time, further tests can be done using a larger database with the inclusion of the various distortions.

Other image processing techniques may be investigated to be implemented such as image thresholding and filtering to enhance features of the spectrogram image so that even if the image is further compressed, the features would still be apparent. The ORB prototype can also be improved in order to retain the robust features while recording the sample for query using the microphone as quality may be lost this way and would affect the spectrogram image. Since initial experiments conducted used the Brute-Force matching method, other more efficient matching methods can be investigated for the comparison of spectrogram images (e.g., nearest neighbor, histogram comparison). This would be a novel and innovative approach to audio fingerprinting.

6 ENDNOTES

The experimental setup included the available computer hardware which was a 1.7 GHz Intel i5 processor with 4 GB RAM. The software environment used was Python 2.7 and OpenCV 3.0 (for ORB) on a Linux system. The program and various tests were coded and executed using Python script modules.

ACKNOWLEDGEMENTS

The authors would like to acknowledge the contribution of Aniel Maharajh for his assistance in the experimental tests conducted.

AUTHORS' INFORMATION

DW completed his B.Sc. Degree with First Class Honors at the Department of Electrical and Computer Engineering from the University of the West Indies (UWI), St. Augustine Campus (STA) in 2016. His area of interest includes audio signal processing, image processing, software development and also in audio engineering. AP is a lecturer in Computer Systems at the Department of Electrical and Computer Engineering. He is a member of the IEEE. He completed his M.Sc. in Communications Systems with Distinction in 2005 and his Ph.D at the Department of Electrical and Computer Engineering of the University of the West Indies (UWI) St. Augustine Campus (STA) in 2012. His area of interest includes sport engineering, image processing and video analysis of sport broadcasts. JS completed his B.Sc. Degree at the Department of Electrical and Computer Engineering from the University of the West Indies (UWI), St. Augustine Campus (STA) in 2015. He has a deep interest in software development and mobile application development. He also has a keen interest in image processing and researching innovative and efficient methods in image processing applications for mobile phones.

COMPETING INTERESTS

The authors declare that they have no competing interests.

PUBLISHER'S NOTE

Springer Nature remains neutral with regard to jurisdictional claims in published maps and institutional affiliations.

REFERENCES

1. M Huber, Music reception in the digital age—empirical research on new patterns of musical behaviour. Int. J. Music. Res. 2, 6–35 (2013)
2. A Lin, Understanding the market for digital music. Stanf. Undergr. Res. J. 4, 50–56 (2005)
3. Sen A (2010) Music in the Digital Age: Musicians and Fans Around the World "Come Together" on the Net. Glob. Media J. 9.16
4. V Venkatachalam, L Cazzanti, N Dhillon, M Wells, Automatic identification of sound recordings. IEEE Signal Process. Mag. 21, 92–99 (2004).
5. Y Liu, HS Yun, NS Kim, Audio fingerprinting based on multiple hashing in DCT domain. IEEE Signal Proc. Lett. 16, 525–528 (2009).
6. S Baluja, M Covell, Waveprint: efficient wavelet-based audio fingerprinting. Pattern Recognit. 41, 3467–3480 (2008).
7. Wang A (2003) An industrial-strength audio search algorithm. ISMIR 2003, 4th Int Conf Music Inf Retr.
8. Zhang X, Zhu B, Li L, Li W, Li X, Wang W, Lu P, Zhang W (2015) SIFT-based local spectrogram image descriptor: a novel feature for robust music identification. EURASIP J. Audio Speech Music Proc.
9. Rublee E, Rabaud V, Konolige K, Bradski G (2011) ORB: An efficient alternative to SIFT or SURF. ICCV '11 Proceedings of the 2011 International Conference on Computer Vision 2564–2571.
10. P Cano, E Batlle, T Kalker, J Haitsma, A review of audio fingerprinting. J. VLSI Signal Proc. 41, 271–284 (2005).
11. A Wang, J Smith, *System and methods for recognizing sound and music signals in high noise and distortion* (Publ, U.S. Pat. Appl, 2006)
12. Cano P, Batle E, Kalker T, Haitsma J (2002) A review of algorithms for audio fingerprinting. Proc 2002 IEEE Work Multimed Signal Process MMSP 2002 169–173.
13. Haitsma J, Kalker T (2002) A highly robust audio fingerprinting system. Proc 3rd Int Soc Music Inf Retr Conf 107–115. doi:10.1.1.103.2175
14. S Kharat, S Modani, S Pujari, M Shah, Audio fingerprinting and review of its algorithms. Int. J. Comput. Technol. Appl. 5, 662–667 (2014)
15. S Lee, D Yook, S Chang, An efficient audio fingerprint search algorithm for music retrieval. IEEE Trans. Consum. Electron. 59, 652–656 (2013).
16. Burges C, Platt J, Jana S (2002) Extracting noise-robust features from audio data. Acoust Speech, Signal ... 1:I-1021-I-1024.
17. Doets PJO, Menor Gisbert M, Lagendijk RL (2006) On the comparison of audio fingerprints for extracting quality parameters of compressed audio. Proc SPIE - Int Soc Opt Eng 60720L–60720L–12.
18. Covell M, Baluja S (2006) Content fingerprinting using wavelets. 3rd Eur Conf Vis Media Prod (CVMP 2006) Part 2nd Multimed Conf 2006 198–207.
19. A Wang, The Shazam music recognition service. Commun. ACM 49, 44–48 (2006).
20. N Instruments, *Understanding FFT and windowing* (White Pap, In, 2015). http://www.ni.com/white-paper/4844/en/, Accessed 13 Mar 2016

21. J Figat, T Kornuta, W Kasprzak, Performance evaluation of binary descriptors of local features. Comput. Vis. Graph. (2014).
22. Miksik O, Mikolajczyk K (2012) Evaluation of local detectors and descriptors for fast feature matching. Pattern Recognit (ICPR), 2012 21st Int Conf 2681–2684. doi:978-1-4673-2216-4
23. A Kulkarni, J Jagtap, V Harpale, *Object recognition with ORB and its Implementation on FPGA* (Theaccents, Org, 2013)
24. S Worner, *Fast Fourier Transform* (Numer. Anal, Semin, 2008)
25. M Calonder, V Lepetit, C Strecha, P Fua, BRIEF : Binary Robust Independent Elementary Features. Eur. Conf. Comput. Vis. 2010, 778–792 (2010).
26. PL Rosin, Measuring corner properties. Comput. Vis. Image Underst. 73, 291–307 (1999).
27. HB Kekre, N Bhandari, N Nair, A review of audio fingerprinting and comparison of algorithms. Int. J. Comput. Appl. 70, 24–30 (2013)

CHAPTER 7

Speaker-Adaptive-Trainable Boltzmann Machine and Its Application to Non-Parallel Voice Conversion

Toru Nakashika* and Yasuhiro Minami

Graduate School of Information Systems, University of Electro-Communications, 1-5-1 Chofugaoka, Chofu, 182-8585 Tokyo, Japan

ABSTRACT

In this paper, we present a voice conversion (VC) method that does not use any parallel data while training the model. Voice conversion is a technique where only speaker-specific information in the source speech is converted while keeping the phonological information unchanged. Most of the existing VC methods rely on parallel data—pairs of speech data from the source and target speakers uttering the same sentences. However, the use of parallel data in training causes several problems: (1) the data used for the training is limited to the pre-defined sentences, (2) the trained model is only applied to the speaker pair used in the training, and (3) a mismatch in alignment may occur. Although it is generally preferable in VC to not use parallel data, a non-parallel approach is considered difficult to learn. In our approach, we realize the non-parallel training based on speaker-adaptive training (SAT). Speech signals are represented using a probabilistic model based on the Boltzmann machine that defines phonological information and speaker-related information explicitly. Speaker-independent (SI) and speaker-dependent (SD) parameters are simultaneously trained using SAT. In the conversion stage, a given speech signal is decomposed into phonological and speaker-related information, the speaker-related information is replaced with that of the desired speaker, and then voice-converted speech is obtained by combining the two. Our experimental results showed that our approach outperformed the conventional non-parallel approach regarding objective and subjective criteria.

Keywords: Voice conversion Boltzmann machine Unsupervised training Energy-based model Speaker adaptation Non-parallel training SAT

1 INTRODUCTION

In recent years, voice conversion (VC), which is a technique used to change speaker-specific information in the speech of a source speaker into that of a target speaker while retaining linguistic information, has been garnering much attention since the VC techniques can be applied to various tasks [1, 2, 3, 4, 5]. Most of the existing approaches rely on statistical models [6, 7], and the approach based on the Gaussian mixture model (GMM) [8, 9, 10, 11] is one of the mainstream methods used nowadays. Other statistical models, such as non-negative matrix factorization (NMF) [12, 13], neural networks (NNs) [14], restricted Boltzmann machines (RBMs) [15, 16], and deep learning [17, 18], are also used in VC. However, almost all of the existing VC methods require parallel data (aligned speech data from the source and the target speakers so that each frame of the source speaker's data corresponds to that of the target speaker) for training the models, which leads to several problems. First, the data is limited to pre-defined articles (both speakers must utter the same articles). Second, the trained model is only applied to the speaker pair used in the training, and it is difficult to reuse the model on the conversion of another speaker pair. Third, the training data (the parallel data) is not the original speech data anymore because the speech data is stretched and modified in the time axis when aligned. Furthermore, it is not guaranteed that each frame is aligned perfectly, and the mismatching may cause some errors in training.

Several approaches that do not use *parallel data from the source to the target speakers* [1] have been also proposed [19, 20, 21, 22, 23]. In [19], for example, the authors model the spectral relationships between two arbitrary speakers (reference speakers) using GMMs and convert the source speaker's speech using the matrix that projects the feature space of the source speaker into that of the target speaker through that of the reference speakers. As a result, parallel data from the source and target speakers is not required. In [21, 22], codebooks (eigenvoice) are obtained using the parallel data of the reference speakers, and a many-to-many VC is achieved by mapping the source speaker's speech into an eigenvoice and the eigenvoice into the target speaker's speech. The multistep VC [24] is also proposed to reduce the training cost of estimating the mapping functions for each speaker pair.

In this paper, we propose a totally-parallel-data-free[2] VC method using an energy-based probabilistic model and speaker adaptive training (SAT). The idea is simple and intuitive. A speech signal of an arbitrary speaker is composed of neutral speech (the speech with the averaged voice calculated from a collection of speech samples from multiple speakers) that directly links to the phonological information belonging to no one, accompanied with the speaker-specific information. In this assumption, VC is achieved by three steps: decomposing a speech signal into neutral speech and speaker-specific information, replacing the speaker-specific information with that of the desired speaker, and composing a speech signal using the neutral speech and the replaced speaker information. The proposed model, called a speaker adaptive trainable Boltzmann machine (SATBM), is designed to help such a decomposition. The above VC steps can be viewed as a simplified version of the combination of automatic speech recognition (ASR) and text-to-speech (TTS) systems: text estimation from the input speech using the ASR system, followed by speech generation of the target speaker from the text using the TTS system. Although the VC can be realized by this approach, our VC scheme has several advantages. First, in our approach, we can reduce (or omit) the cost of training two different systems. Second, the combination approach requires a large amount of training data of the target speaker in TTS, while our approach does not. Third, the latent phonological features in our approach can be optimized for the VC. Fourth, ideally, the voice-converted speech can be generated in real time by our approach due to the frame-wise conversion.

We attempted the non-parallel training using another probabilistic model named the adaptive restricted Boltzmann machine (ARBM) [25] in our previous work. The architecture is different from the proposed model in this paper, which makes some differences, e.g., while an ARBM is based on the model-space transformation, a SATBM is based on the constrained model-space transformation. In the following sections, we will discuss this in more detail.

2 FORMULATION

In general, it is known that the differences of speech signals in terms of speakers can be represented as multiplication in the cepstrum-based domain. After the general form, we define an acoustic feature vector[3] $\left[\hat{x}_{rt}^{1}, \cdots, \hat{x}_{rt}^{D}\right]^{\top} \in \mathbb{R}^{D}$ (D is the number of dimensions) of a speaker r at time t as follows:

$$\hat{\boldsymbol{x}}_{rt} = \mathbf{A}_r \boldsymbol{x}_t + \boldsymbol{b}_r, \tag{1}$$

where xt $\boldsymbol{x}_t = \left[x_t^1, \cdots, x_t^D\right]^\top \in \mathbb{R}^D$, $\mathbf{A}_r \in \mathbb{R}^{D \times D}$, and br∈RDbr∈RD denote the speaker-normalized acoustic feature vector (acoustic features of the neutral speaker or the averaged speaker), a speaker adaptation matrix, and a bias vector of the speaker r, respectively. Note that $\mathbf{A}_r$ is a global matrix for all the phonemes or kinds of speech sounds unlike in MLLR or similar techniques. Here, we assume that $\boldsymbol{x}_t$ is normally distributed with time-varying (phoneme-dependent) mean $\boldsymbol{\mu}_t \in \mathbb{R}^D$ and time-invariant diagonal variance $\Sigma = \text{diag}(\boldsymbol{\sigma}^2), \boldsymbol{\sigma}^2 = \left[\sigma_1^2, \cdots, \sigma_D^2\right]^\top \in \mathbb{R}^D$ given a latent phonological vector $\boldsymbol{h}_t = \left[h_t^1, \cdots, h_t^H\right]^\top \in \mathbb{B}^H$ ($\mathbb{B}$ is a binary space and H is the number of dimensions of the latent vector). At this time, $\hat{\boldsymbol{x}}_{rt}$ is also normally distributed; that is,

$$\begin{aligned} \hat{\boldsymbol{x}}_{rt} | \boldsymbol{h}_t &\sim \mathcal{N}(\hat{\boldsymbol{\mu}}_{rt}, \hat{\Sigma}_r), \\ \hat{\boldsymbol{\mu}}_{rt} &= \mathbf{A}_r \boldsymbol{\mu}_t + \boldsymbol{b}_r \\ \hat{\Sigma}_r &= \mathbf{A}_r \Sigma \mathbf{A}_r^\top. \end{aligned} \tag{2}$$

The dependence on $\boldsymbol{h}_t$ in Eq. (2) is explained as follows. The speech of the neutral speaker at a certain time is supposed to be determined by the latent, phonological information that must exist behind but is not observable. For example, if the phoneme /e/ is intended at time t, then the neutral speech at t should correspond acoustically to the phoneme /e/. Therefore, we assume that the mean vector of the neutral speaker $\boldsymbol{\mu}_t$ is determined using a latent phonological vector $\boldsymbol{h}$ as

$$\boldsymbol{\mu}_t = \mathbf{W} \boldsymbol{h}_t + \boldsymbol{b}, \tag{3}$$

where $\mathbf{W} \in \mathbb{R}^{D \times H}$ and $\boldsymbol{b} \in \mathbb{R}^D$ are a matrix and a bias vector, respectively, that project the phonological space into the acoustic space. Furthermore, $\boldsymbol{b}$ is also regarded as a bias vector to realize the speaker characteristics of the neutral speaker. Incidentally, the conditional probability $p(\hat{\boldsymbol{x}}_{rt} | \boldsymbol{h}_t)$ given $\boldsymbol{h}_t$ given $\boldsymbol{h}_t$ in Eq. (2) can be calculated as follows:

$$p(\hat{\boldsymbol{x}}_{rt}|\boldsymbol{h}_t) = \mathcal{N}(\hat{\boldsymbol{\mu}}_{rt}, \hat{\Sigma}_r)$$
$$\propto e^{-\frac{1}{2}(\hat{\boldsymbol{x}}_{rt}-\hat{\boldsymbol{\mu}}_{rt})^\top \hat{\Sigma}_r^{-1}(\hat{\boldsymbol{x}}_{rt}-\hat{\boldsymbol{\mu}}_{rt})} \tag{4}$$
$$\propto e^{-\left\{\frac{1}{2}(\hat{\boldsymbol{x}}_{rt}-\hat{\boldsymbol{b}}_r)^\top \hat{\Sigma}_r^{-1}(\hat{\boldsymbol{x}}_{rt}-\hat{\boldsymbol{b}}_r)-\hat{\boldsymbol{x}}_{rt}^\top \hat{\Sigma}_r^{-1}\hat{\mathbf{W}}_r\boldsymbol{h}_t\right\}},$$

where we introduce $\hat{\boldsymbol{b}}_r = \mathbf{A}_r\boldsymbol{b} + \boldsymbol{b}_r$ and $\hat{\mathbf{W}}_r = \mathbf{A}_r\mathbf{W}$.

On the other hand, in this paper, we assume that the phonological information can be determined by the acoustic features as well. It means hjthtj is Bernoulli-distributed and its parameter $\pi_t^j \in \boldsymbol{\pi}_t \ (j = 1, \cdots, H)$ that represents the probability $p\left(h_t^j = 1\right)$ is assumed to be a function of $\boldsymbol{x}_t$. In this formulation, it is beneficial in terms of reducing the number of parameters to use the already-defined parameters. We define $\boldsymbol{\pi}_t$ as follows:

$$\boldsymbol{\pi}_t = \boldsymbol{\phi}\left(\mathbf{W}^\top \Sigma^{-1}\boldsymbol{x}_t + \boldsymbol{c}\right), \tag{5}$$

where $\boldsymbol{\phi}(\cdot)$ denotes an element-wise sigmoid function and $\boldsymbol{c} \in \mathbb{R}^H$ is a bias term for the phonological information that is independent of time. Considering that $\mathbf{A}_r^{-1}(\hat{\boldsymbol{x}}_{rt} - \boldsymbol{b}_r)$ and $\Sigma^{-1} = \mathbf{A}_r^\top \hat{\Sigma}_r^{-1}\mathbf{A}_r$, the conditional probability, p(ht|x^rt)p(ht|x^rt) forms incidentally as follows:

$$p(\boldsymbol{h}_t|\hat{\boldsymbol{x}}_{rt}) = \mathcal{B}(\boldsymbol{\pi}_t)$$
$$\propto e^{\left(\mathbf{W}^\top \Sigma^{-1}\mathbf{A}_r^{-1}(\hat{\boldsymbol{x}}_{rt}-\boldsymbol{b}_r)+\boldsymbol{c}\right)^\top \boldsymbol{h}_t} \tag{6}$$
$$= e^{-\left(-\hat{\boldsymbol{x}}_{rt}^\top \hat{\Sigma}_r^{-1}\hat{\mathbf{W}}_r\boldsymbol{h}-\hat{\boldsymbol{c}}_r^\top \boldsymbol{h}\right)},$$

where we use the replacement of $\hat{\boldsymbol{c}}_r = \boldsymbol{c} - \hat{\mathbf{W}}_r^\top \hat{\Sigma}_r^{-1}\boldsymbol{b}_r$.

Now, we consider the joint probability of $\hat{\boldsymbol{x}}_{rt}$ and $\boldsymbol{h}_t$. From Eqs. (4) and (6), we notice that the same term $-\hat{\boldsymbol{x}}_{rt}^\top \hat{\Sigma}_r^{-1}\hat{\mathbf{W}}_r\boldsymbol{h}$ appears in the exponential. Consequently, the following joint probability satisfies Eqs. (4) and (6):

$$
\begin{aligned}
p(\hat{\boldsymbol{x}}_{rt}, \boldsymbol{h}_t) =& \frac{1}{Z} e^{-E(\hat{\boldsymbol{x}}_{rt}, \boldsymbol{h}_t)} \\
E(\hat{\boldsymbol{x}}_{rt}, \boldsymbol{h}_t) =& \frac{1}{2} (\hat{\boldsymbol{x}}_{rt} - \hat{\boldsymbol{b}}_r)^\top \hat{\Sigma}_r^{-1} (\hat{\boldsymbol{x}}_{rt} - \hat{\boldsymbol{b}}_r) \\
& - \hat{\boldsymbol{x}}_{rt}^\top \hat{\Sigma}_r^{-1} \hat{\mathbf{W}}_r \boldsymbol{h}_t - \hat{\boldsymbol{c}}_r^\top \boldsymbol{h}_t,
\end{aligned}
\tag{7}
$$

where Z $Z = \int^D \sum_{\boldsymbol{h}_t} e^{-E(\hat{\boldsymbol{x}}_{rt}, \boldsymbol{h}_t)} d^D \hat{\boldsymbol{x}}_{rt}$ is a normalization term. Furthermore, substituting Eq. (1) for Eq. (7) forms

$$
\begin{aligned}
p(\boldsymbol{x}_t, \boldsymbol{h}_t) &= \tfrac{1}{Z} e^{-E(\boldsymbol{x}_t, \boldsymbol{h}_t)} \\
E(\boldsymbol{x}_t, \boldsymbol{h}_t) &= \frac{\|\boldsymbol{x}_t - \boldsymbol{b}\|_2^2}{2\sigma^2} - \left(\frac{\boldsymbol{x}_t}{\sigma^2}\right)^\top \mathbf{W} \boldsymbol{h}_t - \boldsymbol{c}^\top \boldsymbol{h}_t,
\end{aligned}
\tag{8}
$$

which is nothing more than the definition of a Gaussian-Bernoulli restricted Boltzmann machine (GB-RBM) [26]. In other words, the model defined in Eq. (7) implies that it adapts the neutral speech to that of a speaker *r* when using a GB-RBM with the visible units of acoustic features of the neutral speaker (or the averaged speaker) and the hidden units of latent phonological features, as shown in Figure 1 a. In another viewpoint, it can be regarded as a sort of semi-RBM [27] since there are shared connections W^rW^r between x^rtx^rt and $\boldsymbol{h}_t$ and connections Σ^−1rΣ^r−1 among x^rtx^rtbut no connections among h^th^t (Figure 1 b). The difference is that the model in Eq. (7) assumes the existence of the neutral speaker and defines additional parameters that enable speaker-adaptive training. In this paper, we call the probabilistic model defined in Eq. (7) speaker-adaptive-trainable Boltzmann machine (SATBM). In our previous work [25], we have proposed another probabilistic model named adaptive restricted Boltzmann machine (ARBM), that is an extension of an RBM where only the connection weights between the visible and hidden units are speaker-adaptive. The ARBM is based on a model-space transformation, whereas the SATBM is based on both a model-space transformation and a feature-space transformation (i.e., constrained model-space transformation), as Eqs. (1) and (2) indicate. Specifically, in the SATBM, the speaker-dependent parameters (means and covariance matrix) of Gaussian visible units are represented as $\mathbf{A}_r \mathbf{W} \boldsymbol{h}_t + \mathbf{A}_r \boldsymbol{b} + \boldsymbol{b}_r$ of means and ArΣATrArΣArT of a covariance matrix. On the other hand, in ARBM, the speaker-dependent parameters of Gaussian visible units are represented as $\mathbf{A}_r \mathbf{W} \boldsymbol{h}_t + \boldsymbol{b} + \boldsymbol{b}_r$ of means and $\mathbf{\Sigma}$ of a covariance matrix. This indicates that the speaker-dependent Gaussian parameters in the SATBM are more strongly influenced by the speaker and changed to adapt to the speaker more than those in the ARBM. In another perspective, the SATBM directly models the correlations between the dimensions in the observed features while the ARBM does not. The observed features take different values every time a specific speaker pronounces the same phoneme, and the extent of the variation depends on the speaker. The SATBM also represents such characteristics of each speaker. For this reason, we expect the SATBM would be superior in acoustic modeling to the ARBM.

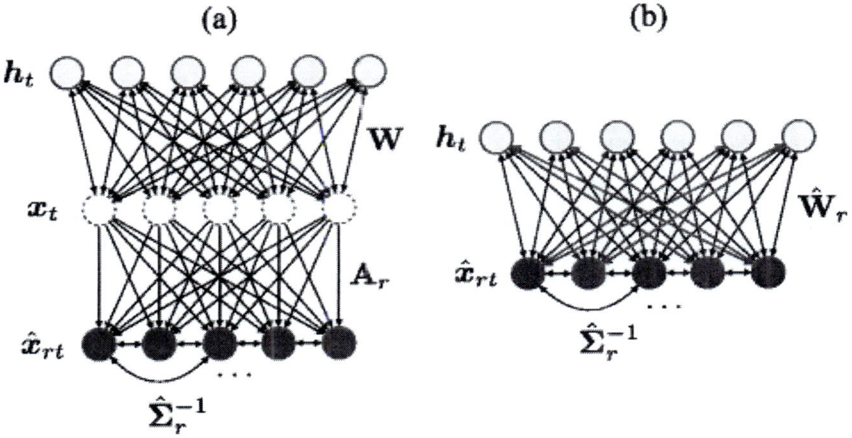

Figure 1. **a** Proposed model: speaker-adaptive-trainable Boltzmann machine (SATBM) and **b** its simplified representation, which can be seen as a type of semi-RBM

2.1 One-hot activation of $\boldsymbol{h}_t$

We can further add constraints ∑ $\sum_{j=1}^{H} h_t^t = 1$ to our model resulting in a one-hot vector $\boldsymbol{h}_t$, which indicates that only a certain phonological component is activated. In the real speech, only one phoneme, such as /a/ and /e/, should be activated in the background at a certain frame. Therefore, this modification may give better representation for speech. The use of a one-hot representation is inspired by such a phonological reason.

Such constraints give the following conditional probability that hjthtj is activated (that is, π_t^j) as) as

$$\pi_t^j = p\left(h_t^j = 1|\hat{\boldsymbol{x}}_{rt}\right)$$
$$= \frac{e^{\hat{\boldsymbol{w}}_r^{j\top} \hat{\Sigma}_r^{-1}\hat{\boldsymbol{x}}_{rt}+\hat{c}_r^j}}{\sum_{j'} e^{\hat{\boldsymbol{w}}_r^{j'\top} \hat{\Sigma}_r^{-1}\hat{\boldsymbol{x}}_{rt}+\hat{c}_r^{j'}}} \quad (9)$$
$$= \psi\left(\hat{\boldsymbol{w}}_r^{j\top} \hat{\Sigma}_r^{-1}\hat{\boldsymbol{x}}_{rt} + \hat{c}_r^j\right),$$

where $\hat{\boldsymbol{w}}_r^j$ and $\hat{c}_r^j$ indicate the *j*th column vector in W^rW^r and the *j*th element in c^rc^r, respectively, and $\psi(\cdot)$ denotes a softmax function (we also define $\boldsymbol{\psi}(\cdot)$ as an element-wise softmax function for convenience). Equation 9 is used when we sample $\boldsymbol{h}_t$ instead of Eq. (5), as discussed in the following sections.

3 PARAMETER ESTIMATION BASED ON SAT

In this section, we describe the method of the parameter estimation in the previously defined model, a SATBM, based on SAT [28]. For convenience, we use symbols $\Theta^{SD} = \{\mathbf{A}_r, \boldsymbol{b}_r\}_{r=1}^R$ for SD parameters and $\boldsymbol{\Theta}^{SI}=\{\mathbf{W},\sigma^2,\boldsymbol{b},\boldsymbol{c}\}$ for SI parameters. Given a collection of the speech data, $\boldsymbol{X} = \{X_r\}_{r=1}^R$, $\boldsymbol{X}_r = \{\hat{\boldsymbol{x}}_{rt}\}_{t=1}^{T_r}$ that is composed of *R* speakers, these parameters are simultaneously estimated so as to maximize the likelihood as

$$(\hat{\Theta}^{SD}, \hat{\Theta}^{SI}) \triangleq \underset{(\Theta^{SD},\Theta^{SI})}{\text{argmax}} \prod_{r=1}^{R}\prod_{t=1}^{T_r} p(\hat{\boldsymbol{x}}_{rt}). \quad (10)$$

According to the SAT paradigm, the SD parameters $\boldsymbol{\Theta}^{SD}$ undertake the speaker-induced variation, and the SI parameters $\boldsymbol{\Theta}^{SI}$ capture the remaining information, i.e., phonetically relevant variation. Unlike the conventional SAT+MLLR (maximum likelihood linear regression), the SATBM explicitly models the relationships between the speaker-normalized acoustic features and the phonological information, which implies the possibility that the model represents the speech data better than SAT+MLLR.

The parameters are iteratively updated based on gradient descent. The partial differential of the log-likelihood $l = \log \prod_r \prod_t p(\hat{\boldsymbol{x}}_{rt}) = \sum_r \sum_t \log \sum_h p(\hat{\boldsymbol{x}}_{rt}, \boldsymbol{h}_t))$ in terms of a parameter $\theta \in \{\boldsymbol{\Theta}^{SD}, \boldsymbol{\Theta}^{SI}\}$ is derived as follows:

$$\frac{\partial l}{\partial \theta} = \sum_r \left(\left\langle \frac{\partial E(\hat{\boldsymbol{x}}_{rt}, \boldsymbol{h}_t)}{\partial \theta} \right\rangle_{\text{data}} - \left\langle \frac{\partial E(\hat{\boldsymbol{x}}_{rt}, \boldsymbol{h}_t)}{\partial \theta} \right\rangle_{\text{model}} \right),$$

where $\langle \cdot \rangle_{\text{data}}$ and $\langle \cdot \rangle_{\text{model}}$ denote expectations of the empirical data and the inner model, respectively. It is generally difficult to compute the expectations of the inner model; however, we can still use contrastive divergence (CD) [29] and efficiently approximate them with the expectations of the reconstructed data. We can analytically calculate the partial gradients $\frac{\partial E(\hat{\boldsymbol{x}}_{rt}, \boldsymbol{h}_t)}{\partial \theta}$ for each parameter as follows:

$$\begin{aligned}
\frac{\partial E(\hat{\boldsymbol{x}}_{rt}, \boldsymbol{h}_t)}{\partial \mathbf{A}_r} &= -\frac{1}{2} \left(\mathbf{A}_r^{-1} \mathbf{C}_{rt} \hat{\Sigma}_r^{-1} + \hat{\Sigma}_r^{-1} \mathbf{D}_{rt} \mathbf{A}_r^{-\top} \right) \\
\frac{\partial E(\hat{\boldsymbol{x}}_{rt}, \boldsymbol{h}_t)}{\partial \boldsymbol{b}_r} &= -\hat{\Sigma}_r^{-1} (\hat{\boldsymbol{x}}_{rt} - \hat{\boldsymbol{b}}_r - \hat{\mathbf{W}}_r \boldsymbol{h}_t) \\
\frac{\partial E(\hat{\boldsymbol{x}}_{rt}, \boldsymbol{h}_t)}{\partial \mathbf{W}} &= -\mathbf{A}_r^\top \Sigma_r^{-1} (\hat{\boldsymbol{x}}_{rt} - \boldsymbol{b}_r) \boldsymbol{h}_t^\top \\
\frac{\partial E(\hat{\boldsymbol{x}}_{rt}, \boldsymbol{h}_t)}{\partial \sigma^2} &= -\frac{1}{2} \text{diag} \left(\mathbf{A}_r^\top \hat{\Sigma}_r^{-1} \mathbf{E}_{rt} \hat{\Sigma}_r^{-1} \mathbf{A}_r \right) \\
\frac{\partial E(\hat{\boldsymbol{x}}_{rt}, \boldsymbol{h}_t)}{\partial \boldsymbol{b}} &= -\mathbf{A}_r^\top \hat{\Sigma}_r^{-1} (\hat{\boldsymbol{x}}_{rt} - \hat{\boldsymbol{b}}_r) \\
\frac{\partial E(\hat{\boldsymbol{x}}_{rt}, \boldsymbol{h}_t)}{\partial \boldsymbol{c}} &= -\boldsymbol{h}_t,
\end{aligned}$$

where

$$\begin{aligned}
\mathbf{C}_{rt} &= (\hat{\boldsymbol{x}}_{rt} - \boldsymbol{b}_r)(\hat{\boldsymbol{x}}_{rt} - \hat{\boldsymbol{b}}_r - 2\hat{\mathbf{W}}_r \boldsymbol{h}_t)^\top \\
\mathbf{D}_{rt} &= (\hat{\boldsymbol{x}}_{rt} - \hat{\boldsymbol{b}}_r)(\hat{\boldsymbol{x}}_{rt} - \boldsymbol{b}_r)^\top \\
\mathbf{E}_{rt} &= (\hat{\boldsymbol{x}}_{rt} - \hat{\boldsymbol{b}}_r)(\hat{\boldsymbol{x}}_{rt} - \hat{\boldsymbol{b}}_r)^\top - 2(\hat{\boldsymbol{x}}_{rt} - \boldsymbol{b}_r)(\hat{\mathbf{W}}_r \boldsymbol{h}_t)^\top.
\end{aligned}$$

4 APPLICATION TO VC

To use the proposed model for the VC, we follow three stages of training, adaptation, and conversion. In the training stage, speaker-independent parameters Θ^SIΘ^SI are obtained as in Eq. (10) using R reference speakers' speech (we discard the speaker-dependent parameters Θ^SDΘ^SD). In the adaptation stage, new speaker-dependent parameters $\Theta_i^{SD} = \{\mathbf{A}_i, \boldsymbol{b}_i\}$ and $\Theta_o^{SD} = \{\mathbf{A}_o, \boldsymbol{b}_o\}$ are estimated using adaptation data of the source and the target speaker $\{\hat{\boldsymbol{x}}_{it}\}_{t=1}^{Ti}, \{\hat{\boldsymbol{x}}_{ot}\}_{t=1}^{To}$ while keeping $\hat{\Theta}^{SI}$ fixed. That is,

$$\hat{\Theta}_r^{SD} \triangleq \underset{\Theta_r^{SD}}{\mathrm{argmax}} \prod_{t=1}^{T_r} p\left(\hat{\boldsymbol{x}}_{rt}; \Theta_r^{SD}, \hat{\Theta}^{SI}\right), \ r \in \{i, o\}. \tag{11}$$

To convert the frame-wise acoustic feature vector of the source speaker $\boldsymbol{x}_{it}$ into that of the target speaker $\boldsymbol{x}_{ot}$, we take an ML-based approach. In this approach, $\boldsymbol{x}_{ot}$ is computed so as to maximize the probability given $\boldsymbol{x}_{it}$, formulated as

$$\begin{aligned}
\boldsymbol{x}_{ot} &\triangleq \underset{\boldsymbol{x}_{ot}}{\mathrm{argmax}}\, p(\boldsymbol{x}_{ot}|\boldsymbol{x}_{it}) \\
&= \underset{\boldsymbol{x}_{ot}}{\mathrm{argmax}} \textstyle\sum_{h_t} p(\boldsymbol{h}_t|\boldsymbol{x}_{it})p(\boldsymbol{x}_{ot}|\boldsymbol{h}_t) \\
&\simeq \underset{\boldsymbol{x}_{ot}}{\mathrm{argmax}}\, p(\hat{\boldsymbol{h}}_t|\boldsymbol{x}_{it})p(\boldsymbol{x}_{ot}|\hat{\boldsymbol{h}}_t) \\
&= \underset{\boldsymbol{x}_{ot}}{\mathrm{argmax}}\, p(\boldsymbol{x}_{ot}|\hat{\boldsymbol{h}}_t) \\
&= \mathbf{A}_o \mathbf{W} \psi\left(\mathbf{W}^\top \Sigma^{-1} \mathbf{A}_i^{-1}(\boldsymbol{x}_{it} - \boldsymbol{b}_i) + \boldsymbol{c}\right) + \mathbf{A}_o \boldsymbol{b} + \boldsymbol{b}_o,
\end{aligned} \tag{12}$$

where we give h $\hat{\boldsymbol{h}}_t \triangleq \mathbb{E}[p(\boldsymbol{h}_t|\boldsymbol{x}_{it})]$. It is worth noting that the conversion function is based on the non-linear transformation.

5 EXPERIMENTAL EVALUATION

5.1 System configuration

In our VC experiments, we evaluated the performance of our model, a SATBM, using ASJ Continuous Speech Corpus for Research (ASJ-JIPDEC[4]). In the training stage where the SI parameters are estimated, we randomly selected and used the speech data of five sentences (approx. 160 k frames) uttered by 56 speakers (26 males and 30 females) from set A in the corpus. For adaptation and evaluation, a male (identified as "ECL0001") and female ("ECL1003") speakers that were not included in the training were used as source and target speakers, respectively, unless otherwise stated. We also evaluated the proposed SATBM using the other speaker pairs, which will be discussed in Section 5.4. The amount of adaptation data was five sentences for each person. As an acoustic feature vector, we used 32-dimensional mel-cepstral features that were calculated from the 513-dimensional WORLD [30] spectra without dynamic features. In the training of the system, we used up to 64 softmax hidden units, a learning rate of 0.01, a momentum of 0.9, and a batch-size of $R\times100(=5600)$ and set the number of iterations as 200. For the evaluation of the proposed method, we used parallel data (of 10 different sentences from the training and adaptation data) of the source and the target speakers, which was created using dynamic programming. But again, note that all speech data used for the training and the adaptation was NOT parallel.

Mel-cepstral distortion (MCD) is generally used for objective evaluation in the VC. However, we used the mel-cepstral distortion improvement ratio (MDIR) instead in this paper because it does not make sense to view the distance between the spectral features in the mel scale of the source and the target speakers when we want to recognize the differences in speaker identities and because the scale of the MCD varies in the evaluation data. For more discussion about the differences between MDIR and MCD, see Section 5.4. The MDIR is defined as follows:

$$\mathrm{MDIR}\ [\mathrm{dB}] = \frac{10\sqrt{2}}{\ln 10}(\|\boldsymbol{m}_o - \boldsymbol{m}_i\|_2 - \|\boldsymbol{m}_o - \boldsymbol{m}_c\|_2)$$

where $\boldsymbol{m}_i$, $\boldsymbol{m}_o$, and $\boldsymbol{m}_c$ are mel-cepstral features at a frame of the source speaker's speech, target speaker's speech, and converted speech, respectively. The higher the value of MDIR is, the better the performance of the VC is. The MDIR was calculated for each frame from the parallel data of 10 sentences and averaged.

5.1.1 Methods to be compared

It is difficult and unfair to evaluate the proposed method because most of the existing VC approaches use parallel data in training and our method does not. Nevertheless, we can still compare the proposed method with our earlier model, ARBM [25]. In addition, a linear-transform-based approach, which has not been proposed, is interesting to compare with. This approach is simple: the vector $\boldsymbol{x}_{ot}$ is calculated as

$$\boldsymbol{x}_{ot} \triangleq \mathbf{A}_o \mathbf{A}_i^{-1}(\boldsymbol{x}_{it} - \boldsymbol{b}_i) + \boldsymbol{b}_o, \tag{13}$$

which was derived from the equation $\boldsymbol{x}_t = \mathbf{A}_i^{-1}(\boldsymbol{x}_{it} - \boldsymbol{b}_i) = \mathbf{A}_o^{-1}(\boldsymbol{x}_{ot} - \boldsymbol{b}_o)$) starting with Eq. (1). However, it is under the assumption that the *true* feature space of the neutral speaker was obtained. The parameters $\mathbf{A}_r$ and $\boldsymbol{b}_r$ are estimated in SAT using the gradient decent, the same as our proposed method. So, the difference between the linear-transform approach and the proposed model is whether the latent phonological features are modeled or not.

For reference, we also compared our proposed model with a popular GMM-based VC with 8, 16, 32, and 64 mixtures using the parallel data of five sentences.

5.1.2 Optimal number of hidden units

From the pre-experiment, we see the effects of changing the number of softmax hidden units. Figure 2 shows the performance when changing the number of hidden units between 8, 16, 32, and 64. From Figure 2, the optimal number was 16, and the performance degraded as the number of hidden units increased more than 16. This is since the hidden layer becomes speaker-dependent with a large number of units, and hence, it cannot convert the voice properly. To verify this, we examined how the hidden units were speaker-dependent by analyzing the distribution of the hidden units with the cases of H=16 (the optimal number of units) and H=64 (too large a number of units). Figures 3 and 4 show examples of the expected values of the hidden units for the cases of H=16 and H=64, respectively, comparing the distributions obtained from the source and target speakers. From Figs. 3 and 4, we observed that more hidden units when H=64 were speaker-dependent than those when H=16. To measure objectively how close the distributions are to each other, we further calculated the Euclidean distances and the cosine similarities between the two distributions obtained from the source and target speakers' speech, as shown in Table 1. Obviously, Table 1 shows that the two hidden activations of H=16 are close to each other, more than those of H=64. A similar discussion can be seen in our previous work using the ARBM [25].

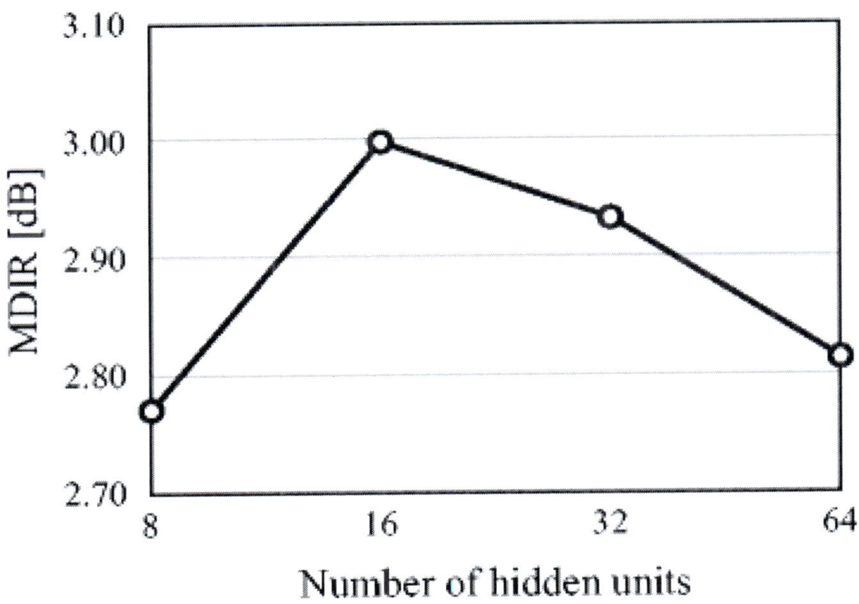

Figure 2. VC performance when changing the number of hidden units

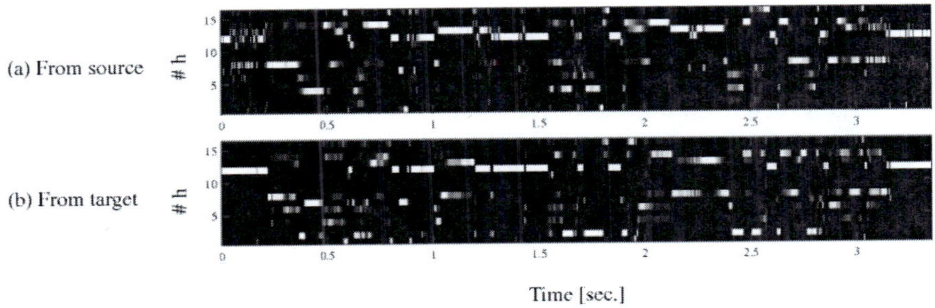

Figure 3. The expected values of hidden units obtained from **a** the source speaker's features and **b** the target speaker's features of the same sentence /ureshi: hazuga yuQkuri netemo irarenai/ when H=16. The *white* and *black* indicate the high and low values, respectively

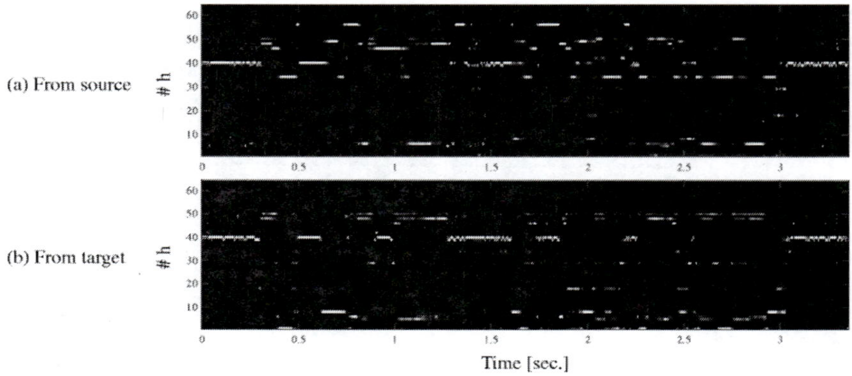

Figure 4. The expected values of hidden units obtained from **a** the source speaker's features and **b** the target speaker's features of the same sentence /ureshi: hazuga yuQkuri netemo irarenai/ when *H*=64. The *white* and *black* indicate the high and low values, respectively

Table 1. Euclidean distance and cosine similarity between the hidden distributions obtained from the source and target speakers' speech of Figs. 3 (*H*=16) and 4 (*H*=64)

	Euclidean dist.	Cosine sim.
$H = 16$	0.660	0.526
$H = 64$	0.869	0.337

In speech recognition in Japanese, 43 phonemes are often used [31], which consists of seven short vowels, five long vowels, 28 consonants, and three special symbols. These kinds of Japanese phonemes were defined by the Acoustical Society of Japan (ASJ) committee. Comparing these artificial numbers with the optimal number of hidden units as *H*=16, we could state that this is reasonable because using the static short-term acoustic features does not represent the consonants and long vowels sufficiently and because the natural speech should contain some allophones.

Considering the above, we will use 16 softmax hidden units in the following experiments unless otherwise stated.

5.2 Objective comparison

The VC performance of the linear-transform-based approach, the ARBM, and the proposed model (SATBM) is compared using objective criteria, as shown in Figure 5. Each method was evaluated by varying the number of diagonals of the adaptation matrices used as 1 (that means diagonal matrices), 3 (tridiagonal), 5 (pentadiagonal), 7 (heptadiagonal), and 9 (nonadiagonal). In this experiment, we used 16 softmax hidden units for the SATBM and the ARBM. As shown in Figure 5, the proposed model performed best with any type of the adaptation matrix. The performance of the SATBM and the ARBM was improved when adding the diagonals up to seven. On the other hand, the linear approach barely improved with the number of diagonals. Interestingly, the proposed model achieved a high MDIR even when the diagonal adaptation matrices were used, unlike the ARBM and linear approaches. In the linear approach, the diagonal matrix could not capture the correlations between the dimensions of the mel cepstrum, which makes it impossible to match the vocal tracts among the speakers. Meanwhile, the SATBM could make the source speech resemble the target voice more or less even when a diagonal adaptation matrix was used, due to modeling the latent phonological information. The ARBM models the latent phonological information as well; however, the speaker-dependent Gaussian parameters of the ARBM are not sufficient and failed to represent the speech correctly with the diagonal adaptation matrices.

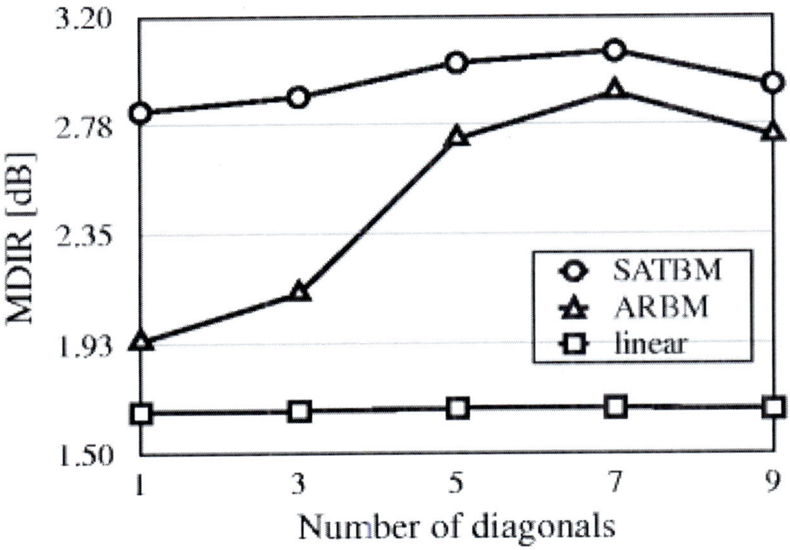

Figure 5. Comparison of VC performance of non-parallel approaches

We also found that the SATBM and the ARBM degraded with nine diagonals and more. This is due to the over-fitting caused by the large number of parameters. In some literature, such as [32, 33, 34], it is known that warping cepstral-based features between different speakers is achieved by linear transformation with an adaptation matrix, and a few diagonal elements (such as tridiagonal, pentadiagonal, and heptadiagonal) of the adaptation matrix are sufficient for warping the cepstral features. Therefore, it does not make sense to use adaptation matrices with many diagonal elements (more than seven diagonals) in terms of efficient learning for this speaker pair. For more discussion using the various speaker pairs, see Section 5.4.

The average MDIR of the GMM-based approach was 3.93 with 32 mixtures, which was the best in the GMM-based approach. Unfortunately, it performed better than our approach. However, again, such an approach benefits from using parallel data and should not be compared with the non-parallel approach, just in terms of VC quality.

5.3 Subjective comparison

We also conducted subjective experiments, comparing our method with the ARBM and the linear-based approaches. We decoded the converted mel cepstra back to the WORLD spectra using the filter theory [35] and generated signals using the original F0 and aperiodic features of the target speaker since we wanted to compare each method in the spectra. In this experiment, seven participants listened to 10 sentences of converted speech using the linear-based, the ARBM, and the SATBM approaches accompanied with the target speech and voted for the most preferable method for each sentence in terms of the speaker specificity of the target speaker. The number of votes for each method are shown in Figure 6. The SATBM performed the best of all. It can be said that the SATBM has the ability to produce sounds auditorily closer to the target speech than the other methods.

For reference, we also compared the proposed method with the GMM-based VC in a subjective manner. In this experiment as well, the seven participants were asked to rank the converted speech using a 5-scale (1 poor, 2 fair, 3 good, 4 very good, and 5 excellent) in terms of speech quality (naturalness) and speaker specificity (similarity). The results are shown in Table 2. From Table 2, the GMM-based VC outperformed the proposed method in both criteria; however, again, the GMM-based VC uses parallel corpora, while the proposed method does not.

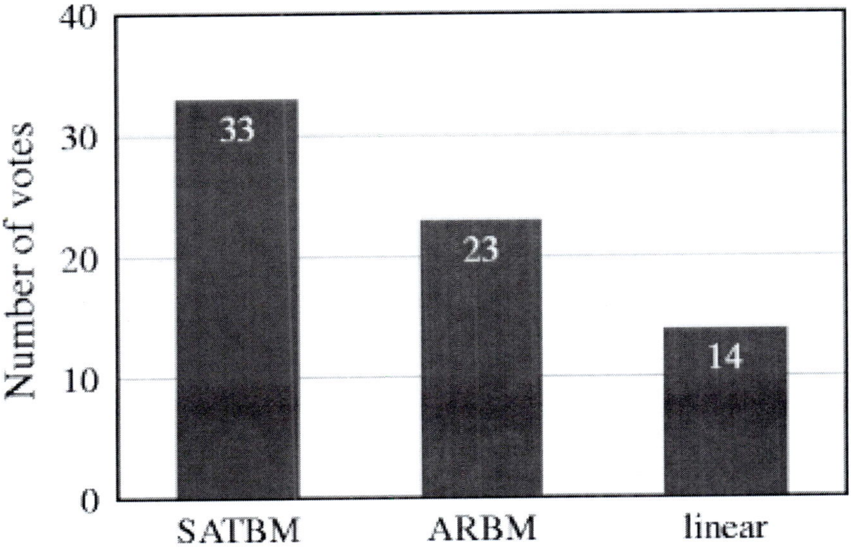

Figure 6. Subjective performance of non-parallel VC methods

Table 2. Subjective comparison of parallel VC (GMM) and non-parallel VC (SATBM) using the 5-scale tests in terms of speech quality and speaker specificity

	Speech quality	Speaker specificity
GMM	3.37	3.66
SATBM	2.11	1.91

5.4 Evaluation using various speaker pairs

We also investigated the performance of the proposed SATBM using various speaker pairs that include four gender types: male-to-female (M2F), female-to-male (F2M), male-to-male (M2M), and female-to-female (F2F). For this evaluation, we randomly chose eight pairs from the corpus that were not included in the training, whose identities and the gender types are listed in the first and the second columns of Table 3, respectively. Table 3 compares the performance for each speaker pair with different criteria of the MDIR and MCD, using the SATBM with heptadiagonal adaptation matrices. When we compare the VC performance of different speaker pairs using the MCD, we may conclude that the model performed best when converting "ECL0001" to "MIT0001" because this conversion provided the smallest MCD. However, the speech of "ECL0001" and "MIT0001" was already close to each other. To see how effective the model is, we should focus on how much the model improves the original speech. The MDIR measures the extent of how much the model improves, and we can say that the VC model was the most effective when converting "MIT0001" to "ECL1003" according to the MDIR. The MDIR of the cross-gender conversion is higher than that of the within-gender conversion. This is natural because, in general, we can feel the extent of how much the source speech was converted from the converted speech of the cross-gender more than from that of the within-gender.

Table 3. MDIR and MCD from various speaker pairs

Source → target	Type	MDIR [dB]	MCD [dB]
ECL0001 → ECL1003	M2F	3.12	6.87
MIT0001 → ECL1003	M2F	4.03	7.00
ECL1003 → CAN0001	F2M	2.77	7.32
NEC1002 → MIT0002	F2M	3.48	6.98
ECL0001 → MIT0001	M2M	1.48	6.09
ECL0001 → MIT0002	M2M	2.02	6.46
CAN1001 → ECL1003	F2F	1.28	6.85
NEC1001 → ECL1003	F2F	1.55	6.14

Finally, Figure 7 shows the VC performance of the proposed method for each gender type when changing the types of the adaptation matrix. Each MDIR was averaged within the same gender type. As shown in Figure 7, we achieved better results as the number of diagonals in the adaptation matrices increased and the best when using the heptadiagonal adaptation matrices, except for F2F conversion. The nonadiagonal adaptation matrices performed the worse for all gender types. This is because too many parameters are included in the adaptation matrices even though it is not needed for the linear transformation across the speakers and caused overfitting, as discussed in Section 5.2. We also noticed from Figure 7 that when comparing the cases with F2F and M2M, the diagonal matrix was not so bad for the F2F conversion. This is because the female voice in general varies with the speaker less than the male voice, and only the diagonal elements in the adaptation matrix were enough to represent the differences in the female speakers.

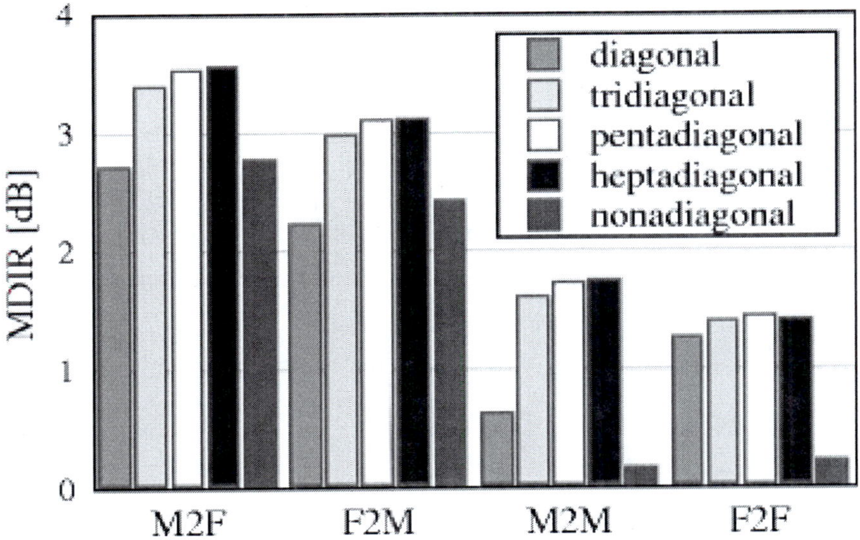

Figure 7. Comparison of VC performance of the proposed model with changing the type of adaptation matrices for each gender type

6 CONCLUSIONS

In this paper, we presented a VC method that does not require any parallel data during training and adaptation according to the basic idea of dividing a speech signal into phoneme-relevant and speaker-relevant information and replacing only the speaker-relevant information with the desired one. To model this, we assumed that the neutral speaker's acoustic features are normally distributed, and its mean is affine-transformed from the latent phonological features that are Bernoulli-distributed. As a result, we showed that the joint probability of the acoustic features and the phonological features forms a type of Boltzmann machine. We also showed the method of estimating the target speaker's features given the source speaker's features in a probabilistic manner. In our VC experiments, we obtained better performance with our model than the other non-parallel VC approaches in both objective and subjective criteria. However, we still have concerns that the proposed approach fell short of the GMM-based approach that uses parallel data in training. In the future, we will continue to improve the system (hopefully, to the performance level of the GMM-based approach) in the non-parallel VC because non-parallel training has several merits, e.g., we can freely use most of the existing speech data.

7 ENDNOTES

[1] Note that they still require parallel data among the reference speakers.

[2] It means that the method requires neither the parallel data of a source speaker and target speaker nor the parallel data of the reference speakers.

[3] In our experiments, we used mel cepstra as the acoustic feature vector.

[4] http://research.nii.ac.jp/src/ASJ-JIPDEC.html

AUTHORS' CONTRIBUTIONS

TN designed the speaker-adaptive-trainable Boltzmann machine, performed the experimental evaluation, and drafted the manuscript. YM reviewed the paper and provided some advice. Both authors read and approved the final manuscript.

COMPETING INTERESTS

The authors declare that they have no competing interests.

Publisher's Note

Springer Nature remains neutral with regard to jurisdictional claims in published maps and institutional affiliations.

REFERENCES

1. A Kain, MW Macon, in ICASSP. Spectral voice conversion for text-to-speech synthesis (IEEE, 1998), pp. 285–288.
2. C Veaux, X Robet, in INTERSPEECH. Intonation conversion from neutral to expressive speech (ISCA, 2011), pp. 2765–2768.
3. K Nakamura, T Toda, H Saruwatari, K Shikano, Speaking-aid systems using GMM-based voice conversion for electrolaryngeal speech. Speech Commun.**54**(1), 134–146 (2012).
4. L Deng, A Acero, L Jiang, J Droppo, X Huang, in ICASSP. High-performance robust speech recognition using stereo training data (IEEE, 2001), pp. 301–304.
5. A Kunikoshi, Y Qiao, N Minematsu, K Hirose, in INTERSPEECH. Speech generation from hand gestures based on space mapping (ISCA, 2009), pp. 308–311.
6. R Gray, Vector quantization. IEEE ASSP Mag. **1**(2), 4–29 (1984).
7. H Valbret, E Moulines, J-P Tubach, Voice transformation using PSOLA technique. Speech Commun. **11**(2), 175–187 (1992).
8. Y Stylianou, Cappe, Ó, E Moulines, Continuous probabilistic transform for voice conversion. IEEE Trans. Speech Audio Process. **6**(2), 131–142 (1998).
9. T Toda, AW Black, K Tokuda, Voice conversion based on maximum-likelihood estimation of spectral parameter trajectory. IEEE Trans. Audio Speech Lang. Process. **15**(8), 2222–2235 (2007).
10. E Helander, T Virtanen, J Nurminen, M Gabbouj, Voice conversion using partial least squares regression. IEEE Trans. Audio Speech Lang. Process. **18**(5), 912–921 (2010).
11. D Saito, H Doi, N Minematsu, K Hirose, in INTERSPEECH. Application of matrix variate Gaussian mixture model to statistical voice conversion (ISCA, 2014), pp. 2504–2508.
12. R Takashima, T Takiguchi, Y Ariki, in SLT. Exemplar-based voice conversion in noisy environment (IEEE, 2012), pp. 313–317.
13. R Takashima, R Aihara, T Takiguchi, Y Ariki, in SSW8. Noise-robust voice conversion based on spectral mapping on sparse space (SynSIG, 2013), pp. 71–75.
14. S Desai, EV Raghavendra, B Yegnanarayana, AW Black, K Prahallad, in ICASSP. Voice conversion using artificial neural networks (IEEE, 2009), pp. 3893–3896.
15. LH Chen, ZH Ling, Y Song, LR Dai, in INTERSPEECH. Joint spectral distribution modeling using restricted Boltzmann machines for voice conversion (ISCA, 2013), pp. 3052–3056.
16. Z Wu, ES Chng, H Li, in ChinaSIP. Conditional restricted Boltzmann machine for voice conversion (IEEE, 2013).
17. T Nakashika, R Takashima, T Takiguchi, Y Ariki, in INTERSPEECH. Voice conversion in high-order eigen space using deep belief nets (ISCA, 2013), pp. 369–372.
18. T Nakashika, T Takiguchi, Y Ariki, Voice conversion using RNN pre-trained by recurrent temporal restricted Boltzmann machines. IEEE/ACM Trans. Audio Speech Lang. Process. **23**(3), 580–587 (2015).
19. A Mouchtaris, J Van der Spiegel, P Mueller, Nonparallel training for voice conversion based on a parameter adaptation approach. IEEE Trans. Audio Speech Lang. Process.**14**(3), 952–963 (2006).
20. C-H Lee, C-H Wu, in INTERSPEECH. Map-based adaptation for speech conversion using adaptation data selection and non-parallel training (ISCA, 2006), pp. 2254–2257.
21. T Toda, Y Ohtani, K Shikano, in INTERSPEECH. Eigenvoice conversion based on Gaussian mixture model (ISCA, 2006), pp. 2446–2449.
22. Y Ohtani, T Toda, H Saruwatari, K Shikano, in NTERSPEECH. Many-to-many eigenvoice conversion with reference voice (ISCA, 2009), pp. 1623–1626.

23. D Saito, K Yamamoto, N Minematsu, K Hirose, in INTERSPEECH. One-to-many voice conversion based on tensor representation of speaker space (ISCA, 2011), pp. 653–656.
24. T Masuda, M Shozakai, in ICASSP. Cost reduction of training mapping function based on multistep voice conversion (IEEE, 2007), pp. 693–696.
25. T Nakashika, T Takiguchi, Y Ariki, in MLSLP 2015. Parallel-data-free, many-to-many voice conversion using an adaptive restricted Boltzmann machine (ISCA, 2015), pp. 1–4.
26. K Cho, A Ilin, T Raiko, in ICANN. Improved learning of Gaussian-Bernoulli restricted Boltzmann machines (ENNS, 2011), pp. 10–17.
27. R Salakhutdinov, Learning and evaluating Boltzmann machines. Technical report, Technical Report UTML TR 2008-002, Department of Computer Science, University of Toronto (2008).
28. T Anastasakos, J McDonough, R Schwartz, J Makhoul, in ICSLP 96, 2. A compact model for speaker-adaptive training (WASET, 1996), pp. 1137–1140.
29. GE Hinton, S Osindero, YW Teh, A fast learning algorithm for deep belief nets. Neural Comput.**18**(7), 1527–1554 (2006).
30. M Morise, in *Proc. the Stockholm Music Acoustics Conference (SMAC)*. An attempt to develop a singing synthesizer by collaborative creation (Logos VerlagBerlin, 2013), pp. 287–292.
31. T Kawahara, A Lee, T Kobayashi, K Takeda, N Minematsu, K Itou, A Ito, M Yamamoto, A Yamada, T Utsuro, K Shikano, Japanese dictation toolkit. J. Acoust. Soc. Japan (E). **20**(3), 233–239 (1999).
32. M Pitz, H Ney, Vocal tract normalization equals linear transformation in cepstral space. IEEE Trans. Speech Audio Process. **13**(5), 930–944 (2005).
33. E Variani, T Schaaf, in INTERSPEECH. VTLN in the MFCC domain: band-limited versus local interpolation (ISCA, 2011), pp. 1273–1276.
34. T Emori, K Shinoda, Vocal tract length normalization using rapid maximum-likelihood estimation for speech recognition. Syst. Comput. Japan. **33**(5), 30–40 (2002).
35. B Milner, X Shao, in INTERSPEECH. Speech reconstruction from mel-frequency cepstral coefficients using a source-filter model (ISCA, 2002), pp. 2421–2424.

CHAPTER 8

Video Processing for Panoramic Streaming Using HEVC and Its Scalable Extensions

Y. Sánchez de la Fuente [1,2] & R. Skupin[1] & T. Schierl [1]

1 Multimedia Communications Group, Video Coding and Analytics Department, Fraunhofer HHI, Einsteinufer 37, 10587 Berlin, Germany

2 Image Communication Group, Department of Telecommunication Systems, Technische Universität Berlin, 10587 Berlin, Germany

ABSTRACT

Panoramic streaming is a particular way of video streaming where an arbitrary Region-of-Interest (RoI) is transmitted from a high-spatial resolution video, i.e. a video covering a very "wide-angle" (much larger than the human field-of-view – e.g. 360°). Some transport schemes for panoramic video delivery have been proposed and demonstrated within the past decade, which allow users to navigate interactively within the high-resolution videos. With the recent advances of head mounted displays, consumers may soon have immersive and sufficiently convenient end devices at reach, which could lead to an increasing demand for panoramic video experiences. The solution proposed within this paper is built upon tile-based panoramic streaming, where users receive a set of tiles that match their RoI, and consists in a low-complexity compressed domain video processing technique for using H.265/HEVC and its scalable extensions (H.265/SHVC and H.265/MV-HEVC). The proposed technique generates a single video bitstream out of the selected tiles so that a single hardware decoder can be used. It overcomes the scalability issue of previous solutions not using tiles and the battery consumption issue inherent of tile-based panorama streaming, where multiple parallel software decoders are used. In addition, the described technique is capable of reducing peak streaming bitrate during changes of the RoI, which is crucial for allowing a truly immersive and low latency video experience. Besides, it makes it possible to use Open GOP structures without incurring any playback interruption at switching events, which provides a better compression efficiency compared to closed GOP structures.

Keywords: Panoramic streaming HEVC SHVC MV-HEVC Tiles Stitching

1 INTRODUCTION

Panoramic streaming is a specific case of video streaming, in which an arbitrary Region-of-Interest (RoI) of a high-spatial resolution video is transmitted. Users navigate within a wide-angle video (e.g. 180° or 360°) by choosing at any time the RoI they are interested in. Figure 1shows an example of a high-resolution video, where the spatial plane of the panorama video is shown with two RoIs marked as blue rectangles. The two rectangles show two different RoIs displayed at two different time instants: namely at time t_0 (left rectangle) and at time t_1 (right rectangle) after user interaction, i.e. after a RoI switch event.

Figure 1. RoI before (t_0) and after (t_1) user interaction

There are prototypes and deployed systems already showing panoramic streaming's feasibility [2, 27]. Taking into account that there exist techniques and commercial products that allow capturing 360° video in real time [28], by stitching multiple HD views from multiple cameras, and the recent market availability of plenty of head mounted consumer displays such as the Oculus Rift [6], Samsung Gear VR [7] or Google

Cardboard [8], we envision that interactive panoramic streaming will be a popular application in a few years from now. In fact, consumers may soon have immersive and sufficiently convenient end devices and content at reach, which could lead to an increasing demand of panoramic video experiences.

Panorama (or very wide-angle) videos require a very high-spatial resolution in order to allow for a truly immersive experience. Although, there is no specification yet about the formats required for Virtual Reality (VR) and panoramic streaming, there is some discussion ongoing about the proper formats for such services in order to have a good QoE. In (http://dashif.org/wp-content/uploads/2015/08/4a-Harmonic-5G-Video.pdf) potential formats for VR are described. More concretely the formats described have a spatial resolution of 2560x1440 pixels at 60 or 120 fps or even 3840x2160 pixels at 120 fps for the section shown at the Head Mounted Displays (HMD), i.e. the RoI. Although current HMDs do not yet support ultra-high resolution formats, the trend points towards such a direction. Taking into account that the field-of-view of HMDs cover around 110°, a more than three times larger panorama video can be expected in the horizontal resolution. This accounts to an 8Kx2K or even higher-resolution video for the full panorama. Despite the better coding efficiency of new video codecs such as H.265/HEVC, there is a need of optimization in the way the panorama video is coded and transmitted in order to reduce the very high throughput that would be required if the whole panorama was transmitted. In fact, transmitting the whole panorama at full resolution would waste resources since only a smaller part of it, i.e. the RoI, is used at the receiver side.

The most basic approach to tackle the aforementioned problem consists of a fully client-server coupled system. In such a system, each user indicates to the panorama streaming system the desired RoI at any time and an encoder associated with each user encodes only the desired RoI. Then, the RoI is transmitted back to the user. Since having a dedicated encoder per user does not scale well, tile-based panoramic streaming (introduced by Mavlankar et al. in [12]) has drawn the attention of the research community and standardization bodies (see [10]). The main idea is to divide the panorama picture horizontally and vertically into smaller regions that are encoded independently. Then the regions that contain the content belonging to the RoI are transmitted to the user. Therefore, the number of streams encoded only depends on the granularity, with which the content has been tiled, and not on the number of users and trajectories chosen by them when making use of the interactivity.

However, while tiled streaming solves the scalability issue described before, it assumes instantiation of a decoder per received spatial region, typically using software decoders that have an impact on power consumption or real-time decoding capability. Power consumption is a very critical issue for head mounted displays based on mobile devices such as the case of Samsung Gear VR or Google Cardboard, since without power supply the battery life would be too short to be able to provide a satisfactory service. Additionally, UHD software decoding can be challenging in software, especially looking at the resolution requirements that are discussed in the field for VR. Therefore, even for HMDs with power supply such as Oculus Rift, hardware decoding is an important component of the end-to-end chain, since GPU decoding can be used. Note, for instance, that for PlayStation VR, where power consumption is not an issue, video decoding is done in hardware. Typically, devices only use a single hardware-accelerated decoder to achieve real-time decoding capabilities and save battery life. Therefore, in order to provide a good technical solution, it is a requirement that a single bitstream is provided to the end-device so that hardware decoding can be performed. An alternative to the solution presented within this paper is definitely to use multiple parallel decoders, which is currently not widely supported in hardware and seems not to be realistic for software decoding taking into account the upcoming trends in terms of resolutions and their impact for real-time decoding.

The goal of this paper is to provide a technique that makes use of tiled streaming for scalability, but allows using a single decoder for efficiency considerations, i.e. real-time decoding of high resolution videos and power efficiency. In addition, several aspects are investigated in order to provide an efficient way of encoding the panorama video.

The technique, described within this paper, overcomes the multiple decoding issue described above. It operates in the compressed domain and generates a single H.265/HEVC [26] bitstream (or H.265/SHVC [25] or H.265/MV-HEVC [25]) that can be fed into a single hardware decoder. The novel method processes the video bitstreams of the different tiles in the compressed domain, by performing a simple manipulation of some information in the header. This simple manipulation is key component for the system scalability. The proposed solution consist of merging coded video bitstreams into a common output bitstream by re-writing some high-level syntax of the bitstreams and inserting some potentially pre-encoded, inter-predicted pictures. This process is of a very low-complexity, which allows doing it either in the network with no scalability issue or at the clients prior to the decoding process. It simply requires that an application is available before the decoding to perform the described process. In any case, the presence of an application is required to take care of the streaming of the video and to serve as an interface to the display. An example of such applications is a DASH player written for a browser. With this respect, the described technique can be implemented at the file parsing level and has been standardized in [14].

In addition, several aspects that allow for a more efficient encoding and transmission of the data are discussed within this paper. One of the aspects proposed within the paper focuses on avoiding or reducing peak bitrates at RoI switch events, which are detrimental for low-latency services such as panorama streaming. This is achieved by reducing the Random Access Points (RAPs) of the bitstreams. Reducing the number of RAPs has the clear benefit of reducing the overall bitrate of the bitstreams and the peak rates. However, there is always a trade-off between the coding efficiency and the availability to random access a stream when seeking or tuning-in when the services are broadcasted. This paper describes how the proposed technique enables usage of open GOP structures, which provide a higher coding efficiency than closed GOP structures, while maintaining seamless playback of the content during RoI switch events.

The remainder of this paper is organized as follows. Section 2 gives an overview of related work in the field. Section 3 describes the system considered for tile-based panoramic streaming. In section 4, the general concept of compressed domain bitstream processing is explained. Section 5 to Section 7 explain the techniques in detail and report on the experiments and results. Finally, the conclusion is shown in section 8.

2 RELATED WORK

As aforementioned, research has been carried out during past years on panorama streaming. In [4, 5], authors describe a real-time system for panoramic video that allows for zooming and panning. They present the whole transmission chain from panorama video generation to the interactive view presentation. For the (potentially zoomed) video, a pin-hole camera model is used to project the per-user camera view to a cylindrical panorama video.

Since it allows for not sending the whole panoramic video at high-resolution and it solves the scalability issue as mentioned above, tile-based streaming has drawn the attention of many researchers. When tile-based streaming is used, two factors have to be taken into account. On the one side, splitting the high-resolution content into different tiles leads to a reduction of the prediction efficiency, since a smaller part of the video can be used as reference for each of the tiles. On the other side, it allows for a better fit of the RoI. Clearly, the smaller the tiles the smaller is the amount of unnecessary pixels (pixel overhead) that are transmitted but also the lower is the compression efficiency of the transmitted pixels. On the contrary, spatially large tiles increase compression efficiency but also lead to the transmission of higher amount of additional data that is not part of the RoI, i.e. higher pixel overhead. The pixel overhead issue is illustrated in Figure 2. Note that borders of the regions/tiles do not necessarily coincide with the RoI borders and therefore some extraneous data (not RoI) might be transmitted, depicted in blue in the figure. For a deeper insight on how to dimension tiles in an optimum way, the reader is referred to [13, 15], where authors present an optimization of the dimension of the tiles in which the panorama video is split.

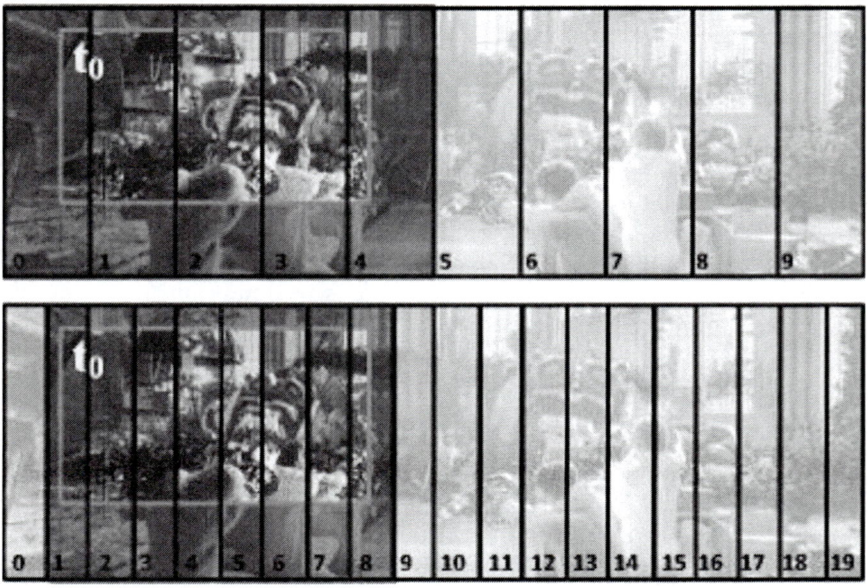

Figure 2. Finer (*bottom*) and coarser (*top*) tiling and impact on pixel overhead

When multiple decoders are used in parallel and several tiles are presented simultaneously together with a thumbnail of the panorama video at lower resolution, it might become an implementation drawback to synchronize the different videos. With this regard, authors in [9] propose to use H.264/MVC to have multiple parts (encoded into layers) of the video. Layers are encoded without coding dependency and are properly synchronized. One of the layers corresponds to the navigation video (video thumbnail). The rest of the layers (with a given view_id) correspond to the different tiles of the high-resolution panorama video offered at different bitrates. Thus, the users can select a set of view_ids that correspond to a given RoI at a given bitrate that matches the available throughput.

Similarly, some approaches that use some hierarchical prediction of a thumbnail view have been pursued in the past, see [13]. The authors use a similar procedure as H.264/SVC. However, in their solution, enhancement layers do not use temporal prediction but only inter-layer prediction. However, since H.264/SVC is not used, only proprietary software decoding can be used.

In [21] a system using multi-resolution panorama streaming is described. The main idea is to encode the panorama video into tiles and at different resolutions. Then the client downloads one or another resolution depending on the zoom factor. Based on the user interactivity, if the desired RoI is not available at the desired resolution, a lower resolution might be still obtained and is upscaled to the proper resolution for display. In [17], authors show the impact of using tiles in an interactive system that allows for panning and zooming in terms of overhead.

An alternative solution to tile-based streaming is described in [15], referred to as monolithic streaming. The idea is to encode videos as done conventionally, without splitting it into tiles. Then all macroblocks required for decoding a RoI are transmitted to the user. In order to do so, a dependency map has to be built for each RoI. This dependency map, determines all macroblocks required for decoding a given RoI. It follows the dependencies of each macroblock that corresponds to a given RoI. Additionally, the encoding process can be constrained in such a way that the dependency maps can be built with a reduced complexity. Note that if the encoder is not constraint, a full search needs to be performed to find all macroblocks of previous frames that a given RoI depends on. However, although the transmission bandwidth savings are similar to the tile-based approach, this approach has two main drawbacks. First, it has a higher complexity than the tile-based approach. But more important is the fact that the subset of macroblocks transmitted cannot be decoded by a standard-conform decoder, since they do not form a rectangular representation and therefore they do not form a valid bitstream.

There has been further work on tile-based streaming (e.g. [16]) that in contrast to [13] consider overlapping tiles. While in [13] all tiles are non-overlapping, in [16] tiles might have some overlapping content. The focus of such works lay on how to optimize the video transmission, for instance, by multicasting some of the tiles while transmitting others via unicast connections. However, we focus only on non-overlapping tiles, since our objective is to generate a single bitstream in the compress domain that contains the RoI of each user, which is not feasible with overlapping tiles.

3 STREAMING SYSTEM OVERVIEW

The solution described within this paper consists of a low-complexity video processing technique that generates a single bitstream out of multiple independently encoded tiles. Besides, a key contribution of this paper is the way the content is generated so that the content is encoded efficiently. With this respect, the target of the proposed technique is to reduce the peak-bitrate during switching events, and to be able to use open GOP structures. The technique entails stitching the videos of the tiles belonging to the RoI and the insertion of Generated Reference Pictures (GRP), Multiview Generated Reference Pictures (MGRP) or Multi-Layer Generated Reference Pictures (ML-GRP) as described in sections 5, 6 and 7 respectively.

Figure 3 provides an overview of the considered system, which consists of an encoder array located at server side, a single video decoder instance at the client side and an Interactive Bitstream Stitching (IBS) device. The figure shows the case, where stereoscopic content is considered. After synchronous tiling of the two views of the panoramic video, individual H.265/MV-HEVC compliant Multiview video encoders create video bitstreams from every pair of two corresponding left and right view tiles. The user RoI, as illustrated with a blue rectangle, determines which pairs of tiles a user requires, e.g. the dashed tiles 0 to 3 in Figure 3. The corresponding bitstreams are processed by the IBS device to form a single bitstream that can be decoded on the end device by a single MV-HEVC decoder instance.

Note that the mentioned H.265/MV-HEVC encoder array can be replaced by H.265/HEVC or H.265/SHVC depending on the use case considered, as seen later. Note also that the physical location of the IBS in the system can be either on server side, client side or within the network, if the bitstreams are unencrypted and therefore accessible for modification. As the processing steps are of low complexity, usage of cloud infrastructure should scale well. Even low-end client devices would be able to handle the operation alongside decoding.

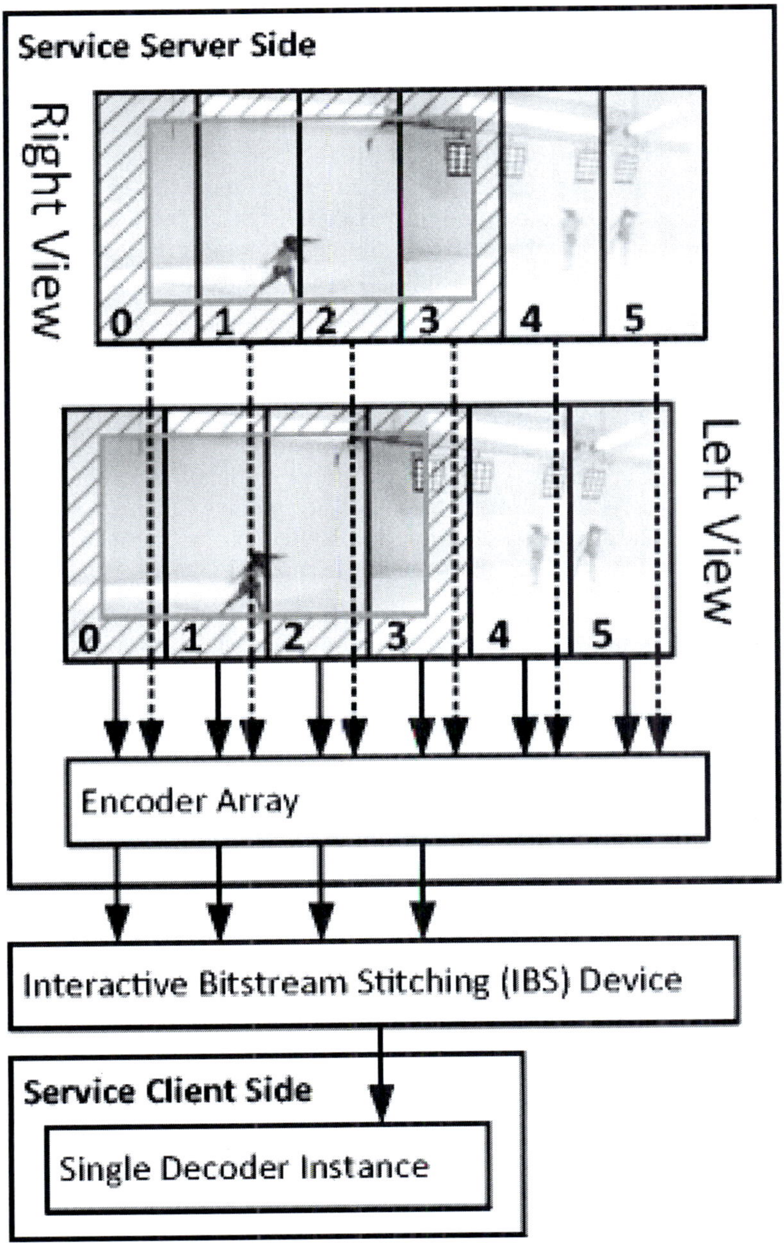

Figure 3. System overview

4 COMPRESSED DOMAIN VIDEO PROCESSING OVERVIEW

The proposed compressed domain video processing technique, IBS, is based on the stitching process described in [18] used to generate a single bitstream. Each of the independently encoded spatial regions belonging to the RoI is converted into an HEVC tile of a common bitstream. For this purpose, only adjustments to high-level syntax are required, which are lightweight to carry out.

First, the parameter sets need to be rewritten, mainly to reflect the spatial picture dimensions, level and tile setup of the RoI bitstream. Second, adjustments on slice level are necessary, e.g. slice addresses in the slice headers of the merged bitstream, which identify the HEVC tile that a slice belongs to. Each tile corresponds to the position of the independently encoded tiles within the merged RoI picture plane. Slice delta Quantization Parameters (QPs) might also need adjustment to reflect the common initial QP value as signaled in the rewritten parameter set.

Additionally, in order to be able to stitch the different bitstreams in the compressed domain, it is a requirement that the original videos are encoded according to a set of constraints:

- Motion vectors (MVs) cannot require samples that lie outside picture boundaries for temporal prediction.
- The rightmost Prediction Units (PU) cannot use the MV prediction candidate that corresponds to the Temporal MV Prediction (TMVP) candidate if it exists or that would correspond to the TMVP candidate if it existed.
- In-loop filters across slices and tiles have to be disabled.

The coding efficiency loss of these constraints was reported to be around 1 % [22] when applied to a single picture border and 3 % for all picture borders [18]. For more information the reader is referred to [18].

The technique described in [18] requires some extensions in order to be used for H.265/SHVC and H.265/MV-HEVC. In case of H.265/MV-HEVC it is a straightforward extension where MVs are constraint so that no sample that lies outside picture boundaries are used for inter-layer prediction. For H.265/SHVC this is not an issue since the MVs for inter-layer prediction are constrained to be equal to zero. However, in case of H.265/SHVC with spatial scalability, when inter-layer sample prediction is performed and the described technique is applied, the resampling process could use samples from multiple tiles. Therefore, the second constraint has to be rewritten as follows:

- The rightmost Prediction Units (PU) cannot use the MV prediction candidate that corresponds to the Temporal MV Prediction (TMVP) candidate if it exists or that would correspond to the TMVP candidate if it existed. Furthermore, the rightmost PU cannot use inter-layer prediction to a lower layer that is resampled.

An advantage of using H.265/SHVC is that users can download a larger region at the base than at the enhancement layer. The additional base layer data can be prefetched and presented when a RoI change event occurs and the higher layer data is not available. Prefetching only the lower layers reduces the downloading throughput while enabling the data to be presented at a slightly lower quality. The described approach with a different number of tiles in an H.265/SHVC stream with two layers is illustrated in Figure 4.

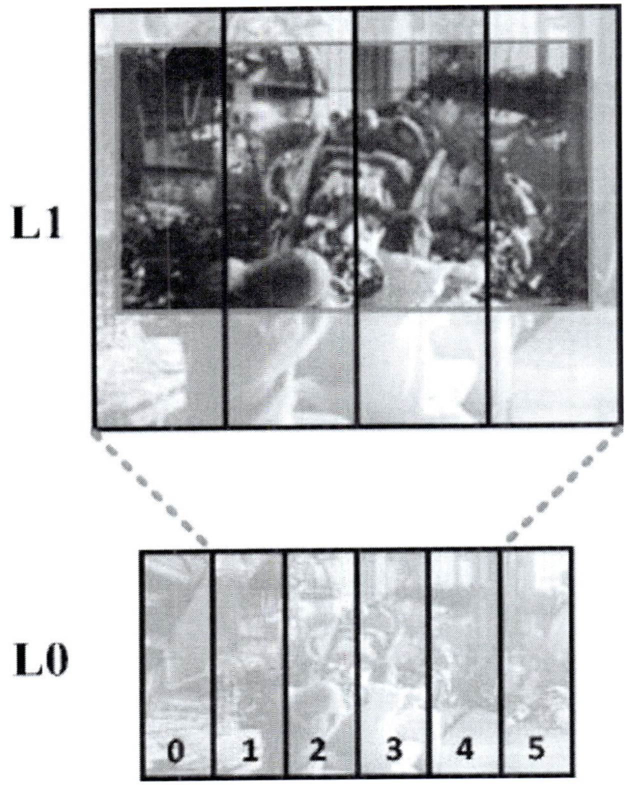

Figure 4. Tile setup for 2 layers n H.265/SHVC with a larger amount of tiles in L0

If a larger area is downloaded at the base layer, it is important that the IBS process adjusts signaling to indicate the area, which the enhancement layer uses as prediction. This is done by including the region reference offsets in the PPS.

The following sections describe the presented techniques in detail: namely GRP [19], ML-GRP [20] or MGRP [23]. The work in [19, 20, 23], has been extended by additional simulation results, i.e. a higher number of sequences have been tested. Besides, the work has been extended by combining GRPs with open GOP structures (see Section 5.1) and by extending the usage of ML-GRP for a full non-tiled base layer with unequal RAPs periods (see Section 7).

5 GENERATED REFERENCE PICTURES (GRP)

The technique presented hereafter aims to reduce the transmission bitrate during RoI switch events and was first introduced in [19]. The main idea behind it is to insert some pictures into the bitstream that are not output and perform a content displacement of reference pictures at occurrences of RoI switch events. Thus, temporal prediction can still be used for some parts of the video from the RoI switch event onwards.

Figure 5 illustrates a RoI switching event. Time instant t_1 represents the switching point at which the presented RoI changes compared to t_0. It can be seen that the position of the received spatial regions at the receiver screen (RoI view) changes over time (see dashed tiles 3 and 4 within the blue rectangles representing the RoI at different time instants).

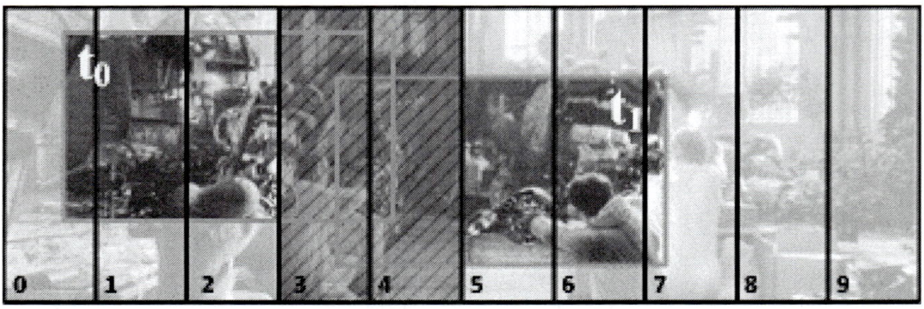

Figure 5. Overlap of RoIs before user interaction (t0) and after (t1)

Obviously, new spatial regions (see non-shaded tiles with index 5 to 7 in Figure 5) require random access, since they were not present in the RoI view previously. However, the set of tiles that remains displayed albeit displacement (tiles 3 and 4) would benefit from using temporal prediction. Since their position changes in the stitched picture based on the user movement, temporal prediction cannot be used in a straightforward manner. Figure 6 illustrates the effect of using temporal prediction for the stitched picture at time t_1 for a RoI switch event as depicted in Figure 5. The figure shows spatial regions using random access depicted with an I (I slices) while spatial regions using temporal prediction are depicted with a P (P slices in this example). The MV for a block at the encoder side is shown at the top of the figure for the tile with index 3. The bottom part of the figure shows that after the stitching process, the block of the tile with index 3 uses a wrong reference at the decoder side, due to the change of the position of tile 3 within the stitched picture.

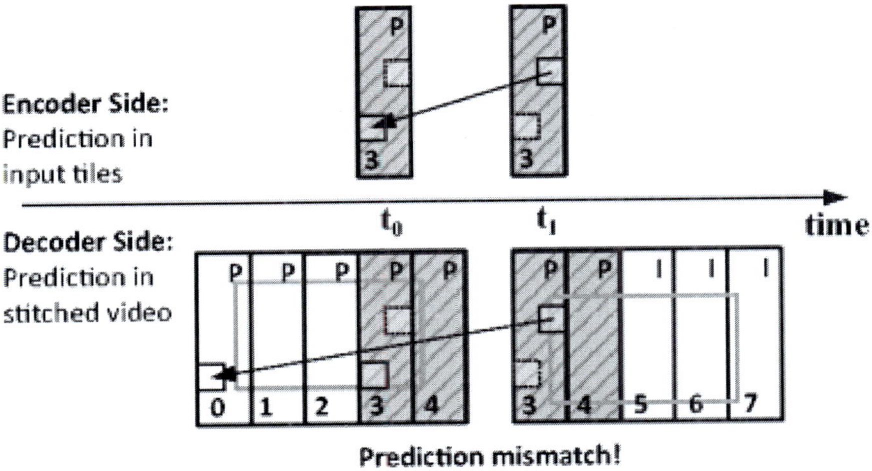

Figure 6. Prediction mismatch after IBS without GRP

In order to avoid random access for all spatial regions, which would lead to large transmission bitrate peaks at switching points, we propose to insert Generated Reference Pictures (GRP): one per reference picture at the Decoded Picture Buffer (DPB). A GRP is a picture that performs a displacement of the content of a regular reference picture and substitutes it so that following pictures (from the RoI switching point onwards) can use temporal prediction.

Figure 7 shows how the block in tile 3 at t_1 uses the block in the GRP that has the same content as the block from t_0 (belonging to tile 3 as well) that is used at the encoder side. For more information on how to generate a GRP the reader is referred to [19].

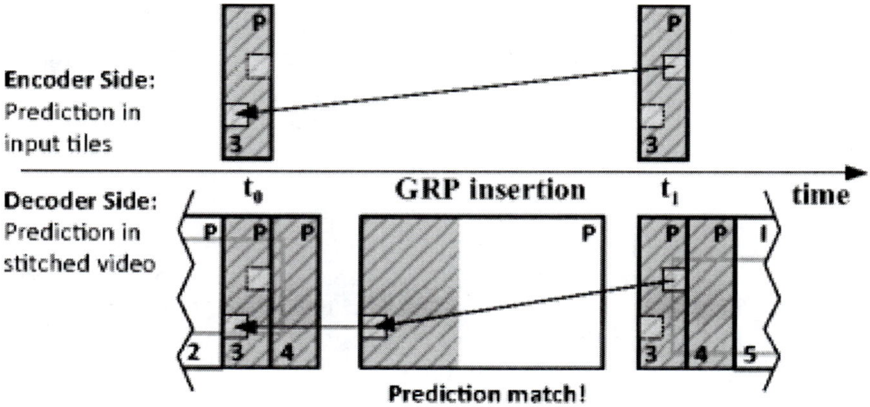

Figure 7. Prediction match after IBS with GRP

In order to avoid any decoding drift, in addition to the constraints listed in Section 4, the original bitstreams have to fulfill the following constraint:

- Temporal Motion Vector Prediction (TMVP) has to be restricted so that no pictures that may be reference-wise substituted by GRPs are used for TMVP.

Motion Vector (MV) prediction in H.265/HEVC [11] is performed from neighbor or temporal MV candidates. The latter (TMVP candidate) refers to the right-bottom collocated block in a reference picture. If the reference picture substituted by a GRP were used for TMVP, the TMVP predictors derived after GRP insertion would be wrong. Note that the derived TMVP predictor would belong to the GRP instead of to the substituted reference picture. Therefore, the constraint above must be fulfilled. An effective way to achieve it is to define switching points, at which the reference pictures at the Decoded Picture Buffer (DPB) are never selected for TVMP.

Figure 8 shows a typical hierarchical Group Of Pictures (GOP) structure of 4 pictures and three temporal levels (TL0, TL1 and TL2). The solid arrows in the figure represent the sample prediction and the dashed arrows represent the dependencies for MV prediction when TMVP is used. It can be seen that no TL0 picture is used for TVMP. Therefore, pictures from TL0 can be defined as switching points and can be used for RoI switching and GRP insertion.

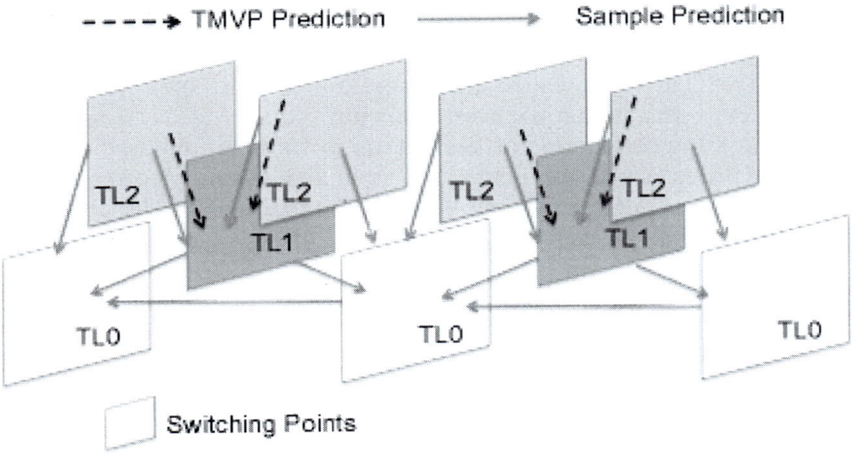

Figure 8. Example of TMVP restriction

In [19], GRPs were used so that only Random Access Points (RAPs) were only inserted for tiles that correspond to areas of the panoramic video that are new when a RoI switch event occurs. A drawback of the proposed solution is that for each potential RAP offered to the clients a new version of the content needs to be encoded and made available at the server. This is not practical in a real scenario. In a practical scenario, it is necessary to set Random Access Points (RAPs) with a given granularity. In the following subsection it is discussed how the solution in [19] can be extended to enhance the coding efficiency of streams using frequent RAPs.

5.1 Open GOP RoI switching with GRP

As aforementioned, only having RAPs at switching events would require encoding a separate stream per potential switching point, which would not be feasible. A solution is to offer a limited number of bitstreams with a given RAP interval, e.g. 5 seconds, and offer at each of alternative bitstreams RAPs at different positions. Thus, when required RAPs for new tiles could be obtained by switching from one of the alternative bitstreams to another where an RAP is available. I.e., RoI switching can be performed at a finer granularity than the RAP interval at the price of having multiple alternatives offered at the server side.

In H.265/HEVC, there are two possibilities to encode RAPs. The first one is to use Instantaneous Decoding Refresh (IDRs) as RAPs, which correspond to closed GOP structures. It means that any picture following a RAP (in decoding order) does not use any picture preceding the RAP (in decoding order) as a reference (see Random Access Decodable Leading – RASL – pictures in the figure). The second one is to use Clean Random Access (CRAs) as RAPs, which correspond to open GOP structures. Open GOP structures mean that pictures, following a RAP in decoding order, but preceding it in presentation order, can use pictures preceding the RAP in decoding order as reference (see prediction arrows and pictures marked as Random Access Skip Leading – RASL - in the figure). The prediction structure of both approaches is illustrated in Figure 9, for a GOP of size 4.

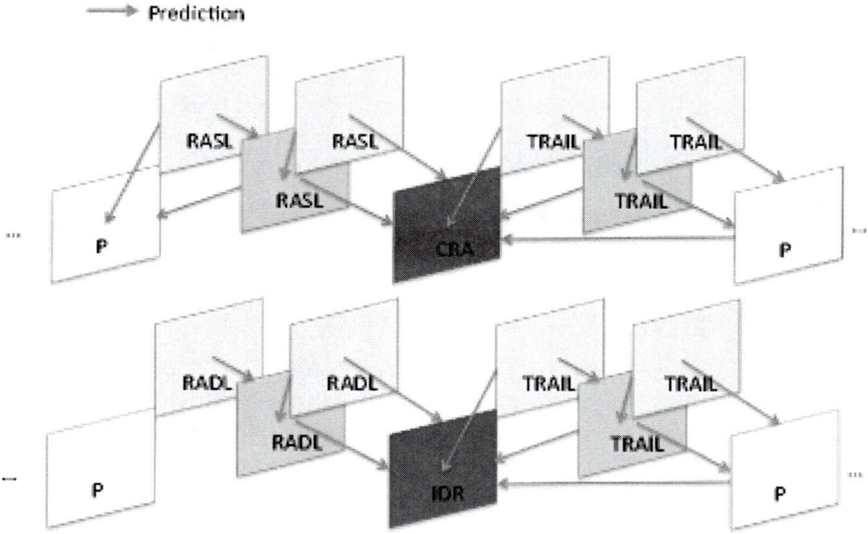

Figure 9. Closed GOP (*bottom*) and Open GOP (*top*) structures in H.265/HEVC

It is well known that using open GOP structures with CRAs provide a better compression efficiency (around 5 % as reported in [3]). During the Random Access procedure using CRAs, some pictures, namely the RASL pictures in Figure 9, must be discarded from output, since they require a previous picture (leftmost picture in the figure) that is not available at Random Access procedure. This is not an issue with traditional video services where skipping whole video pictures is only done when tuning-in into a service. However, it is a problem in context of tiled panoramic streaming, where switching from a RoI to another is considered. Such a switch must happen seamlessly without any interruption, i.e. without pictures being discarded or parts thereof corrupted.

If a Random Access procedure were started using CRAs for a newly encompassed tile of the new RoI, some pictures corresponding to that tile would not be able to be presented and would have to be discarded. This would prevent a seamless playout and thus open GOP structures. Therefore, it is necessary to use only closed GOP structures (i.e. IDRs) with the corresponding lower compression efficiency for the newly encompassed tiles. However, for the set of tiles that remains displayed in the RoI albeit displacement, the same issue as described above occurs. In a similar manner as described previously, GRPs can be used so that RASL pictures that use CRAs can reference the correct region when a RoI switch occurs, thus allowing for open GOP structures.

5.2 Experiments with GRP

In the following, the experiments and results for the proposed techniques using GRPs are described. Four panorama videos (captured with [28]) have been used for the GRP experiments. Two panorama videos have a resolution of 8192x1600 pixels and the other two have a resolution of 6912x1920. All of them consist of 1425 frames at 25fps. All sequences correspond to fixed cameras. The first 2 sequences have low-motion content where several people play different instruments but stay at the same position for the whole sequence. The last 2 sequences have higher-motion with people dancing and moving around the stage, among which the first one (referred to as 3rd video in the results) has the highest motion. The HEVC reference software HM-14 was modified to include the constraints described before. The default random access configuration has been used with a GOP size of 4 and a single RAP at the beginning. The GOP size of 4, which corresponds to a 160 ms reordering delay at the decoding, has been chosen exemplarily. A higher GOP size could have been chosen in order to achieve a higher efficiency but this would increase the reordering delay, as well as the download time of GOPs due to its larger size. Although, it has not been analyzed in this work, a larger GOP size would require downloading a larger amount of non-displayed pixels to compensate for the higher end-to-end latency. In the end the selected GOP size is a compromise about encoding efficiency and additional data that needs to be downloaded (prefetch). Two tiling variants have been used to analyze the impact of a finer or coarser tiling process. The videos have been tiled only vertically, to limit parameter space, into spatial regions of 512 pixels width and spatial regions of 256 pixels width. These sizes have been exemplarily selected. The reader is referred to [13, 15] if interested in how to perform optimization of the tile sizes.

For the GRP experiment, the peak bitrate reduction during RoI switch events has been measured using the following metrics:

- B_w is the bitrate of the whole RoI sequence.

- B_r is the bitrate within the RoI change interval, time during which the user carries out the RoI movement.
- B_s is the bitrate of GOPs within the RoI change interval in which the tile setup changes.
- B_n is the bitrate of the remaining GOPs within the RoI change interval for which the tile setup does not change in comparison to the previous GOP.

B_s and B_n, are of a high relevance since they describe the bitrate variability during RoI switching intervals. The motivation of such an analysis is of special interest when considering HTTP streaming techniques such MPEG-DASH [24]. In MPEG-DASH based streaming, media segments are transmitted. The larger the media segments the higher the end-to-end latency. In order to reduce the latency to the minimum the smallest possible segment would be selected and this is a single GOP. GOPs could be mapped to video segments, without requiring an IDR picture at segment start allowing individual transmission and thus reduction of the end-to-end latency of the video transmission. The bitrate peaks of interests are the ones that correspond to the downloaded chunks of data, i.e. the response to each of the requests that correspond to a GOP. In fact, it is crucial to minimize peak bitrates, since the downloaded quality selected by the client would follow the worst-case, which correspond to the biggest segments.

For these two cases, a simple interactivity model has been simulated. It is based on patterns with limited interactivity but sufficient to prove the validity of the proposed techniques. In fact, the proposed technique aims at reducing the RAPs within the session due to RoI interaction. Other movement patterns would lead to different regions requiring RAPs. However, the factor that plays the most important role is the speed with which the user navigates around the panorama video. Therefore, two client screen movement patterns with different movement speeds have been considered. Both consist of a movement towards the right picture border: a constant movement at high or low speed for a given time interval of 1.2 seconds, referred to as switching interval in the experiments. These patterns were selected to be easily parameterizable. They correspond to a complete RoI change within 1.2s for the fast movement, since the considered client screen is 1080p. The slow movement pattern, on the other hand, results in a change of half of the RoI within the switching interval.

Figure 10 illustrates, for each tile dimension and movement speed, the frequency of switching point GOPs, i.e. GOPs where the tile setup changes and either full random access (IDRs) or GRP are used.

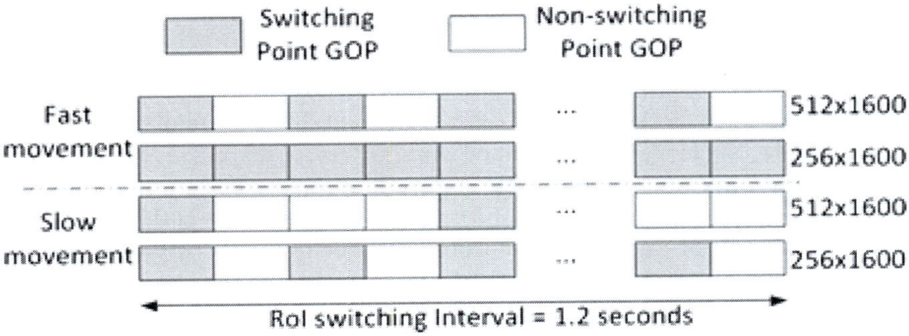

Figure 10. Switching point GOP distribution

RoI switching has been performed at different times in the bitstream, every 248 frames and the average bitrates have been computed and are presented in subsection 5.3. For this purpose, several streams have been encoded. As aforementioned each of these streams is encoded with a single IDR at the beginning and no more RAPs within the stream. For tiles of width 256, the panorama videos have been encoded starting at frame number $240 + 4\,i + 248\,j$, where $0 \leq i \leq 8$ and $0 \leq j \leq 4$, until the end of the sequences. For the wider tiles, the starting frame corresponds to $240 + 8\,i + 248\,j$, where $0 \leq i \leq 5$ and $0 \leq j \leq 4$. With this encoding, the switching point GOP distribution in Figure 10 can be achieved.

5.3 Results for GRPs

Figures 11 and 14 summarize the performance of GRPs as shown in [19]. They show the average transmission overhead during RoI switching intervals of 1.2 s of the full random access (RA) solution compared to usage of GRPs. The test sequences have been encoded with QP 22 and 32 to show the impact of the QP on the results.

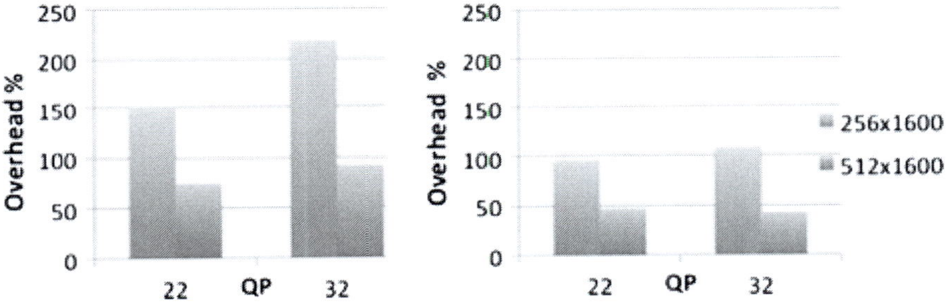

Figure 11. Transmission overhead RA vs. GRP for fast movement (*left*) and slow movement (*right*) for 1st video

Figure 11 shows the average overhead for a fast and slow screen movement on the left and right plot respectively. It shows that the faster the screen movement is or the higher the QP is, the higher is the overhead of RA compared to the usage of GRPs. Additionally, the smaller the spatial regions are, the larger is the gain of using GRPs, which is reasonable as the number of switching point GOPs is higher (see Figure 11). In general, it can be seen that a transmission bitrate of around a 100–200 % higher for 256x1600 spatial regions or 50–100 % higher for 512x1600 regions can be expected if RA is used instead of GRPs.

Similar conclusions can be drawn from the results of the other three videos shown from Figs. 12, 13 and 14 with respect to the influence of the tile sizes and speed of the movement.

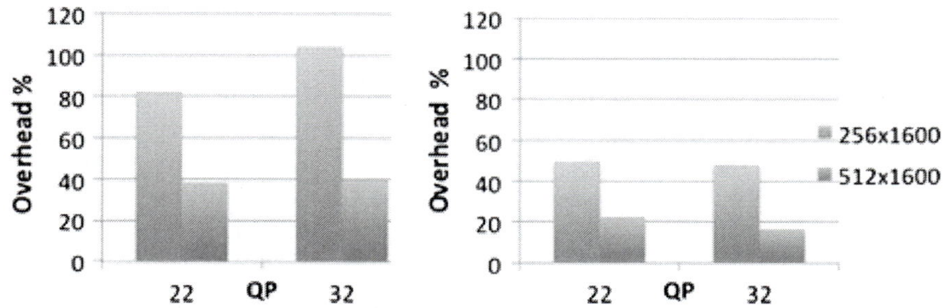

Figure 12. Transmission overhead RA vs. GRP for fast movement (*left*) and slow movement (*right*) for 2nd video

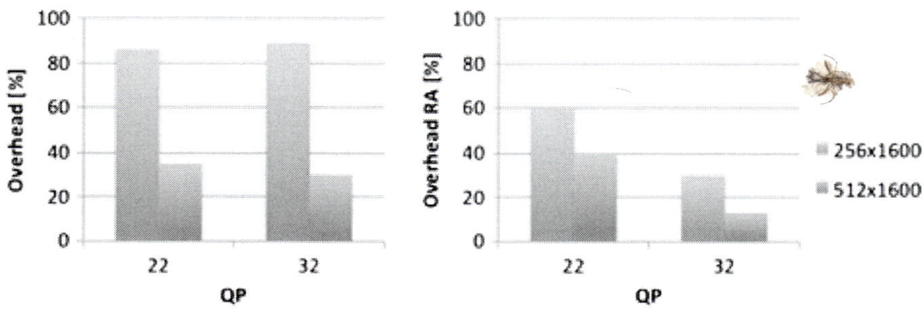

Figure 13. Transmission overhead RA vs. GRP for fast movement (*left*) and slow movement (*right*) for 3rd video

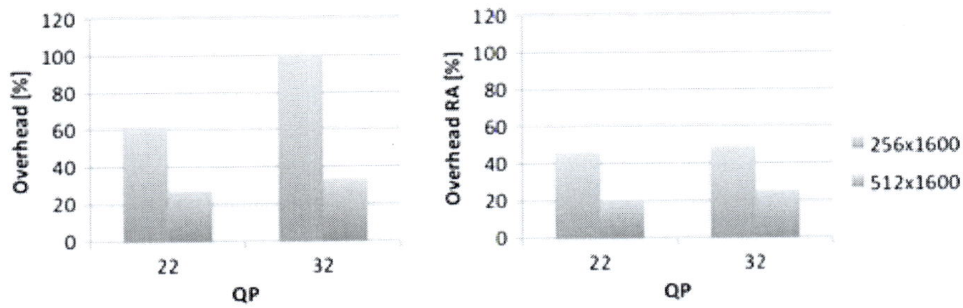

Figure 14. Transmission overhead RA vs. GRP for fast movement (*left*) and slow movement (*right*) for 4th video

However, as shown in figure, the overhead is slightly smaller: 50–100 % for 256 pixels width spatial regions and 20–60 % for 512 pixels width regions. In any case, the gains provided by GRP are significant.

Table 1 shows the standard deviation of the Br overheads shown in Figure 11, 12, 13 and 14. In general, it can be seen that the reported values are small, which means that the variability of Br overhead is not so high and the reported values in previous figures are of high reliability.

Table 1. Standard deviation for Br overhead of the 4 videos

Table 1 Standard deviation for Br overhead of the 4 videos

Movement speed	Tile width	Video 1		Video 2		Video 3		Video 4	
		QP22	QP32	QP22	QP32	QP22	QP32	QP22	QP32
Fast	256	.09	.06	.21	.27	.39	.41	.09	.22
	512	.03	.03	.09	.09	.16	.14	.04	.08
Slow	256	.15	.04	.24	.20	.32	.17	.06	.09
	512	.06	.04	.11	.06	.15	.07	.04	.09

In order to analyze this issue in more detail, we focus on the absolute values of the transmitted bitrate, taking only the values for the second video and large tiles for brevity. Table 2 shows the average bitrates over the whole sequence B_w, over RoI switching interval B_r, over the switching point GOPs B_s and over the non-switching point GOPs B_n. It can be seen that most of highest bitrate values correspond to the switching point GOPs, for which the gain of GRP is even higher than the values discussed before.

Table 2. Comparison of average bitrates (Mbps) for the 2nd video

	QP =32				QP = 22			
	B_w	B_r	B_s	B_n	B_w	B_r	B_s	B_n
RA	1.3	2.3	3.4	1.2	6.0	10.6	13.8	7.3
GRP	1.2	1.3	1.5	1.0	5.3	5.8	6.5	5.1

Due to the lack of space the numbers for the other cases are not presented. However, very similar values have been obtained. In the case of slow movement, the transmission bitrate for the switching interval is slightly lower but still very similar values have been obtained for switching point GOPs. Overall, a reduction from around 1.9 up to 7.3 Mbps at the switching point GOPs was achieved for the studied sequences and QPs.

6 MULTIVIEW GENERATED REFERENCE PICTURE (MGRP)

Multiview Generated Reference Pictures (MGRPs) are a straightforward extension of GRPs for stereo video and were presented first in [23]. The only extension that needs to be mentioned in comparison to the GRP is that the Temporal Motion Vector Prediction (TMVP) restriction aforementioned can be relaxed if used for an inter-layer predicted picture. In other words, for the switching points previously defined (TL0 pictures) which are not used for TVMP candidates, this restriction only applies when temporal prediction is considered. For higher layers, a TL0 picture can use the TL0 picture from a lower layer for TMVP. This is due to the fact that replacement of that picture happens after decoding the given whole Access Unit and therefore is not affected by MGRPs. As described in Section 5.1, open GOP switching is facilitated through MGRP likewise.

6.1 Experiments for MGRP

Experiments for MGRP follow the setup of experiments in section 5.2 in spirit. However, a single stereoscopic video sequence has been used with a resolution of 5760 × 1664 pixels. The sequence consists of 1000 frames at 30fps. For this case, the video has been tiled into spatial regions of 640x1664 pixels and spatial regions of 320x1664 pixels and a GOP size of 8 has been chosen exemplarily, which corresponds to a 267 ms reordering delay at the decoding. This parameter selection corresponds to the common test conditions used by JCT-VC during standardization. Correspondingly, these parameters result in a complete RoI change in 1.6 s for the considered fast movement pattern. Therefore, the switching interval in this experiment is slightly larger compared to the experiment for GRP. RoI switching has been performed at different times in the bitstream, every 152 frames and the results are averaged over these instances. Similar to the experiments in Section 5.2, the test sequence has been encoded with QP 22 and 32 to show the impact of the QP on the results. As for the experiments in Section 5.2, several streams have been encoded. For tiles of width 320, the panorama video has been encoded starting at frame number $120 + 8i + 152j$, where $0 \leq i \leq 8$ and $0 \leq j \leq 5$. For 640 pixels width tiles, the starting frame corresponds to $120 + 16i + 152j$, where $0 \leq i \leq 5$ and $0 \leq j \leq 5$.

6.2 Results for MGRPs

This section summarizes the performance of MGRP as shown in [23]. Table 3 below provides the four bitrates B_w, B_r, B_s and B_n in kbps at QP 22. Results are summarized for both views, i.e. independent layer L0 and dependent layer L1. It can be seen that in particular the critical peak bitrates within the RoI change interval are considerably reduced using the proposed MGRP technique, which is sensible keeping in mind that much of the unnecessary intra-coded data is omitted from the bitstream.

Table 3. Summary of bitrates in Mbps for QP 22

RoI change with	Movement speed	Tile width	B_w	B_r	B_s	B_n
IDR	Fast	320	2.45	4.73	4.73	0[a]
MGRP			2.39	2.87	2.87	0[a]
IDR		640	2.36	3.61	4.56	2.65
MGRP			2.32	2.80	3.10	2.5
IDR	Slow	320	2.52	3.83	4.91	2.75
MGRP			2.47	2.75	2.94	2.55
IDR		640	2.39	3.27	4.68	2.57
MGRP			2.36	2.69	3.17	2.46

[a] The RoI change interval in this particular case contains only GOPs in which RoI change events occur

Figure 15 visualizes the overhead (in percent) of the IDR-based RoI change with respect to the proposed MGRP solution, showing B_r on the left and B_s on the right. It can be seen that by not using MGRPs, around 60

% or 20 % more bits needs to be transmitted during the RoI switching interval for the fast movement for the finer and coarser tiles respectively. For the slow movement, a 40 % higher bitrate needs to be transmitted for the coarser tiling approach. It can be seen that the faster the movement the more effective is the MGRP approach in terms of saved bitrate. However, if we focus on the peak bitrate values, it can be seen how the gain obtained by the proposed approach does not depend so much on the moving speed. The overhead of using IDRs instead of MGRPs based on the bitrate of the switching GOPs (B_r) is around 60 and 40 % for finer and coarser tiles respectively, irrespective of the moving speed.

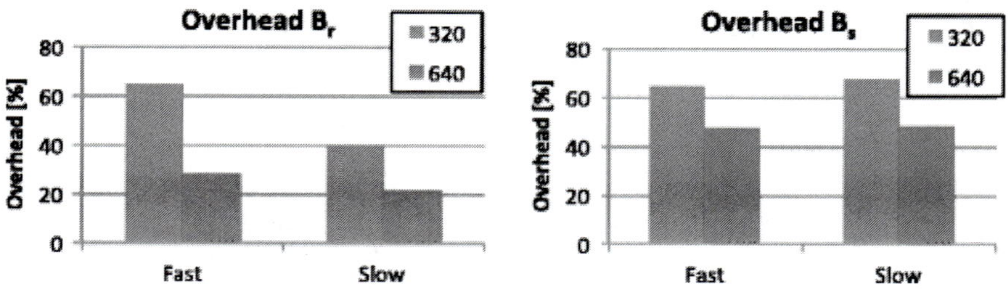

Figure 15. IDR bitrate overhead in B_r and B_s for QP 22

Analogously, bitrate results for QP32 are reported in Table 4. Overall, the effect of MGRP at such low bitrate is even more pronounced in the relevant bitrates B_r and B_s, while B_n for example does not exhibit significant impact. As seen in Figure 16, the relative overhead of IDR based RoI changing is even more significant at low quality.

Table 4. Summary of bitrates in Mbps for QP 32

RoI change with	Movement speed	Tile width	B_w	B_r	B_s	B_n
IDR	Fast	320	.484	1.12	1.12	0[a]
MGRP			.456	.574	.574	0[1]
IDR		640	.414	.726	1.02	.434
MGRP			.404	.523	.609	.437
IDR	Slow	320	.488	.825	1.17	.480
MGRP			.473	.542	.599	.485
IDR		640	.423	.639	1.06	.428
MGRP			.415	.498	.632	.431

[a] The RoI change interval in this particular case contains only GOPs in which RoI change events occur

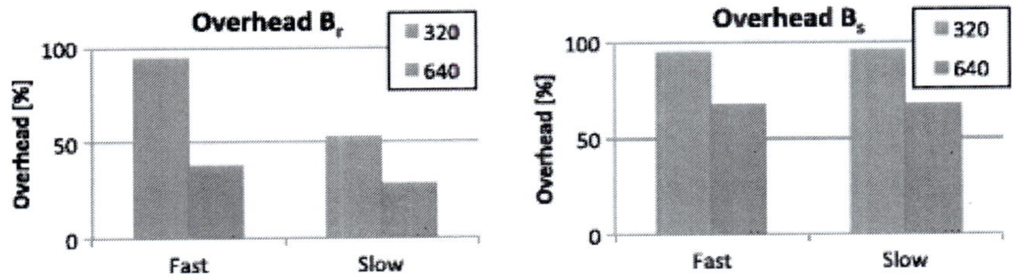

Figure 16. IDR bitrate overhead in B_r and B_s for QP 32

Overall it can be seen that a denser tile grid, i.e. small tiles, benefits more from use the MGRP technique as they implicate more frequent RoI change event that introduce intra-coded pictures without MGRP. The overhead in B_r increases with the movement speed as more RoI change events occur while the overhead in B_s itself, i.e. during RoI change events, is mostly independent of the movement speed.

Table 5 shows the standard deviation of the overhead of Br when comparing the solution using IDRs with the proposed MGRP. It can be seen that the values are low, which means that the average Br overhead shown in Figure 16 is of high reliability.

Table 5. Standard deviation for Br overhead

Movement speed	Tile width	QP22	QP32
Fast	320	.077	.140
	640	.045	.071
Slow	320	.071	.122
	640	.032	.063

Of interest for the present stereoscopic use case with MV-HEVC is particularly the distribution of bitrate between the two views or layers as well as the effect of MGRP on each layer. Results of the per-layer IDR overhead relative to MGRP are reported in Table 6. It can be seen that the benefits from MGRP in the independent view, i.e. layer L0, are quality, tile grid and speed dependent over the switching interval (B_r), as for the single layer case. While overhead in B_r is in some respect weighted by the distribution of RoI change events (or speed) as illustrated in Figure 10, it can be seen from the behavior of B_S, which omits this weighting, that the QP is the main determining factor for MGRP benefits on GOP level.

Table 6. IDR overhead percentage per layer

QP	Movement speed	Tile width	Overhead B_r	Overhead B_s		
			L0	L1	L0	L1
22	Fast	320	60.4	74.4	60.4	74.4
		640	27.4	32.0	44.5	53.0
	Slow	320	37.4	44.3	63.2	75.6
		640	20.6	23.7	45.7	53.0
32	Fast	320	105.0	74.2	105.0	74.2
		640	43.5	28.6	74.1	50.9
	Slow	320	57.4	41.6	105.0	74.5
		640	32.0	20.3	74.9	51.3

On the other hand, in the dependent view, i.e. layer L1, again focusing on B_S, the IDR overhead almost only depends on the tiling grid granularity and the benefits are independent of QP.

7 MULTI-LAYER GENERATED REFERENCE PICTURE (ML-GRP)

Although GRP and MGRP techniques described above are sufficient to allow for using open GOP structures and thus reduce the transmitted bitrate in interactive panoramic streaming scenarios, they have two limitations. First, it is necessary to encode and store at the server side two different versions of the content: one using open GOP structures and one using closed GOP structures. Second, the faster the movement, the less effective is the usage of GRPs and MGRPs. This is due to the fact that for fast movements, it is more probable that the RoI after a RoI switching event is a fully new RoI or a RoI with very few content present both before the switch event and after.

H.265/SHVC allows for an enhancement of the described technique that overcomes the aforementioned limitations, as explained below. Additionally, H.265/SHVC provides a good alternative for efficiently coping with fast RoI movements. Note, that it is very inefficient to offer the content encoded with very frequent RAPs. Therefore, RAPs are usually offered at a given granularity, e.g. every 1 second. For interactive panoramic streaming the RAP frequency might be higher (RAP interval lower than 1 second) but still not so frequent that at each picture a new tile can be random accessed. This implies that a user has to compensate the RAP granularity by downloading additional data that is not intended to be shown. This additional data acts as a backup in case respective user interaction shifts it into the RoI. This additional data downloaded only as backup can be offered in a lower resolution when using H.265/SHVC as shown in Figure 17, where tiles with index 1 to 4 (intended to be shown in the user RoI) are encoded at the highest resolution, i.e. at the higher layer, while tiles with index 0 and 5 are only included in the base layer in case they are required during a RoI switch event.

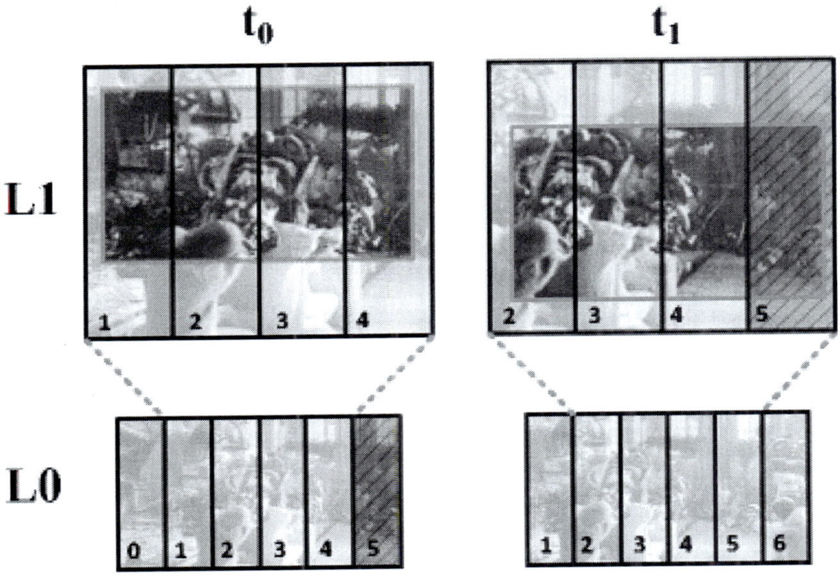

Figure 17. Tile setup during a RoI change to the right

The extension of GRPs described here and first proposed in [20], allows for using open GOP structures even for content that was not present at the highest resolution but present in the low-resolution layer. The proposed solution consists in inserting so-called Multi Layer Generated Reference Picture (ML-GRP). The main motivation is shown in Figure 17, where a RoI switch event is depicted. The RoI change represents a move to the right by an amount equal to the width of a tile. As can be seen in the figure, there is a tile that is new at the enhancement layer (see tile with index 5 marked in red), which has its corresponding base layer tile present in previous pictures in the stream.

Multi-Layer Generated Reference Pictures (ML-GRPs) aims at exploiting this fact and using that data available at the base layer so that open GOP switching at RoI switch events can be used at the enhancement layers. ML-GRPs consist of several tiles, which contain the GRP information, i.e. movement information to compensate the RoI change event. I.e., as for GRP, tiles that are presented before the RoI switch event and after need to the shifted. Besides, for newly encompassed tiles an ML-GRP contains a copy slice for those tiles that reference to a lower layer, which leads to inheritance of the sample values from the correct region of the lower layer. Since the reference layer is at a lower resolution, the process is not a simple sample copy but entails a resampling process as defined in H.265/SHVC. It requires indication of the scaled reference layer offsets and referenced region offsets defined in the PPS that indicate, which region of the base layer is to be upsampled. The resulting L1 ML-GRP picture area can then be used as reference by the RASL picture as illustrate in Figure 18. Depending on the quality of the ML-GRP used as reference by the RASL picture, no noticeable or only minor decoding drift may occur, despite significant coding efficiency gains.

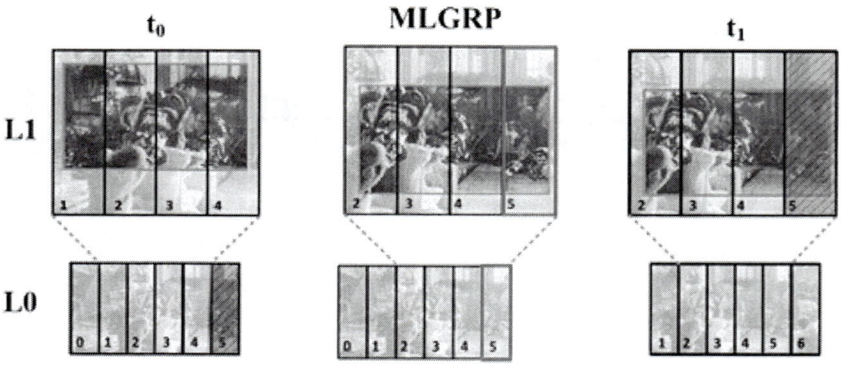

Figure 18. MLGRP with open GOP in tile-based panorama streaming

ML-GRP are inserted into the bitstream only at RoI change events and only for reference by following pictures, i.e. ML-GRP are not output by the decoder, as for the GRPs. For more information the reader is referred to [20].

An issue of the solution provided in [20] is that when the potential movement speed is very high the whole base layer will be needed and tiles at the base layer will add an unnecessary overhead. In this paper, the technique in [20] is extended so that only the enhancement layer is tiled and the whole base layer is always transmitted. In order to achieve a higher coding efficiency, it is combined with unequal RAP periods.

H.265/SHVC allows, besides having different types of RAPs at different layers as discussed above, having a different RAP periodicity. This is of especial interest when the base layer at low resolution contains the whole panoramic video. In fact, RAPs periodicity at the base layer can be of a much coarser granularity than at higher layers, since no random access to new regions is required, as the whole panoramic video is always present. Still, the RAPs at the enhancement layer needs to be frequent enough (as frequent as in previous cases) to allow for random access of new tiles at highest resolution.

The ML-GRP is extended to so that a non-tiled whole base layer is used in combination with unequal RAP periods. Thus, open GOP switching is available at the base layer and enhancement layer as well. In comparison to the ML-GRP technique presented in [20], the constraint that the rightmost PU cannot use inter-layer prediction to a lower layer that is resampled mentioned in Section 4 is removed. This leads to a better compression efficiency than for the ML-GRP encoding described in [20]. The results corresponding to this new feature are presented in Section 7.2.

7.1 Experiments for ML-GRPs

The experiments carried out for ML-GRPs are again similar in fashion to the experiments carried out for GRP. Particular differences in terms of parameters or test sequences are described hereafter. Results for this experiment are reported applying the Bjontegaard metric [1], aka. BD-rate.

In order to analyze the benefits of using ML-GRP, the same four sequences as in Section 5.2have been used. They have been encoded with a GOP size of 8 and at four different QPs: 22, 27, 32 and 37, which corresponds to the common test conditions using in standardization in JCT-VC. A single vertical tiling variant of 512 pixels width at the enhancement layer has been considered. The vertical resolution is 1600 for the first 2 videos and is 1920 for the last 2 videos. The sequences have been encoded with 2 layers and a layer configuration that corresponds to an upsampling factor of 2. The base layer in section 7.2 consists of tiles of 256x800 and 256x960 pixels respectively. For these experiments, the base layer covers a larger area than the enhancement layer. More concretely, there are 2 more tiles at the base layer than at the enhancement layer, as shown in Figure 17. If the RoI is not the leftmost or rightmost possible position, i.e. the RoI corresponds to the leftmost or rightmost position, the two additional tiles correspond to the side at which further tiles are available, i.e. right and left respectively. As in the previous experiments, these sizes have been exemplarily selected without optimization. In case of the results for section 7.3, the whole base layer is always present and, therefore, the whole base layer is encoded as a single tile.

A RoI of 1080p has been targeted, which means that the enhancement layer of the bitstream, produced by the IBS, is conformed by 4 tiles. Streams have been produced for RoIs at different positions. This leads to 13 bitstreams with a size of 2048x1600 pixels or 10 streams of 2048x1920 pixels. Bitstreams contain tiles (i, i + 1, i + 2 and i + 3) with i = 0...12 for the first two videos or with i = 0..9 for the last two videos.

7.2 Results for ML-GRPs

Although the quality of the Random Access Skip Leading (RASL) pictures when using the ML-GRPs has not been subjectively measured, our assessment by looking at the resulting videos is that the technique performs very good. In Figure 19, a small part of the first picture that belongs to a new tile after a RoI change event is shown for comparison. The left picture corresponds to the proposed method when the RASL picture uses ML-GRP as reference and the right picture shows the same are of the picture when closed GOP is used. That is, the figure on the left is a part of a picture using the ML-GRP as reference instead of its original reference picture (which is shown on the right).

Figure 19. Example of quality comparison of proposed method

It can be seen that the quality of the picture when the proposed method is used is slightly lower but still very good. This slightly lower quality is the result of using another reference that entails upsampling of part of the base layer for being used as reference. It can be argued that such a low quality degradation does not affect the streaming experience, especially because it only happens for a few leading pictures when RoI change events occur.

The Random Access Point period used for the results shown below is 24 pictures, which corresponds to around 1 second. As a reference, we use the setup with the base layer and enhancement layer RAPs using a closed GOP structure, i.e. IDRs. We compare it with the case where the base layer RAPs have been encoded as IDRs, while enhancement layer RAPs have been encoded as CRAs with an open GOP structure. The latter is the one used in combination with the ML-GRPs. The BD-rate [1] of all the bitstreams described above when using closed GOP structures vs. the proposed solution has been measured. The ML-GRPs show to provide an average BD-rate reduction of around 3 to 10 %, in comparison to using closed GOP structures without the proposed ML-GRP insertion. Results in [20] (shown in Tables 7 and 8) have been extended with new sequences, as shown in Tables 9 and 10.

Table 7. BD-rate comparison using the first sequence and GOP size 8 and 512x1600 size tiles

Leftmost tile index for RoI	BD-rate (%) of proposed method
0	3.267
1	3.506
2	3.707
3	3.724
4	3.859
5	3.909
6	3.919
7	4.062
8	4.061
9	4.028
10	3.904
11	3.538
12	2.882

Table 8. BD-rate comparison using the second sequence and GOP size 8 and 512x1600 size tiles

Leftmost tile index for RoI	BD-rate (%) of proposed method
0	8.867
1	8.846
2	9.051
3	7.569
4	7.857
5	7.792
6	6.773
7	6.042
8	6.712
9	6.625
10	7.582
11	9.591
12	9.421

Table 9. BD-rate comparison using the third sequence and GOP size 8 and 512x1920 size tiles

Leftmost tile index for RoI	BD-rate (%) of proposed method
0	5.561
1	5.633
2	4.362
3	4.293
4	4.606
5	4.123
6	5.665
7	5.995
8	6.280
9	7.188

Table 10. BD-rate comparison using the fourth sequence and GOP size 8 and 512x1920 size tiles

Leftmost tile index for RoI	BD-rate (%) of proposed method
0	8.249
1	9.117
2	9.171
3	7.817
4	7.263
5	7.149
6	6.793
7	7.638
8	8.151
9	7.985

Table 7 shows the BD-rate values of the proposed technique against the solution using closed GOP for the resulting 13 streams described above at different RoIs of the first 8192x1600 video sequence with 512x1600 tiles.

On average a 3.72 % BD rate reduction has been measured for the first sequence. Table 8 shows the BD-rate values of the proposed technique against the solution using closed GOP for the resulting streams at different RoIs of the second 8192x1600 video with 512x1600 tiles. The results shown for the second 8192x1600 stream are much higher: between 6.0 and 9.6 % approximately. For this sequence, a 7.902 % BD rate reduction on average can be seen when using the ML-GRPs.

Table 9 shows the BD-rate values of the proposed technique against the solution using closed GOP for the resulting streams at different RoIs of the first 6984x1920 video sequence with 512x1920 tiles. The results shown for this video are between 4.1 and 7.2 % approximately. For this sequence, an average of 5.371 % BD rate reduction can be seen when using the ML-GRPs

Table 10 shows the results for the last video sequence of a resolution of 6984x1920 pixels. The BD-rate values shown in this table correspond to higher values than for the previous sequence corresponding to an average of 7.93 %.

In any case, it can be seen that the reported gains are content dependent. For some sequences, gains up to 9 % can be obtain while for other gains up to 4 %. This depends on the temporal correlation of the pictures within a video sequence. The more temporal prediction can be used for the RASL pictures from previous pictures in presentation order the more effective the technique is. However, the gains shown between 3 % and almost 10 % show that the proposed technique can achieve a higher compression efficiency.

7.3 Results for RoI switching with ML-GRP and unequal RAP period

The results in Tables 11, 12, 13 and 14 show the benefits of using ML-GRPs for open GOP switching with unequal RAP periods. The same four sequences as in Sections 5.2 and 7.2 have been used. The Random Access Point period used for the results shown in Tables 11–14 is 24 pictures for the enhancement layer and 48 or 96 pictures for the enhancement layer. As a reference, we use the setup with the enhancement layer RAPs using a closed GOP structure, i.e. IDRs. We compare it with the case where the enhancement layer RAPs have been encoded as CRAs with an open GOP structure. For both cases the base layer is encoded using an open GOP configuration, i.e. encoded with RAPs of type CRA. As already mentioned, for this case the base layer has not been tiled and therefore consist of a single tile.

Table 11.BD-rate comparison using the first sequence and GOP size 8 and 512x1600 size tiles

Leftmost tile index for RoI	BD-rate (%) for RAP period 48	BD-rate (%) for RAP period 96
0	6.48	6.74
1	6.97	7.25
2	7.92	8.13
3	8.67	8.69
4	9.31	9.33
5	9.66	9.73
6	9.68	9.87
7	10.13	10.16
8	10.11	10.23
9	9.78	10.20

Table 12. BD-rate comparison using the second sequence and GOP size 8 and 512x1600 size tiles

Leftmost tile index for RoI	BD-rate (%) for RAP period 48	BD-rate (%) for RAP period 96
0	7.39	7.25
1	7.47	8.01
2	7.67	8.32
3	8.11	8.68
4	8.42	8.00
5	8.59	7.89
6	8.44	7.89
7	8.27	7.89
8	8.22	7.87
9	8.50	8.05

Table 13. BD-rate comparison using the third sequence and GOP size 8 and 512x1920 size tiles

Leftmost tile index for RoI	BD-rate (%) for RAP period 48	BD-rate (%) for RAP period 96
0	4.80	4.95
1	4.18	4.08
2	3.72	3.72
3	3.52	3.61
4	3.32	3.59
5	3.46	3.72
6	3.83	4.11
7	4.39	4.41
8	4.62	4.58
9	4.91	4.98

Table 14. BD-rate comparison using the fourth sequence and GOP size 8 and 512x1920 size tiles

Leftmost tile index for RoI	BD-rate (%) for RAP period 48	BD-rate (%) for RAP period 96
0	5.72	5.73
1	5.83	5.84
2	5.94	5.95
3	5.90	6.03
4	4.32	4.54
5	4.38	4.39
6	4.20	4.37
7	5.10	5.18
8	5.23	5.27
9	5.26	5.30

The results shown in Tables 11–14 show that the gains of ML-GRP do not almost vary with respect to the periodicity of the RAPs in the base layer. In general, ML-GRP with unequal RAP shows a gain of around 4 % up to 10 % in BD-rate. However, a RAP period of 96 provides between 8.5 % and 20.1 % bitrate savings in comparison to a RAP period of 48 in the base layer.

8 CONCLUSION

In this paper, we have proposed a technique to perform stitching of multiple H.265/HEVC bitstreams of a tiled panoramic video, so that devices with a single hardware decoder can be used. We have described how this works for streams encoded with H.265/HEVC, as well as for streams encoded with its scalable versions H.265/SHVC and H.265/MV-HEVC. We provide a solution that reduces the transmission bitrate at RoI switching points significantly. It consists of inserting Generated Reference Pictures (GRP) that allows using temporal prediction even at RoI switching points for some spatial regions instead of requiring full random access for the single layer case.

We showed that transmission peak bitrate savings between 80-200 % or 40-100 % during the RoI moving interval can be achieved depending on the video content and movement speed. Such bitrate savings are very beneficial for switching events where a drastic increase in the bitrate can lead to a big delay that can make an interactive streaming system unfeasible.

Since we consider that the success of head mounted displays is imminent and this is going to come along with stereo panorama streaming, tile-based panorama streaming for stereoscopic panorama video has been analyzed. Therefore we have used H.265/MV-HEVC and have extended the GRP technique towards stereo with MGRPs. Results are reported and the effect of MGRP is analyzed in context of a layered codec scenario. Results show that the MGRP technique allows for significant peak bitrate reduction, which can be a key in future panoramic video services with particularly strict latency requirements such as head mounted displays.

Such techniques can be implemented very easily without any concerns about real-time constraints since are of low complexity. They can be implemented in an application before feeding the decoder. For instance, they can be performed at the demultiplexing stage as discussed in the paper. In fact, such a technique can be implemented easily following the ISO base Media File Format [14]. One of the issues of GRPs and ML-GRPs is that they require different versions of the content at the server side, increasing the storage capacity that would be required, for instance, at CDNs.

In order to overcome this issue H.265/SHVC can be used. With this regard, we present Multi-Layer Generated Reference Pictures (ML-GRP). An ML-GRP allows using open GOP encoding structures, instead of requiring usage of closed GOP structures. We show that with the proposed solution the average BD-rate performance can be improved by around 3 to 10 %. Such bitrate savings happen mainly at random access points, which are very beneficial for switching events where a drastic increase in the bitrate can lead to a big delay that can make an interactive streaming system unfeasible.

REFERENCES

1. Bjøntegaard G (2001) Calculation of average PSNR differences between RD-curves. Proc VCEG-M33 Meeting: 1–4

2. ClassX, Stanford University (2015) http://classx.stanford.edu/. Accessed 18 December 2015
3. Fujibayashi A, Tan TK (NTT DOCOMO) (2011) Random access support for HEVC. JCTVC-D234, 4th JCT-VC Meeting, Daegu
4. Gaddam VR, Langseth R, Ljødal S, Gurdjos P, Charvillat V, Griwodz C, Halvorsen P (2014) Interactive zoom and panning from live panoramic video. Proc Netw Operating Syst Support Digit Audio Video Workshop (p. 19). ACM
5. Gaddam VR, Langseth R, Stensland HK, Gurdjos P, Charvillat V, Griwodz C, Halvorsen P (2014, March) Be your own cameraman: Real-time support for zooming and panning into stored and live panoramic video. Proc 5th ACM Multimed Syst Conf (68–171). ACM
6. http://www.oculus.com/rift/. Accessed 18 December 2015
7. http://www.samsung.com/global/microsite/gearvr/. Accessed 18 December 2015
8. https://www.google.com/get/cardboard/. Accessed 18 December 2015
9. Inoue M, Kimata H, Fukazawa K, Matsuura N (2010) Interactive panoramic video streaming system over restricted bandwidth network. Proc Int Conf Multimed (1191-1194). ACM
10. ISO/IEC 23009-1:2014/Amd 2:(2015) Spatial relationship description, generalized URL parameters and other extensions
11. Lin J, Chen Y, Huang Y, Lei S (2013) Motion vector coding techniques for HEVC. IEEE J Sel Top Sign Proces 7(6):957–968
12. Mavlankar A, Agrawal P, Pang D, Halwa S, Cheung N, Girod B (2010) An interactive region-of-interest video streaming system for online lecture viewing. special session on advanced interactive multimedia streaming. Proc 18th Int Packet Video Workshop (PV), Hong Kong
13. Mavlankar A, Baccichet P, Varodayan D, Girod B (2007) Optimal slice size for streaming regions of high resolution video with virtual Pan/Tilt/Zoom functionality. Proc 15th Europ Sign Process Conf (EUSIPCO), Poznan, Poland
14. MPEG#115, Text of ISO/IEC FDIS 14496-15 4th edition, W16169
15. Quang N, Ravindra G, Ooi WT (2011) Adaptive encoding of zoomable video streams based on user access pattern. MMSys 2011, San Jose
16. Ravindra G, Ooi WT (2012) On tile assignment for region-of-interest video streaming in a wireless LAN. Proc NOSSDAV '12, 22nd Int Workshop Netw Operat Syst Support Digit Audio Video, Toronto, Canada
17. Reddy Gaddam V, Ngo HB, Langseth R, Griwodz C, Johansen D, Halvorsen P (2015) Tiling of panorama video for interactive virtual cameras: overheads and potential bandwidth requirement reduction. Pict Coding Sym (PCS), 2015 (204-209). IEEE
18. Sanchéz Y, Globisch R, Schierl T, Wiegand T (2014) Low complexity cloud-video-mixing using HEVC. Proceedings of IEEE Consumer Communications and Networking Conference, Las Vegas
19. Sanchéz Y, Skupin R, Schierl T (2015) Compressed domain video processing for tile based panoramic streaming using HEVC. Imag Process (ICIP), 2015 22nd IEEE Int Conf. IEEE
20. Sanchéz Y, Skupin R, Schierl T (2015) Compressed domain video processing for tile based panoramic streaming using SHVC. Proc Immersive Med Exper 2015 Workshop - ACM Multimed, Brisbane, Australia
21. Seo D, Kim S, Park H, Ko H (2014) Real-time panoramic video streaming system with overlaid interface concept for social media. Multimedia Systems 20(6):707–719
22. Skupin R, Sanchez Y, Schierl T (2015) Compressed domain video compositing with HEVC. Picture Coding Sym (PCS 2015), Cairns, Australia
23. Skupin R, Sanchez Y, Schierl T (2015) Compressed domain processing for stereoscopic tile based panorama streaming using MV-HEVC. Proc IEEE Int Conf Consumer Electron-Berlin (ICCE-Berlin), Berlin, Germany
24. Stockhammer T (2011) Dynamic adaptive streaming over HTTP--: standards and design principles. Proc Second Ann ACM Conf Multimed Syst. ACM

25. Sullivan GJ, Boyce JM, Chen Y, Ohm J-R, Segall CA, Vetro A (2013) Standardized extensions of high efficiency video coding (HEVC). Select Topics Sign Process, IEEE J 7(6):1001–1016
26. Sullivan GJ, Ohm J-R, Han W-J, Wiegand T (2012) Overview of the High Efficiency Video Coding (HEVC) standard. IEEE Trans Circ Syst Video Technol, December 2012, Best Paper Award
27. van Brandenburg R, Niamult O, Prins M, Stokking H (2011) Spatial segmentation for immersive media delivery, 15th International conference on Intelligence in Next Generation Networks (ICIN), Oct. 2011
28. Weissig C, Schreer O, Eisert F, Kauff P (2012) The ultimate immersive experience: panoramic 3D video acquisition. Adv Multimed Model, Lect NotesComput Sci 7131:671–681

CHAPTER 9

ALECSO Mobile Apps Initiative

Mohamed Jemni* and Mohamed Koutheair Khribi

ICT Department Arab League Educational, Cultural and Scientific Organization ALECSO, Av. Med Ali Akid, Centre Urbain Nord, BP11201003 Tunis, Tunisia

ABSTRACT

Technological advancements in wireless and broadband networks infrastructures have promoted the widespread distribution of mobile devices. Accordingly, content and software developers rushed to adapt their products, and to innovate and create appropriate services and applications to be used in the everyday life of mobile devices' users. Recent stats from the International Telecommunication Union (ITU) unveiled that mobile broadband is the fastest-growing ICT service in history, and around 4 billion of the global mobile phone population have Internet access using their mobile devices. In light of these considerations, there is no doubt that mobile technologies are entirely changing our lives, including particularly the way we learn. Nevertheless, when trying to draw up the status of Arab mobile Apps development and use, several difficulties show up, mainly in relation to the very few available Arab mobile applications in international apps stores. Therefore, recognizing the potentials of mobile technologies and its status in the region, the Arab League Educational, Cultural, and Scientific Organization (ALECSO), has proposed a Pan-Arab wide mobile initiative, aiming to promote the use and development of mobile applications in the Arab world, particularly in the fields of education, culture, science, and serious games. In this paper, we present an overview of the ALECSO mobile initiative, and we describe in details its related activities and implementations.

Keywords: Mobile Apps Mobile Markets Mobile learning Cross-Platform Development Smart Learning

BACKGROUND

Recent years have witnessed an increasing interest in the mobile computing realm. Gartner says that mobile device (smartphones and tablets) sales are on a continuous rise from year to year, and the future of enterprise applications, both for enterprise workers and consumers, is mobility. According to ITU[1] stats, more than 90% of the global population are covered by a mobile-cellular signal, and more than the half of the population of the Earth are using now mobile communications. This means that mobile devices, to which access has become ubiquitous, are extremely influencing national economies worldwide, and thus empowering people and society, especially in the areas of job creation, entrepreneurship and economic growth in both developed and developing regions (GSM Association 2015a). In the Mobile Economy report authored by GSMA,[2] it was stated that: "There are still many adults and young people who would appreciate the social and economic benefits of mobile technology but are unable to access it, highlighting a huge opportunity for future growth and a challenge to all players in the industry ecosystem to expand the scope of products and services to tap this demand." (Association GSM and ATKEARNEY 2013). This statement refers to the ongoing need for mobile services, while plenty of opportunities remain unexploited, but can be seized thanks to the large scope of mobile technologies and resulting positive impacts on society and economy. So what is the status of mobile technologies in Arab countries? Are there sufficiently suitable Arab Mobile Apps? Is there a global mobile Arab market suitable for gathering and promoting these apps?

Actually, all of these questions were raised in the Arab League Educational, Cultural and Scientific Organization (ALECSO) precisely, during the preparation of its forthcoming ICT projects for the two-year financial plan 2015–2016. Within this context, ALECSO launched an internal study to assess the status of Mobile technologies in Arab countries. This study showed that the mobile industry has grown rapidly over the last few years in the Arab world. Official stats (GSM Association 2015b) revealed that 54% of the population is subscribed to a mobile service as of mid-2015. In 2014, mobile technologies and services generated 4% of GDP in the Arab States, a contribution that amounted to around $115 billion of economic value across 18 Arab countries. Naturally, with such rapid increase in mobile devices adoption, apps have become increasingly more popular. Indeed, around half of users in Egypt, Lebanon, Saudi Arabia and the UAE downloaded more than five apps (both paid and free) in June 2015, the most popular application types are tied to gaming and social media. It is worth noting that most customers who paid for apps have also made in-app purchases (G. Business 2015). Then, what's about the remaining half? In fact, the main reasons, preventing the remaining half of mobile devices' users in these countries (and mostly in all Arab countries) from using and purchasing apps, are the following:

- Lack of the required and suitable apps;
- Very few number of appropriate available applications in Arabic language existing so far;
- No availability of online payment using credit cards and foreign currencies in international mobile markets in several Arab countries. (Actually, the latter reason is even prohibiting some Arab Mobile developers to submit their apps and to get profits)

Knowing also that mobile apps and content continue to be dominated by a few major languages, most significantly English. Whereas Arabic language, as well as a significant number of other national languages, is only represented by less than 0.1% over the Internet. Moreover, according to ITU, future first-time Internet and mobile users are likely to come mainly from less well-represented languages and dialects, less well-educated, and less urban backgrounds.

For all of these aforementioned considerations, ALECSO has proposed the Arab mobile Apps initiative and has accordingly launched a set of promising related projects aiming to support the Arab Mobile Apps use and development, especially, in relation to the areas of education, culture and science in the Arab region (Jemni 2014). The overall goal of this initiative is to promote the Arab mobile industry and to prepare the Arab digital ecosystem for the new mobile technology opportunities, harnessing region's assets (common language, global market, youth population, decent mobile use penetration, etc.) and mobile benefits (economic growth and entrepreneurship, and major improvements in education, financial, healthcare, social, services and other priority sectors) (ALECSO and ITU 2015). This paper is arranged in the following way: In section 2, we evoke the main existing initiatives and works related to Mobile technologies promotion. In section 3, we describe the ALECSO Mobile Apps initiative. In section 4, we focus on the ALECSO Apps initiative projects and activities, namely, the ALECSO Apps Store, Editor, Award and training projects. In section 5, we present an ongoing multimodal training program called ALECSO M-Developer Program aiming to build and reinforce capacities in the region in the field of mobile applications' development harnessing online learning facilities. In section 6, we present first exploration of the impact of the initiative in the region and to which extent people in Arab countries react and adhere to its underlying projects and activities. Finally, a conclusion is presented.

MOBILE INITIATIVES

In the last decade, several projects regarding the use of mobile technology especially in education have been carried out all over the world. The primary motives are the widespread use of mobile devices thanks to their low cost and their multiple and diverse functionalities. There has been also a growing recent interest in experimenting with mobile devices especially tablets in schools adopting BYOD (Bring Your Own Device), BYOT (Bring Your Own Technology), and mobile learning approaches. Many pilot projects have been conducted in this context whether through personal initiatives driven by enthusiastic leaders (e.g. teachers) at small scales or within regional/national initiatives and/or policies to promote mobile learning and ICT use in education. These initiatives aim generally to promote the use of mobile technologies whether at an educational level and/or at a larger scale. However, all of these practices are still emergent, and differ from one country to another.

In fact, mobile learning involves the use of mobile technology, either alone or in combination with other information and communication technology (ICT), in order to enable learning anytime and anywhere. Learning can unfold in a variety of ways: people can use mobile devices to access educational resources, connect with others, or create content, both inside and outside classrooms. Mobile learning also encompasses efforts to support broad educational goals such as the effective administration of school systems and improved communication between schools and families

In the European union for instance, the European Commission has funded a number of successful projects related to mobile technologies and smart learning, mostly dedicated to develop a primarily technological infrastructure with respect to the learner-centered approach, in which mobile technologies play a part, alongside more fixed technologies, in supporting ubiquitous learning (The United Nations Educational Scientific and Cultural Organization UNESCO 2012a). In (Kukulska-Hulme et al. 2011), Kukulska-Hulme et al. describe the most important EU-funded R&D projects over the past decade. MOBIlearn is a mobile learning initiative that ran from 2002 to 2005 with funding from the European Commission involving nine European countries as well as several countries outside of Europe. Universities and mobile phone and telecommunications companies are the main actors in this programme. The main objective is to enhance learning using mobile technologies, which would support and develop learning outside of traditional schools and classrooms. The eMapps programme is another mobile initiative that ran from 2005 to 2008 with support of the European Commission. The eMapps project aims to develop the skills of creativity and innovation among communities of technologically-savvy and internationally-minded children who would generate digital content about their local culture and exchange experiences and communicate with peers in other countries through eMapps' platform and network. The project aims also to build adaptable interactive tools, mainly serious games played on a mobile platform, in order to thrive children' abilities for analysis, interpretation, problem solving, memory exercises, etc. The United Nations Educational Scientific and Cultural Organization UNESCO 2012a).

As for the Asia region which is one of the largest and most diverse region of the globe, ranging from countries as large as China and India, already the two largest mobile markets in the world, to a number of small islands and territories (GSMA Intelligence 2015). In this region, majority of people own and use mobile phones and devices. In 2010, according to ITU stats, there were nearly 70 mobile phone subscriptions per 100 inhabitants in this region (The United Nations Educational Scientific and Cultural Organization UNESCO 2012b). However, it has been shown in a study conducted by UNESCO in 08 Asian countries (China, Indonesia, Japan, Malaysia, South Korea, Singapore, Taiwan and Thailand) that few projects and policies tied specifically to the use of mobile devices, particularly for education, exist (The United Nations Educational Scientific and Cultural Organization UNESCO 2012b), covering different countries and territories with a broad range of languages and cultures. Knowing that there is a tremendous diversity of the Asian countries, the UNESCO review reveals that these countries tend generally to fall into one of the following three main categories in terms of their engagement with mobile learning: "(1) countries with a mature mobile market, high penetration of mobile phones and strong ICT infrastructure: Mobile learning is included under the broad context of national-level ICT policies. (2) Countries with a growing mobile market, medium to high penetration of mobile phones and basic ICT infrastructure: Mobile phones are used for distance learning and in informal learning contexts. (3) Countries with an emerging mobile market, low to medium penetration of mobile phones and weak or basic ICT infrastructure : Mobile learning activities are scarce" (The United Nations Educational Scientific and Cultural Organization UNESCO 2012b).

Regarding the North America region, many educational institutions provide mobile devices for all students, to ensure equity and consistent access to mobile opportunities. In the United States, two main initiatives deserve to be quoted: the first, Qualcomm's Wireless Reach initiative, created in 2006, and the second is the FCC's Learning On-the-Go pilot programme, launched in 2010 (The United Nations Educational Scientific and Cultural

Organization UNESCO 2012c). Both programmes are BYOT (Bring Your Own Technology) based initiatives aiming to support and encourage students to experience new modes of active learning by bringing and using their mobile devices at school and outside (Quillen 2011).

Many other broader mobile initiatives also exist with the aim to promote mobile applications and content creation via training, education, and competitions. As examples, we can cite the Youth Mobile[3] project, one of the UNESCO's projects for sustainable development via education and technologies. With such initiative, UNESCO and partners strive to provide young people with the high-level skills and confidence to develop, promote, and sell locally relevant mobile apps that solve local issues of sustainable development and provide employment.

Imagine Cup[4] is another project led by Microsoft Company. It is an international student technology competition offering to students all over the world the chance to get involved in mobile technology field and to win awards. Many Arab students are participating regularly in this competition and won several times many prices. Unfortunately, there is no similar Pan-Arab initiative to promote mobile apps and content targeting Arab people, except some local projects that did not yet gain a Pan-Arab dimension and mostly are not comprehensive. For example, we can cite the Arab Mobile Application Challenge (AMAC)[5] initiative, which aims to promote mobile application development in Arab countries, but did not yet cover capacity building activities and technical issues.

As can be seen, the mobile technology realm has witnessed amazing advancements and synergistic opportunities with several priority sectors such as education and social and economic development. In light of drivers and benefits of mobile technologies, there is a real need to create initiatives and policies in order to highlight and benefit from the multiple advantages of this technology and its positive impact on education and employability and other sectors. Nevertheless, in the Arab region, there is a luck of such regional and common Pan Arab initiatives and/or policies to promote mobile technology harvesting its potential for education and employability and other priority sectors, and to overcome barriers (mostly related to global markets, Arabic Language, technical infrastructure, skills, regulation, etc.). Therefore, ALECSO has launched a regional comprehensive initiative in order to go a step further in the massive use and production of Arab mobile apps and content in education, culture, science and serious games. This initiative spans some required aspects related to the Mobile ecosystem namely the technical infrastructure, soft and tools, markets, trainings, incentives, etc.

ALECSO MOBILE APPS INITIATIVE

As shown previously, in spite of an increasing techie Arab young population, highly interested and even addicted to mobile devices and smartphones, the number of Arabic language based mobile applications developed so far is still few. Endeavoring to address this issue, ALECSO organization has proposed a comprehensive and strategic initiative[6] (ALECSOApps) aiming to provide the necessary technological and institutional environment for the promotion of an emerging digital creative Arab Mobile industry, related to the fields of education, culture, science and serious games (Jemni and Khribi 2016a). The ALECSO mobile apps initiative has started in 2015 and it is still running. This initiative involves 22 Arab countries members in the Arab league. Some partners including ministries of education and ICT, universities, and mobile phone and telecommunication companies in the Arab region are involved likewise. In general, the key objectives of that initiative, ranging from the raising awareness and capacity building features to the implementation of appropriate tools and technical environment and financial boost, cover the following:

- Taking advantage from mobile technologies since it can deliver many important social and economic benefits in the region, especially by improving access to education, and culture and financial services and healthcare and other priority sectors;
- Supporting the mobile industry in the Arab region, which will yield economic growth and entrepreneurship, and major improvements in education, financial, healthcare, social, etc. services;
- Preparing the digital ecosystem for the new mobile opportunities, particularly in the areas of job creation, and business prospects, and economic growth.
- Offering to the 400 million Arab population a Pan-Arab wide market with advanced technical infrastructure for the hosting and exchanging of a selection of Arab mobile Apps, with new business models and opportunities.
- Introducing mobile technologies to all in the Arab region through a specific training program and material available in several learning modes (face to face, online, blended, etc.) for a large spectrum of learners (from newbies to experts);
- Encouraging the Arab youth to be more competitive and innovative by offering possibilities to reach specific mobile learning programs providing required knowledge and skills;

- Providing a suitable technical environment for developing and testing and hosting mobile applications;
- Promoting Mobile Learning in the Arab region, especially by empowering mobile learning opportunities by proposing low-cost and easy-to-implement solutions to make education more accessible to all students;
- Motivating the Arab mobile developers and give them the opportunity to create and innovate by organizing a Pan Arab wide mobile competition to generate more profound mobile innovations and select annually the best apps in the fields of education, culture, science and serious games.

Given these points, many projects and activities have been proposed to let the initiative come to fruition quickly and efficiently. Indeed, the following flagship projects[7] are delivered (Jemni et al. 2015):

- ALECSO Apps Store;
- ALECSO Apps Editor;
- ALECSO Apps Award,
- ALECSO Apps training programs.

ALECSO apps store

The ALECSO Apps Store is a web-based application intended for hosting and gathering Arab Mobile Applications (Figure 1). This platform is also installable on supported mobile devices that run Android OS.[8] This Arab marketplace provides the opportunity to Arab developers involved in Mobile Technology to innovate and to share their creations without any fees, restrictions or barriers. To ensure a good quality of applications on the store, a strict publishing process is adopted. Indeed, before publishing a submitted application, a team of experts must assess it and ensure the checkup phase. The architecture of the ALECSO Apps store platform is designed to ensure a high quality of services. It is composed of two main modules hosted on two different servers. The first module is web based and it ensures the management of the web interface of the store. The second module is Cloud based. It ensures all features that need processing the binary files such as metadata, size, signature, etc. This architecture is intended to be gradually entirely cloud based.

Figure 1. The ALECSO Apps Store

ALECSO apps editor

Recently, many developers are relying more and more on hybrid techniques for the development of mobile applications. In fact, they are using generally combination of web languages (e.g. HTML5, JavaScript and CSS3). To do so, developers tend to use hybrid development tools. Phonegap[9] is one of the most well-known tool which allows the compilation of web source code embedded in mobile apps, using the potential of mobile devices and their features, and can be run for Android or iOS or Windows Phone operating system (Shotts 2013).

Review of cross-platform development

Currently, with over than four millions of existing mobile applications in leading app stores, developers are facing new daily challenges to innovate, create, develop, deploy, manage, publish, and disseminate mobile applications. The complexity of such situation makes it difficult to estimate the development's cost and time of mobile applications suitable at least to the most used and leading app stores and related platforms. The Cross Platform Mobile App Development's concept has tremendously simplified this process since developers can run seamlessly their apps across multiple mobile platforms. So it looks like "one code fits all" since it is possible to code an application that can be run on multiple platforms without tweaking the code belonging to each obtained native version.

Many tools are available to develop flexible mobile applications with seamless compatibility, like: PhoneGap, Appcelerator, Sencha Touch, MonoSync, Corona, Adobe Air, Xamarin, RhoMobile, etc.

- PhoneGap (Apache Cordova): an open source tool that enables developers to create mobile applications compatible with Android, iPhone, iPad, Palm, BlackBerry, and Symbian.
- Sencha Touch: HTML5 based cross platform framework that provides fully functional APIs and offers a component based approach for building mobile applications.
- MonoSync: This framework supports C and C++, PHP, Java, JavaScript, Python, and Ruby on Rails for mobile development apps.

To be able to choose the most suitable tool a developer can lean on, besides local needs and requirements, a well-defined list of criteria should be taken into consideration. Those criteria cover, among others, what follows: cost, platform support, access to hardware and device API's, performance, architecture, technical aspects, leaving curve, productivity, user interface, usability, efficiency, supported languages, testing tools and debugging, etc (Holzer and Ondrus 2011).

DISCUSSION

The cross platform development technological ground is constantly shifting with each tool introducing new functionalities and facilities to the communities of developers and users. In the ALECSO Apps project, one of the major criteria by which we are concerned is related to the no support of RTL (Right to Left) languages, and especially Arab language, in addition to other technical matters related mainly to the multi-users, multi-tasks and compilation issues. There is no doubt that all the aforementioned existing cross-platform mobile development tools are actually covering most of the required components to create apps (such as pages creation, media integration, rich text editors, app personalization, etc.), but they don't support Arab language neither in the interface nor in the content of applications. Whereas our main need, in the ALECSO Apps project, is to provide non-expert users with a comprehensive framework enabling them to create and build intuitively Arabic language based mobile apps.

ALECSO apps editor: arab-based cross-platform apps development studio

The ALECSO Apps Editor (Figure 2) is a web based platform that provides an environment of Rapid Application Development (RAD) (James 1991). It represents a comprehensive mobile applications development Studio. It enables users to create their applications in few intuitive steps. The Editor is mainly proposed for people whom do not master programming languages such as JAVA or objective C and includes a real time previewer based on WYSIWYG. The main specificity of ALECSO Apps editor is its ability to build Arabic mobile apps based on a set of embedded easy-to-use tools. Those tools cover actually the most requested components by the Arabic community and among them, we can mention the pages creation tool, the rich text editor, the video gallery tool and photo album tool (Figure 3). Since this Editor is based on web technologies like HTML5, CSS3 and JavaScript, it becomes easy for users to integrate new plug-ins in addition to the pre-built plugins provided by default. The process of generating the final mobile app is done in a transparent way where the user receives the compiled app according to the target platform that she/he specifies. Therefore, the generated app is a hybrid mobile app that takes the advantages at a time of web and native applications. The application is subsequently able to access to sensors and other hardware features available on mobile devices such as the rear and front cameras, the GPS and the gyroscope, etc. The technical details about the Editor's software architecture will be presented in the next section.

As explained above, applications generated by the ALECSO Apps Editor are able to run on any device since they are built using web technologies and wrapped and compiled with Apache Cordova. Thus, these applications can access to all native device capabilities and features. Thereby, advanced users can then use the source code of the app and add more plugins in order to enrich the application with native functionalities.

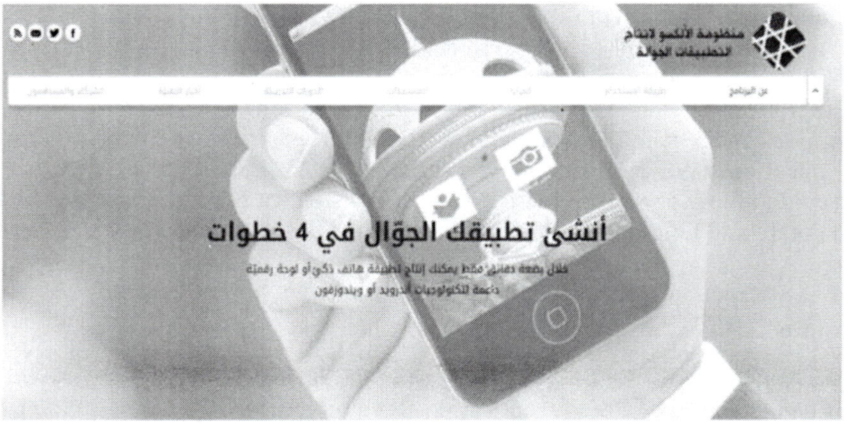

Figure 2. The ALECSO Apps Editor

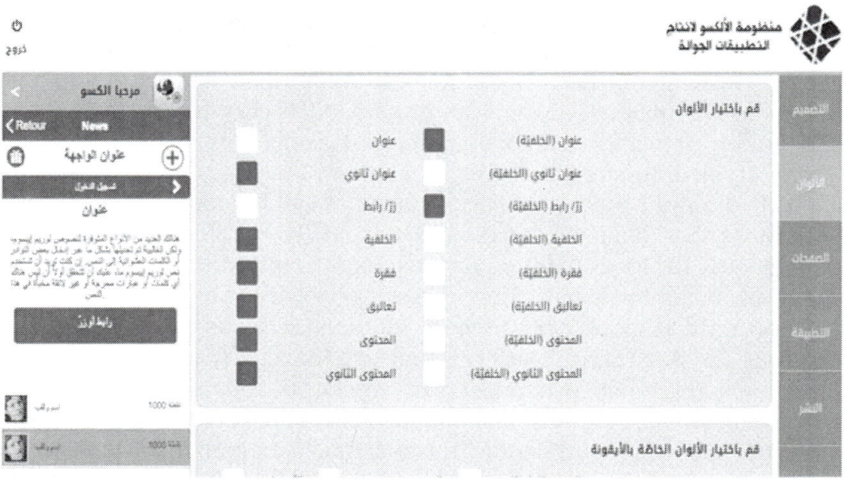

Figure 3. Creation of mobile applications intuitively in few steps

Architecture overview

The Editor connects the user interface with the back-end system. This system adopts a very flexible visual approach to provide final users with high level of customization. Indeed, users can benefit from the web-based visual platform to collaborate and share the application view in order to tune the application simultaneously. As illustrated in Figure 4, the platform of the editor is based on four layers: Editor Front, Libraries, Back-end system and the integration framework. The Front is the user interface service which allows developers to select the provided components and build the application's pages. We should notice that other third-party tools like online picture processing are provided as well. Moreover, a set of predefined templates and plugins are provided, otherwise the developer can customize and/or add new developed templates.

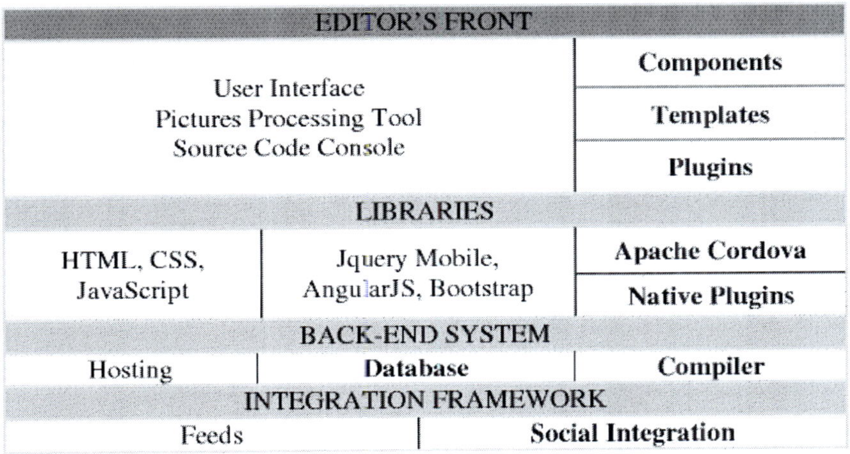

Figure 4. ALECSO Apps Editor Architecture

In the next layer, we find libraries that represent mainly the basic web technologies that will be used to render the web version of the mobile app. The apache Cordova, which is a Javascript library, allows the creation of plugins ensuring access to native features like storage, network, camera, etc. The following layer is the Back-end system, which is the engine of the Editor. In Fact, this part of the platform represents the components used to manage users' accounts, authentication as well as apps compiling. As for the last layer, it represents the integration functionalities gathering the most known APIs which allow developers to embed external data resources natively. Indeed adding a map from google, a video from YouTube or a feed from any website is possible thanks to the integration framework.

Infrastructure

Actually, the Editor is deployed on a cloud based-infrastructure. Two main instances are dedicated to both the Editor's Front and the Editor's compiler. To guarantee a high level of availability the editor's platform is built behind a very scalable Cloud DNS lookup service. This service, called "Cloud Front" automatically roots the traffic to zone2 (Ireland) where the whole platform is cloned. The compiler is an intensive service in term of computation requirements. It allows the editor's Front to convert the generated apps form HTML5 into WP8 and Android binaries, which are composed, of native containers that embed Web views. The average time necessary to compile an application is around 45 s on a single instance. The compilation average time can cause bottlenecks especially during rush hours and simultaneous access (e.g. during training sessions). Subsequently, a mechanism of auto scaling and load balancing are necessary in order to handle excessive simultaneous calls to the compilation process. The detailed infrastructure is shown in the following figure (Figure 5).

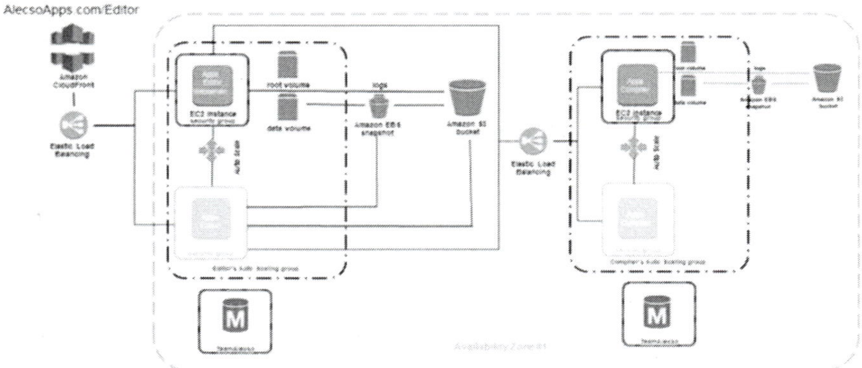

Figure 5. ALECSO Apps Editor: Cloud infrastructure

ALECSO apps award

The ALECSO Apps Award is an annual Pan-Arab competition aiming to motivate and encourage Arab developers to meet high-level standards in term of Mobile Applications quality, innovation and Entrepreneurship. The competition is set over two stages: The first stage is national, lead and held locally in each Arab countries to select the best national Mobile Applications, in the areas of Education, Culture, Science and serious games. The second stage is rather at a Pan-Arabic level: wining applications are selected among those getting successfully the first round. The amount of the ALECSO Apps Awards is about 50 000 $US. The submission and the evaluation of applications are done online (Figure 6).

Figure 6. The ALECSO Apps Award web site

Many reviewers from different Arab countries participated in the evaluation of each application. The evaluation is based on many criteria such as innovation, creativity, features, content, user interfaces, technology and even application packaging. During this phase, Internet users can choose and so nominate the winner of the audience award applied through the voting system. The first edition of the ALECSO APPS Award was held in Qatar (Doha 2015), the second edition was held in UAE (Dubai 2016), and the third edition is going to be held in Tunisia (Tunis 2017).

ALECSO apps training programs

In order to introduce adults and youth people in the Arab region to the mobile technologies realm, and build, and reinforce capacities in Mobile Apps development, ALECSO offers varied training programs ranging from short workshops, to specific and advanced mobile development programmes for a wide spectrum of trainees from all the Arab countries. ALECSO Apps training programs provide trainees with continuous and consistent access to training, technology, and networks. The educational resources, material and activities used during training workshops, and covering the required skills for the development of Mobile Apps, are available online via the ALECSO online training platform.[10] So that discussions and interactions via the platform can continue after the official duration of workshops. Trainees are mainly teachers, students and developers from Arab countries. The ALECSO Apps training Programs are ensured basically via three modes:

- Face to face training workshops using e-learning facilities to enhance the quality of training;
- Online learning, in the form of Small Private Online Courses (SPOCs) and Massive Open Online Courses (MOOCs);
- Blended learning, in partnership with Academic and industrial partners in the region.

A set of learning and training online environments with necessary technical cloud computing based infrastructure are used to ensure these training programs, including e-learning platforms, SPOCs and MOOCs platforms (Jemni and Khribi 2016), and a compiler which is a specific tool allowing the conversion of generated HTML5 apps to specific mobile OS format binaries (Android, Window Phone, etc.).

As for training material, and as we opt for a mobile cross-platform development, the material focuses mainly on the creation of cross platform hybrid mobile apps with native look using known technologies i.e. HTM5, CSS3 and JavaScript. So that all the trainees whether they are web developers or beginner in web development, can easily pitch into mobile apps development. Moreover, with hybrid apps development, developers can write the hybrid mobile app once and run it on every platform without any extra efforts. The HTML5 UI frameworks provide many components that help a lot in the design of responsive web app that fits all devices' screens, and it is also possible to access all native hardware components such as Camera or GPS thanks to JavaScript APIs, whether already existing like those offered by Cordova (PhoneGap) or newly written and compiled. All the educational resources and environments used in this project are under open license.

Furthermore, a specific training programme (called ALECSO M-Developer) based on blended learning was launched earlier in 2015. The pilot experience of this programme was held in Tunisia with the partnership of the Tunisian Ministry of communication technologies and digital economy, and Tunisian universities, aiming to train 500 students enrolled in graduating class or newly graduated, on mobile apps development. The programme includes a training of Trainers workshop, a face-to-face training phase, an online learning phase via a dedicated SPOC and a coaching phase to define the Apps' ToRs and to develop and finally deliver and publish the Apps. As a second stage, ALECSO organization intend to duplicate this pilot project for Arab countries expressing an interest in disseminating and localizing mobile technologies.

M-DEVELOPER PROGRAMME

The M-Developer Program is a specific hybrid training program whose first edition has just been finished (December 2016). The pilot experience of this programme initiated by ALECSO, is the result of a fruitful and successful collaboration between the organization and the Tunisian Ministry of Technologies of Communication and Digital Economy. Co-financed and monitored by both entities, the project aims to build a capacity in the realm of Mobile technology for a young audience of regular students enrolled in Tunisian universities. ALECSO is in charge of designing and implementing the program. For this purpose, a specific hybrid model of training is setup taking into consideration a number of constraints related mainly to students' attendance, technical aspect of the course, etc., and taking full advantages of ICT use in education. In fact, 500 Tunisian students among those enrolled in graduating class or newly graduated, belonging to the ICT major, are selected to attend such a specific training on mobile apps development (it is worth noting this number was raised later to 569 enrolled students). These students are, then, grouped into 20 cohorts (Figure 7), each of which is taken up by an instructor who is in charge of all the training phases, ranging from face to face workshops, to online training and coaching sessions. For this purpose, a set of platforms and tools are used in order to offer appropriate learning experience to students.

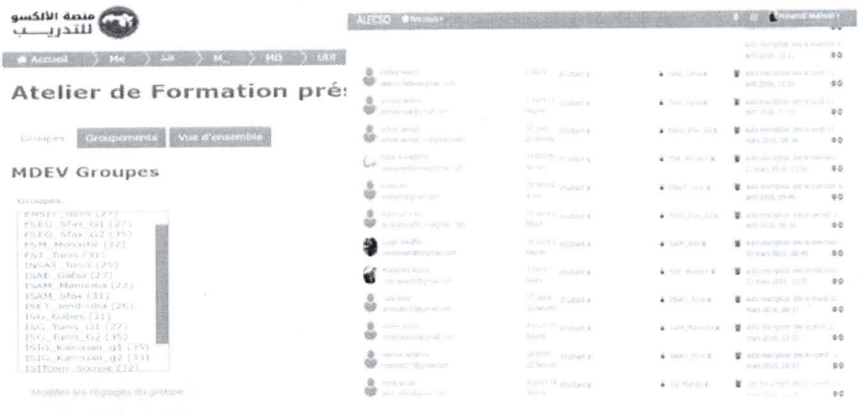

Figure 7. Registered students and cohorts

As a second stage, ALECSO organization intends to duplicate this pilot project for other Arab countries expressing an interest in disseminating and localizing mobile technologies, and especially, preparing new generations of skilled and competitive mobile developers in the Arab region.

M-Developer core activities

The program includes primarily five milestones in terms of training:

- Training of trainers' workshop, with the aim of providing to trainers a profound description of the program and its specificities, and to explore deeply the training material (Figure 8). Twenty instructors among interested teachers in Tunisian universities, experts in the field of ICT and mobile development, are hired as contractual trainers under M-Developer program to ensure all the training phases for a duration of six months.

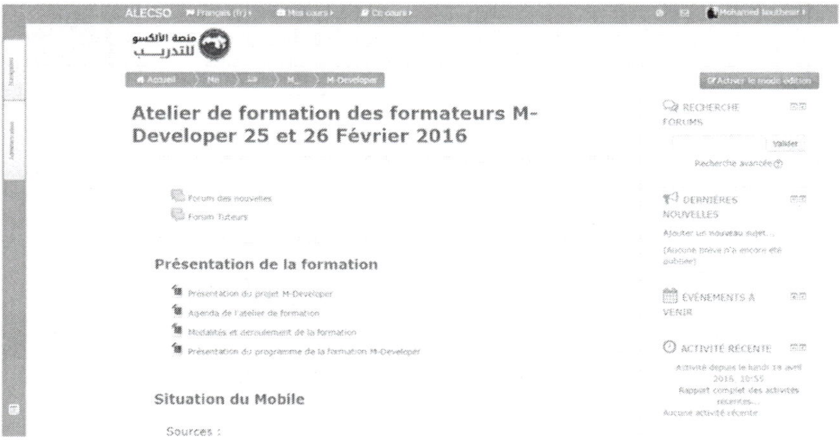

Figure 8. Training of Trainers Online Course

- Face-to-face phase training, each trainer is asked to organize a five-days face-to-face training workshop for his/her group of students. Even in these face-to-face workshops, an online learning platform is used in order to host the training material designed and developed by ALECSO to conduct in total twenty five-days face-to-face workshops throughout Tunisian universities and Tunisian regions, with several possibilities to use communication and collaborative tools whether between students themselves and/or with instructors (Figure 9). It is to be noted that first face-to-face workshops are three-days based. Then, there one-day workshop held in the mid of the online phase and finally, last one-day workshops at the end of the online phase.

Figure 9. ALECSO Online Training Platform

- Online phase via a dedicated Small Private Online Course SPOC, this phase lasts six weeks during which students access to several videos and different learning resources. They are also asked to make Quizzes and assignments. During this phase, students are supervised and guided by their instructors (tutors).
- First coaching phase lasting one month with the aim to help students finding appropriate project's ideas and defining properly their mobile apps' ToRs;
- Second coaching phase lasting one month aiming to develop and finally deliver and publish the required mobile apps.

M-Developer SPOC

It is noteworthy that M-Developer project represents actually a kind of results-based project, which means that at the end of the program, we should get as concrete outcomes, besides the students' completion of all training phases, dozens of decent mobile apps developed and published. Moreover, given that the program was initially designed for a relatively small number of regular students throughout Tunisian universities, gathered in several groups, with focus on the instructor role during the training phases, This would avoid somehow students' potential dropouts or disinterest. It was therefore agreed that the online phase would be ensured using a SPOC course type instead of MOOC, even though in terms of content, there are almost no differences between both types, except the "massiveness" and "openness" dimensions. Indeed, the M-Developer SPOC is only accessible for those who are registered via the M-Developer program, and thus not open for all, and the number of registered students is relatively small, added to that, gathered in tiny groups, with an instructor for each.

M-Developer syllabus

The SPOC lasts six weeks, it is a 42 h equivalent semester module in university. Each week includes specific tasks to ensure progressively week by week the completion of the entire training phase and then be able to step ahead to the next stage in the Program. During each week of the SPOC, students are asked to get through the following (Figure 10):

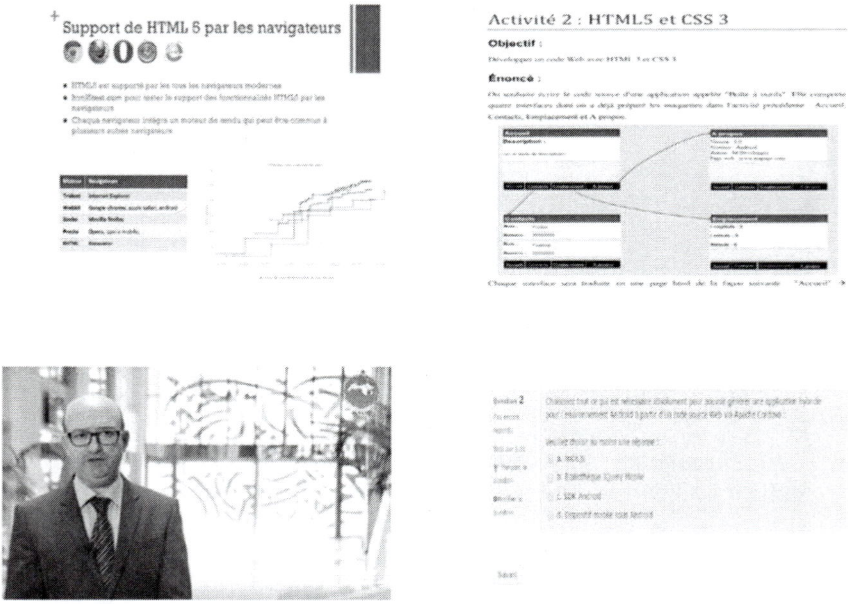

Figure 10. M-Developer SPOC material

- Access available short video lectures,
- Explore available presentations, documents, tutorials, and extra learning resources if any,

- Answer to Quizzes (involving corrections to better understand learning material),
- Make assignments, problem sets, and submission in due date,
- Pass a final Quiz test (weekly and at the end of the SPOC).

Obviously, students can interact with each other, ask for clarifications, launch discussions, and put questions using available Forums within the course. Basically, lecture topics are organized among the six-weeks SPOC as follows:

- Week 1 :
  - Welcome address and Introductory remarks
  - M-Developer Syllabus
  - Pitching Project Ideas
  - Mobile Apps Opportunities
  - Status of Mobile technology
  - Mobile Operating Systems
- Week 2:
  - Mobile Development
  - Native and Hybrid Programming
  - Design and Interfaces
- Week 3:
  - Web Programming Languages HTML5, CSS3, JavaScript, JQuery
  - Mobile Apps Ads
- Week 4:
  - Cordova Environment
- Week 5:
  - Interactions with eternal services (Client–server Architecture, JSON, Examples, etc.)
- Week 6:
  - Cordova Plugins
  - Mobile Apps Sample Project
  - Mobile Apps publishing

- Business Models

Grading policy

In this SPOC course, as shown above, there are varied types of assignments. The obtained final grade is weighted average of the following:

- Problem sets : 40%
- Weekly Quiz : 30%
- Final Quiz: 30%

In order to earn a certificate at the end of the SPOC, students must pass the course with a grade of C or better. The following grading breakdown will apply:

- >= 80%: A
- >= 70%: B
- >= 60%: C

In order to earn a certificate at the end of the Whole M-Developer Programme, students must:

- Attend all the training phases,
- Earn a SPOC certificate,
- Prepare and pitch a project idea,
- Prepare and submit the project's ToRs,
- Develop and publish the developed mobile Application.

It is noteworthy that, following the new ALECSO vision to open up digital content and training material, all developed learning resources are planned to be openly licensed using creative common licenses (Butcher 2011).

USE AND IMPACT OF THE ALECSO APPS INITIATIVE

Despite being launched in 2015, the ALECSO mobile apps initiative is still alive and well progressing, and all relevant stakeholders from many Arab countries have adhered to its values ever since. Moreover, many contacts have been initiated with international organizations, associations and companies working in the area of mobile technologies and telecommunication with the aim to create partnerships and to collaborate in order to enhance the quality of projects and to enlarge the scope of the initiative. In this respect, we have networked with GSMA aspiring to involve ALECSO APPs Awards within the Global Mobile Awards and to extend the competition policy accordingly. Furthermore, discussions with a couple of known companies working in the field of mobile technologies are ongoing, these companies are interested in the installation and use of the ALECSO APPs store initially on their smartphones, which will offer fruitful commercial opportunities to improve their sales rate and thus penetration in the Arab market (more than 400 million users). In the same vein, ALECSO is participating in the UNESCO mobile learning week held in March of each year in the UNESCO headquarters in Paris. By attending such international events, ALECSO aims to promote its Mobile Initiative, and consequently to expand international understandings of how such initiative can help, especially in the developing world, to open and enrich opportunities for developers (especially youth, girls, and women) to create and innovate. Which has an important impact on the growth of economy and entrepreneurship, and improvements in education, financial, healthcare, social, etc. services. In this context, other countries and regions were interested in this valuable experience, and how would it be possible to replicate it successfully overseas.

Many relevant indicators are used to help out in measuring the scope of the use and impact of the initiative in Arab countries so far (e.g. enrolment, number of mobile apps in the ALECSO Apps store, usage stats, sentiment analysis, interactions in terms of comments and feedback and various requests, number of mobile apps submitted in each session of the ALECSO Apps Award, number of mobile apps created with the ALECSO Apps editor, number of training sessions, number of trainees, etc.). To this end, some dashboard interfaces were developed in order to give the required assistance in analyzing the use and impact of the initiative and all its components.

Regarding the ALECSO APPs store, current key figures indicate the availability of 458 mobile applications so far, more than 200 K downloads, more than 440 K views, more than 21 K ratings of different Apps, 756 comments, and 1898 registrants, as shown in Figure 11, which reflects the progress status of mobile apps in the ALECSO APPs store and its use and dissemination since its creation recently.

Figure 11. ALECSO Apps Store stats

As for the ALECSO APPS Award, the first edition of this unprecedented competition in the region was held in Qatar, and the closing ceremony was organized in Doha in January 14th 2016. This first edition witnessed the submission of more than 1164 applications from 19 Arab countries via the Award web site. The reviewing committee composed of 13 members, whom are experts in the field from Arab countries, ensured a preliminary selection of the best submitted apps at a national level in the fields of education, culture, science and serious games. The result of this process provided 244 selected applications from 16 Arab countries. Eventually, during the closing ceremony, reviewers selected the best applications at a Pan-Arabic level. There were 10 chosen awarded apps, some of which were equally ranked and thus equally awarded. Winners are from 09 Arab countries: Qatar, KSA, UAE, Kuwait, Sudan, Tunisia, Jordan, Algeria, and Morocco. The second edition of the ALECSO Apps Award 2016 was held in Dubai, with the support and collaboration of the Telecommunications Regulatory Authority (TRA) in UAE. The Closing ceremony was held in November 20th 2016 during the UAE innovation week. This second edition has already witnessed the submission of more than 1300 applications from 19 Arab countries via the Award web site (Figure 12). A preliminary selection of the submitted applications based on technical and relevance issues to the competition has led to some 516 appropriate mobile apps ready to be reviewed by the international board of experts in order to select best mobile apps in the fields of education, cultural, science and educational games, first, at national levels and then, at a Pan Arabic level. At the national level, 56 mobile apps were selected as the best apps. And during the closing ceremony, reviewers selected the best applications at a Pan-Arabic level i.e. among these 56 final candidates. There were 12 chosen awarded apps, some of which were equally ranked and thus equally awarded. Winners are from 10 Arab countries: Qatar, KSA, UAE, Palestine, Tunisia, Syria, Jordan, Egypt, Algeria, and Morocco.

Figure 12. ALECSO APPs Award stats, Dubai 2016 edition

Moreover, a dedicated page to the ALECSO APPs Award is created on Facebook with more than 41000 subscribers so far (Figure 13). Other social networks are used likewise in order to raise the spectrum of interested people and to promote more and more the initiative and all its components.

In regard to the ALECSO APPs Editor, which is used to build Arabic based mobile apps in few intuitive steps based on a set of embedded tools and environments, especially the compiler which allows the editor's Front to convert and generate apps form HTML5 into WP8 and Android binaries. The editor's front and back are mostly used in the context of training sessions. There are actually 1546 generated mobile apps, and some 308 users (Figure 14) from all over the Arab world (Figure 15).

Figure 13. ALECSO APPs Award Facebook page

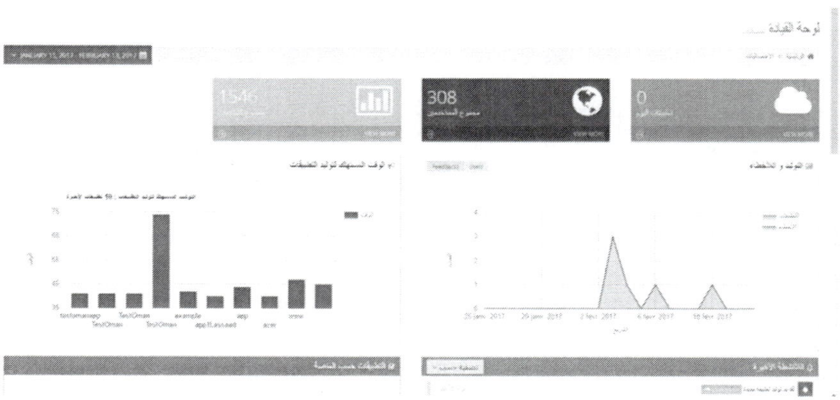

Figure 14. ALECSO APPs Editor's Front and back stats

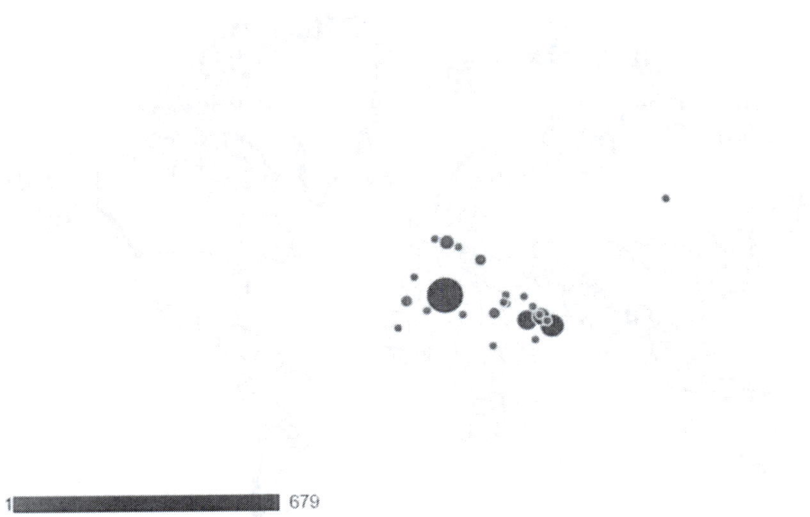

Figure 15. ALECSO APPs Editor user's distribution map

Regarding the capacity building issue, many training sessions were organized with collaboration of national committees in Arab countries. There were 07 face-to-face training workshops so far using e-learning facilities to enhance the quality of training. These workshops were held in Tunisia, Doha, UAE, and Oman (Figure 16). Some 150 participants from different majors, basically students and teachers, attended these sessions. Besides the training programme M-Developer, described above in section 4, with more than 500 beneficiaries, all students from Tunisian universities. ALECSO plans to duplicate this program in other Arab countries with collaboration of local ministries of education and ICT. Another MOOC on mobile development entirely in Arabic language is still under preparation and will be launched shortly for all interested people from Arab countries.

Figure 16. ALECSO training workshops on Mobile Development available online on the ALECSO training platform

CONCLUSION

The last recent years have witnessed tremendous growth of ICT and increasing availability of high bandwidth mobile network infrastructures, which has opened up new opportunities for all sectors at all levels. Mindful of these major advancements in mobile technologies and big shifts in digital economy, ALECSO Organization committed to prepare and boost the ecosystem in the region in order to advance opportunities further for citizens especially in the education, culture and science fields. To this end, a comprehensive mobile initiative has been formulated and implemented by ALECSO since 2015, with special focus on building capacities aspects in order to empowering new generations of Arab developers with all required skills and competencies to innovate, create and develop Arab mobile applications and push forward towards Arab knowledge societies. In this paper, we presented the ALECSO Mobile initiative aiming to promote the mobile applications development and use in the Arab region. We put the focus on all its related projects and activities, especially the ALECSO Apps Store, Editor, Award, and training programs.

FOOTNOTES

1 https://itunews.itu.int/En/6266-The-State-of-Broadband-2015-.note.aspx

2 http://www.gsma.com/

3 http://en.unesco.org/youthmobile

4 https://www.imaginecup.com

5 http://www.arabmobilechallenge.com/

6 http://www.alecsoapps.com

7 http://http://www.alecsoapps.com

8 http://www.android.com

9 http://www.phonegap.com

10 http://training.alecso.org/

ACKNOWLEDGEMENTS

We would like to thank Prof. Abdullah Hamad Muharib, the Director General of the Arab League Educational, Cultural and Scientific Organization (ALECSO), who provided insight, wisdom and engagement that greatly helped in achieving ALECSO ICT projects to come to fruition. We also thank Mr. Oussema Elghoul, Mr. Achraf Othmen, Mr. Kabil Jaballah, the team of experts that worked on the ALECSO mobile initiative.

AUTHORS' CONTRIBUTIONS

Both authors read and approved the final manuscript.

PUBLISHER'S NOTE

Springer Nature remains neutral with regard to jurisdictional claims in published maps and institutional affiliations.

REFERENCES

1. GSM Association. The mobile economy. 2015a.
2. Association GSM and ATKEARNEY. The mobile economy 2013. 2013.
3. GSM Association. The mobile economy - arab states 2015. 2015b.
4. G. Business. Taping the App market. 2015.
5. Jemni M. Promoting the Effective Use of ICT for Enhancing Education in the Arab World. In: The 14th IEEE International Conference on Advanced Learning Technologies - ICALT2014 Advanced Technologies for Supporting Open Access to Formal and Informal Learning. 2014.
6. ALECSO and ITU. Guidelines for formulating national strategies on smart learning. 2015.
7. Butcher N. A basic guide to open educational resources OER, Commonwealt of learning and UNESCO. 2011.
8. The United Nations Educational Scientific and Cultural Organization UNESCO. TURNING ON MOBILE LEARNING : illustrative initiatives and policy implications. 2012a.

9. Kukulska-Hulme A, Sharples M, Milrad M, Arnedillo-Sanchez I, Vavoula G. The genesis and development of mobile learning in Europe. In: Hershey P, Parsons D, editors. Combining E-learning and M-learning: New applications of blended educational resources. 2011.
10. GSMA Intelligence. The mobile economy - Asia pacific 2015. 2015.
11. The United Nations Educational Scientific and Cultural Organization UNESCO. TURNING ON MOBILE LEARNING in Asia : illustrative initiatives and policy implications. 2012b.
12. The United Nations Educational Scientific and Cultural Organization UNESCO. TURNING ON MOBILE LEARNING in north america : illustrative initiatives and policy implications. 2012c.
13. Jemni M, Khribi K, Achraf O, Oussama E, Kabil J. ALECSOApps: Toward Empowering Mobile Applications Development in the Arab World. In: International Conference on Smart Learning Environments (ICSLE 2015). p. 87–93.
14. Quillen I. Districts tackle questions regarding BYOT policy. 2011. [Online]. Available:
15. Holzer A, Ondrus J. Mobile application market: A developer's perspective. 28. Netherlands: Telemat. Informatics, Elsevier B.V; 2011. p. 22–31.
16. Shotts K. PhoneGap 2.x mobile application development hotshot. 2013.
17. James M. Rapid application development. 1991.
18. Jemni M, Khribi MK. The ALECSO Smart Learning Framework. In: Proceedings of International Conference on Smart Learning Environments (ICSLE 2016). p. 28–30.
19. Jemni M, Khribi MK. Toward empowering Open and Online Education in the Arab world through OER and MOOCs". In: Jemni M, Kinshuk, Khribi MK, editors. Open Education: from OERs to MOOCs, Springer Lecture Notes in Educational Technology series. 2016.

CHAPTER 10

Interactive Live-Streaming Technologies and Approaches for Web-Based Applications

Luis Rodriguez-Gil[1,2] · Pablo Orduna˜ [1,2] · Javier Garc´ıa-Zubia[1,2] · Diego Lopez-de-Ipi ´ na˜ [1,2]

[1].*Faculty of EngineeringUniversity of DeustoBilbaoSpain*

[2].*DeustoTech - Deusto FoundationBilbaoSpain*

ABSTRACT

Interactive live streaming is a key feature of applications and platforms in which the actions of the viewers affect the content of the stream. In those, a minimal capture-display delay is critical. Though recent technological advances have certainly made it possible to provide web-based interactive live-streaming, little research is available that compares the real-world performance of the different web-based schemes. In this paper we use educational remote laboratories as a case study. We analyze the restrictions that web-based interactive live-streaming applications have, such as a low delay. We also consider additional characteristics that are often sought in production systems, such as universality and deployability behind institutional firewalls. The paper describes and experimentally compares the most relevant approaches for the study. With the provided descriptions and real-world experimental results, researchers, designers and developers can: a) select among the interactive live-streaming approaches which are available for their real-world systems, b) decide which one is most appropriate for their purpose, and c) know what performance and results they can expect.

Keywords: Webcam Live streaming Remote laboratories Online learning tools Rich interactive applications

1 INTRODUCTION

The latest social trends and technological advances have led to the emergence of various popular web-based live streaming platforms, such as YouTube Live,[1] TwitchTV,[2] Instagram Livestream[3] and Facebook Live.[4] These platforms are designed to maximize scalability and, though they are indeed live, they still allow a relatively high delay (several seconds or more). This enables them to use a larger buffer, heavier compression and more effective transcoding techniques than they otherwise could. The work in [48] provides further detail on these issues and outlines the TwitchTV architecture, which is a good example. Specifically, the measured broadcast delay of that platform varies between 12 to 21 seconds. The negative impact on user experience is not too high, because for non-interactive live-streaming applications —such as live sports—, such a delay is acceptable.

However, there are also many applications of live streaming which need to be interactive. In interactive live streaming systems, the viewers affect the content of the stream. A common example is a videoconference application, in which viewers interact with each other. Other example are remote laboratories, which will be used in this work as the main case study. These labs allow remote students to view specific hardware through a webcam and interact with it remotely in close to real time. Figure 1 characterizes the different types of streaming and some of its applications.

Interactive live-streaming systems share some challenges with standard live-streaming platforms. One of those is the importance of being web-based. Throughout the last years there has been a powerful trend towards shifting applications to the Web. However, certain features, such as multimedia, have traditionally had more limited support [31, 41]. Applications that depended on them had to find workarounds: many chose to rely on non-standard plugins [9], such as Java Applets[5] or Adobe Flash.[6] Others accepted a significant decrease in their quality or performance, or could not be migrated at all. Today, with HTML5 [16] and with other related Web standards such as WebGL [44], this is starting to change. One of the features for which applications have traditionally had to rely on external plug-ins was video streaming. Now, as an example, large websites such as Youtube or Netflix[7] rely by default on HTML5 [47].

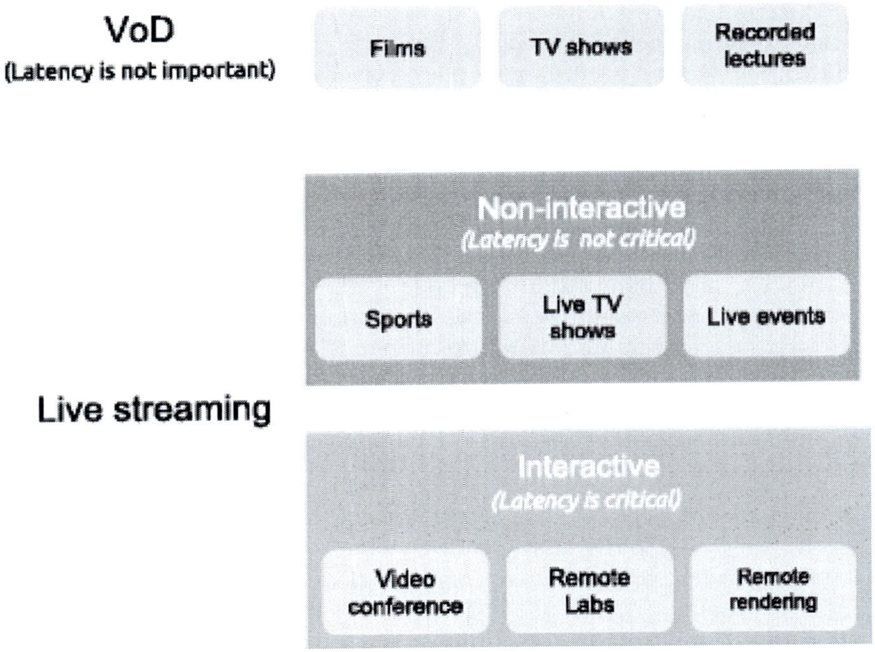

Figure 1. Characterization of the different types of streaming and some of its applications

Applications that require interactive live-streaming, however, have additional requirements, expectations, and limitations. VOD (Video-On-Demand) streaming applications, such as Youtube or Netflix, are the most common platforms. Because videos exist far in advance before the users view them, they can be preprocessed at will. They can use heavy compression and prepare the video for different qualities and transmission rates. Also, they can be streamed through adaptive streaming with relative ease. Also, they rely on buffering to provide a greater quality despite network issues, and to be able to use a larger compression frame. Live applications, however, have limitations at those respects. As previously mentioned, those that are not interactive (e.g., broadcasting a live sports event), can withstand several seconds delay without issues. For those that are interactive (e.g., remote laboratories, collaborative tools, video conferencing applications) more than a second delay is already high: according to some HCI analysis, beyond a 0.1 seconds delay the user can notice a system is not reacting instantaneously, and beyond 1 second the user's flow of thought is interrupted [27].

In this context, researchers and system designers and developers that want to implement interactive live-streaming systems face certain difficulties. Major live-streaming platforms are closed and proprietary. It is difficult to use them for learning and research purposes [48], and they are not suitable for interactive live-streaming or as middleware for other applications. Moreover, the schemes that are available for implementing interactive live-streaming are complex. For a real-world usage, the adequacy of a scheme may depend on the video format, on the communication scheme, on the compatibility of different browsers, on the resources and bandwidth available, etc. Most of those aspects, individually, are examined in the literature. However, the real-world performance and limitations of the different real-world schemes cannot be readily predicted from it. There is little real-world experimental data that researchers and developers may use to take a truly informed decision on the approaches they choose. The main goal of this work is to provide them with that information.

In this paper, in Section 2, we describe the goals and contributions of this work and the particular requirements of web-based interactive applications that rely on live-streaming that we will consider. To illustrate the case practically, we put special focus on remote laboratories and educational applications. We propose some criteria through which the effectiveness of each approach can be compared. Then, in Section 3, we examine and describe several approaches that Web-based interactive applications may use for providing live-streaming capabilities. The five of them that seem potentially more relevant according to the previously defined criteria are described in more detail, and selected for further experimental comparison. In Section 4 we describe the experiments that have been conducted to measure the effectiveness and real-world performance of those five approaches. In Section 5, we compare the results of the different experiments. In Section 6 we examine the results and comparison and we offer an interpretation and some guidelines for potential application. Finally, in Section 7 we draw a number of conclusions and we outline some possible future lines of work.

2 MOTIVATION

2.1 Challenge and purpose

In a live streaming system the content is typically produced while it is being broadcast. That is, essentially, what differentiates it from non-live systems. However, there is still a very significant delay between the moment a frame is captured and the moment it is displayed in the target device [1, 15]. This delay is not only the result of network or hardware latency. It is built into the design to achieve a higher scalability [43]. In non-interactive live streams, a delay of seconds does not typically harm the QoE (Quality of Experience), and it makes it possible to leverage techniques such as buffering, video segmentation and high-compression motion codecs. An example of this is the case of the Twitch[8] platform. It relies on different techniques depending on the target device, but it tends to have a higher than 10 seconds delay [48]. Other example is the YouTube[9] live streaming platform, which lets users choose between better quality or lower latency. Even in the lower latency mode a capture-display delay higher than 20-30 seconds is, reportedly, not unexpected.[10] This is appropriate for several types of applications, such as broadcasting a sports event. However, for certain interactive applications, delays higher than a second, as previously established, can already be considered high.

An *interactive* live streaming application differs from a non-interactive one. Users are not simply passive spectators to the content. Instead, they are able to interact with it or through it, affecting the stream [48]. This imposes a strong constraint on the maximum acceptable capture-display delay that is not present in other types of live streaming. It could thus also be considered as *near-real-time* streaming. Some of the potential applications for interactive live streaming (see also Figure 1) are the following:

- **VIDEOCONFERENCING SOFTWARE**, such as Skype,[11] Google Hangouts,[12] or Apple Facetime,[13] in which users view, listen and react to each other in *near-real-time*.

- **SURVEILLANCE SYSTEMS**, in which the viewer should be able to see what is happening in almost real-time.

- **REMOTE RENDERING SYSTEMS**, in which the server handles the rendering and sends the video to the client in real time. An example is cloud-based gaming [36]: rendering a videogame in the server-side and forwarding the input from the client. Other example is free-viewpoint rendering [40]: in such a system, with many video inputs, the server has a huge amount of video data. To reduce bandwidth requirements, only the relevant portions are served to the client in real time.

- **INTERACTIVE REMOTE LABORATORIES**, in which users interact with real physical equipment located somewhere else with a webcam stream as their main input.

The contributions of this work are intended to be useful for any web-based interactive live streaming application. However, due to the experience and background of the authors, the examples of this work will mainly relate to this fourth type of application: remote laboratories. Nowadays, remote laboratories often rely on relatively old technologies and approaches to provide interactive live streaming. Examples of such an approach is refreshing an image from JavaScript, or relying on the M-JPEG codification scheme. It is currently not clear, however, which of these relatively old approaches are more effective. Also, it is not clear whether newer approaches are not being used due to:

- Inertia and developer preference.
- More advanced technologies (such as adaptive streaming, video segmentation, or high-compression codecs) not being effective for near-real-time streaming.
- Newer approaches having significant real-world issues, such as portability issues, low reliability or difficulties to deploy behind institutional proxies.
- No literature available on the approaches available, their effectiveness, and the expected real-world outcome.

This work thus aims to shed more light in that area. The goal is that the remote laboratory community in particular and other interactive live streaming applications in general have the information to make better decisions on which streaming approaches to implement. And, moreover, so that they can know what effectiveness and performance they can expect by doing so. It also aims, specifically, to describe the currently used approaches and their architecture, and to propose some novel ones.

2.2 Contributions

The contributions of this work are thus the following:

- A brief analysis of which characteristics are important for interactive live streaming applications.

- Description and architecture of the most common interactive live streaming approaches that are currently used by remote laboratories (JavaScript-based image refreshing, and native M-JPEG).
- Description and architecture of some more advanced approaches, which, to our knowledge, have not been used in real-world remote laboratories but which could be superior. (JavaScript-based M-JPEG, JavaScript-based MPEG-1 and JavaScript-based H.264/AVC, all three relying on Web Sockets as a transport).
- Experimental analysis of the support for these approaches across all major desktop and mobile browsers.
- Experimental performance comparison of those described approaches that are most relevant.
- Scientific knowledge for existing developers of systems that rely on interactive live-streaming, that enables them to make educated decisions on the feasibility and convenience of incorporating alternative technical approaches into their implementations.
- Conclusions, based on the results of the experiments, on which approaches would be more appropriate depending on the type of remote laboratory required.

Of all of those contributions, the main one is the experimental performance comparison among the most relevant web-based approaches.

2.3 Remote laboratories

A remote laboratory is a software and hardware tool. It allows students to remotely access real equipment located somewhere else [9, 13, 24]. They can thus learn to use that equipment and experiment with it without having it physically available. Research suggests that learning through a remote laboratory, if it is properly designed and implemented, can be as effective as learning through a hands-on session [5]. Additionally, they can offer advantages such as reducing costs [26] and promoting sharing of equipment among different organizations [29]. Many remote laboratories feature one or several webcams. Through them, users can view the remote equipment. Simultaneously, they can interact with the physical devices using means such as virtual controls that are physically mapped to them. (e.g., [14, 20, 42, 46]). Some remote laboratories are even designed to allow access from mobile devices [8]. An example of remote laboratory is depicted in Figure 2. In this particular case,[14] the students experiment with the Archimedes' principle. They can interact with 6 different instances of equipment, for which 6 simultaneous webcam streams are needed.

2.4 Technical goals and criteria

We propose a set of technical goals and criteria to compare and evaluate the different interactive live streaming approaches that will be examined.

The key technical goals that will be considered are the following:

- **NEAR-REAL-TIME**: The delay between the actual real-life event and the time the user perceives it —the latency— should be minimum for the interaction to be smooth.
- **UNIVERSALITY**: The applications should be deployable under as many platforms, systems and networks and as easily as possible.
- **SECURITY**: The applications should be secure.

Though less critical, the following traits significantly affect the Quality of Experience and will be taken into account when evaluating the different possible approaches:

- **FRAME RATE**: The higher the better.
- **QUALITY**: The higher the better.
- **NETWORK BANDWIDTH USAGE**: The lower the better.
- **CLIENT-SIDE RESOURCES**: CPU and RAM usage. The lower the better.

SERVER-SIDE PROCESSING is also an important consideration, especially for production systems. Though it will be considered and discussed evaluating it quantitatively is beyond the scope of this work — which focuses mainly on the client-side. Therefore, the experiments themselves include no server-side measurements.

A last consideration is the **IMPLEMENTATION COMPLEXITY** of each approach. Beyond the previously mentioned criteria, in practise, the knowledge, cost and effort required for implementing a specific interactive live-streaming approach is also, in many cases, a determining factor. Evaluating this complexity quantitatively is beyond the scope of this work.

In the following subsections we briefly describe a simplified streaming platform model. Additionally, we provide further detail and rationale about the aforementioned technical goals and criteria.

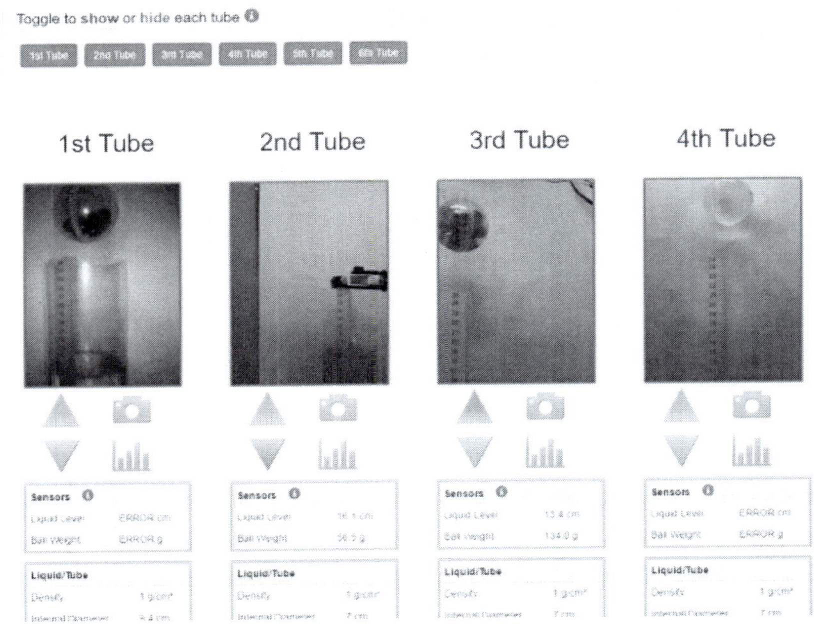

Figure 2. Archimedes principle remote laboratory at the University of Deusto

2.4.1 Simplified live-streaming platform model

Different live-streaming platform models may exist. A simplified one is shown in Figure 3. It is also the general model that is considered in this work. A set of IP cameras provide their input to the streaming platform through a camera output format. The particular format will vary, because different camera models support different formats. Common ones are, for instance, JPG snapshots, M-JPEG streams, and, in newer models, the H.264 format. The streaming platform receives the input and transcodes it into the target format. Often, the platform will also briefly act as a cache server for the input, so that it can scale for an arbitrary number of users without increasing the load on the webcams. The transcoded output is served through the server-client channel protocol (e.g., standard HTTP, AJAX, Web Sockets) to the client's browser. Depending on the approach, the browser will render it natively or through other means.

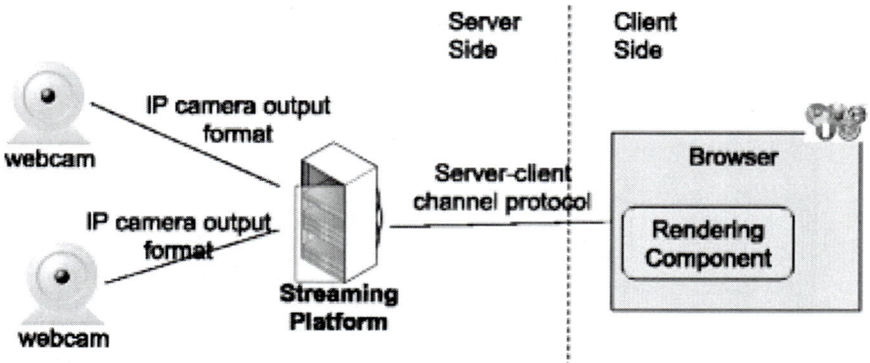

Figure 3. Simplified live-streaming platform model

2.4.2 Near-real-time

In a live-streaming context end-to-end latency (sometimes also known just as *latency*), is generally considered to be the time that elapses between the instant a frame is captured by the source device and the time it is displayed on the target device. For most types of live streaming applications a relatively high (some seconds) latency can be tolerated without significantly harming the user's experience [6, 32]. Latency is introduced in each stage of the process. Noteworthy delays are the latency introduced by the camera, the latency introduced by the server-side encoding, the latency introduced by the network and the latency introduced by the client (decoding and displaying). These sources of latency are analyzed and discussed in detail in the white paper by Axis Communications [22]. Tolerating a relatively high delay is a significant advantage. Especially in a bandwidth-constrained network, codecs that provide large compression but which require heavy pre-processing can be used. Issues such as *jitter* can be solved with a longer buffer. Most HTTP streaming methods rely on buffering to provide adaptation for bandwidth fluctuation, and often separate the stream into multiple media segments. This adds an unavoidable capture-display delay [23].

Interactive live-streaming applications are much less tolerant to latency. The actions of the users depend directly on what they are currently seeing on the stream. A few seconds delay is enough to severely harm their Quality of Experience. Exactly how much latency can be tolerated and how much it affects user experience varies depending on the application. For example, some works report that in conversational applications (e.g., IP telephony, videoconferencing) 150 ms is a good latency, while 300-400 ms is not acceptable [32]. For cloud-based games some studies suggest that approximately for each additional 100 ms latency there is a 25%

decrease in player performance [3]. For many other types of common interactive live streaming applications, such as remote laboratories, there is, to our knowledge, little specific research available on how much increased latency affects user experience. However, the interaction style and pace of many of them, such as remote laboratories themselves, is generally similar to that of a standard application or interactive website. Thus, it is reasonable to assume that generalist interaction conclusions are appropriate. In this line, according to works such as [27], beyond a 0.1 seconds delay the user can notice that a system is not reacting instantaneously, and beyond 1 second the user's flow of thought is interrupted.

Due to all this, supporting near-real-time (which for the purpose of this work, we will consider as being able to provide a relatively low end-to-end latency) is a particularly important requirement for an effective interactive live streaming approach, and the set of techniques that can be applied are significantly different than those that are applied for standard live-streaming or for VoD (Video on Demand). Modern techniques which are very popular and effective for standard streaming are sometimes not an option anymore, or are severely limited:

- **BUFFERING**: Would add a delay of at least the buffer length, so it can't be used or needs to have a minimal length.
- **SEGMENTED STREAMS**: Would add a delay of at least the segment length.
- **PRE-TRANSCODING**: Not really an option if a small delay is required.

2.4.3 Universality

The meaning and usage of *universality* varies between contexts, but in this paper we will use it to refer to the degree to which an application is technically available to those who may want to use it. Aspects which increase universality are, among others, the following:

- Being cross-platform
- Being web-based
- Being available across many types of devices (PCs, mobile phones, tablets)
- Having less technical requirements to run properly
- Requiring less user privileges to run

- Being deployable behind more strict institutional firewalls and proxies

Universality is generally positive, but it is important to note that, in practise, it often implies important trade-offs. Depending on the particular context, needs and requirements of an application, the actual importance of universality will vary. In the case of remote laboratories, research suggests that it is one of the most important characteristics [9], but in other cases this might differ. It is noteworthy that this work aims to contribute to web-based interactive applications, which, for being web-based, already tend to provide relatively high universality.

2.4.4 Security

Being secure can be considered a goal of any application. However, the importance will vary depending on the context. Some technologies tend to provide greater security than others. For example, remote laboratories and other educational applications are often hosted by universities. Their IT teams are often hesitant to offer intrusive technologies to students to avoid exposing them to security risks, for which the university could be liable [9]. All things equal, *non-intrusive* technologies are thus preferred.

2.4.5 Frame rate

The frame rate is measured through the frames-per-second (FPS) metric. In some contexts, 50-60 FPS is considered to be a satisfactory visual quality at which increases can hardly be noticed. However, in practise, in many cases, significantly lower frame rates are used [32]. This is often in fact the case for many interactive live streaming applications.

2.4.6 Quality

Quality is hard to measure because it is actually a qualitative perception that is affected by many (qualitative and quantitative) variables. Sometimes (e.g., in Youtube) it is used as a synonym for *resolution* or *pixel density*. For simplification, in the comparison of the different approaches, we will rely the most on the *resolution*. The particular video codec that is used also has great influence in the final quality of the stream.

2.4.7 Network bandwidth usage

Live-streaming applications consume significant amounts of network bandwidth. This is because video content tends to consume significant bandwidth itself, and because often it has to be provided to many users [38]. Bandwidth usage can thus be a significant cost and limitation, and all things equal approaches that preserve network bandwidth are preferred. Unfortunately, there tends to be an inverse correlation between network bandwidth usage and required server-side and client-side processing. That is, the codecs that require the less bandwidth tend to also be the ones that require the more processing power to code (server-side) and to decode (client-side). Sometimes specialized hardware is relied upon to provide more efficient decoding. Adding to the difficulty, some network setups, particularly mobile ones, are inherently unstable and their bandwidth capacity cannot be predicted reliably [23, 39].

2.4.8 Client-side resources

Different approaches and implementations require different amounts of CPU power and RAM. The codecs used, particularly, have a very significant influence at that respect. Client-side processing effort tends to be higher for the codecs that require the less bandwidth. To compensate for this, however, many devices also provide hardware-level support for particular codecs. Relying on hardware-level support is most of the time significantly more efficient, in terms of processing and energy usage. At the same time, because support tends to vary between different devices, it can sometimes make portability harder. In this work, the client-side processing effort will be measured in terms of CPU and RAM usage, though additional variables could be taken into account, such as energy cost, I/O usage or discrete graphic card usage. It is noteworthy that some applications have different client-side processing restrictions than others. All things equal, lower resources usage is better: A Video on Demand (VoD) application, for instance, could admit a relatively high usage in exchange of low bandwidth and high quality. There is a single active stream and the user is not expected to be multi-tasking. However, a remote laboratory or an IP surveillance application which requires being able to observe many cameras at once would often have stricter limits. See for instance the remote laboratory in Figure 2. The students have access to 6 different simultaneous streams. Through them, they must be able to interact with the equipment in real-time. Thus, the resource usage of an individual stream must be significantly conservative.

2.4.9 Server-side processing

Server-side processing can be very high due to the pre-processing, compression and encoding that is sometimes used. Large media servers and systems, and especially those that aim to scale to many concurrent users per stream, such as Wowza,[15] YouTube and Netflix, encode a given source video into many separate formats and qualities. Thus, they can dynamically adapt the stream to the bandwidth and technical restrictions of each user. A higher or lower quality stream can be served depending on the bandwidth that the user has available. Also, one format or another can be served depending on whether the user's device or browser supports that format or not, and depending even on whether the user's device supports hardware acceleration for that format. For interactive applications the possible choice of codecs and formats is more limited, because the latency cannot exceed certain values. Also, it is noteworthy that for applications which do not aim to scale to many concurrent users per stream, but which instead aim to serve a relatively high number of different streams (such as many remote laboratories) it is sometimes convenient to accept a higher bandwidth usage in exchange of a lower processing effort.

Though server-side processing could thus be an important consideration, this paper focuses on the client-side and therefore, though server-side considerations will be briefly described, experiments will focus on the client-side.

2.4.10 Implementation complexity

In practise, in production systems, the main factor for choosing an interactive live-streaming approach will often not be the technical characteristics or performance, but its implementation complexity. Technically superior approaches may be overlooked in favour of approaches that require less knowledge and effort and have a lower cost to implement. The quantitative evaluation of the implementation complexities of each of the different approaches is beyond the scope of this work. It would be hard to do and very difficult to reach meaningful results, due to its often developer-specific and subjective nature. Nonetheless, the architecture used for each experiment will be described and thus the implementation complexity may be partially inferred from it.

3 INTERACTIVE LIVE-STREAMING APPROACHES

In this section we will describe and analyze some of the different approaches that are available for web-based interactive live streaming. The first of them (image-refreshing and native M-JPEG based approaches) are often used by the architectures, use-cases and implementations of live streaming applications that can be found in the literature. Additionally, we include some novel approaches which are more rarely used, some of which have only recently become available due to their reliance on new or under-development Web standards.

The diagram in Fig 4 shows the generalized (and simplified) process that the interactive live streaming platforms follow from the time a frame is captured to the time it is displayed. The flow starts when the IP webcam captures a frame. Many different IP webcam models exist, and different models support different output formats. Some of the most common are JPG (discrete images), M-JPEG and H.264 streams. Through those formats, the output from the cameras is forwarded to the streaming platform. Depending on the source and target formats, it might or might not be necessary to transcode it into a different format. Transcoding can take a significant amount of processing power and adds some latency. The cameras server will briefly store these images, and will be responsible of serving them to the browser. Different server-client channel protocols are available. Once delivered, the browser will render the provided data to the user. Depending on the particular scheme, it will rely on a native component (such as for native M-JPEG videos or for image refreshing) or it will process, decode and render the data through JavaScript.

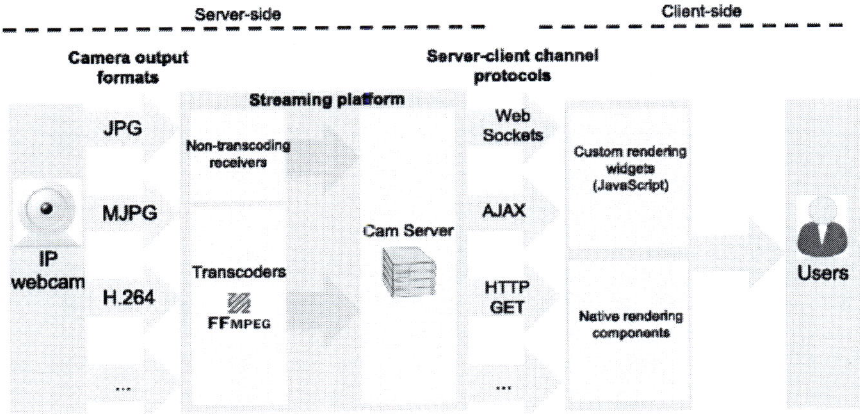

Figure 4. Interactive live-streaming platform process

In the following subsections we will describe in more detail the different schemes. We will describe more thoroughly those schemes which best seem to meet the criteria described in Section 2, and which we will select for the experimental comparison. For most schemes, we will describe separately the server-side and client-side.

3.1 JavaScript-based image refreshing

This is a mature technique which is technically very simplistic, both in the client and the server-side. The server simply provides individual access to the current frame and the client repeatedly asks for a new frame using JavaScript. Despite its technical shortcomings it is used by many applications in the literature, sometimes as a fallback. Particularly, it is used by many remote laboratories for which a high FPS isn't absolutely necessary, including most of the remote laboratories of WebLab-Deusto,[16] LabsLand[17] and RemLabNet[18] [34].

3.1.1 Client-side

In the client-side only a browser with JavaScript support is required. The HTML contains an <img> tag which points at the webcam image. Then, from JavaScript, the image tag's srcattribute is constantly modified. Under all modern browsers —and most legacy ones— when the src tag is changed the new image is loaded. To prevent some technical issues, generally some additional low-level considerations are taken:

- To modify the webcam image's URL in some way (such as by adding a random number to the *GET query* parameters) so that no cache issues occur.
- To query for a new image only after the load event has fired, sometimes after a small delay, so that requests don't accumulate on slow networks.

3.1.2 Server-side

Server-side this particular approach is also relatively simple. Most IP webcams provide an image URL that serves one frame, so that URL just needs to be made available either directly or through a standard web server. Some applications require several concurrent users and the hardware of webcams is sometimes not particularly powerful, so a cache server can be used. In that case, a cache server in the same network would continuously request frames to the camera. Then, whenever the web server asks for a frame, the last cached frame is served.

3.2 Motion JPEG

Motion JPEG, often known as just M-JPEG, is a video format with intraframe-only compression: each frame is essentially a separately compressed JPEG image. Because of this, its compression rate tends to be significantly lower than that of most modern interframe formats [4] (e.g., H.264/MPEG-4 AVC [19], H.265 [18], VP8 [2], VP9 [11]). However, it does have some significant advantages [21]: it is simple to implement, it requires little memory and processing power, it responds better than other formats to packet loss, fast image changes [4], and network jitter [28]. Many IP webcams provide native support for M-JPEG streaming, and M-JPEG is supported by most modern browsers, including the desktop and mobile versions of Google Chrome, Mozilla Firefox, Apple Safari and Microsoft Edge. It is not natively supported, however, by Microsoft Internet Explorer, and there have been significant issues with the implementations of most of these browsers. Examples of interactive live streaming applications that currently rely on M-JPEG are the RexLab.[19] Other example are laboratories based on the iSES[20] SDK [33], which support both browser-native M-JPEG and a JavaScript-based M-JPEG decoder which receives the frame from the server through WebSockets.

Natively, browsers and HTTP servers implement M-JPEG by sending the videos through special mimetypes such as multipart/x-mixed-replace and using the Chunked Based Coding feature of HTTP 1.1 (RFC2616 [7]), which is a data transfer mechanism that allows the transmission of dynamically generated content. When the request is started the total length does not need to be known. Instead, an undetermined number of *chunks* can be sent, and the request can be completed any time by a final zero-length chunk. In the case of a M-JPEG stream, servers keep a long-running request, sending the separate JPEG images that compose the video as separate chunks.

3.2.1 Limitations of browser-native M-JPEG implementations

Although the M-JPEG video format itself is relatively effective for live streaming [10, 21] and it is indeed a popular format for applications such as webcams, digital cameras or remote laboratories, there are in practise some technical and reliability issues with the native M-JPEG implementations of current browers.

Though most major browsers nominally support M-JPEG natively, it fails to work under certain versions of Google Chrome, Mobile Safari and Firefox. Also, when the stream is interrupted or fails, browsers do not recover. Under some circumstances, such as receiving at a higher FPS than the bandwidth allows, Chrome and Firefox often stop displaying the image but keep internally receiving them.

Motion-JPEG has no particular bandwidth-control or timing provisions. Browsers tend to render the frames just as they are received. This works as expected when the bandwidth is high enough for the FPS. The latency is even particularly low when compared to modern formats such as H.264 because there is no interframe compression or buffering delay. However, when the server is sending frames at a higher rate than the client can receive and display, the frames tend to accumulate and thus a significant and growing latency is introduced. Avoiding this is non-trivial and is not always possible, and the implementations observed in this work do not make any particular provision at this respect.

3.2.2 Client-side

The client-side is, at least in principle, straightforward for those browsers that natively support M-JPEG, because including an <img> tag is all that is needed. In practise, some implementations will provide a fallback mechanism (e.g., in [25]) for browsers that do not support it or that encounter issues, which is not uncommon.

As described in the previous section, reliability and bandwidth control is often an issue. Browsers provide no particular Motion-JPEG-related functionality or semantics through JavaScript, so detecting and recovering from failures is non-trivial. Under the tested browsers (Google Chrome, Mozzilla Firefox) no *load* or *error* events are raised on the <img> element that hosts the M-JPEG image when the stream is interrupted. In principle, the binary data of the image could be repeatedly accessed in JavaScript through the HTML5 APIs and explicitly compared to verify whether it has changed or not. In practise, however, this is very costly in terms of performance and is by default disallowed for externally hosted images due to CORS restrictions. Furthermore, browsers seem to have issues handling high FPS, with Chrome, for instance, soon using 100% CPU on that tab and showing a blank image.

Most observed implementations simply choose to stream at a fixed and relatively low FPS to partially avoid these issues, or let the user or administrator configure the FPS.

An alternative is to avoid relying on the native M-JPEG capability of the browsers (which tends to be flawed) and to receive and render the stream through JavaScript instead.

3.2.3 Server-side

Many IP webcam models support M-JPEG natively, so some implementations simply redirect that stream to the end-users. However, if the system should support several concurrent users, a caching server is required to achieve an acceptable Quality of Service. The server can try to adapt to available bandwidth by avoiding to queue frames and instead sending always the latest captured frame. Thus, theoretically, if the client received and displayed the latest frame just when it is received, the capture-display delay would be minimized and the server and client would be mostly synchronized. In practise, however, intermediate systems (including the browsers themselves) often buffer the TCP stream, so this scheme does not always work as well as expected.

To avoid relying on the (often flawed) native M-JPEG browser support, and to rely on JavaScript instead, the server will have to send the stream through an alternative means, such as Web Sockets, WebRTC or AJAX. This way, the previously mentioned glitches can be bypassed, and it becomes feasible to adapt to the available bandwidth. This comes at the cost of a higher client-side processing.

3.3 High-compression formats

Image-refreshing and M-JPEG, as discussed, provide relatively poor compression, but they are nonetheless often used for certain types of real-time interactive applications. That seems to be, mostly, because:

- They require little client-side and server-side processing power.
- They are simple to implement and maintain.
- Encoding and decoding takes very little time so very little capture-display latency is added.
- They can be used in almost any platform and browser.

In other contexts, however, such as non-interactive live streaming, or such as VoD, those formats are generally not used and would often be regarded as suboptimal formats. Instead, those contexts often favour formats and approaches that take higher processing time, require a more complex architecture, and add some latency; but that require lower bandwidth and provide higher quality. Example formats are, for instance: MPEG-1 [17], H.264/MPEG-4 AVC [19], H.265 [18], VP8 [2], or VP9 [11]. Today, some of those are natively supported by some browsers and systems —though not necessarily for live-streaming—, and some formats can be decoded, at a potentially high processing cost, through JavaScript. Therefore, in the current state of things, approaches that rely on this kind of codecs could today be an effective alternative for near-real-time live video streaming. Especially, since they offer a particularly high compression-rate and a relatively high quality [12].

3.3.1 Client-side

Client-side there are, again, two possibilities. First, in the most ideal case, the browser and hardware will support the format natively through the HTML <video> tag, and the support will also provide enough facilities for near-real-time live streaming of that format. Unfortunately, this is not always a valid approach due to the following:

- The HTML5 standard provides the <video> tag but it does not include live-streaming support. Though that is likely to change in the future through the MediaExtensions API.

- Each browser supports a different set of codecs, so the server needs to generate different streams to be truly cross-platform.

As an alternative, or as a fallback, it is possible to use JavaScript-based decoders for some of the formats. Such a system receives the stream data through Web Sockets, AJAX, or similar; decodes it through JavaScript, which depending on the format can require significant resources; and then renders it into an HTML5 canvas. Though more costly in terms of processing power, it is truly cross-platform and compatible with any modern browser.

3.3.2 Server-side

Server-side this approach tends to be significantly more costly in terms of resources, especially if several streams need to be provided. If a single stream is provided, it is also more costly than in the case of image-refreshing or M-JPEG due to the compression and intra-frame nature of these formats. A significant difference is also that for an user to be able to join an ongoing stream, initialization steps are required. That sometimes involves sending initialization packets through a secondary data channel, and/or waiting for specific periodic frames before being able to join.

3.4 Non-standard plugins

Traditionally, multimedia features in the browser have been limited. This has led many media-dependant applications to rely on non-standard plugins such as Adobe Flash or Java Applets. The remote laboratory described in [37], for instance, displays a webcam through the YawCam[21] Java Applet.

Adobe Flash, Java Applets and similar plug-ins have access to native TCP and UDP sockets, which makes it possible to use non-web streaming protocols such as RTSP [35]. Although this makes this approach particularly powerful, it also implies that it is less universal. The plugins themselves need to be previously installed, which requires administrator privileges that are not always available. Also, Java Applets, for instance, are not supported in mobile devices, and Flash support is very limited. Support in desktop browsers is better, but still, Chrome has dropped support for Java Applets, and Firefox is expected to drop it soon. Other browsers are likely to follow similar paths. These issues are also discussed in [30]. Furthermore, the plugins themselves and the usage of non-HTTP protocols have security implications. As a result, applications that rely on those would be unable to be deployed under many institutional firewalls and proxies without significant configuration and policy changes [9].

3.5 WebRTC

WebRTC (Web Real-Time Communication) is an API standard that is currently under development by the W3C. It is oriented for peer-to-peer multimedia communication. This technology can be very useful for certain applications, such as videoconferencing ones, which can benefit from being decentralized and peer-to-peer. However, it has certain constraints:

- It still requires a server to handle the connection process and signalling; and to route all data for those cases where the NATs or firewalls of the clients prevent them from directly connecting to each other.
- It is oriented towards peer-to-peer connections, so its usefulness is limited when the source of the content is a traditional centralized server.
- It is not yet an accepted standard, and it is not yet supported by every major browser.
- For these reasons, WebRTC-based approaches will not be considered for the purposes of this work, though it may be useful to also compare them in the future.

3.6 HLS and MPEG-DASH

HLS (HTTP Live Streaming) is a protocol created by Apple which is intended to answer some of the challenges described in this work. However, it is, at least for now, not natively supported by all browsers, and it is not standard, so *universality* is limited.

MPEG-DASH (Dynamic Adaptive Streaming over HTTP) is an adaptive bitrate streaming standard that is currently in draft form. Support is growing and in the future it is likely to be a very effective alternative.

3.7 Limitations

Though several approaches were described in the previous section, there are many more potential ones which could be feasible, and more are likely to appear in the future. Thus, it is noteworthy that the previous list or this comparison is not meant to be exhaustive.

4 EXPERIMENTAL WORK

In this section, we experimentally evaluate the performance of the five most relevant schemes (described in the previous section). First, we detail the experimental setup and methodology. Next, for each scheme, we:

- Implement the scheme.
- Conduct qualitative experiments to verify whether the scheme does indeed run under different systems and devices.
- Conduct quantitative experiments to evaluate its performance.

4.1 Experimental setup

At this stage we have selected 5 approaches to be compared quantitatively (which we will refer to as image-refreshing, native M-JPEG, JS M-JPEG, MPEG-1, H.264/AVC). We are interested in measuring the performance under real-world conditions. Thus, beyond the specific scheme being analyzed, there are several other variables which may affect the measurements. Some of these are the following:

- **FPS:** Target Frames Per Second.
- **CLIENT DEVICE:** Computer or mobile device to render and take measurements in.
- **NETWORK:** Latency, available bandwidth, etc.
- **BROWSER:** Browser and specific version.

Conducting experiments for every combination would be impractical, and not particularly meaningful. Certain restrictions have been applied for each of these variables, and will be described next.

4.1.1 FPS

Though some systems rely on a variable FPS, in this case we will set a target FPS. This makes it possible to obtain comparable results for RAM, CPU and bandwidth, and is consistent with real-world usage. When applicable,[22] we will conduct the experiments against three different FPS values: 5, 10 and 25. For some schemes, we will also measure the maximum average FPS they can achieve.

4.1.2 Client device

All the quantitative experiments have been conducted under *Device A*. In addition to the quantitative experiments, several qualitative ones were conducted to verify whether the specific schemes are indeed cross-platform. For those, two additional devices were used. The specification of the three devices are the following:

- **DEVICE A** Mac Book Pro 13' Mid 2014: 2.6 GHz Intel Core i5, 8 GB RAM, 256 GB SSD, Intel Iris 1536 MB Graphics Card. Running OS X 10.11.5).
- **DEVICE B** Desktop PC. Intel Core i7, 8 GB RAM. Running Windows 10.
- **DEVICE C** Samsung Galaxy S7 Edge (SM-G935F).

4.1.3 Network

There are mainly two network parameters which could be considered: bandwidth and latency. The experiments were conducted in a local network, with around 100 Mbps of bandwidth and around 20 ms of latency. Though both parameters are important, preliminary experiments suggest that they do not significantly affect the comparison.

In those preliminary experiments, the bandwidth did not affect the measurements, except when the measured bandwidth usage started getting close to the maximum network bandwidth. In these cases, either the target FPS could not be met (image-refreshing scheme) or the capture-render delay started growing beyond what could be reasonable for an interactive live-streaming system (the other schemes). Differences in latency seemingly have no effect in RAM, CPU or bandwidth. As expected, however, an increased network latency results in an increased capture-render delay. The relationship seems to be, as expected, mostly linear. So, though the measurements would vary on a slower network, the comparison and the conclusions should not.

4.2 Methodology and measurements

The implementations have been deployed in a server in the local network. The video feed is obtained from a local IP webcam. The metrics that will be measured are the RAM usage, CPU usage, downstream bandwidth and capture-render latency. They all will be measured in relation to a target FPS. We have kept them as separate metrics because, depending on the specific application, the most significant ones might vary. For instance, in certain mobile networks minimizing the bandwidth usage could be the most important criteria [39]. In other cases, such as in networks with more bandwidth, minimizing RAM or CPU usage could be more appropriate.

Bandwidth measurements are incoming-only, and have been obtained either through the Chrome Task Manager or the Mac OS activity monitor (because web socket bandwidth usage is not shown in Chrome). RAM and CPU were measured through the Chrome Task Manager. 5 measurements were taken in each case. The highest and lowest measurement were discarded. The 3 remaining measurements were used to compute the average and the standard deviation, which are listed in tables for each scheme.

For measuring the latency, an IP webcam was pointed towards a desktop computer displaying a clock on the screen. Then, the test laptop (Device A) was placed next to it, rendering the webcam image through the experimental streaming system, using the particular settings of each experiment. The latency is thus equal to the difference between the live clock (in the desktop) and its image rendered in the test laptop. For each experimental combination (FPS and streaming approach) 5 pictures were taken of both screens, and the difference measured. For these 5 measurements, the average and standard deviation was computed. Figure 5 shows a picture of this setup. The screen (in the middle) shows a clock. An IP webcam (in the lower left) is pointing to it and forwarding the stream to our interactive live-streaming platform. Then, the stream is being rendered in the laptop (to the right), using one of the schemes and configurations. When a picture is taken of both screens, the capture-render delay, at that moment, will thus be the difference between the clock and its render.

4.3 JavaScript-based image refreshing

The setup for this set of experiments can be observed in Figure 6. The live images are retrieved from the IP camera and stored into a Redis cache server. A Python-Flask-based server serves those images to the browser, which simply applies the image refreshing technique from JavaScript to obtain the images through standard HTTP and then displays them at a given frame rate.

The implementation was run on device A (with Chrome, Firefox, Safari), device B (with Chrome, Firefox, Internet Explorer and Edge) and device C (with mobile Chrome and mobile Firefox). Works as expected and without noticeable issues in all of them.

Figure 5. Picture measuring the capture-render delay

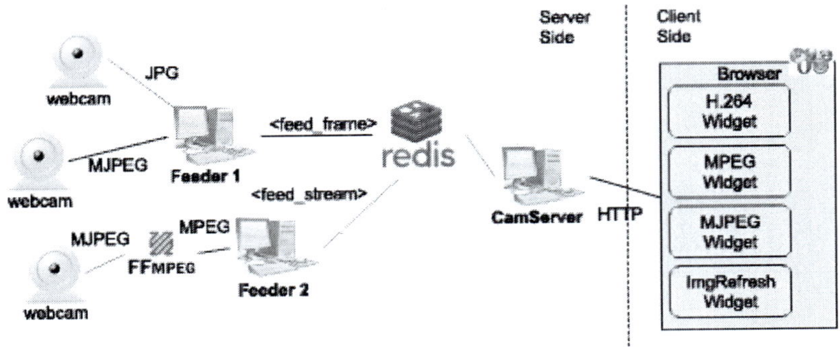

Figure 6. Architecture and deployment setup for the different experiments

The performance of the experimental implementation (conducted under device A and Chrome) is summarized in Table 1. It is noteworthy that RAM usage is particularly high. It increases steadily since the first image is loaded, and, after a while, it stabilises at around 600 MB. It is hypothesised that this is because of the Chrome caching and memory optimization schemes, which retains copies of the previously loaded images up until a certain point. The latency (capture-display delay) is relatively low. For all the tested frame rates, it is within the 223ms to 316ms range. The latency is lowest for 25 FPS. Although not covered in the table, it is noteworthy that at 10 FPS but with a constrained, simulated *Good 2G* connection, the delay is stable at around 1726 ms.

Table 1. JavaScript-based image refreshing performance

		Mean	S.D.
5 FPS	RAM	618.0 MB	2.646
	CPU	16.57%	0.115
	Bandwidth	233.0 KB/s	4.359
	Latency	316 ms	104.083
10 FPS	RAM	634.7 MB	0.577
	CPU	31.8%	0.100
	Bandwidth	461.3 KB/s	0.577
	Latency	246 ms	104.083
25 FPS	RAM	649.67 MB	17.098
	CPU	85.5%	0.709
	Bandwidth	1130.3 KB/s	1.528
	Latency	223 ms	107.480
Max	Achieved FPS	41 FPS	
	RAM	671 MB	
	CPU	116.9%	
	Bandwidth	2100 KB/s	

4.4 Native M-JPEG

The setup for these experiments is similar to the previous ones, and also depicted in Figure 6. The live images are retrieved from the IP camera and stored into a Redis cache server. A Python-Flask-based server provides a M-JPEG stream from them to the client at a fixed target frame rate. The client displays the M-JPEG stream natively by simply using an <img> element to the stream. No particular JavaScript is needed. Thus, no particular 'Native M-JPEG' widget is present in the figure.

The implementation was tried on device A (with Chrome, Firefox, Safari), device B (with Chrome, Firefox, Internet Explorer and Edge) and device C (with mobile Chrome and mobile Firefox). Runs in all browsers except on Internet Explorer.

The performance of the experiment (conducted under device A and Chrome) is summarized in Table 2. Similarly to the previous experiment, the RAM raises steadily since the first image is rendered, and increases steadily until it reaches around 600 MBs. When not bandwidth-constrained, the capture-display delay is in the 218-515 ms range, being lowest for 25 FPS. When bandwidth-constrained, the delay steadily increases and can be higher than 60 seconds. No data for a maximum FPS is provided, because at higher FPS the stream fails sooner. This is likely due to the native M-JPEG limitations described in Subsection 3.2.1. Particularly, it seems that once a single image fails, the browser stops updating the image. And because there is no JavaScript API and no JavaScript error event raised, recovery is non-trivial.

4.5 JavaScript-based M-JPEG

The setup for this set of experiments is also depicted in Figure 6. The live images are retrieved from the IP camera and stored into a Redis cache server. A Python-Flask-based server provides a M-JPEG stream from them to the client at a fixed target frame rate through Web Sockets and the *socket.io* library. The client renders each frame to an HTML5 Canvas through JavaScript.

The implementation was tried on device A (with Chrome, Firefox, Safari), device B (with Chrome, Firefox, Internet Explorer and Edge) and device C (with mobile Chrome and mobile Firefox). Runs in all browsers. No particular issues were observed in any of them.

The performance of the experiment (conducted under device A and Chrome) is summarized in Table 3. The RAM usage seems to increase slowly but it lowers periodically, and does not increase proportionally to the FPS. When not bandwidth-constrained the latency is relatively low and quite stable. It is within the 284-289 range, and it is lowest for 10 FPS, though given the small difference, it might be due to random fluctuations.

Higher than 115 FPS could be reached, and, strangely, in that case the CPU usage was actually lower than at 25 FPS.

Table 2. Native M-JPEG

		Mean	S.D.
5 FPS	RAM	605.3 MB	1.155
	CPU	12.40%	0.265
	Bandwidth	235.3 KB/s	4.726
	Latency	515 ms	149.921
10 FPS	RAM	617.3 MB	6.658
	CPU	24.5%	0.866
	Bandwidth	445.7 KB/s	32.624
	Latency	356 ms	51.394
25 FPS	RAM	625.3 MB	1.155
	CPU	60.13%	0.503
	Bandwidth	1126.7 KB/s	12.014
	Latency	218 ms	55.426

4.6 JavaScript-based MPEG-1

MPEG-1 [17] is a very mature format and in many traditional streaming contexts it could be considered *legacy*. More modern formats such as H.264 —which will also be tested in later sections,— provide better quality and compression [45]. However, potentially, its simplicity also implies a lower processing cost and a lower latency. Considering this and that currently many applications (such as most remote laboratories) still rely on apparently less efficient approaches such as image-refreshing or M-JPEG; MPEG-1 could still be an effective option in some current contexts.

The setup for this set of experiments is also depicted in Figure 6. It is slightly more complex than the previous ones because a transcoding component (from M-JPEG to MPEG) is necessary. Thus, in the server, a *ffmpeg* instance retrieves the live stream from the IP webcam (through M-JPEG), transcodes it into MPEG-1 and sends it to a *feeder* server. The *feeder* forwards the stream to the web server through Redis channels. The client receives the stream from that server through Web Sockets and *socket.io*. The stream is decoded using a JavaScript decoder and rendered into an HTML5 canvas. The MPEG-1 standard supports a limited number of FPS options, so in this case, the experiment was conducted only with 25 FPS (5 FPS and 10 FPS are not really allowed by the standard). The codec was configured to use an 800 Kbps constant bitrate.

Table 3. JavaScript-based M-JPEG

		Mean	S.D.
5 FPS	RAM	166.0 MB	11.136
	CPU	6.867%	0.058
	Bandwidth	315.7 KB/s	3.215
	Latency	289 ms	71.924
10 FPS	RAM	430.0 MB	18.330
	CPU	12.5%	0.100
	Bandwidth	528.0 KB/s	34.511
	Latency	216 ms	57.735
25 FPS	RAM	306.3 MB	47.480
	CPU	28.433%	0.231
	Bandwidth	1494.3 KB/s	92.376
	Latency	284 ms	54.262
Max	Achieved FPS	115-127 FPS	
	RAM	263 MB	
	CPU	20.8%	
	Bandwidth	8434.3 KB/s	

Specifically, the system relies on the following ffmpeg command to transcode the stream:

```
ffmpeg -r 30 -f mjpeg -i <webcam_mjpeg_url> -f mpeg1video
-b 800k -r 25 pipe:1
```

Client-side, a pure JavaScript decoder has been used. The decoder is Open Source and was originally created by Phoboslab.[23] It has been modified to add support for the *socket.io* library, which is a wrapper around Web Sockets but falls back to a long-polling system if the specific deployment does not support the former. The modified decoder is available at Github.[24]

The setup was tried on device A (with Chrome, Firefox, Safari), device B (with Chrome, Firefox, Internet Explorer and Edge) and device C (with mobile Chrome and mobile Firefox). Runs in all browsers. No particular issues were observed in any of them. It is noteworthy, though, that MPEG-1 quality was lower than the previous approches (which was to be expected due to the higher compression).

The performance of the experiment (conducted under device A and Chrome) is summarized in Table 4. The RAM usage is very steady. The latency is on average 610 ms when not bandwidth-constrained. Though not included in the table summary, it is noteworthy that when simulating a *Good 2G* connection under Chrome, the latency is similar, probably because due to its low bandwidth requirements, the restricted bandwidth is not really constrained either.

Table 4. JavaScript-based MPEG-1

		Mean	S.D.
25 FPS	RAM	104.0 MB	0.000
	CPU	6.9%	0.351
	Bandwidth	39.57 KB/s	3.066
	Latency	610 ms	325.087

4.7 JavaScript-based H.264/MPEG-4 AVC

H.264/MPEG-4 AVC [19] is currently a popular high-compression format, which is particularly appropriate for streaming, and is commonly supported as an output format for many modern IP webcams. The performance of a system relying on H.264 will vary significantly depending on the specific codec implementation, on the specific parameters for the codec, and on other factors. Thus, these experiments are not intended to evaluate the performance of the H.264 format itself, but, instead, the potential performance of a real-life interactive live streaming system that relies on it.

The setup for these experiments is depicted in Figure 6. Its architecture is similar to the one that was used for the MPEG-1 experiment, and it also relies on a transcoding component (from M-JPEG to H.264). Thus, in the server, a *ffmpeg* instance retrieves the live stream from the IP webcam (through M-JPEG), transcodes it into H.264 and sends it to a *feeder* server. The *feeder*forwards the stream to the web server through Redis channels. The client receives the stream from that server through Web Sockets and *socket.io*. The stream is decoded using a JavaScript decoder and rendered into an HTML5 canvas.

The *ffmpeg* instance was configured to use the *libx264* codec, with the baseline profile, constant bitrate mode (set to 1500Kbps) and with several low latency flags enabled. Specifically, the *ffmpeg* commandline that was used is:

```
ffmpeg -r 30 -f mjpeg -i <webcam_mjpeg_url> -flags +low_delay
-probesize 32 -c:v libx264 -tune zerolatency -preset:v ultrafast
-r <target_fps> -f h264 1500k pipe:1
```

The client renders the stream through a modified *Broadway.js* decoder. *Broadway.js* is a heavily optimized, Open Source, H.264 JavaScript decoder, which has been compiled through Emscripten and is futher optimized to use WebGL. To it, we have added *socket.io* support, so that it can gracefully fall back to AJAX under systems and deployments where Web Sockets are not functional. The modified decoder is Open Source and is hosted at GitHub.[25]

The setup was tried on device A (with Chrome, Firefox, Safari), device B (with Chrome, Firefox, Internet Explorer and Edge) and device C (with mobile Chrome and mobile Firefox). Runs in all browsers. No particular issues were observed in any of them.

The performance of the experiment (conducted under device A and Chrome) is summarized in Table 5. RAM usage is steady despite the FPS. CPU usage increases with the FPS. Latency is highest at 5 FPS (under which it averages 1083 ms) and lowest at 25 FPS (under which it averages 417 ms). This difference is quite significant, and, in part, is probably due to internal buffers in the codec being filled faster at higher framerates.

5 COMPARISON

Table 6 summarizes the browser support for each chosen approach and implementation. For the most part, it is very wide. This is to be expected because they were chosen, precisely, for providing relatively high *universality*.

Table 5. JavaScript-based H.264/AVC

		Mean	S.D.
5 FPS	RAM	177.3 MB	1.528
	CPU	11.67%	1.155
	Bandwidth	90.9 KB/s	22.848
	Latency	1083 ms	29.445
10 FPS	RAM	178.3 MB	5.859
	CPU	15.67%	1.155
	Bandwidth	96.2 KB/s	1.258
	Latency	734 ms	27.731
25 FPS	RAM	176.0 MB	1.000
	CPU	27.0%	2.646
	Bandwidth	100.3 KB/s	8.314
	Latency	417 ms	160.728

Table 6. Browser support for each approach and implementation

	Chrome	Safari	IE	Edge	Firefox	Chrome Mobile	Samsung Mobile	Firefox Mobile
Image Ref.	✓	✓	✓	✓	✓	✓	✓	✓
Native M-JPEG	✓	✓	✗	✓	✓	✓	✓	✓
JS M-JPEG	✓	✓	✓	✓	✓	✓	✓	✓
JS MPEG-2	✓	✓	✓	✓	✓	✓	✓	✓
JS H.264	✓	✓	✓	✓	✓	✓	✓	✓

Figure 7 compares the client-side RAM usage observed during the experiments. In the case of image refreshing and native M-JPEG it is, apparently, very high. However, it is noteworthy that when the page loads it starts small, and progressively grows until it stabilizes at the figures that are displayed. That is likely due to Chrome's caching and RAM management scheme. In the case of JavaScript-rendered M-JPEG RAM usage is significantly smaller, and it is rather volatile —which probably explains why for 25 FPS the measured RAM usage is smaller. The MPEG-1 and H.264 implementations consume, by far, the least RAM.

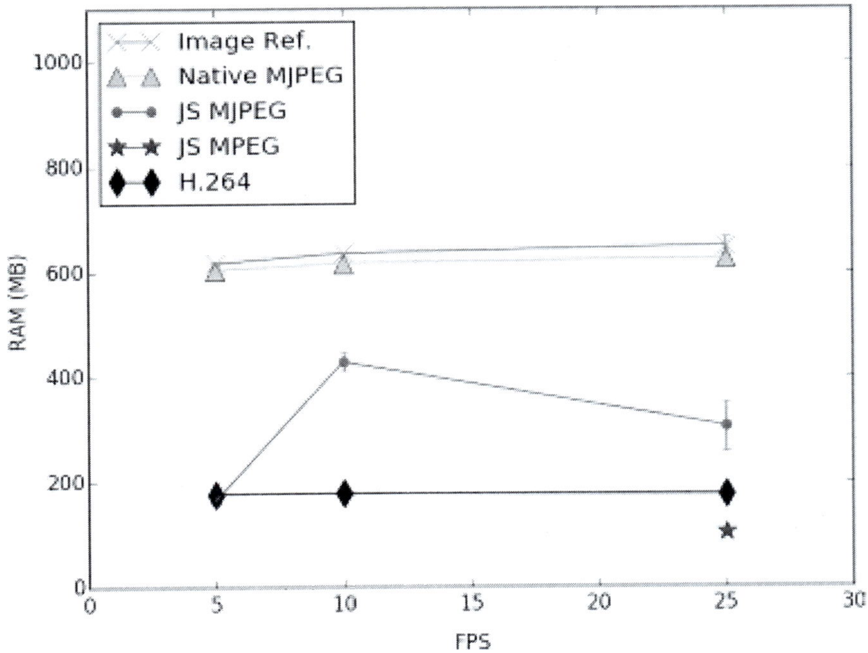

Figure 7. Client-side RAM usage comparison

Figure 8 compares CPU usage. As one would normally expect, it seems to increase almost linearly with the FPS. Interestingly, however, native M-JPEG and image-refreshing consume the most CPU, while JavaScript-based M-JPEG and the high-compression-based methods —MPEG-1 and H.264— consume the least. This could be considered counter-intuitive, because MPEG-1 and H.264 have a significantly more powerful and complex, interframe compression. Although explaining these results would require further analysis and is not within the scope or target of this work, some of the factors involved could potentially be:

- Higher bandwidth-requirements of the lower-compression formats increase the CPU usage as compared to the higher-compression but lower-bandwidth ones, especially in a browser environment where probably the buffers involved are copied several times.
- Image-refreshing is not what the browsers' image component and system was designed for, and modifying an image repeatedly is not necessarily meant to be efficient: it involves cache and DOM operations which are appropriate for single images but not so much for videos.

- The native M-JPEG implementation of Chrome might be significantly suboptimal, while the JavaScript engine is very heavily optimized, which would explain the difference between the JavaScript-based M-JPEG and the native M-JPEG experiments.
- The H.264 decoder has the advantage of being heavily optimized (compiled into JavaScript through Emscripten, and even using WebGL for some specific tasks such as color conversion) while the MPEG-1 decoder has the advantage of being relatively simple.

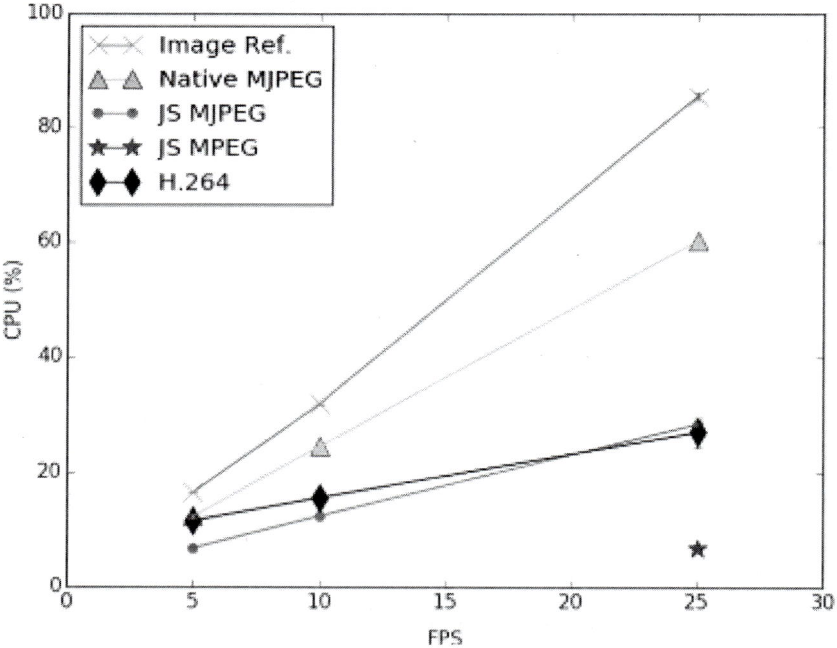

Figure 8. Client-side CPU usage comparison

Figure 9 compares downstream bandwidth usage. Comparatively, MPEG-1 and H.264 consume a very small amount of bandwidth. Image-refreshing, native M-JPEG and JavaScript-based M-JPEG, which do not rely on interframe compression, consume several times more bandwidth and it increases proportionally to the FPS. JavaScript-based M-JPEG seems to consume slightly more than native, specially at higher framerates, possibly due to *socket.io* or WebSocket overheads.

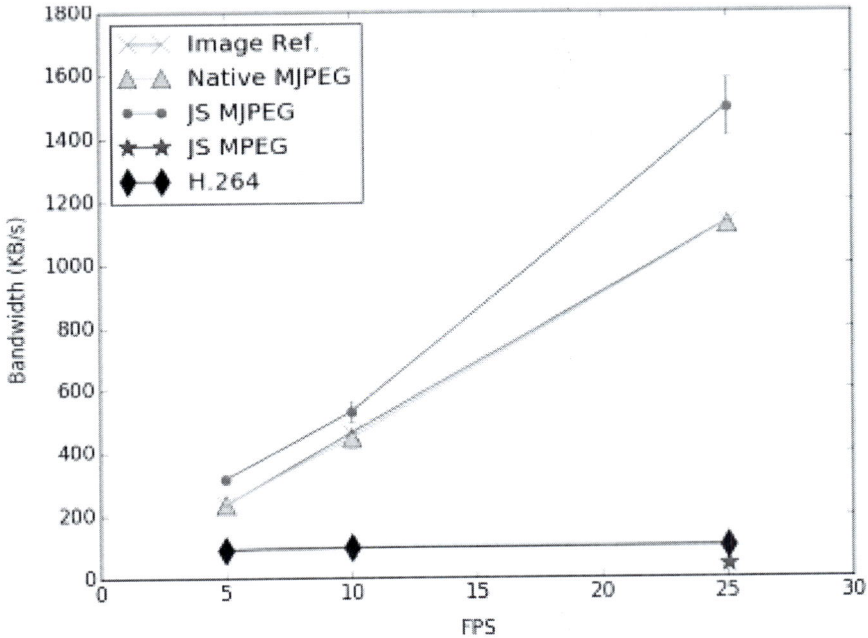

Figure 9. Client-side downstream bandwidth usage comparison

Figure 10 compares the latency of the different approaches. For the low framerates image-refreshing and JavaScript-based M-JPEG are the fastest. H.264 is the slowest. However, for the higher framerates, the difference among the difference approaches decreases. The change is most apparent for H.264, which goes from an around 1100 ms delay at 5 FPS to a quite low around 500 ms delay at 25 FPS. This non-linear change is probably due to the codec's implementation details. Particularly, internal buffers are probably being filled faster at the higher framerates.

6 DISCUSSION

We have examined and compared some techniques and implementations for web-based near-real-time interactive live streaming. Of cross-platform web-based techniques, image refreshing and native M-JPEG are currently among the most commonly used ones for applications such as remote laboratories. We have also examined and compared some approaches (Java-Script based M-JPEG rendering, JavaScript-based MPEG-1 rendering, and JavaScript-based H.264/AVC rendering) which as far as we know, have not been used for remote laboratories (and possibly not for similar purposes such as IP camera servers).

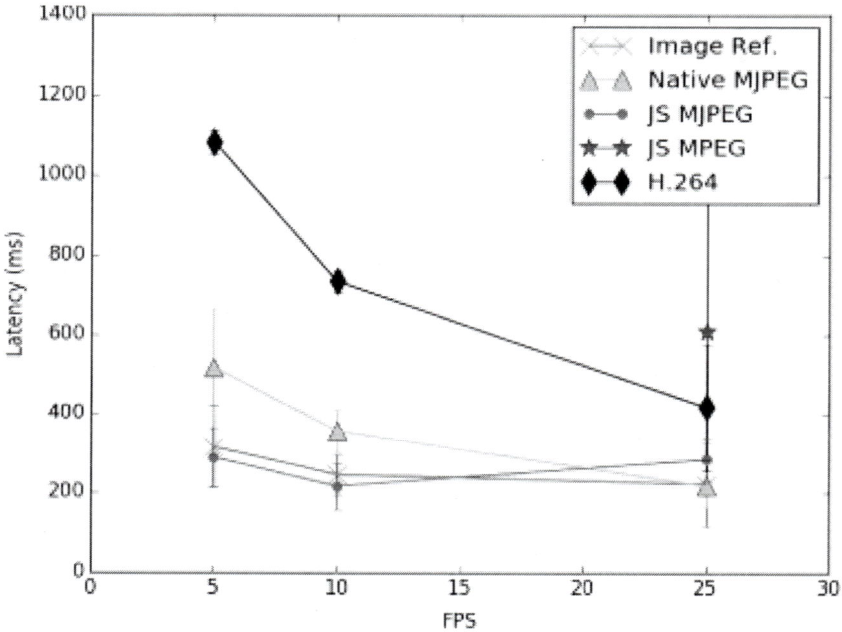

Figure 10. Latency comparison

The formats that some of those approaches rely on (particularly, M-JPEG and MPEG-1) are far from new. However, M-JPEG is still very popular for interactive live streaming because of its simplicity and because of the low capture-display latency that it provides. MPEG-1, similarly, is very mature. Before the appearance of newer formats, it used to be popular for web streaming. Some of those newer formats are H.264 AVC [19], H.265 [18], VP8 [2] and VP9 [11]. They provide a significantly better quality and compression rate, but they are more complex. They generally have a higher processing cost. Of those newer formats, we have considered an approach relying on JavaScript and H.264.

The results of the experiments show that no single approach is necessarily the best for all cases. They show, however, that some approaches can probably be significantly more advantageous than others for certain purposes.

One of the first conclusions that we learn from the experiments is that relying on the native M-JPEG scheme does not seem to be convenient in any case. This is remarkable because, currently, many remote laboratories and other applications, such as IP camera servers, rely on it. However, the only advantage seems to be a slightly lower bandwidth usage than JavaScript-based M-JPEG. In exchange:

- A major browser lacks support (Internet Explorer)
- Other browsers have several reported bugs and a relatively poor track-record at supporting it
- It consumes significantly more RAM
- It consumes significantly more CPU power

Additionally, other significant observation is that the performance of the most simplistic approach —image refreshing— is as good as that of native M-JPEG in RAM and bandwidth usage, and is not far in CPU power. Considering the aforementioned issues that come with native M-JPEG, and the significant advantages of image refreshing such as simplicity and trivial error-recovery and bandwidth-adaptation capabilities, we conclude again that in most cases, there would be no advantage in relying on native M-JPEG.

Other significant observation is that JavaScript-based MPEG-1 and JavaScript-based H.264 seem to be significantly advantageous in many of the evaluated variables. This is remarkable because, as far as we know, they have not been used in the context of remote laboratories. They require much less RAM, extremely lower amounts of bandwidth than the other approaches, and also less CPU power —especially in the case of MPEG-1—. The lower bandwidth requirement is expected due to their interframe compression, and the fact that a fixed bitrate was used. However, it is still noteworthy that it can be achieved while maintaining a (subjectively) good image quality. The lower CPU requirement is less obvious (some possible explanations are suggested in Section 5). These results suggest that, for some remote laboratories, particularly those that require a high FPS and which are particularly bandwidth-constrained (for example, because they are intended to be used on mobile devices, or because they feature many simultaneous webcams) relying on MPEG-1 and H.264 could be a very effective choice.

These formats, however, do have some disadvantages. First, the image quality —with the constant-bitrate, low-latency configuration that was chosen— is not bad, but is worse than for the other approaches. Second, they do indeed raise the latency. Nonetheless, by choosing the appropriate low-latency configuration, most measurements remain lower than 1 second. This is still acceptable for many interactive live streaming applications. However, it is certainly higher than with other more *traditional* approaches such as image refreshing or M-JPEG. Thus, despite the mostly superior results, they are not necessarily the best choice for all applications. It is also noteworthy that they have some additional disadvantages:

- The implementation and deployment is more complex. It requires a transcoding server, and a specific JavaScript-based player in the client.
- Deployment is more complex due to the transcoding server that is required. Server-side, more processing resources are required.
- Error recovery and bandwidth adaptation is harder than with other approaches such as image-refreshing (for which it is trivial).

7 CONCLUSIONS AND FUTURE WORK

In this work we have described two of the most common approaches that are nowadays used for web-based near-real-time interactive live streaming (image refreshing and native-M-JPEG). Additionally, we have proposed and compared three additional approaches (JavaScript-based M-JPEG, JavaScript-based MPEG-1 and JavaScript-based H.264). Those last, to our knowledge, are not currently used in this context.

The results suggest that, in many cases, avoiding the native M-JPEG scheme in favour of one of the other four would be advisable. It seems to provide very little benefit over the alternatives. They also suggest that the three JavaScript-based alternative approaches (JavaScript-based M-JPEG, JavaScript-based MPEG-1 and JavaScript-based H.264/AVC) provide comparatively good performance.

The schemes based on MPEG-1 and H.264/AVC could be the most appropriate for certain types of interactive applications. Particularly, for those, such as certain remote laboratories, which can withstand a relatively high latency (around 1 second) but which require a low bandwidth usage at a high FPS. Nonetheless, the image-refreshing scheme, despite its simplicity, could still be the most appropriate scheme for those interactive applications which require a very low latency, especially at lower FPS rates.

In the future, it would be interesting to compare new approaches. MPEG-DASH is a promising HTML5-related standard which will likely provide near-real-time live-streaming. Once the support for it is wider, it would be useful to evaluate whether a low capture-display delay can be achieved, and how its performance compares against the alternatives.

Additionally, it would be interesting to evaluate more modern interframe compression formats, and with more configurations. Although the most modern formats (such as VP-9) are expected to require a much higher amount of resources, especially if decoding through JavaScript, a format such as VP-8 could still give interesting results. Especially, if the implementation was heavily optimized and relied on *asm.js* or a similar scheme.

FOOTNOTES

1 https://www.youtube.com/live

2 https://twitch.tv

3 https://instagram.com/livestream

4 https://live.fb.com

5 http://java.com

6 http://www.adobe.com/es/products/flashplayer.html

7 https://www.netflix.com

8 http://www.twitch.tv

9 http://www.youtube.com

10 Though no official figures are provided by YouTube, several observations and informal tests are available, such as those found at http://blog.ptzoptics.com/youtube-live/low-latency-streaming/ or at the Google product forum (https://productforums.google.com/forum/).

11 https://www.skype.com

12 https://hangouts.google.com

13 https://apple.com/facetime

14 The Archimedes' principle remote laboratory is usually publicly available at: https://weblab.deusto.es/weblab/labs/Aquatic%20experiments/archimedes/

15 http://www.wowza.com

16 https://weblab.deusto.es

17 http://labsland.com

18 http://remlabnet.eu

19 Brazillian consortium headed by the Federal University Santa Catarina (UFSC) remote laboratories. On 21th April 2016 at least 8 different remote laboratories are available at http://relle.ufsc.br, all of which rely on browser-native M-JPEG.

20 http://www.ises.info

21 http://www.yawcam.com/

22 As described in more detail in later subsections, MPEG-1 will only be measured with 25 FPS, because its standard does not allow 5 or 10 FPS.

23 http://phoboslab.org

24 https://github.com/zstars/jsmpeg

25 https://github.com/zstars/h264-live-player

ACKNOWLEDGMENTS

This work has received financial support by the Department of Education, Language policy and Culture of the Basque Government through a Predoctoral Scholarship granted to Luis Rodriguez-Gil.

OPEN ACCESS

REFERENCES

1. Akhshabi S, Begen AC, Dovrolis C (2011) An experimental evaluation of rate-adaptation algorithms in adaptive streaming over HTTP. In: Proceedings of the second annual ACM conference on multimedia systems. ACM, pp 157–168
2. Bankoski J, Wilkins P, Xu Y (2011) Vp8 data format and decoding guide. Tech. rep., available: http://tools.ietf.org/html/rfc6386 (accessed: 2016-07-07)

3. Claypool M, Finkel D (2014) The effects of latency on player performance in cloud-based games. In: 2014 13th annual workshop on Network and systems support for games (netgames). IEEE, pp 1–6
4. Cozzolino A, Flammini F, Galli V, Lamberti M, Poggi G, Pragliola C (2012) Evaluating the effects of mjpeg compression on motion tracking in metro railway surveillance. In: Advanced concepts for intelligent vision systems. Springer, pp 142–154
5. De Jong T, Linn MC, Zacharia ZC (2013) Physical and virtual laboratories in science and engineering education. Science 340(6130):305–308
6. Deshpande H, Bawa M, Garcia-Molina H (2001) Streaming live media over a peer-to-peer network. Tech. rep
7. Fielding R, Gettys J, Mogul J, Frystyk H, Masinter L, Leach P, Berners-Lee T (2006) Hypertext transfer protocol–HTTP/1.1, 1999. RFC2616
8. Garcia-Zubia J, López-de-Ipiña D, Orduña P (2008) Mobile devices and remote labs in engineering education. In: 2008 eighth IEEE international conference on advanced learning technologies. IEEE, pp 620–622
9. García-Zubia J, Orduña P, López-de-Ipiña D, Alves GR (2009) Addressing software impact in the design of remote laboratories. IEEE Trans Ind Electron 56(12):4757–4767
10. Golparvar-Fard M, Bohn J, Teizer J, Savarese S, Peña-Mora F (2011) Evaluation of image-based modeling and laser scanning accuracy for emerging automated performance monitoring techniques. Autom Constr 20(8):1143–1155
11. Grange A, Rivaz P, Hunt J (2016) Draft vp9 bitstream and decoding process specification. Tech. rep., available: http://www.webmproject.org/vp9/ (accessed: 2016-07-07)
12. Grois D, Marpe D, Mulayoff A, Itzhaky B, Hadar O (2013) Performance comparison of H.265/mpeg-hevc, vp9, and H.265/MPEG-AVC encoders. In: Picture coding symposium (PCS), 2013. IEEE, pp 394–397
13. Harward VJ, Del Alamo JA, Lerman SR, Bailey PH, Carpenter J, DeLong K, Felknor C, Hardison J, Harrison B, Jabbour I et al (2008) The ilab shared architecture: a web services infrastructure to build communities of internet accessible laboratories. Proc IEEE 96(6):931–950
14. Hashemian R, Riddley J (2007) Fpga E-lab, a technique to remote access a laboratory to design and test. In: Microelectronic systems education, 2007. IEEE International Conference on MSE'07. IEEE, pp 139–140
15. Hei X, Liang C, Liang J, Liu Y, Ross KW (2007) A measurement study of a large-scale P2P IPTV system. IEEE Trans Multimed 9(8):1672–1687
16. Html5 specification (2016) Tech. rep., W3, available: https://www.w3.org/TR/html5
17. ISO/IEC (2015) Iso/iec 11172:1993. coding of moving pictures and associated audio for digital storage media at up to about 1.5 mbit/s. Tech. rep., available: http://www.iso.org/iso/catalogue_detail?csnumber=19180 (Accessed: 2016-07-07)
18. ITU-T (2015) High efficiency video coding. Tech. rep., available: https://www.itu.int/rec/t-REC-h.265-201504-i/en (accessed: 2016-07-07)
19. ITU-T (2016) Advanced video coding for generic audiovisual services. Tech. rep., available: http://www.itu.int/rec/T-REC-H.264-201602-I/en (Accessed: 2016-07-07)
20. Jara CA, Candelas FA, Torres F (2008) Virtual and remote laboratory for robotics e-learning. Comput Aided Chem Eng 25:1193–1198
21. Kaspar M, Parsad NM, Silverstein JC (2010) Cowebviz: interactive collaborative sharing of 3D stereoscopic visualization among browsers with no added software. In: Proceedings of the 1st ACM international health informatics symposium. ACM, pp 809–816
22. Latency in live network video surveillance (2015) Tech. rep., axis communications, available: http://bit.ly/2izYVOb (accessed: 2016-07-07)

23. Kim K, Cho BY, Ro WW (2016) Server side, play buffer based quality control for adaptive media streaming. Multimed Tools Appl 1–19
24. Ma J, Nickerson JV (2006) Hands-on, simulated, and remote laboratories: a comparative literature review. ACM Comput Surv (CSUR) 38(3):7
25. Martinez G, Angulo I, Garcia-Zubia J (2016) Weblabmicroscope: A remote laboratory for experimenting with digital microscope. In: 2016 13th international conference on remote engineering and virtual instrumentation (REV). IEEE, pp 159–162
26. Nedic Z, Machotka J, Nafalski A (2003) Remote laboratories versus virtual and real laboratories. In: FIE 2003 33rd annual, vol 1. IEEE
27. Nielsen J (1994) Usability engineering. Elsevier
28. Nishantha D, Hayashida Y, Hayashi T (2004) Application level rate adaptive Motion-JPEG transmission for medical collaboration systems. In: Proceedings of 24th international conference on distributed computing systems workshops, 2004. IEEE, pp 64–69
29. Orduña P, Bailey PH, DeLong K, López-de-Ipiña D, García-zubia J (2014) Towards federated interoperable bridges for sharing educational remote laboratories. Comput Hum Behav 30:389–395
30. Quax P, Liesenborgs J, Barzan A, Croonen M, Lamotte W, Vankeirsbilck B, Dhoedt B, Kimpe T, Pattyn K, McLin M (2016) Remote rendering solutions using web technologies. Multimed Tools Appl 75(8):4383–4410
31. Rodriguez-Gil L, Orduña P, García-Zubia J, Angulo I, López-de-Ipiña D (2014) Graphic technologies for virtual, remote and hybrid laboratories: Weblab-fpga hybrid lab. In: 2014 11th international conference on remote engineering and virtual instrumentation (REV). IEEE, pp 163–166
32. Salkintzis A, Passas N (2005) Emerging wireless multimedia: services and technologies. Wiley
33. Schauer F, Lustig F, Ožvoldová M (2009) Ises-internet school experimental system for computer-based laboratories in physics. Innovations 109–118
34. Schauer F, Krbecek M, Beno P, Gerza M, Palka L, Spilaková P (2014) Remlabnet-open remote laboratory management system for e-experiments. In: 2014 11th international conference on remote engineering and virtual instrumentation (REV). IEEE, pp 268–273
35. Schulzrinne H, Rao A, Lanphier R (1998) Rtsp: real time streaming protocol. IETF RFC2326, april
36. Shea R, Liu J, Ngai ECH, Cui Y (2013) Cloud gaming: architecture and performance. IEEE Netw 27(4):16–21
37. Soares J, Lobo J (2011) A remote fpga laboratory for digital design students. In: 7th portuguese meeting on reconfigurable systems (REC 2011). pp 95–98
38. Sripanidkulchai K, Ganjam A, Maggs B, Zhang H (2004) The feasibility of supporting large-scale live streaming applications with dynamic application end-points. In: ACM SIGCOMM computer communication review, vol. 34. ACM, pp 107–120
39. Tan WL, Lam F, Lau WC (2008) An empirical study on the capacity and performance of 3g networks. IEEE Trans Mob Comput 7(6):737–750
40. Ueberheide M, Klose F, Varisetty T, Fidler M, Magnor M (2015) Web-based interactive free-viewpoint streaming: a framework for high quality interactive free viewpoint navigation. In: Proceedings of the 23rd ACM international conference on multimedia. ACM, pp 1031–1034
41. Van Lancker W, Van Deursen D, Mannens E, Van de Walle R (2012) Implementation strategies for efficient media fragment retrieval. Multimed Tools and Appl 57(2):243–267
42. Vargas H, Farias G, Sanchez J, Dormido S, Esquembre F (2013) Using augmented reality in remote laboratories. Int J Comput Commun Control 8(4):622–634
43. Wang B, Zhang X, Wang G, Zheng H, Zhao BY (2016) Anatomy of a personalized livestreaming system. In: Proceedings of the 2016 ACM on internet measurement conference. ACM, pp 485–498

44. Webgl specification (2014) Tech. rep., khronos webGL working group, available: https:// www.khronos.org/registry/webgl/specs/1.0/
45. Wiegand T, Sullivan GJ, Bjontegaard G, Luthra A (2003) Overview of the h. 264/avc video coding standard. IEEE Trans Circuits Syst Video Technol 13 (7):560–576
46. Yazidi A, Henao H, Capolino GA, Betin F, Filippetti F (2011) A web-based remote laboratory for monitoring and diagnosis of ac electrical machines. IEEE Trans Ind Electron 58(10):4950–4959
47. Youtube now defaults to HTML5 video (2016) https://youtubeeng. googleblog.com /2015/01/youtube-now-defaults-to-html5_27.html https://youtubeeng. googleblog.com/2015/01/youtube-now-defaults-to-html5_27.html (accessed: 2016-07-07)
48. Zhang C, Liu J (2015) On crowdsourced interactive live streaming: a Twitch.TV-based measurement study. In: Proceedings of the 25th ACM workshop on network and operating systems support for digital audio and video. ACM, pp 55–60

CHAPTER 11

Virtual Reality in Medicine — Going Beyond the Limits

Florin Graur[1, 2]

[1] *University of Medicine and Pharmacy "Iuliu Hatieganu" Cluj-Napoca, Romania*

[2] *Regional Institute of Gastroenterology and Hepatology "Octavian Fodor" Cluj-Napoca, Romania*

1. INTRODUCTION

In the last years technology had an explosive evolution in the development of new minimal invasive medical instruments and led to a novel need and a brand new field: virtual medicine.

Virtual reality is an "in silico" simulation of a real situation. In particular, in surgery, dimensional modeling of deformable objects with spatial characteristics and specific elastic-dynamic behavior is required. In addition, simulation of tools and their action against the organs in the virtual environment is also required.

The purpose of virtual medicine is to minimize the direct exploration of the human body in order to provide a virtual model for those who want to learn new techniques and to provide advanced treatment options for those who perform delicate maneuvers or in areas inaccessible by conventional methods: in short to minimize the invasiveness of treatment.

Also a number of virtual techniques tend to be held in the virtual environment of the Internet, allowing remote accessibility and an increased number of users.

This chapter is a literature review that explores the current virtual techniques used in research, education, treatment and development trends of these methods in the future.

2. SHORT HISTORY

First virtual system proposed in medicine was developed by Robert Mann in 1965 [1]. It was used to decide what the best procedure for a orthopedic disease would be. Also this system was used for training residents [2].

In the 60s, the first simulators with 3D images appeared. In the 80s the head mounted display (HDM) were developed and the term “virtual reality” was defined. Over a decade later came the application of virtual reality used in medical education (simulator of colonoscopy and upper gastrointestinal endoscopy) and the first simulator for laparoscopy appeared. The simulation systems became more advanced in time, but it was necessary to develop tactile interaction between man and machine. Haptic systems involve the transmission of information from human to computer and vice versa. Virtual reality nowadays is closely linked to haptic devices with force-feedback [2].

3. RESEARCH METHODS USING VIRTUALIZATION IN MEDICINE

Among research methods using virtual medicine there are a number of examples of software that is used for the three-dimensional reconstruction of protein molecules. Understanding how proteins (whose structure of amino acids is known) are "packed" to reach the three-dimensional structure of the molecule and especially understanding errors of "packing", helps researchers in deciphering the molecular biology of diseases such as: Alzheimer's disease, mad cow disease, Huntington's disease, Parkinson's disease, cystic fibrosis and cancers.

The need for high computing power has led to the creation of online communities such as Rosetta@Home, Human Proteome Folding and Folding@Home. Within these communities an internet user can offer their unused computing capacity of its personal computer to participate in these projects [3-5].

The usefulness of these programs is to understand the physico-chemical properties of different types of proteins and different types of interactions between amino-acids, as well as the evaluation of local energy of short sequences of amino acids. This way the researchers could identify the structures with the lowest energy (i.e., the greatest stability) resulting in the most stable structure of the native protein. Moreover, one can understand the most predictable possibilities of packing for abnormal proteins that can cause diseases. Using computational power of multiple systems generates more structures and several search strategies are tested in order to identify the most effective one.

Foldit game is based on the Rosetta platform. The player or groups of players are able to manipulate the amino acid chain to achieve minimum energy conformations, those that achieve the most favorable energy structure win [6].

Another application helps to identify ways in which a number of drugs bind to a receptor of known 3D structure of a HIV component [7].

4. METHODS IN MEDICAL EDUCATION THAT UTILIZES VIRTUALIZATION

As a method of education, virtual medicine is used in various ways: either to explore the human body, without interacting with the analyzed structures, or by performing maneuvers on simple or complex structures (up to simulate human organs) to quantify gestures.

Satava describes the features of ideal simulator: high fidelity, capacity to simulate the physic-dynamic characteristics of organs, to be interactive and to provide haptic feedback [8].

Some examples of the exploration of the human body for anatomical study are: Visible Human Project [9, 10], The Virtual Body [11]; The Virtual Human Embryo [12]; The Visible Human Server [13]. Most of these resources are online atlases of three-dimensional reconstruction images obtained from computerized tomography or MRI. These sites allow interactive navigation and detailed anatomical study of the structures concerned, including relations with other organs.

Three-dimensional reconstruction of intracellular organelles for a better understanding of physiology is another area in which the research was conducted, allowing visualization of how these structures interact [14].

Rapid development of laparoscopic techniques require the implementation of special training and acquisition of special technical skills. Design and modeling of three-dimensional virtual environments that respect the anatomy and intraoperative conditions require close collaboration between dedicated surgeons and engineers in order to develop such platforms. The virtual environment is connected to a console that allows the surgeon to manipulate the virtual instruments through a dedicated joystick. Also some devices use a system for haptic feedback simulation. Simulation is now an integrated part of medical education. These simulators allow the trainee to make mistakes and to learn how to avoid or to solve them, in order to reduce complications in the real procedures.

Of these simulators the best known are: MIST-VR, The LaparoscopyVR [15]; LapMentor [16]; LapSim [17].

MIST-VR system allows the surgeon's training in a virtual space assimilated to a three dimensional cube where the student can perform different moves with a cylinder and balls and the difficulty can be graded in 6 steps. The time to accomplish the tasks as well as the errors are quantified. The system is used to learn simple gestures in laparoscopic surgery, but does not have force-feedback [18].

The surgical simulator LaparoscopyVR (LapVR™) is a virtual reality simulation system that enables learning and updating skills needed in laparoscopic surgery. The LapVR™ system combines laparoscopic simulation software with haptic hardware, providing a complete unit for the virtual reality training. LapVR™ was designed to help surgeons in acquiring, maintaining, preserving and assessing movement skills and knowledge necessary to perform various laparoscopic surgery procedures. Clinical studies show that novice surgeons trained by laparoscopic simulation have skills that help them in real procedures. LapVR™ system allows both individual and team training and provides a basic technical module composed of five skills steps with increasing levels of difficulty: camera navigation, using the hook electrode, cutting, clipping, suturing and knot tying. The system also contains a module for laparoscopic cholecystectomy with 18 variants of cases and three levels of difficulty as well as one of obstetrics and gynecology that allows simulation of laparoscopic operations performed for ectopic pregnancy, tubal occlusion and adnexa's pathology [12].

Multidisciplinary laparoscopic surgical simulator LapMentor™ provides training opportunities for beginners and experienced surgeons from basic laparoscopic skills to complete laparoscopic operations. LapMentor™ was designed to meet the needs of training and practice of physicians as well as the assessment and management of their instructors. The system is characterized by life-like view of human anatomy and perception of tactile sensations using laparoscopic instruments that mimic reality (haptic system). Application modules provide a relaxing environment outside the operating room to help learning essential skills for a variety of laparoscopic procedures: basic techniques module, suturing module, laparoscopic cholecystectomy module, ventral hernia module, gastric bypass module and gynecology module. The basic techniques module was designed to train surgeons in basic skills in minimally invasive procedures: camera navigation (with 0º and 30º laparoscope), handling of usual instruments, manipulating objects, clipping and cutting. Suture techniques module allows surgeons to learn intracorporeal suturing and knot tying, providing a perfect training environment similar to real-life practice. Laparoscopic cholecystectomy module includes virtual patient reconstructions obtained from CT / MRI images of real patients with multiple anatomical variants and thus training surgeons in recognition of anatomical variants and successful resolution of surgical complications. The Ventral hernias module represents the first opportunity to train surgeons with skills necessary to perform laparoscopic hernia repair procedures and inserting prostheses of different shapes and sizes. The gastric bypass module helps surgeons accustomed with basic laparoscopic surgery in learning, performing and perfecting stages of this bariatric procedure in a safe and monitored environment. The gynecological laparoscopic module trains surgeons in learning different methods applied in the treatment of ectopic pregnancy, tubal sterilization and adnexal disease. Videos of all laparoscopic interventions are available before or during simulation. The skills and knowledge acquired during the virtual training increases surgeon's experience, allowing them to cope with intraoperative complications, such as: bleeding from the implantation site of trocars, organ rupture, flooding the abdominal cavity with blood. LapMentor™system provides all the elements necessary to validate acquired skills and recorded performances. Detailed information on handling tissue, handling tools, time and movements efficiency are collected during the training session to allow evaluation of the level of skill. Performance indicators are recorded in a file and can be viewed on simulator [19].

LapSim™ system provides a virtual environment very similar to the real one as well as extremely useful simulations for common practice. The skills acquired through this system are directly transferable to the operating room. The interface is easy to use and practical sessions vary in complexity depending on the chosen level. Courses can be modified by an instructor according to specific needs. Functions can be imported and exported to be transferred between instructors and institutions. Standard modules of this system are: the basics skills, anastomosis and suture, laparoscopic cholecystectomy and one dedicated to gynecology [14].

SINERGIA is a new type of simulator for laparoscopic surgery composed of seven teaching modules: eye-hand coordination, handling the camera, grasping, pulling, cutting, dissection and section. It also can achieve differentiation between levels of student skills. Yet, even this simulator does not have an integrated haptic system [20].

Compared to physical simulators (artificial or animal model), virtual simulators stimulate the learner to perform all duties listed and evaluated by software, it does not require the presence of a permanent trainer to verify the correctness of performing the tasks and evaluates more accurate the gestures of the surgeon. Virtual systems for surgical training can be used for assessing the competence of the surgeon. In addition, warm-up concept can bring increased surgical performance. This concept allows the warm-up by making virtual preoperative procedure and later, the surgeon will perform the actual procedure. To improve this concept for preoperative phase in virtual environment, three-dimensional reconstructions created from CT of the patient to be operated can be used, thus simulating more accurately the patient's own anatomical variations in the virtual environment.

The VERT system is a virtual environment used in the training of radiotherapy physician and provides a platform for acquiring the skills necessary for doctors, nurses and auxiliary staff [21, 22].

VirRAD project is an online platform that includes a virtual laboratory where the radiopharmacy community members can experience and learn different aspects of practice [23].

A team from the United States has developed a virtual learning system used for EndoStitch device suture learning and performing laparoscopic nodes. It includes in addition to the virtual environment a working console and a haptic feedback [24].

The usefulness of virtual medicine as a diagnostic method is exemplified through a relatively known example: virtual colonoscopy. This examination allows inspection of virtual colonic lumen obtained using three-dimensional reconstruction based on computed tomography images acquired from a patient. The range of examinations is currently expanded to virtual gastrointestinal exploration, three-dimensional assessment of vascular lumen-especially if coronary obstruction. Also the new geometry of the damaged heart wall after a myocardial infarction could be explored.

For intravenous catheter insertion, CathSim system was developed, that provides the student, besides the virtual environment, with a working console with tactile feedback and a series of simulations of complications that may occur during the real procedure [25].

A large number of simulators were developed for: endoscopic sinus surgery, endoscopic gastrointestinal procedures, bronchoscopy, arthroscopy, cardiac catheterization and ophthalmic surgery [26-29].

By integrating knowledge in the field of acupuncture and three-dimensional reconstruction based on images obtained from computer tomography,

Chinese Visible Human was created, which is useful in education and research in Chinese medicine [30].

In dentistry there are 3D models of teeth or of an entire human head simulating the details of anatomy of the teeth or mouth. The trainee could perform drills having a haptic feedback. Also a Virtual Reality Dental Chair system (HapTEL) enables the trainee to test and learn various skills [31].

5. METHODS OF DIAGNOSTIC AND TREATMENT USING VIRTUALIZATION IN MEDICINE

There are a number of softwares for three-dimensional reconstruction of organs using 3D ultrasound images or 4D CT or MRI images, acquired for a more accurate evaluation of diseases. Some software even allows a simulation of the proposed intervention thus achieving preoperative planning.

During remote interventions, the surgeon acts on a virtual environment, the operation itself is performed by a surgical robot. This kind of procedure was performed in September 7, 2001 and was called „Lindbergh operation" during which Professor J. Marescaux located in Strasbourg performed a laparoscopic cholecystectomy on a patient who was in New York (at a distance of approx. 15000 km) using a ZEUS robot (Computer Motion), the surgeon's presence being virtual [32].

The utility of this technology is to use the expertise of a specialist at a great distance (i.e. space station) to perform surgery (telemedicine) or to help a less experienced surgeon during interventions with high difficulty (telementoring).

The use of robots in surgery allows more accurate movements, avoiding surgeon's tremor, smaller incisions, decreased blood loss, quicker postoperative recovery, etc.

The new models of modified DaVinci robot uses three-dimensional immersion type image, allowing detailed visualization of the operative field, besides haptic feedback [33].

Virtual reality refers not only to virtualization of visual perception but also to virtualization of tactile perception, the touch feeling being essential in surgery. Haptic systems are designed as a virtual environment for the sense of touch, allowing artificial tactile perception of objects created in the virtual environment or of real objects touched by surgical robot, the sensations being transmitted to the interface with the surgeon.

VerroTouch system is an extension of DaVinci robot proposed by Kuchenbecker et al [34] which makes transfer of vibrations measured by surgical instruments attached to the robot-surgeon interface, allowing haptic sensation to the operator.

Augmented reality facilitates surgical intervention by projecting in the operative field inner images of the organs located in the visual field. These images are obtained by three-dimensional reconstruction from CT or MRI after acquisition and processing. The projected images are adjusted according to the position of organs, instruments and actions of the surgeon in the operating field. For example, large intrahepatic vessels can be projected on the surface of the liver capsule, showing a useful map to the surgeon in order to avoid injuries. This is called also „intraoperative navigation" and it shows the surgeon where he can find important elements and also the anatomic variations.

Navigation systems have been proposed for NOTES (Natural Orifice Transluminal Endoscopic Surgery) surgery [35, 36] which reduce intraoperative accidental injuries. It uses three-dimensional reconstruction from images captured by CT and data of real-time location of the endoscope. The main problem with augmented reality is identifying common reference points of real images and of those obtained by preoperative three-dimensional reconstruction. Augmented reality is very useful during minimally invasive interventions, where the visual field is diminished and thus the orientation of the surgeon in the operating field is hampered.

The current systems of virtual reality and augmented reality fail to perfectly simulate the interaction between surgical instruments and organs. In the future, the researchers aim to improve the interaction between surgeon and interface with the virtual system, getting feedback for surgeons, synchronization of virtual reality with operative field, etc.

Virtual reality can be very useful in bridging the gap between food and social behavior of patients with diabetes and/or obesity and the rules that they should follow. The software allows interaction with virtual environments that simulate both video and tactile sensations and other sensations (smell, taste). Patients can learn new habits such as the amount of food they should ingest, food choices and given encouragement to perform physical activities. Also in people with heart disease or morbid obesity it may stimulate performing progressive physical activity at home, even by increasing motivation.

Another direction in which virtual medicine interferes with spectacular results is the treatment of phobias. The patient is connected to a virtual environment that simulates situations that produce phobic states, everything being controlled and can be interrupted at any time of the simulation [37]. Phobias treated with such reality simulation programs are: post-traumatic stress, public speaking, arachnophobia, agoraphobia, acrophobia, claustrophobia, panic, social phobia, stress secondary vehicle crush accidents etc. [38]. A number of applications have also been developed, dedicated to various phobias or posttraumatic stress syndromes (Virtual Iraq/Afghanistan, Virtual Airplane, Virtual Nicotine, Virtual Elevator, Hurricane Katrina Virtual, Virtual World Trade Center and Virtual Vietnam) [39]. Virtual Iraq / Afghanistan is used in more than 60 clinics and has demonstrated efficacy in reducing symptoms of posttraumatic stress [40].

STRIVE (Stress Resilience in Virtual Environments) is an application that is used to adapt future soldiers to fight stress. The body reactions to stress are described to the soldier and also he can learn how to cope with this stress [40].

VirtualPatients is an application used for the clinician involved in the learning process and interaction with the patient [40].

For trypanophobia treatment (fear of needles) a system with two lenses was developed which shows images to the patient. It can project different scenarios such as a visit to a health center where a nurse shall pick a blood sample. The whole system also provides feedback on the mental and emotional reactions [41].

To help patients with disabilities, along with dedicated systems which allow the patients to learn how to use wheelchairs in crowded cities, he can also use Second Life type virtual environments, where through an avatar, these patients can interact with others without the limitations encountered in the real world [42].

To avoid animal experiments there were developed digital models of rats, pigs and humans. For example, a virtual pig head [41] and also a model of a physiological rat [43] was developed, in order to use these models in virtual experiments.

Three-dimensional virtual reality combined with haptic feedback is used for motor recovery of patients with stroke sequelae. This technology is currently used in experimental studies, but it might extend in recovery clinics and even at home recovering. There are commercial systems used for related purposes with the ability to develop complex movements of the hand. These applications provide an assessment of movements and skills acquired in order to follow-up the evolution of these patients [44, 45].

A new area of research with direct implications in the therapy is currently developing: virtual rehabilitation. Also looming as a subdomain, virtual tele-rehabilitation allows the therapist to interact with the patient through a 3D avatar and guide them during therapy sessions. Haptic systems attached to such systems allow the doctor to examine the patient's muscle tone [46, 47].

Another application is the virtual prototyping technology that combines virtual modeling with rapid prototyping in order to be used in biomedical engineering (eg. for the development of prosthetic or medical devices) [48, 49].

6. ETHICS IN VIRTUAL REALITY MEDICINE AND TELEMEDICINE

The rapid evolution of virtual reality and telemedicine may result in overcoming limits, more so in this area as yet there are no law or ethics rules. As the interactions between people from different countries become more and more globalized, the implementation of ethical codes should be considered. .

Implementation of very expensive virtual reality and augmented reality systems for use in therapy can create disparities in specialist's presence who will migrate toward the best equipped centers. Also there will be an imbalance in patients addressability, which also would prefer clinics with superior performance [50, 51].

Training therapists in centers with the possibility of using virtual reality will also be more efficient and also preoperative simulations leading to superior results. These issues are already visible in Eastern European countries with subfinanced health systems, where both patients and physicians migrate to Western European states.

Funding the development of such performant systems of virtual reality and telemedicine is not currently covered by health systems or government agencies but more often through projects or private sponsorships. These facts may lead to impairing of projects on long-term [52].

As virtual systems will gain autonomy in different degrees, the responsibility of creators and users of these systems will increase. There is currently no legislation to use autonomous robots or virtual systems. There arises the problem of such systems errors and who will be punished for them.

Some cultural and social problems may occur in telemedicine. Because the distance between doctor and patient, the latter can be reduced to a mere "beneficiary" or, worse, "data source" [53].

Differences between health legislations in different countries may lead to situations such as: doctor without a license in a country may provide remote treatment in another country; some illegal procedures (cloning, abortion) in a country can be remotely performed in another country where they are allowed. These differences can lead to self-limitation of experts performing remote therapies in countries where laws are not familiar. It is therefore necessary to implement a symmetric legislation.

Storing data in information systems can lead to loss of confidentiality with repercussions on both the patient and the service providers.

Patients are usually informed of these systems by mass-media (stimulated by the industry) and these information is incomplete or insufficient.

7. FUTURE DIRECTIONS

Development of virtual reality in medicine aims in the following directions: increasing fidelity in order to reproduce the reality, haptic systems integration in the usual simulators and surgical robots, identifying new standards for evaluating student performance, expanding the use of simulators in the educational field, research and therapy. Virtual reality is likely to become the most common method of learning and training young surgeons and also for senior surgeons to acquire new skills [2].

The researchers also seek solutions to lower the costs of information systems and especially with force feedback haptic devices, but its price makes them prohibitive for general use.

A new direction is predicted, combining virtual reality with holographic projection which would improve the three-dimensional vision.

The combination of autonomous systems with virtual reality will be able to step into the future for autonomous surgical robots, autonomous systems for rehabilitation of people with disabilities, autonomous educational systems and complex software for virtual research.

8. CONCLUSION

The spectrum of applications of virtual reality in medicine widens permanently and it is developing in various unexpected directions. The contribution of IT support in the development of medicine is huge but the possibilities and applications that will shape the future of medicine are still unknown.

Virtual reality finds its applications in various fields and its usefulness becomes more predominant in training, preoperative evaluation and preparation of surgeons. Learning with virtual simulators increases the dexterity of the surgeons and reduces the number and severity of intraoperative complications. Also, in computer-assisted research, virtual reality brings benefits that other methods could not reach. Various models are developed for research purposes at different levels, from macro-models to micro-or even nano-levels allowing researchers to perform “in silico” experiments more rapidly and more cheaply.

The combination of virtual reality with the power of multiple computers as in online communities enhances the speed of research to a level otherwise unachievable at this time.

The use of virtual reality in the diagnosis and especially in treatment of certain diseases, widens the range of therapeutic procedures, increases operator safety, patient compliance and reduces the duration of applied treatment. Virtual environments used to treat phobias could not be achieved by any other means, leading to a unique mode of treatment in this field.

Using robot technology as well as telemedicine and telementoring systems will increase surgical accuracy and will reduce hospitalization and complications and on the other hand will increase medical expertise in disadvantaged areas or with difficult access (including inaccessible areas for experts: stations space, underwater).

As in all newly developed fields, the virtual reality domain needs some sound rules to be applied during its use, in order to avoid mistakes and/or injuries, especially in the field of diagnostics and therapeutics.

REFERENCES

1. Mann, R.W. *The evaluation and simulation of mobility aids for the blind.* in *Rotterdam Mobility Research Conference.* 1965. New York: American Foundation for the Blind.
2. Custura-Craciun, D., et al., *Surgical virtual reality-highlights in developing a high performance surgical haptic device.* Chirurgia (Bucur), 2013. 108(6): p. 757-63.
3. *Folding@Home.* 2014 [cited 2014 24 August]; Available from: http://folding.stanford.edu/.
4. *Rosetta@Home.* 2014 [cited 2014 24 August]; Available from: http://boinc.bakerlab.org/rosetta/.
5. http://www.worldcommunitygrid.org/. *Human Proteome Folding Project* 2014 [cited 2014 28 August]; Available from: http://www.worldcomm unity grid.org/research/hpf2/overview.do.
6. Wikipedia. *Rosetta@home.* 2014; Available from: http://en.wikipedia.org/w/index.php?title=Rosetta@home&oldid=616140030.
7. *FightAIDS@Home.* [cited 2014 24 August]; Available from: http://www. World communitygrid.org/research/faah/overview.do.

8. Satava, R.M., *Historical review of surgical simulation--a personal perspective.* World J Surg, 2008. 32(2): p. 141-8.
9. NLM. *The Visible Human Project.* 2014 [cited 2014 24 August]; Available from: http://www.nlm.nih.gov/research/visible/visible_human.html.
10. NLM. *Visible Human.* 2014 [cited 2014 24 August]; Available from: http://www.madsci.org/~lynn/VH/.
11. *The Virtual Body.* 2014 [cited 2014 24 August]; Available from: http://medtropolis.com/virtual-body/.
12. LSUHSC. *Virtual Human Embryo Project.* 2011 [cited 2014 24 August]; Available from: http://virtualhumanembryo.lsuhsc.edu/.
13. visiblehuman.epfl.ch. *Visible Human.* 2014 [cited 2014 24 August]; Available from: http://visiblehuman.epfl.ch/index.php.
14. *Organelle View.* 2014 [cited 2014 24 August]; Available from: http://www.nformationdesign.com/portfolio/portfolio01.php.
15. caehealthcare.com. *LapVR Surgical Simulator.* 2014 [cited 2014 24 August]; Available from: http://www.medsimlab.com/brochuras/lap.pdf.
16. Simbionix. *LAP Mentor.* 2014 [cited 2014 24 August]; Available from: http://simbionix.com/simulators/lap-mentor/.
17. SurgicalScience. *http://www.surgical-science.com.* 2014 [cited 2014 24 August]; Available from: http://www.surgical-science.com.
18. Tarcoveanu, E., R. Moldovanu, and A. Vasilescu, *ÎNVĂȚĂMÂNTUL VIRTUAL ÎN CHIRURGIA MINIM INVAZIVĂ.* Jurnalul de Chirurgie, 2010. 6(3): p. 230-236.
19. Saunders, N.R., *The Celestin tube in the palliation of carcinoma of the oesophagus and cardia.* Br J Surg, 1979. 66(6): p. 419-21.
20. Lamata, P., et al., *SINERGIA laparoscopic virtual reality simulator: didactic design and technical development.* Comput Methods Programs Biomed, 2007. 85(3): p. 273-83.
21. www.virtalis.com. *VERT: Virtual Environment Radiotherapy Training.* 2014 [cited 2014 24 August]; Available from: http://www.virtalis. com/files /articles /flier_whatisvert.pdf.
22. www.vertual.co.uk. *VERT.* 2014 [cited 2014 24 August]; Available from: http://www.vertual.co.uk/.
23. VirRAD. *VirRAD.* 2014 [cited 2014 24 August]; Available from: http://www.virrad.org/.
24. Kurenov, S.N., et al., *Simulation for training with the Autosuture Endo Stitch device.* Surg Innov, 2006. 13(4): p. 283-7.
25. *CathSim Intravenous Simulator.* 2014 [cited 2014 24 August]; Available from: http://www.pennstatehershey.org/web/simulation/equipment/cathsim.
26. Bro-Nielsen, M., et al., *PreOp endoscopic simulator: a PC-based immersive training system for bronchoscopy.* Stud Health Technol Inform, 1999. 62: p. 76-82.
27. Cotin, S., et al., *ICTS, an interventional cardiology training system.* Stud Health Technol Inform, 2000. 70: p. 59-65.
28. Mabrey, J.D., et al., *Development of a virtual reality arthroscopic knee simulator.* Stud Health Technol Inform, 2000. 70: p. 192-4.
29. Rudman, D.T., et al., *Functional endoscopic sinus surgery training simulator.* Laryngoscope, 1998. 108(11 Pt 1): p. 1643-7.
30. Heng, P.A., et al., *Virtual acupuncture human based on chinese visible human dataset.* Stud Health Technol Inform, 2006. 119: p. 194-7.
31. *THE Awards: Virtual reality chair helps drill trainee dentists.* 2013 [cited 2014 25 August]; Available from: http://www.reading.ac.uk/sse/news/sse-newsarticle-2013-11-25.aspx.
32. Marescaux, J., *OPERATION LINDBERGH-A World First in TeleSurgery: The Surgical Act Crosses the Atlantic!* September 19, 2001: New York-Strasbourg.
33. Okamura, A.M., *Haptic feedback in robot-assisted minimally invasive surgery.* Curr Opin Urol, 2009. 19(1): p. 102-7.

34. Kuchenbecker, K.J., et al. *VerroTouch: High-Frequency Acceleration Feedback for Telerobotic Surgery.* in *EuroHaptics'10 Proceedings of the 2010 International Conference on Haptics: Generating and Perceiving Tangible Sensations.* 2010.
35. Vosburgh, K.G. and R. San Jose Estepar, *Natural Orifice Transluminal Endoscopic Surgery (NOTES): an opportunity for augmented reality guidance.* Stud Health Technol Inform, 2007. 125: p. 485-90.
36. Fernandez-Esparrach, G., et al., *The role of a computed tomography-based image registered navigation system for natural orifice transluminal endoscopic surgery: a comparative study in a porcine model.* Endoscopy, 2010. 42(12): p. 1096-103.
37. VBI. *Virtual Reality Software Programs for Phobias, Substance Use Disorders, Skills Development, PTSD, & Stress/Pain Management.* [cited 2014 24 August]; Available from: http://www.virtuallybetter.com/.
38. VRMC. *Virtual Reality Phobia.* [cited 2014 24 August]; Available from: http://www.vrphobia.com.
39. *Virtual Reality Therapy for Phobias.* 2014 [cited 2014 24 August]; Available from: http://psychiatry.duke.edu/divisions/general-psychiatry/virtual-reality-therapy-phobias.
40. USC-ICT. *Medical Virtual Reality.* [cited 2014 24 August]; Available from: http://medvr.ict.usc.edu/projects/.
41. VRS.ORG.UK. *Virtual reality and trypanophobia (fear of needles).* [cited 2014 18 Aug]; Available from: http://www.vrs.org.uk/virtual-reality-healthcare/ trypanophobia. html.
42. VRS.ORG.UK. *Virtual reality for the disabled.* [cited 2014 18 Aug]; Available from: http://www.vrs.org.uk/virtual-reality-healthcare/disabled.html.
43. *The Virtual Physiological Rat Project.* 2014 [cited 2014 25 August]; Available from: http://virtualrat.org/.
44. Broeren, J., et al., *Assessment and training in a 3-dimensional virtual environment with haptics: a report on 5 cases of motor rehabilitation in the chronic stage after stroke.* Neurorehabil Neural Repair, 2007. 21(2): p. 180-9.
45. Merians, A.S., et al., *Sensorimotor training in a virtual reality environment: does it improve functional recovery poststroke?* Neurorehabil Neural Repair, 2006. 20(2): p. 252-67.
46. Sandlund, M., S. McDonough, and C. Hager-Ross, *Interactive computer play in rehabilitation of children with sensorimotor disorders: a systematic review.* Dev Med Child Neurol, 2009. 51(3): p. 173-9.
47. ScienceDaily. *Pushing boundaries of virtual reality.* 2013 [cited 2014 24 August]; Available from: www.sciencedaily.com/releases/2013/02/130205143336.htm.
48. Choi, S.H. and H.H. Cheung, *Multi-material virtual prototyping for product development and biomedical engineering.* Computers in industry archive, 2007. 58(5): p. 438-452.
49. Clin, J., C.E. Aubin, and H. Labelle, *Virtual prototyping of a brace design for the correction of scoliotic deformities.* Med Biol Eng Comput, 2007. 45(5): p. 467-73.
50. Chen, L.C. and J.I. Boufford, *Fatal flows--doctors on the move.* N Engl J Med, 2005. 353(17): p. 1850-2.
51. Dickens, B.M. and R.J. Cook, *Legal and ethical issues in telemedicine and robotics.* Int J Gynaecol Obstet, 2006. 94(1): p. 73-8.
52. Silverman, R.D., *Current legal and ethical concerns in telemedicine and e-medicine.* J Telemed Telecare, 2003. 9 Suppl 1: p. S67-9.
53. Irvine, R., Mediating telemedicine: ethics at a distance. Intern Med J, 2005. 35(1): p. 56-8.

CHAPTER 12

Understanding People With Human Activities And Social Interactions For Human-Centered Computing

Sangil Choi*

Department of Computer Science, Swaziland Christian University, Mbabane, Kingdom of Swaziland

ABSTRACT

An ultimate goal of human-centered computing is making human beings the center of computing technologies. To make people a core component of the technology, first of all, we need to understand people and society in which people live. In this paper, we propose two important factors in order to understand people and their social interactions. Proposed human activity recognition and neighbor discovery schemes help us comprehend human activities and their social behaviors. In addition, combination of these two mechanisms provide us with an opportunity for better understanding of people in the near future. Finally, it might be worth analyzing correlation between human activities and social interactions for the group of people using our proposed schemes.

HUMAN-CENTERED COMPUTING

Computing technology has changed a lot of things in the world quickly. It is still affecting the way we think, the way we communicate with each other, the way we study, the way we work, and so on. Furthermore, computer hardware and software keep evolving every day and new paradigms and mechanisms continuously emerge into the world. There is no doubt that the main purpose of these technologies make human beings and our daily life convenient. In other word, the center of computing is all mankind.

However, the main purpose of computing technology may not be human beings. Artificial intelligence (AI) could be one of the promising computing technologies in the future. Many AI researchers hope that this technology will help and assist people effectively and efficiently. In addition, they believe that AI dramatically change our life in the near future. Unfortunately, all of the change are not always positive. Rapid and frequent changing of computing technologies could be difficult to use especially for elderly people. Furthermore, it is well known that innovative AI technology could give people a great fear. Some famous movies dealing with AI issues reflected this phenomenon. In addition, there was the fight of the century to play game Go between an AI Go player (AlphaGo) and a professional human Go player in March, 2016. AlphaGo finally defeated the human Go player at that game. It is definitely possible that the result of the game surprised and frightened all of the people in the world.

As we discussed before, one of the fundamental problems in current computing technologies is that there is a gap between human and computing technologies. Most current computing technologies concentrate on improving existing technologies or solving specific technological problems. This approach may not take care of human issues carefully. Originally, a computer was made for better human life, but now experts probably keep developing computing technologies for the enhanced performance of computer itself. In order to minimize the existing gaps, human-centered computing (HCC) has emerged. HCC encompasses all of the studies and efforts regarding making human beings the heart of computing technologies. Because of this reason, HCC could incorporate different types of disciplines such as computer science, sociology, psychology, cognitive science, graphic design, and anthropology. HCC research expects revolutionary movements to happen by dealing with human abilities and needs.

In [1], authors proposed three important factors that form the core of HCC system: First, the HCC system should take into account personal human abilities and limitations. Second, it should consider social and cultural environments. Finally, the system could be properly adjustable to diverse individuals and specific environments. In addition, the authors addressed the following research directions:

- New algorithms and development of diverse HCC systems;
- Integration of multiple sensors, media, and human sciences that make human beings the central point;
- New interdisciplinary academic and industrial programs;
- Discussions on the impact of computing technology that include the social, economic, and cultural contexts in which such technology might be deployed;
- Data collection from culturally diverse social situations;
- Evaluation metrics for theories, design processes, implementations, and systems from a human-centered perspective; and
- Methodologies for privacy protection and the consideration of ethical and cultural issues.

The papers [1, 2] mentioned that a key challenge of developing HCC systems is encompassing diverse disciplines that we have already discussed in computational environments. Especially, in this paper, we propose a potential computational model that focuses on understanding individual and social activities toward future HCC systems.

HUMAN ACTIVITY MONITORING SYSTEM

Human beings have different types of physical activities in their daily life. They could sit on a chair, walk along a street, or sometimes run or jog inside or outside a building. Although there are some different levels or degrees of activity based on their occupations, most people have their own activity styles everyday. In addition, many people are getting interested in their health so that different kinds of activity tracking devices have emerged these days. With the activity trackers, users can keep recording their own daily activities and realize the pattern of physical activities numerically. Furthermore, these activity patterns may indicate their current health status.

We proposed a human activity monitoring system using a wearable sensor in our previous paper [3]. The system consists of two primary components: activity data collection and physical activity recognition. Our system focuses on classifying and monitoring human daily activity. In this section, we briefly introduce our activity monitoring system.

Shimmer: wireless wearable sensor

For collecting and recognizing different human physical activities, we used a tiny and lightweight wireless wearable sensor called Shimmer [4]. It is widely used for studying a lot of phenomenon, implementing diverse algorithms, and making some experiments in wireless sensor networks. The Shimmer device consists of a number of integrated and extended sensors, a central processing unit, wireless communication modules, and storage devices. It can be considered as a tiny personal computer equipped with wireless communication and sensing capabilities. Especially, Shimmer has a triaxial acceleration sensor. By reading and analyzing a series of acceleration data with this sensor, we can recognize a real-time human physical activity. Shimmer has three key features: First, it has a very low power or low energy consumption capability. Second, its size is very small (53 × 32 × 15 mm enclosure). Lastly, its weight is only 15 g. Due to these features, it is currently widely used for wearable sensor applications. In addition, Shimmer is applicable to a variety of areas such as healthcare, rehabilitation, remote patient monitoring and assistive technology, environmental sensing solutions, and biomechanics.

Metrics for activity recognition

There are two typical physical activities in our daily life: static and dynamic activities. Representative static activities consist of standing, sitting, and reclining. Additionally, famous dynamic activities are composed of walking, running, and jumping. With acceleration readings from Shimmer, we compute an inclination angle and a standard deviation with vertical and anterior-posterior accelerations to recognize real-time human physical activities. The inclination angle has been calculated to classify the static activity in previous research [5, 6, 7, 8, 9]. After obtaining each x- and y-axis of acceleration values, we calculate the inclination angle (Φ) with Eq. (1), where A_x and A_y represent accelerations of the x- and y-axis, respectively. In our system, as mentioned before, the inclination angle is used for recognizing standing, sitting, or reclining activities.

$$\Phi = \arctan\frac{A_x}{A_y} \tag{1}$$

Most dynamic activities are closely related to the variation of accelerations in vertical direction. We decided that a standard deviation could be one of the best measurements to distinguish between static and dynamic activities. If the standard deviation value is constantly changing, we can conclude that the activity is dynamic. To get the standard deviation of the y-axis, we collect 10 samples of acceleration values of the y-axis and calculate the standard deviation (σσ) with Eq. (2), where *n* is the number of samples, y_i is the acceleration of the y-axis at time *i*, and y¯y¯ represents the average of the acceleration of the y-axis over *n* samples, respectively.

$$\sigma = \sqrt{\frac{1}{n-1}\sum_{i=1}^{n}(y_i - \bar{y})^2} \quad (2)$$

Activity recognition algorithm

We used two measurements, inclination angle and standard deviation, for activity recognition in our system. The computation needed for these measurements is not complicated. Therefore, our activity recognition algorithm is simple and compact. This is one of the contributions of activity monitoring. The main reason is that a wireless sensor device is a resource-constrained and battery-dependent hardware, and therefore, we need to minimize the battery of sensors for computation in order to decrease energy consumption. If sensor applications consume a lot of energy and require heavy computation, this system might not be useful to collect and monitor daily physical activity in humans.

Figure 1 represents the flow chart of our entire physical activity recognition. First, we collect original acceleration data from the accelerometer in the Shimmer. Second, we perform our own data calibration process to get accurate acceleration data. Then, we calculate the inclination angle and standard deviation with the calibrated acceleration value. Finally, we compare the angle or standard deviation value with some threshold values that we computed to produce a boolean indicator. As a result, we can finally obtain a series of boolean indicators representing '0' or '1'.

How can we get the final activity data from the series of binary numbers consisting of '0' and '1' in the proposed activity recognition algorithm? Here is a concrete example. Let us consider one specific activity like *standing*. We may think that *standing* is a static posture. There is no active movement in this activity, which means that both HIGH and LOW dynamic values from the standard deviation are around zero. From the previous experimental study [3], we found that the inclination angle of *standing* is different from that of *sitting* or *lying*. Therefore, the LIE value in Figure 1 is also zero. The TRAN value comes from the big difference of angles, so that the value is also zero because there is no big angle difference in the *standing* position.

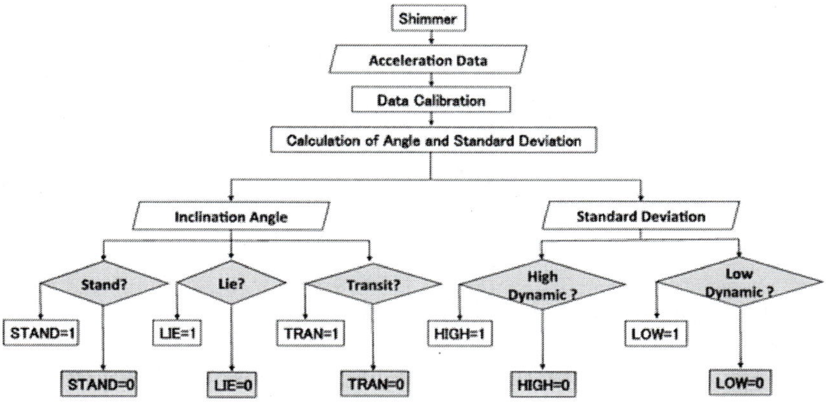

Figure 1. Activity recognition algorithm

Consequently, all values are zero except the first one (e.g., 10,000). After getting these binary data, we can map them into a specific decimal number representing the specific activity and conclude that the current activity is a *standing* posture. This is how the activity recognition algorithm works.

NEIGHBOR DISCOVERY PROTOCOL

Most recent studies of the wireless sensor network (WSN) area focus on energy consumed by wireless sensors [10, 11, 12, 13, 14, 15]. Especially, neighbor discovery has been actively studied for over a decade since the research of WSN began. There are two primary reasons why the topic of neighbor discovery became popular: First, if sensors cannot find neighbors within a certain amount of time, they are unattended or useless. Second, if this situation continues, it makes the entire network partitioned or disconnected. A variety of asynchronous neighbor discovery protocols have been developed in order to address a neighbor discovery problem [16, 17, 18, 19, 20, 21, 22, 23, 24]. In this section, we present an asynchronous neighbor discovery protocol we proposed called *BAND* in the previous paper [25].

Neighbor discovery problem

Most wireless sensors are characterized as a resource-constrained device because they have limited computing power and their power source comes from battery. For the purpose of energy conservation, almost all sensors have their own power-saving mode. In this mode, sensors turn off their communication channel and do noting. Periodically, they turn on their radio and try to communicate with their neighbors. Unfortunately, there is no information regarding when their neighbors wake up. Therefore, each sensor in the network should know how many neighbors are located within its communication range and how often they wake up. Traditionally, using some number of control packets, sensors tried to synchronize the meeting time of their neighbors, but it turned out there is a huge overhead of exchanging these control packets. Therefore, an asynchronous neighbor discovery scheme came into the spotlight these days.

Combinatorial block design

The neighbor discovery mechanism we proposed borrowed the concept of combinatorial block designs. Especially, we developed a neighbor discovery schedule using a *Balance Incomplete Block Design* (BIBD) [26, 27, 28]. As we mentioned before, there are two distinctive modes in a neighbor discovery schedule called active and power-saving modes. We could represent these two modes with a number zero and one. For example, we have '010101' schedule, which means a sensor is in power-saving mode for the first time and then turns on its radio to communicate with its neighbors and continues this pattern repeatedly. One of the most challenging tasks for construing neighbor discovery schedules is how two different schedules have the same active mode at the same time without any further information. In [29], according to Theorem 2.1.2, it has been proved that if a given (v, k, λ)-BIBD is a symmetric BIBD then randomly selected two blocks have exactly common λ points. This Theorem represents a fundamental property showing that two arbitrary discovery schedules could have common active time slots when we apply the symmetric BIBD to the asynchronous neighbor discovery problem without control packets.

Combination of two block designs

Although we could apply BIBD to the construction of an asynchronous neighbor discovery schedule, there is a weakness when simply employing BIBD for creating discovery schedule. The practical challenge of using a block design for asynchronous neighbor discovery is that there is no unified block construction method. That is why we developed a block combination algorithm. A basic concept under the proposed construction technique is combining two block designs.

Let us explain how to combine two designs in detail. For simplicity, two simple designs are used for demonstration purposes. Note that we created these two designs only for the purpose of illustrating the combination process.

***Step 1*: choose two block designs**

First, we select any two well-known block designs. Assume that there are two block designs, $A = (v_a, k_a, \lambda_a)$-*BIBD* and $B = (v_b, k_b, \lambda_b)$-*BIBD*. For the sake of simplicity, we use (4, 3, 2) and (3, 2, 1)-designs to demonstrate the proposed idea of block combination. Figure 2 shows (4, 3, 2) and (3, 2, 1)-designs. Here, we call the (4, 3, 2)-design a *base* design and (3, 2, 1)-design a *replacement* design.

Slot	1	2	3	4
1	0	1	1	1
2	1	0	1	1
3	1	1	0	1
4	1	1	1	0

Slot	1	2	3
1	1	1	0
2	0	1	1
3	1	0	1

Figure 2. (4,3,2) and (3,2,1)-designs

***Step 2:* replace each active slot of the *base* design with the entire blocks of the *replacement* design and every sleep slot of the *base* design with a *sleep schedule* of order 3. Here, a *sleep schedule* is defined as a square matrix of order *n* with all 0's**

In Step 2, for every active slot in the *base* design, we replace it with the entire blocks of the *replacement* design, that is, the (3, 2, 1)-design. In addition, sleep slots are replaced with a *sleep schedule*. Let us assume that we change each active slot from the (4, 3, 2)-design into the entire blocks from the (3, 2, 1)-design.

***Step 3*: generate a new block design for neighbor discovery**

Finally, we can get a $(v_a \times v_b, k_a \times k_b, \lambda_a \times \lambda_b)$-*design* by combining A and B in this step. Figure 3 illustrates the completed (12, 6, 2)-*design* by combining the (3, 2, 1) and (4, 3, 2)-*design*.

Slot	1	2	3	4	5	6	7	8	9	10	11	12
1	0	0	0	1	1	0	1	1	0	1	1	0
2	0	0	0	0	1	1	0	1	1	0	1	1
3	0	0	0	1	0	1	1	0	1	1	0	1
4	1	1	0	0	0	0	1	1	0	1	1	0
5	0	1	1	0	0	0	0	1	1	0	1	1
6	1	0	1	0	0	0	1	0	1	1	0	1
7	1	1	0	1	1	0	0	0	0	1	1	0
8	0	1	1	0	1	1	0	0	0	0	1	1
9	1	0	1	1	0	1	0	0	0	1	0	1
10	1	1	0	1	1	0	1	1	0	0	0	0
11	0	1	1	0	1	1	0	1	1	0	0	0
12	1	0	1	1	0	1	1	0	1	0	0	0

Figure 3. Combination of (4,3,2) and (3,2,1) designs

By using the method in Step 2, we can construct a set of new neighbor discovery schedules (NDS) with a different duty cycle. These combined schedules make the neighbor discovery problem easy to solve. We can generate a new NDS by combing two block designs. If there exists a BIBD with a desired duty cycle, we can just use the BIBD for the neighbor discovery. However, due to the lack of a unified algorithm of generating BIBDs, it is not always possible to generate an NDS with a certain duty cycle. Therefore, the proposed block design scheme gives us more options. For instance, the proposed method can virtually construct a new block design with almost any duty cycle by selecting a proper set of previously known block designs. Figure 4 illustrates the algorithm we designed for combining two block designs.

In the simulation study, we focused on two major criteria of neighbor discovery problems: energy consumption and discovery latency. Related studies of neighbor discovery also dealt with these metrics in their performance evaluation. We have implemented four representative neighbor discovery protocols in the literature and *BAND*. The performance of the proposed algorithm is much better than other competitive protocols. As shown in Figure 5, the energy consumption of *BAND* is less than that of three competitive protocols. Note that *Combinatorial* is the optimal solution and the energy consumption of *BAND* is very close to that of *Combinatorial*.

Algorithm: Combination of Block Designs

```
procedure COMBINING TWO DESIGNS
    Φ := (v1,k1,λ1)-BIBD
    Ψ := (v2,k2,λ2)-BIBD
    Ø := a sleep schedule
    for all p ∈ Φ do
        replace p by Ψ
    end for
    for all q ∉ Φ do
        replace p by Ø
    end for
end procedure
```

Figure 4. An algorithm of combining two block designs

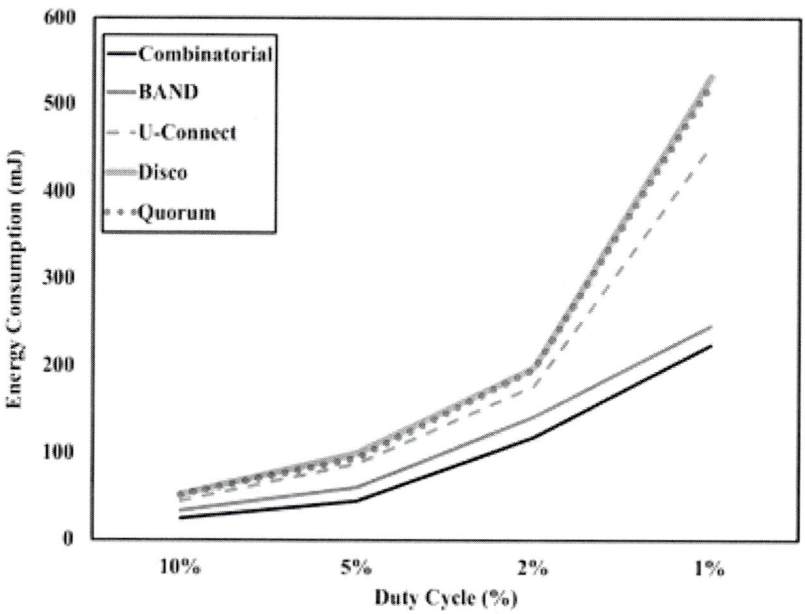

Figure 5. Energy consumption of five neighbor discovery protocols

COMBINATION OF HUMAN ACTIVITY MONITORING AND NEIGHBOR DISCOVERY

We discussed three factors composing the core of HCC system. These factors focus on human abilities and limitations, social and cultural awareness, and adaptability across individuals and specific situations. From a human-centered perspective, one of the most important tasks toward an ideal HCC system is to understand people and society in which people live. In this section, we propose a potential computational model for supporting HCC systems. Based on the research directions that we have discussed in the beginning of this article, we suggest one possible model that can be used for understanding the behavior of individuals and social interactions.

First, we need a data collection mechanism in order to understand and analyze the human's behavior and the relationship with others. According to the purpose of the system, there are many different types of options we can choose. One of the possible choices is the data of human physical activities. Our proposed human activity monitoring system can be applied to collect physical activity data. The monitoring system only requires a small amount of battery and memory space. It was originally developed for sensor applications, so the system is user-friendly and energy-efficient. Through the monitoring system, we could measure the level of physical daily activity of people.

Additionally, we might also collect the social interactions of people with our neighbor discovery protocol. In a wireless sensor network environment, in the beginning phase of the deployment of sensors, they try to find their neighbors and join the network in their communication range for a certain amount of time. Usually, a graph theory can be used for representing sensor nodes and their connectivity graphically. In the graph, each node illustrates a sensor and each vertex expresses a link between sensors. We could apply this concept to represent the interactions of people in communities. If our proposed neighbor discovery protocol finds neighbors frequently then it means that a specific person actively makes a relationship with others. The frequency of fining different neighbors can be used as a metric for the level of sociability of people.

Second, the level of physical activity and sociability of individuals can be used for developing evaluation metrics for HCC systems from a human-centered perspective. Our activity monitoring system can recognize typical human daily activities such as walking, running, standing, or sitting. It is possible that some active group of people usually has combination of running and walking activities. We could imagine that most businessmen or salesmen generally have some busy schedules almost every day. Especially, these type of people frequently meet other individuals in their daily life to make a social or business relationship with their partners. Therefore, we could define the degree of activeness of an individual based on analyzing different kind of physical activities through the proposed activity monitoring system. We could also design the degree of dynamics of social interactions using frequent data exchange for neighbor discovery. These two metrics can be employed for evaluating that a HCC system deeply considers the understanding of people.

Finally, let us think about a feasible application of combining the application-level solution and the network protocol-level approach. The proposed activity monitoring system can measure the level of physical daily activity of people. In addition, we could also apply our neighbor discovery protocol to quantify the level of sociability of people by checking how frequently the sensors detect their neighbors or how many neighbors they find within a certain amount of time. Let us make an assumption: the daily activity of a certain person consists of a lot of dynamic activities (walking or running) and the frequency or the number of neighbor discovery is also high then we could say that he or she is a sociable and an active person. The level of physical activity indicates how people live vigorously during their daily life. Frequent data exchange for neighbor discovery shows how actively people interact with others. Therefore, using the combination between physical activity monitoring and neighbor discovery, we can measure both individual health level and the level of socialized relationship with others.

There is one more possibility on the combination of human activity monitoring and neighbor discovery. We can conduct a correlation analysis between the level of physical daily activity and sociability of people. There are some meaningful hypotheses for better understanding of people. For example, we have the following questions?

- Does the people who has mostly dynamic activities show a vigorous relationship with their friends or partners?
- Does the people who actively interact with others have the high degree of activeness of their daily life?
- Is human daily activity closely related to human social interaction?

CONCLUSION

In conclusion, one of the most significant considerations of designing or implementing HCC systems is understanding people. That is why human beings should be the core component of the system in a HCC environment. In this paper, we propose a computational model quantifying the level of activeness of individuals and the level of social interactions. The combination of human activity monitoring and neighbor discovery could have some promising research works for better comprehension of people in the future. If there is a close relationship between individual physical activities and social interactions through the correlation analysis we suggest, we could adopt this relationship as a meaningful evaluation metric for HCC systems. In addition, by mixing the level of activeness and social interactions, we could characterize a number of groups of people. This clustering approach might give us a better understanding of people when each group indicates its own characteristic. This could be an opportunity of understanding the behavior or characteristic of a group of people.

COMPETING INTERESTS

The authors declare that they have no competing interests.

REFERENCES

1. Jaimes A, G-Perez D, Sebe N, Huang TS (2007) Human-centered computing: toward a human revolution. IEEE Comput 5:30–34
2. Jaimes A, Sebe N, G-Perez D (2006) Human-centered computing: a multimedia perspective. In Proceedings of the 14th ACM international conference on multimedia. ACM, pp 855–864
3. Choi S, LeMay R, Youn J (2013) On-board Processing of acceleration data for real-time activity classification. In Proceedings of the 10th IEEE consumer Communications and networking conference (CCNC), pp 68–73
4. http://www.shimmer-research.com
5. Culhane KM, Lyons GM, Hilton D, Grace PA, Lyons D (2004) Long term mobility monitoring of older adults using accelerometers in a clinical environment. Clin Rehabil 18(3):335–343
6. Karantonis DM, Narayanan MR, Mathie M, Lovell NH, Celler BG (2006) Implementation of a real-time human movement classifier using a triaxial accelerometer for ambulatory monitoring. IEEE Trans Inf Technol Biomed 10(1):156–167
7. Lyons GM, Culhane KM, Hilton D, Grace PA, Lyons D (2005) A description of an accelerometer-based mobility monitoring technique. Med Eng Phys 27(6):497–504
8. Najafi B, Aminian K, Paraschiv-Ionescu A, Loew F, Bula CJ, Robert P (2003) Ambulatory system for human motion analysis using a kinematic sensor:

monitoring of daily physical activity in the elderly. IEEE Trans Biomed Eng 50(6):711–723
9. Veltink PH, Bussmann HBJ, De Vries W, Martens WLJ, Van Lummel RC (1996) Detection of static and dynamic activities using uniaxial accelerometers. IEEE Trans Rehabil Eng 4(4):375–385
10. Meng T, Wu F, Yang Z, Chen G, Vasilakos AV (2015) Spatial resuability-aware routing in multi-hop wireless networks. IEEE Trans Comput 65(1):244–255.
11. Chen L, Li Y, Vasilakos AV (2016) Oblivious neighbor discovery for wireless devices with directional antennas. In Proceedings of the IEEE INFOCOM, San Francisco, 10–15 April 2016
12. Yao Y, Cao Q, Vasilakos AV (2015) EDAL: an energy-efficient, delay-aware, and lifetime-balancing data collection protocol for heterogeneous wireless sensor networks. IEEE ACM Trans Netw 23(3): 810–823
13. Bhuiyan MZA, Vasilakos AV (2015) Local area prediction-based mobile target tracking in wireless sensor networks. IEEE Trans Comput 64(7):1968–1982
14. Zhang XM, Zhang Y, Yan F, Vasilakos AV (2015) Interference-based topology control algorithm for delay-constrained mobile ad hoc networks. IEEE Trans Mob Comput 14(4): 742–754
15. Xiao Y, Peng M, Gibson J, Xie GG, Du D-Z, Vasilakos AV (2012) Tight performance bounds of multihop fair access for mac protocols in wireless sensor networks and underwater sensor networks. IEEE Trans. Mob Comput 11(10):1538–1554
16. McGlynn MJ, Borbash SA (2001) Birthday protocols for low energy deployment and flexible neighbor discovery in ad hoc wireless networks. In Proceedings of the 2nd ACM international symposium on mobile ad hoc networking and computing, pp 137–145
17. Jiang J, Tseng Y, Hsu C, Lai T (2005) Quorum-based asynchronous power-saving protocols for IEEE 802.11 ad hoc networks. Mob Netw Appl 10(1–2):169–181
18. Tseng Y-C, Hsu C-S, Hsieh T-Y (2002) Power-saving protocols for IEEE 802.11-based multi-hop ad hoc networks. In Proceedings of twenty-first annual joint conference of the IEEE computer and communications societies, pp 200–209
19. Dutta P, Culler D (2008) Practical asynchronous neighbor discovery and rendezvous for mobile sensing applications. In Proceedings of the 6th ACM conference on embedded network sensor systems, pp 71–84
20. Kandhalu A, Lakshmanan K, Rajkumar R (2010) U-connect: a low-latency energy-efficient asynchronous neighbor discovery protocol. In Proceedings of the 9th ACM/IEEE international conference on information processing in sensor networks, pp 350–361
21. Zheng R, Hou JC, Sha L (2003) Asynchronous wakeup for ad hoc networks. In Proceedings of the 4th ACM international symposium on mobile ad hoc networking and computing, pp 35–45
22. Bakht M, Trower M, Kravets RH (2012) Searchlight: Won't you be my neighbor. In Proceedings of the 18th annual international conference on mobile computing and networking, Istanbul
23. Meng T, Wu F, Chen G (2014) On designing neighbor discovery protocols: a code-based approach. In Proceedings of the IEEE conference on computer communications, Toronto, 27 April–2 May 2014
24. Chen L, Bian K, Zheng M (2014) Heterogeneous multi-channel neighbor discovery for mobile sensing applications: theoretical foundation and protocol Design. In Proceedings of the 15th ACM international symposium on mobile ad hoc networking and computing, Philadelphia, 11–14 August 2014
25. Choi S, Lee W, Song T, Youn J (2015) Block design-based asynchronous neighbor discovery protocol for wireless sensor networks. J Sens 2015:951652.
26. Anderson I (1988) Combinatorial designs and tournaments. In Chapter 2, Oxford University Press, Oxford
27. Colbourn CJ, Dinitz JH (1996) The CRC handbook of combinatorial designs. CRC Press, Boca Raton

28. Stinson DR (2004) Combinatorial designs: constructions and analysis. Springer, Berlin
29. Godsil C (2010) Combinatorial design theory. http://www.math.uwaterloo.ca/~kpurbhoo/co634/Designs.pdf

CHAPTER 13

Mobile Virtual Reality — An Approach for Safety Management

Dong Zhao[1]

[1] Department of Building Construction, Virginia Polytechnic Institute and State University, Blacksburg, VA, USA

1. INTRODUCTION

Workplace safety is paramount for all production sectors throughout the world. However, every year the number of occupational injuries attracts concerns on the safety management for every industry. Existing studies have endeavored great efforts on injury causations and found that more than half of workplace accidents are due to human errors.

For most human errors, professional training is believed to be an effective safety enhancement and management approach. Active and interactive training is often of higher level of comprehension while the passive methods of learning are not as effective, especially for adult learners. Most current electrical safety training programs in terms of video tape, paper-based handouts or slide shows can hardly present the electrical hazards vividly to trainees and, on the other hand, the trainees are not provided enough opportunity to participate in these activities. In fact, it is believed that an active and interactive training program can lead to a better comprehension of training material [1]. Such participatory training brings a real life aspect into the training in an "it can happen to you" scenario and allows the trainees to relate to conditions and regulations in real life situations and with a life or death importance. The best scenario is when people do not have to consciously think about following safety procedures because it is second nature to them.

Safety training as safety management means has been existing for years, however what type of training can be the effective approach remains a question. Rooney, et al. [2] suggested that effective training should comprise of both the initial skill training and further refreshing training to reduce human mistakes. The initial skill training is generally conducted in the classroom and supplemented with on-the-job experience. It prepares workers for experiences they will routinely encounter and those they will infrequently encounter. If training does not include the infrequent events or situations, the likelihood of successfully handling such situations will depend solely on the problem solving and decision making skills of the worker. In addition to initial training, refresher training on non-routine or modified tasks will minimize worker mistakes and reduce the potential for a worker's skills to deteriorate. A refresher training program is needed to assist workers in developing and maintaining a high skill level. Such a program will address a worker's loss of skills and enhance skills beyond the initial training level.

Following the same logic, virtual reality (VR) technology becomes an innovative method to promote the training effectiveness. VR-based training has been used with varied successes in many industries such as fire-fighter training, mine safety training, safe procedure in surgical training, security in refineries, safe equipment operation, and civil engineering education. Specifically within the construction industry, VR technology has been used for constructability analysis of precast concrete structural analysis application development [3], electrical design and installation [4], construction prototyping.

Mobile virtual reality (MVR) is an adoption of VR simulation on mobile/portable devices connected to cloud technology for end users. Besides the inclusion of features from VR, another important characteristic of the MVR-supported training programs is the flexibility (in terms of time and location) that they offer to the user. In traditional classroom-based training/instruction, availability of the training provider and trainees need to be coordinated to schedule the training session. MVR, especially when designed for use with a mobile device, allows for convenience of location and time. The user can participate in the training in a job trailer, office, or conceivably the back of a truck with a smart phone. There is no limitation to classroom or training schedules. Tracking the user performance can be built into the applications, which reduces the need for direct trainee observation. Taking mining as a MVR example, users are able to explore sights and sounds of a virtual mine shaft where the screen of the iPad or iPhone is a window into the mine and interact with the environment via the touchscreen. Based on their activities, the trainee is sent messages and questions, and the mine shaft environment changes to match the response criteria.

Current training modes do not count for all learning style and result in information transfer losses (see gaps in Figure 1a). In terms of safety training, information transfer losses include the loss between the information to be expressed and the expressed information (gap 1) and the loss between the expressed information and delivered information (gap 2). Current static two-dimensioned training modes limit the types of safety information and the pool of information receivers, leading to gap 1. Some dangerous tasks and safety issues cannot be allowed for trainees to rehearsal and practice in real life, leading to gap 2. On the contrary, MVR increases a third dimension and mobility, expands the portions of both expressed and delivered information, and eventually helps to deduce the gaps of information losses (see Figure 1b).

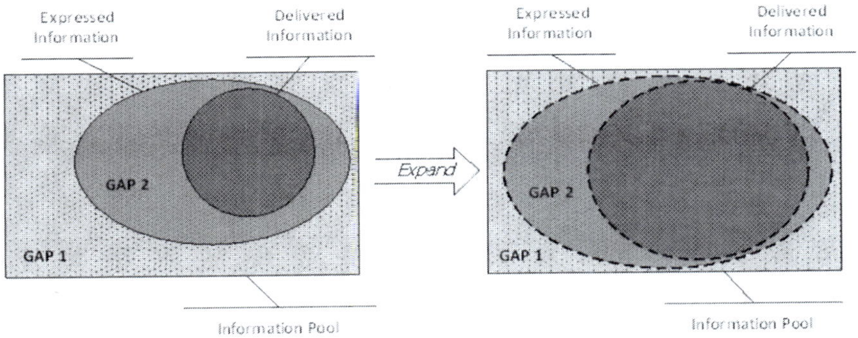

FIGURE 1. Information transfer in traditional training (L) and MVR-supported training (R)

The effectiveness of information perceiving is also confined to traditional training modes. As stated before, for adult trainees, interactive and active training methods instead of passive methods can lead to a better comprehension of training material. Such participatory training brings a real life aspect into the training in an "it can happen to you" scenario and allows the trainees to relate conditions and regulations with real life situations and a life or death importance. The best scenario is when people do not have to consciously think about following safety procedures because it is second nature to them. However, current electrical safety training programs in terms of video tape, paper-based handouts or slide shows can hardly present the electrical hazards vividly to trainees and, on the other side, the trainees are not provided enough opportunity to participate in.

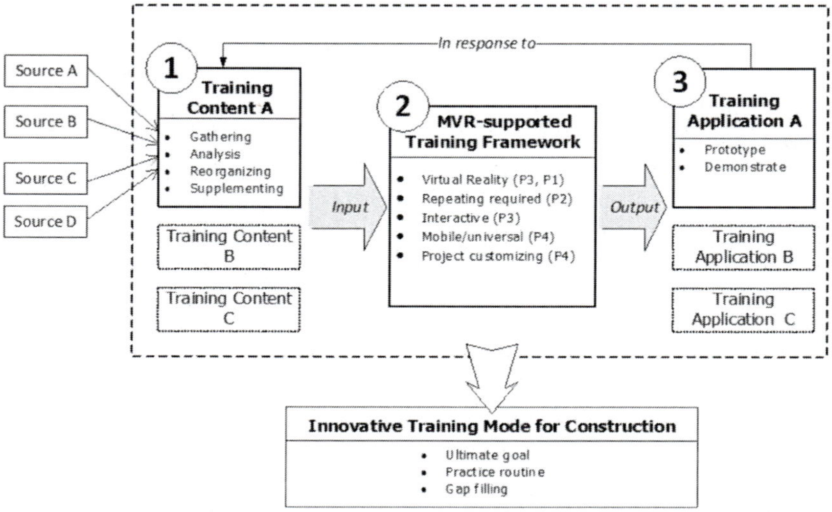

FIGURE 2. Program development framework

This chapter introduces such comprehensive approach that incorporates real-world safety concerns into virtual-world simulations. The approach includes three steps: (1) real-world data collection and coding using a text analysis method; (2) scenarios determination using latent class clustering; and (3) simulation in a virtual environment. The whole process enables to transfer existing safety failures reflected in injuries into training points in a 3D virtual environment for users to practices. This chapter will also provide an example to demonstrate the approach using electrical fatality data from the U.S. construction industry. Mostly, the data and programs demonstrated in this chapter are selected from the author's previous works (Zhao and Lucas, 2014; Zhao et al., 2014b; Zhao et al., 2014c). Figure 2 gives the framework of the demonstration case of electrical safety in the construction industry.

2. REAL-WORLD DATA COLLECTION

This section introduces a systems method to collect real-world accident cases and extract information for building the virtual program. Here, the author takes an example from the electrical safety in the construction industry to demonstrate the data collection process.

2.1. Factor Background

As Figure 3 shows, the ideal solution for integrating construction safety innovation in electrical contracting (EC) needs to fit: 1) the technical and cultural nature of the industry in terms of innovation, 2) the needs of small construction firms and 3) the nature of hazards for ECs. This solution needs to be safer, affordable, accessible, participatory and context/task-specific while integrating technology innovations into practical routines to achieve higher effectiveness and better human habitus in construction. Also, this solution needs to respect human learning behavior and human cognitive rules. As a result, an innovative training approach such as the MVR appears to be a viable solution.

Relevant factors need to be distilled to represent the cases. A fishbone (or Ishikawa) diagram is a helpful tool to complete this step. Based on events and causal factors thinking, the fishbone diagram provides a systematic way of breaking down a complicated problem and identifying areas for data collection. Figure 4 illustrates fishbone diagram to generate factors which are used in the electrical safety example in the next section.

2.2. Data Collection Example

The example choose the data from U.S. electrocution investigation reports. These reports provide an historical perspective from 1989 to 2012. This period of time was also deemed appropriate, as it contains data during many of the years previously reported with alarming statistics on electrical incidents in US construction.

The fishbone mapping tool also provides an accessible process for distilling complex reporting structures into salient categories of data for study. As a result, (previously shown in Figure 4), 13 factors were categorized using five categories which included: when, who, where, what and how. Under each category, 13 related factors were created based on the information gathered from FACE reports as well as from extended literature reviews. Therefore, using these factors, information from narrative text can be coded into an information table (shown in Figure 5).

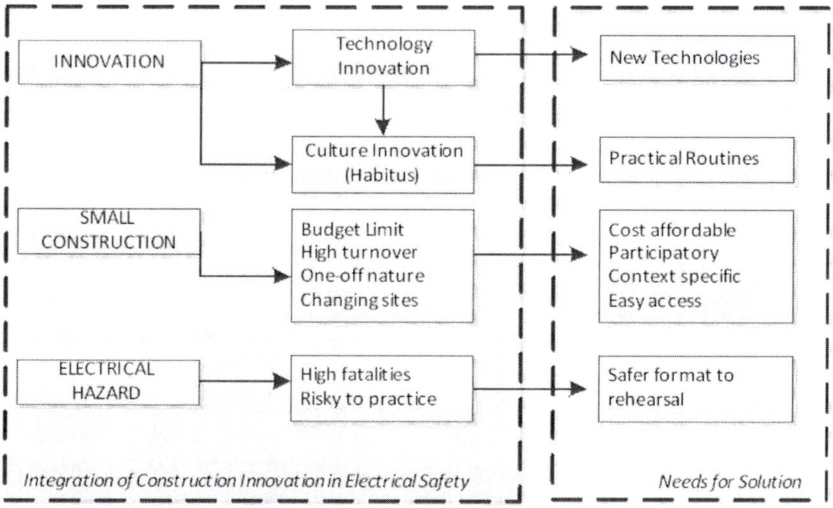

FIGURE 3. Needs for construction innovation in electrical safety

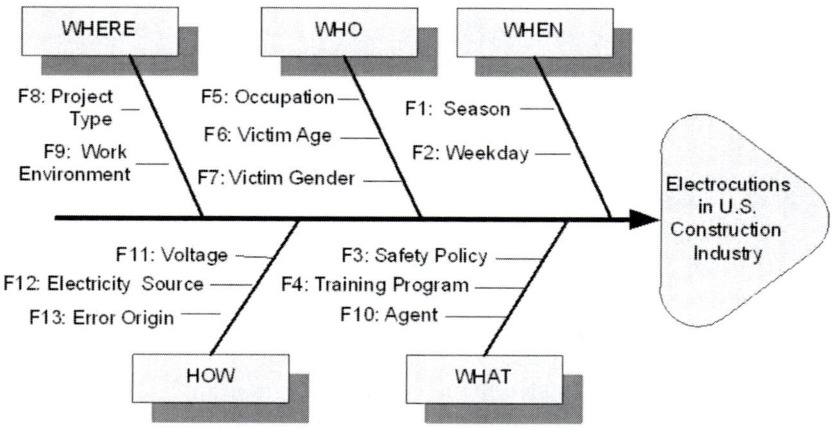

FIGURE 4. An example of fishbone diagram

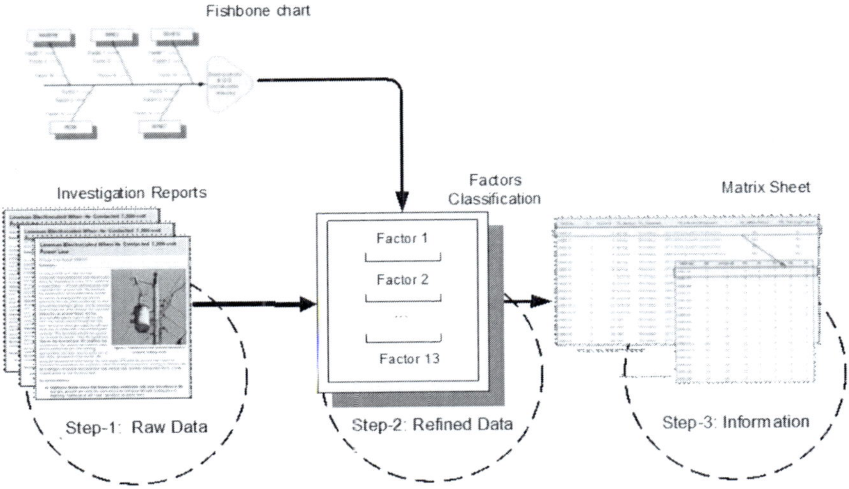

FIGURE 5. Coding process diagram

3. SCENARIOS IDENTIFICATION

This section elaborates a statistical method to build the connection between real-world data and virtual elements. Typical elements in a scenario comprise characters, scenes and events. The characters, including the trainee, represent all roles who participate in the simulation. Here, characters can be created based upon the training target's demographic features. The scenes depict necessary circumstances such as time, place and properties, which are created in accordance with the factor values of a hazardous pattern. The events refer to all the training tasks, hazards associated with the tasks and the respective safety procedures.

3.1. Statistical Analysis

The statistical method is the Latent class analysis (LCA). LCA has some merits over other similar techniques (de Oña et al., 2013): (1) being able to use different type of variables; (2) being able to choose different type of statistical criteria; and (3) being able to using subsequent membership probabilities with maximum likelihood method. Latent classes are unobservable subgroups or segments. Cases are homogeneous within the same latent class while distinctive from each other in different latent classes, depending on certain criteria (Vermunt, 2008). The latent class analysis is a technique to identify the smallest number of latent subgroups or clusters that are sufficient to explain all the associations among manifest variables in a sample group. As shown in Figure 6, a latent class is represented by *N* distinct categories/values of a nominal latent variable.

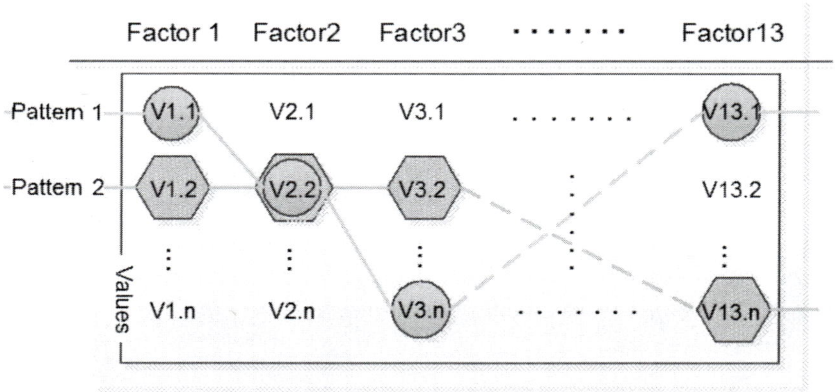

FIGURE 6. Coding process diagram

Recently, LCA is able to include mixed-scale-type variables and covariates, and thus has been adopted in a wide-range of research areas including accident analysis (Collins and Lanza, 2010; Depaire et al., 2008). Given *X* representing the latent variable with value *Y*, and suppose *M* be the LC number and *N*be the variable number. A particular LC is enumerated by the index *x*, *x=1, 2, ..., M*, with value set *Y*(*y1, y2,..., yn*). The aim of LCA is to determine the vector notation *Y*, referring to a complete injury system pattern, by computing the conditional multivariate probabilities *P* (*Y=y*), as:

$$P(Y=y)=\sum_{x=1}^{M}\left[P(X=x)\prod_{n=1}^{N}P(Y_n=y_n\mid X=x)\right] \quad (1)$$

where *P*(*X=x*) denotes the proportion of injury cases belonging to LC *x*.

The most widely used LC fitting criterion is the likelihood ratio chi-squared statistic L^2. L^2 builds on the likelihood of the data under the null hypothesis relative to the maximum likelihood, as:

$$L^2 = 2\sum_{i=1}^{I}\left[C_i \times \ln \frac{C_i}{C \times P(Y = y_i)}\right] \quad (2)$$

where C denotes the total injury case size; Ci denotes the observed frequency of pattern i; $P(Y=yi)$ denotes the probability of having the pattern i; and I denotes the total number of possible patterns in the N-dimensional frequency table, as:

$$I = \prod_{n=1}^{N} n \quad (3)$$

L^2 statistic is advanced on calculations especially for a large number of variables as it enables a decomposition of them into smaller components. Further, this work also incorporates other popular criteria to evaluate the LC model's goodness-of-fit for the sake of research reliability. They are the L^2based Akaike's information criterion (AIC), the Bayesian information criterion (BIC), and the consistent AIC (CAIC). These statistical criteria measure LC's parsimony. A lower criteria value means a higher parsimony, which indicates a better model fitting. An LC model with a lower BIC value is preferred rather than one with a higher BIC value.

3.2. Data Analysis Example

After previously imported coded data into this analysis, the author assigned LC number from 1 to 10 (M=1, 2, ..., 10, see Equation 1) to the LC model and named them model#1 (M=1), model#2 (M=2), ..., and model#10 (M=10), respectively; then evaluated model#1 to model#2 through calculating their fit criteria values. The LC model fit criteria applied in this example included the likelihood ratio chi-squared statistic L^2, BIC(L^2), AIC(L^2) and CAIC(L^2), and usually a lower value of which indicated a better model fitting. The results of model fit evaluation are demonstrated in Figure 2, which indicates that the model#3 (3 LCs, M=3) has better performance (lower BIC, CAIC) than other models. In addition, model #3's *p-value* of 0.056 (good when greater than 0.05) and *Npar* value of 50 (the number of parameters) also indicate a good separation between latent classes.

According to the results, Model 3 with 3 segments provided LC-dependent univariate distributions for each variable, allowing each later class to represent a typical electrocution system pattern. The overall probabilities of falling into LC #1, LC #2, and LC #3 are 41%, 36%, and 23%, respectively. To identify the characteristics of each pattern, the researchers examined values' loadings for each LC. The loading indicates the degree of correlation between the variable values and the designated LC. In multivariate statistical analysis, some research (Stevens, 2002) preferred a cut-off of 0.4 for important loading while some other (Kline, 1994) suggested 0.3 as an acceptable threshold, irrespective of sample size. Here, this work chooses the loading of 0.37 or greater to determine a closer correlation between the variable value and the corresponding LC of model #3. In this way, the significantly related values to each of the three scenarios are identified, alphabetically listed as following three groups:

- **Scenario A**: younger (age<40) male non-electrical workers die due to indirectly contacting high-voltage power lines or powered machines/tools, usually in Summer or Winter at outdoor workplaces. The employers do not have written safety policies nor provide safety training programs. This pattern is particularly related to the residential building construction projects.
- **Scenario B**: middle-aged (age 40-64) male electrical workers die due to directly contacting high-voltage power lines or electrical components, usually in Spring, Fall or Winter weekends at outdoor workplaces. The employers have written safety policies and provide safety training programs. This pattern is particularly related to the heavy and civil construction projects.
- **Scenario C**: adolescent (age<20) male workers died due to directly contacting low-voltage electrical components or powered machines/tools at an indoor workplace. Whether the employer has written safety policies or provides safety training programs is uncertain. This pattern is particularly related to the non-residential building construction projects.

As a result, three scenarios are identified from real-world contexts. Three construction types are coincidently allocated into the three scenarios. It implies that Scenario A is highly correlated to the residential building construction projects; Scenario B is highly correlated to the heavy and civil engineering construction projects; and Scenario C is highly correlated to the non-residential building construction projects. The results can be interpreted in a tri-plot diagram (see Figure 7), showing each scenario's characteristics in a more visual manner. In the diagram, the three angels indicate the three scenarios while the distance between any two points reflects their relationship (the shorter, the closer).

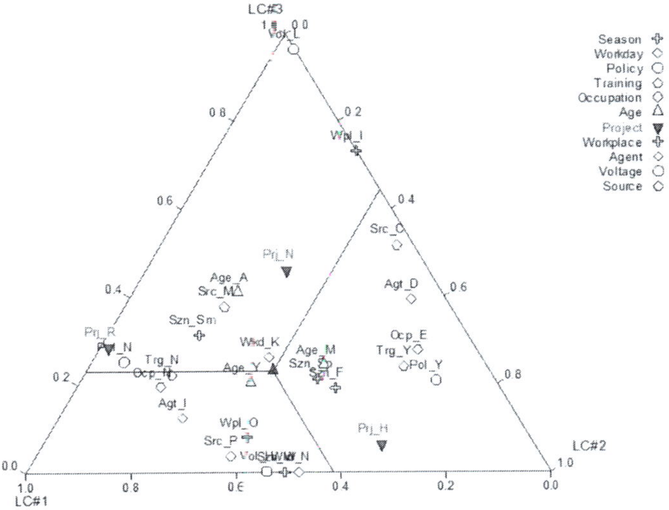

FIGURE 7. LC analysis triangle

4. PROGRAM DEVELOPMENT

This section introduces the program development using mobile virtual reality technology. The example for demonstration is the previously identified scenario B. Given the identification of typical workplace scenario, six training-critical points are created: the potential electrical hazardous awareness; the safe approach distance; the work condition clearance; the lockout and tag out; the suitable personal protective equipment (PPE); and the effective communication. These training points were required by OSHA regulations, National Fire Prevention Association codes (NFPA 70) and FACE report recommendations(Zhao et al., 2012). Based on the prototype simulation, a training point is linked to an event which consists of triggers and outcome animations. Taking the training point of work condition clearance for example, barriers such as waterlogging or storage boxes were added into the scenario. Users can only access the panel safely until they clear these barriers by touching them. If this training point is not completed, an electrical accident such as a shock may be triggered later and the outcome of an electrical shock will be represented via an animation (Zhao and Ye, 2012).

4.1. Design And Modelling

The modeling process includes two separate parts: the 3D object modeling and 3D environment modeling. The 3D objects include buildings, machines, equipment, tools, materials, electrical components, background settings and worker actors. Most of these models were created using Autodesk's 3ds Max, such as a mobile crane and electricity transmission tower. 3D environment modeling includes designs of area terrain, sky clouds, sun point, wind, rain (if necessary), light layout, landscape as well as relative sounds. Prior complete 3D models are imported into the completed 3D working environment, the whole of which resulted in a training scenario. Each electrical hazard and its responding tasks were simulated as interactive events through coding scripts. Scenarios and events were linked by animations. The training scenarios, including 3D objects and 3D environments, and integrated training events are together comprised of a training Module. 3D characters and properties are modeled in Autodesk's 3ds Max. Scenes are designed and compiled in Torque 3D game engine. For mobility, the output is published as an Android application.

4.2. User Interface Design

The User Interface (UI) is designed to connect all previously developed 3D objects and the 3D environment, which can be customized for specific project. The function of UI is to display a distinct set of scenarios, which are further broken down into a series of tasks, such as:

- load the 3D environment and facility model to the user scene;
- receive user input of the 3D character with relevant behavior for the user control in the preset environment;
- load the scenarios, display 3D elements, and activate the storybook;
- track the activities that are performed during the scenario, and response timely.

4.3. Development Example

The training content of this example demonstrates one of construction scenarios in which electrical accidents often occur. The designated scenario is based on the previously identified scenario B: middle-aged male electrical workers die due to directly contacting high-voltage power lines or electrical components at an outdoor highway construction jobsite in September. The example scenario assumes energized indoor electrical components as the hazard. In the way, the storybook is compiled as:

- Character (or avatar): a young male electrician is modeled as the character;
- Time: Sunny day with the heavy sunshine and sun glares;
- Place: an unexposed highway construction surrounded with high-voltage distribution towers.
- Properties: comprise protective equipment, heavy machines like boomed cranes, road roller, and trucks.
- Task: lifting construction materials from truck to pave the road surface.

The prototype incorporated these features into one scenario which was a road construction site with overhead power lines surrounded The scenario development included two major aspects: environment modeling and storybook coding. The environment modeling simulates construction-related objects and characters while the storybook coding linked these objects and characters with hidden electrical hazards. The modeling and coding was completed using Autodesk 3DS max (see Figure 8) and Torque 3D package.

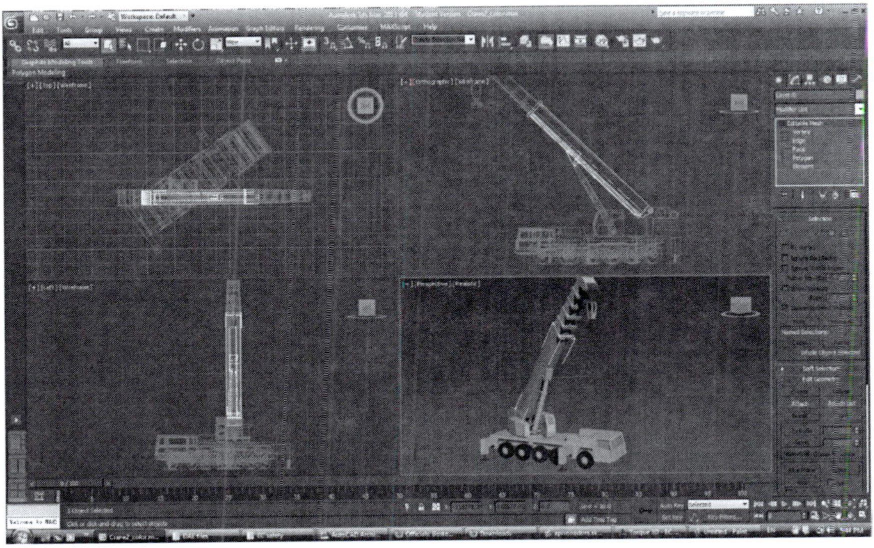

FIGURE 8. Elements Modelling

Simulation is processed on a module basis. Training elements are respectively simulated into virtual reality modules. Each module represents a major hazardous environment that could lead to electrocution. The working conditions, electrical hazards that workers are exposed to, and related work tasks are simulated in modules. The MVR simulations allow the users to recognize the hazards, identify them and intervene in a simulated virtual world. Trainees may participate in the safety working tasks, feel the hazards as well as its crucial outcome of failures (e.g., getting electrocuted), and hopefully transfer this experience to their real life working environment. Also, users are allowed to choose the specific module that is related to their daily work to get trained. This provides users the opportunities to choose which scenarios they would like to complete and allows them to be trained for designated working tasks or work environments.

FIGURE 9. User Interface Testing

The simulation storybook is presented through a thread of independent interactive events. These events are triggered by various approaches depending on the desired reaction. When the user walks through the scenario following instructions, a variety of hazard triggers will be touched and then the pre-programed reactions will be activated as responses. For examples, a touch approach is used to trigger the training event for safety emergency responses on "contact power line" when the user touches a power line. When the user goes close to the 10-feet distance line indicating the distance from the overhead power lines' upright projection allowed by safety regulations, the training element of "safe working distance and clearance" will be triggered and instructions will appear in the text panel explaining this safety regulation. These events are a mixture of animations and text used to present training contents to the user. All information expressing methods used in the scenario are aimed at increasing the learning efficiency and enhancing the training effectiveness. The learning efficiency and training effectiveness will be studied through evaluation processes in future research.

5. MERITS OF MVR

There are several ways to make learning more active and engaging. Training methods like on-the-job training, full scale training mock-ups, and the use of VR simulation offer more engagement. However, due to the dangerous characteristics of electricity, the on-the-job training and mock-ups can hardly allow trainees to fully rehearse electricity-related tasks, access all electrical hazards and experience possible consequences in real life. As a result, the effectiveness of these training methods might be limited. In contrast, a MVR-based training method is not constrained by these limits and instead can provide trainees full participatory experience without the safety risk from electricity.

MVR is advanced contributed to its adoptability. MVR technology provides a new perspective of safety training for dangerous hazards. A MVR-based training program has the ability to create a problem-based learning exercise in an environment that replicates the trainees' actual working environment (McAlpine and Stothard, 2003). It offers an interactive, active, and cognitive learning-by-doing experience for users (Stanney and Zyda, 2002) but without the concern for "real-world repercussions" (Eschenbrenner et al., 2008).

MVR is also advanced ascribed to the flexibility. MVR technology overcomes the training limitations on time and location and facilitates the mandatory and effective rehearsals in the virtual world. As a result, it will help establish the concepts of safety risk mitigation as habitus in workers' minds and place habitus into the context of real world practices.

Combing cloud technology, the safety training scenarios are used to be simulated in 3D interactions and on mobile devices, such as an iPad or a smartphone. The VR simulations allow the user to be exposed to the hazards within the simulated 3D environment so they can recognize those hazards, strengthen proper working memory and transfer the relative experiences into real life work or experience. Meanwhile, the cloud technology allows the user to access the training everywhere, and at any time, using any device (Chen et al., 2014). User data will be stored on remote servers and be automatically synchronized in real time with any authorized delivery devices. In this manner, users are no longer locked to a single device and do not have to transfer their data manually when switching devices.

Outside of the technology, MVR may contribute to the knowledge of safety management in terms of safety culture fostering. Literature suggests that unsafe procedures and violations by workers, such as forgetfulness, negligence and recklessness, are the primary causes leading to OSH injuries (Kletz, 2001). There is opportunity to reduce unsafe behaviors through appropriate and effective training, though, even if they cannot be eliminated completely. Goldenhar et al. (2001) highlighted that the most direct way to change statistics in human mistakes was through effective worker training. Neville (1998) suggested that effective training programs could help save large costs by preventing accidents. Effective training not only saves lives but also eliminates the extra indirect costs associated with accident investigations, insurance rates, equipment downtime and repair and productivity losses.

The MVR application may help to establish the safety culture transferring trainees' safe practices in a virtual world into their routines in real situations. In this perspective, culture is not considered a set of beliefs and values but the "whole way of life" which includes practices and routines(Zhao et al., 2014a) (Manseau and Shields, 2005). Bourdieu (2003) referred to this set of predispositions which guide improvisations in daily routines as the habitus or practical knowledge as repeated routines. One strength in understanding culture as habitus is that routines can be observed and documented, whereas values and beliefs must be inferred, making them less amenable to research. As a result, rather than formulating risk control as a break in habitus, it may prove more useful to conceive of OSH risk mitigation as a process. This process will allow people to show their own propensity toward adoption (decision-adoption process) in an appropriate way, especially when problems are encountered. Therefore, the habitus, a set of practical routines and dispositions towards certain ways of solving problems, is suggested as an innovative approach to the safety-culture-integrated OSH risk management. Combining risk mitigation as a continuous process of controls, rather than a group of static checkpoints of control, with a habitus-based process of safety training could not only mitigate OSH risk but also complement sustainable productivity and growth for the firm.

6. CONCLUSIONS

Workplace safety is paramount for all production sectors throughout the world. However, every year the number of occupational injuries attracts concerns on the safety management for every industry. Existing studies have endeavored great efforts on injury causations and found that more than half of workplace accidents are due to human errors. This chapter introduces an innovative safety management approach and the development process of such MVR-integrated application.

MVR is an adoption of virtual reality (VR) simulation on mobile/portable devices which are connected to cloud technology for end users. It allows safe simulation of real-life events in a digital environment that might otherwise be too dangerous or expensive to create (Haller et al., 1999). VR is described as a 3-dimensional world seen from a first-person view that is under real-time control of the user (Bowman et al., 2005). It also has the ability to create a problem-based learning exercise in an environment that replicates the trainee's actual working environment (McAlpine and Stothard, 2003). Training programs via VR offers an interactive, active, and cognitive learning experience for the user (Munro et al., 2002; Stanney and Zyda, 2002). As a result, they are often used in place of on-the-job training or full size simulation. Applied to the construction industry, MVR overcomes time and location barriers for workers and provides them more flexibility to access.

MVR also benefits trainees with a participatory training environment. Such participatory training brings a real life aspect into the training in an "it can happen to you" scenario and allows the trainees to relate conditions and regulations with real life situations and a life-or-death importance (Zhao et al., 2009). The best scenario is when people do not have to consciously think about following safety procedures because it is second nature to them (Trybus, 2008). Moreover, MVR provide trainees with the ability to experiment without concern for "real-world repercussions" and the ability to "learn by doing." With a MVR program, the user controls the objects and couples this with information and later task-based testing, thus, an interactive and active-learning experience is created.

Most importantly, MVR simulation may contribute to building safety culture in terms of safe practical routines. Through this technology, training programs might allow construction workers to be familiar with common hazards, including dangerous electrical hazards, and to mock up relevant prevention practices without real injury repercussions. It may not only improve trainees' awareness of potential risks in a reality-based working environment, but also unconsciously influence routine behaviors as second nature, which will largely lead to the safety culture. Trainees are expected to be prepared for their future electrical tasks by rehearsing in a virtual environment. The goal of repeated rehearsal is not only to enhance trainees' professional skills but also, more importantly, to help build up their habitus for safe practices. Training goals are achieved when users complete the task repeatedly and with success. As a result, proper safety procedures and responses in the specific scenario are aimed to be enhanced and embedded in trainees' minds.

REFERENCES

1. Kowalski KM, Vaught C. Principles of adult learning: Application for mine trainers US CDC: US Department of Health and Human Services; 2002:1-1
2. Rooney JJ, Vanden Heuvel LN, Lorenzo DK, Stoecklein M, Christensen M. Reduce human error. Quality Progress. 2002;35(9):27-36.
3. Setareh M, Bowman D, Kalita A. Development of a Virtual Reality Structural Analysis System. Journal of Architectural Engineering. 2005;11(4):156-64.
4. Barrett M, Blackledge J, and Coyle E. Using Virtual Reality to Enhance Electrical Safety and Design in the Built Environment. ISAST Transactions on Computers and Intelligent Systems. 2011(3):1-9.
5. Zhao D, Thabet W, McCoy A, Kleiner B. Electrical Deaths in the U.S. Construction: An Analysis of Fatality Investigations. International Journal of Injury Control and Safety Promotion. 2014;21(3):278-88.
6. Zhao D, McCoy A, Kleiner B, Feng Y. Integrating Safety Culture into OSH Risk Mitigation: A Pilot Study on the Electrical Safety. Journal of Civil Engineering and Management. 2014:1-10.
7. Zhao D, Lucas J. Virtual Reality Simulation for Construction Safety Promotion. International Journal of Injury Control and Safety Promotion. 2014:1-11.
8. de Oña J, López G, Mujalli R, Calvo FJ. Analysis of traffic accidents on rural highways using Latent Class Clustering and Bayesian Networks. Accident Analysis & Prevention. 2013;51(0):1-10.
9. Vermunt JK. Latent class and finite mixture models for multilevel data sets. Statistical Methods in Medical Research. 2008;17(1):33-51.
10. Collins LM, Lanza ST. Latent Class and Latent Transition Analysis: With Applications in the Social, Behavioral, and Health Sciences: Wiley; 2010:1-330
11. Depaire B, Wets G, Vanhoof K. Traffic accident segmentation by means of latent class clustering. Accident Analysis & Prevention. 2008;40(4):1257-66.
12. Stevens JP. Applied Multivariate Statistics for the Social Sciences. 5th ed. New York, NY, USA: Routledge; 2002:1-699.
13. Kline P. An Easy Guide to Factor Analysis: Routledge; 1994:1-194.
14. Zhao D, Thabet W, McCoy A, Kleiner B. Managing electrocution hazards in the US construction industry using VR simulation and cloud technology. Ework and Ebusiness in Architecture, Engineering and Construction. 2012:759-64.
15. Zhao D, Ye Y. Using virtual environments simulation to improve construction safety: An application of 3D online-game based training. Future Control and Automation. Lecture Notes in Electrical Engineering. 172 LNEE. VOL. 1 ed. Takamatsu, Japan: Springer Verlag; 2012: 269-77.
16. McAlpine I, Stothard P, editors. Using multimedia technologies to support PBL for a course in 3D modeling for mining engineers. World Conference on Educational Multimedia, Hypermedia and Telecommunications 2003; 2003; Honolulu, Hawaii, USA: AACE: 2449-2455.
17. Chen A., Golparvar-Fard M., Kleiner B., 2014. Saves: An Augmented Virtuality Strategy for Training Construction Hazard Recognition, Construction Research Congress 2014. ASCE:2345-2354.

18. Eschenbrenner B, Nah FF-H, Siau K. 3-D Virtual Worlds in Education: Applications, Benefits, Issues, and Opportunities. Journal of Database Management. 2008;19(4):91-110.
19. Kletz TA. Learning from accidents. Oxford ; Boston: Gulf Professional Pub.; 2001:1-345
20. Goldenhar LM, Moran SK, Colligan M. Health and safety training in a sample of open-shop construction companies Journal of Safety Research. 2001;32(2):237-52.
21. Neville H. Workplace accidents: they cost more than you might think. Industrial Management. 1998;40(1):7-9.
22. Zhao D, Feng Y, Ye Y, Suh M. Integrating Safety Culture into OSH Risk Mitigation via Information Technologies. In: Xu J, Fry JA, Lev B, Hajiyev A, editors. Proceedings of the Seventh International Conference on Management Science and Engineering Management. Lecture Notes in Electrical Engineering. 241. Philadelphia, PA: Springer Berlin Heidelberg; 2014: 335-44.
23. Manseau A, Shields R. Building Tomorrow: Innovation In Construction And Engineering. Burlington, VT: Ashgate; 2005:120-32.
24. Bourdieu P. Outline of a Theory of Practice. New York, NY: Cambridge University Press; 2003:1-63.
25. Haller M, Kurka G, Volkert J, Wagner R. omVR-A Safety Training System for a Virtual Refinery. ISMCR '99, Topical Workshop on Virtrual Reality and Advanced Human-Robot Systems; June 10-11; Tokyo, Japan1999: 24-8.
26. Bowman DA, Kruijff E, Laviola JJ. 3D User Interfaces: Theory and Practice. Boston, MA: Pearson Education; 2005:6-7.
27. Munro A, Breaux R, Patrey J, Sheldon B. Cognitive Aspects of Virtual Evironments Design. In: Stanney K, editor. Handbook of Virtual Environments: Design, Implementation, and Applications. Mahwah, NJ: Lawrence Erlbaum Associates; 2002: 415-34.
28. Zhao D, Lucas J, Thabet W. Using Virtual Environments to Support Electrical Safety Awareness in Construction. Proceedings of the 2009 Winter Simulation Conference; Austin, TX: IEEE; 2009: 2679-90.
29. Trybus J. Making Safety Second Nature: Using Simulation Tools to Practice Safety. Professional Safety. 2008;12(0):54-5.

CHAPTER 14

Smart Technology for Self-Organizing Processes

Marlene Scardamalia* and Carl Bereiter

Institute for Knowledge Innovation and Technology, University of Toronto, Toronto, Canada

ABSTRACT

Learning technology periodically undergoes changes in response to changes in the prevailing models of human cognition and learning. A major shift throughout the behavioral sciences that began in the 1980s is beginning to have effects at the level of classroom learning and its supportive technologies. Inspired by complexity theory, it is a shift that treats all learning and knowledge building as essentially self-organizing processes. The design challenge is not to control the self-organizing process, as some instructional approaches attempt to do, but to facilitate the emergence of higher-level outcomes—e.g., better explanations, more coherent understanding. To foster such higher-level emergents, smart technologies not only need to support people interacting productively with other people but also ideas interacting productively with ideas and feedback systems promoting engagement between people and ideas. This is in contrast to conceptions of smart technology that see it as providing increasingly precise centralized control over learning processes. Smart technology attuned to the emergent character of learning and thinking does not simply turn more control over to the learners but shifts the emphasis from control to productive interaction among learners, teachers, ideas, and technology.

Keywords: Centralized mindset Knowledge building Self-organization Complexity theory Design thinking

We started developing educational technology in 1983, at a time when cognitively-oriented technology was exploiting what was seen as a natural affinity between the mind's logic engine and that of the computer. However, we resisted the temptations of artificial intelligence, expert systems, and instructional management systems, focusing instead on students as epistemic agents in learning. As we put it then,

At first thought it might seem that the key requirement is a highly intelligent tutoring system, capable of performing sophisticated diagnoses of students' learning strategies, providing sensitive coaching and instruction. Such a system, however, is not only unrealistic, given the state of the art; it may also be heading in the wrong direction ... For it is not the computer that should be doing the diagnosing, the goal-setting, and the planning, it is the student. The computer environment should not be providing the knowledge and intelligence to guide learning, it should be providing the facilitating structure and tools that enable students to make maximum use of their own intelligence and knowledge (Scardamalia et al. [1989]), p. 54.

The technology we developed was originally focused on support of intentional learning in a networked social environment—hence the name "Computer-Supported Intentional Learning Environment" or "CSILE". However, we quickly recognized that the young students using CSILE were doing more than helping each other learn. They were in fact engaged in a collective process that in the business world was coming to be called "knowledge creation" (Nonaka & Takeuchi [1995]) but which we had already labeled "Knowledge Building" (Scardamalia et al. [1994])—a collaborative effort to advance the state of knowledge and ideas in a community. As discussed elsewhere (Bereiter & Scardamalia [2014]), the terms knowledge building/knowledge creation are basically interchangeable. Knowledge Building pedagogy, however, deals with the particular issues of pursuing knowledge creation in an educational context. CSILE and its successor, "Knowledge Forum", with more powerful supports for collaborative Knowledge Building, became part of a larger movement in the learning sciences undergirded by sociocultural theory (John-Steiner & Mahn [1996]), realized at a practical level in Computer Supported Collaborative Learning (CSCL), and highlighted by such concepts as "situated learning" (Lave & Wenger [1991]) and "group cognition (Stahl [2006]).

In the meantime, a revolution has been taking place in the behavioral sciences. Its origins are in the 1980s, when two important advances in the behavioral sciences took place. One was research on mental models, which produced evidence that the mind does not function like a logic machine after all but more like a simulation device (Johnson-Laird [1983]; Johnson [2009]). The other was the development of connectionism, which demonstrated how complex adaptive structures can function without the executive control that intelligent systems had been assumed to require (Molenaar [1986]). Later, complexity theory (Kauffman [1995]) provided a coherent basis for both mental models and the emergent cognitive structures. Under this broad theoretical umbrella, single-factor or multifactorial explanations of everything from motor skills to the rise and collapse of civilizations are giving way to systemic explanations in which outcomes are seen as emergents of self-organizing processes among lower-order components. Learning and human development in general call for systemic explanations (Thelen & Smith [1994]). The concept of self-organization, which now plays an essential role in explaining the evolution of complex novel biological structures (Dawkins [1987]), also offers a solution to what Piaget ([1971]) recognized as the ultimate problem for genetic epistemology: "How can one attain to something new?" But complexity theory's role in education has been almost entirely theoretical (Bereiter & Scardamalia [2013]). Since self-organization characterizes learning of all kinds, from the most highly regulated to the most spontaneous, complexity theory cannot help resolve the endless controversies about how best to promote learning. But complexity theory ought at least to have implications for the design of educational technologies. Our purpose in this paper is to explore such implications.

1 TECHNOLOGY ATTUNED TO THE SELF-ORGANIZING CHARACTER OF LEARNING AND THOUGHT

Learning technology attuned to the self-organizing character of learning and thought does not necessarily have to function in a self-organizing manner itself. However, smart educational technology of the future may well do so and thus be able to interact with students in a self-organizing system where neither one controls the other. There is already network analysis technology that situates people and words in the same Euclidian space with emergent properties (Oshima et al. [2012]). This is in contrast to rule-based smart technology, which dominated artificial intelligence in its early decades (cf. Anderson [1993]).

The distinctive nature of the design challenge implicit in the self-organizing character of individual and group cognition may be brought to a more concrete level by considering two formulations of the goal of improving students' thinking—a goal much in evidence in current concerns with innovativeness. One popular formulation, dating from research of the 1950s, is "teach them thinking skills"; the other, dating from much farther back, is “help them become thinking persons”. In the current literature of “21st century skills” programs no distinction is made. Although the long-range goal of such programs is people who think in the creative and critical ways required by citizenship and work in a knowledge-based society, the immediate goal is measurable gains on tests of specific skills. The implicit assumption is that the long-range objective cannot be pursued directly during the formative years. The alternative formulation, which implicitly denies this assumption, is vividly expressed in a frequently quoted passage attributed to Bertrand Russell:

When you want to teach children to think, you begin by treating them seriously when they are little, giving them responsibilities, talking to them candidly, providing privacy and solitude for them, and *making them readers and thinkers of significant thoughts from the beginning.* That's if you want to teach them to think. (Emphasis added.)

There is no mention of skill teaching here. Russell treated “teach them to think” as a matter of enculturating students into the society of "thinkers of significant thoughts". This was to be accomplished by arranging experiences and conditions and, most strikingly, treating children as already junior members of this society of thinkers rather than as trainees.

To the learning technologist, a mandate to “teach thinking skills” immediately brings to mind such functions as presenting problems, teaching reasoning and problem solving strategies, managing inquiry projects, scripting argumentation, tagging items for alignment with curriculum goals, and so forth. By contrast, a mandate to help students develop into “thinkers of significant thoughts” may not immediately bring to mind anything in particular beyond what is already available in an information-rich classroom. Further reflection, however, suggests a number of definite challenges for technology designed for helping learners develop into thinkers:

Higher levels of agency for students (Scardamalia & Bereiter [1991]): turning over to the learners strategic cognitive activity normally confined to the teacher—e.g., priority setting, evaluating progress, trouble-shooting, ensuring inclusiveness.

Promoting collective cognitive responsibility: students functioning like expert teams that go beyond division of labor to making every member responsible for doing whatever is necessary to achieve success in a joint effort (Scardamalia [2002]).

Democratizing knowledge and knowledge-building activity.

Identifying and discussing promising ideas: determining which ideas are most worthy of further work.

Explanation-building discourse (Bereiter [2012]): distinct from argumentation and guided by principles of explanatory coherence.

Metacognitive judgment: evaluating the progress of knowledge-building or problem-solving discourse, critically examining goals, finding ways around obstacles.

Giving ideas a life of their own: School practices and social media both tend to personalize ideas, which is fine at an early stage of idea development; but at some point ideas should become detached from their authors and open to criticism and revision by the whole community without its reflecting on the authors.

Support for tentativeness and risk-taking with ideas.

These are essentially the specifications we have set out elsewhere for knowledge building environments (Scardamalia [2003]; Scardamalia & Bereiter [2006], [in press-b]).

2 SUPPORT FOR KNOWLEDGE BUILDING DISCOURSE: NOT TOO LITTLE, NOT TOO MUCH

Simulations, handy laboratory instruments, robotics, immersive digital environments, technologies that enable students to create movies, games, and now (with 3D printing) physical working models—all these can provide valuable support for knowledge building, but community knowledge building requires that outputs from such sources become objects for group discourse and continuing discovery. In the end collaborative knowledge building rises or fails on the success of that discourse in generating knowledge advances. The central role of discourse has also been recognized in the literature of organizational knowledge creation (von Krogh et al. [2000]; Tsoukas [2009]).

Any communication technology can be a medium for knowledge building discourse as long as it enables people to represent and preserve ideas in a form comprehensible to others and allows for discussion and revision. But this presupposes a community of users already skilled and committed to knowledge building discourse. Education's challenge is getting students up to that level, and for this communication technology could benefit considerably from improved design. Some of it offers so little help that discourse will persist at a low epistemic level. Some of it controls the discourse so much that it affords the users little opportunity to acquire the goal-setting and planning skills needed for them to become active participants in a knowledge building community. Even for quite sophisticated knowledge builders common varieties of discourse technology make collaborative "integrative thinking" (Martin [2009]) unnecessarily awkward and inefficient. Technology that does too little to support knowledge building discourse is represented by the ubiquitous threaded discussion. Technology that takes over too much of what students should be learning to do themselves is represented by the more extreme forms of what Dillenbourg and Jermann ([2006]) called "micro-scripting". Along the continuum from too little to too much we find the following:

3 THREADED DISCOURSE: ICT'S VERSION OF THE MESSAGE IN THE BOTTLE

Technology for asynchronous online discourse has not changed much since the 1990s. It still consists of notes arranged in chronological order, with appended comments, comments on comments, and so on in what usually turns out to be a short chain of indentations. Idea revision is hampered by notes and comments getting lost in strings of messages. Synthesis of ideas into more complex structures is hampered by the fact that only subordination is supported (adding notes under existing notes) and not superordination (introducing a note that stands above and draws together or is supported or elaborated by a set of existing notes). "Integrative thinking", defined by Martin ([2009]) as holding "two conflicting ideas in constructive tension", is impeded by the inability to link to two different notes or to link across different discourse threads. Other technology allows for tagging, grouping, and flexible rearrangement. The challenge, however, is to combine such activity with focus on big ideas, synthesis, and breakthroughs. The common variety of threaded discourse is adequate for question-answer and opinion-reaction exchanges, and these constitute almost the whole of what one finds in the ubiquitous threaded discussions attached to news stories and blog postings on the web. But for people trying to carry on serious constructive work with ideas, threaded discourse technology is a source of continual frustration. Like setting messages afloat in bottles, threaded discourse has the virtue of preserving ideas and getting them out into the world, but is not a good way of getting them to a desired destination or for maintaining a productive exchange. Instructional management systems have started claiming to be collaborative. What this apparently means, however, is that they have handy mechanisms for creating groups. This is a useful capability, especially with thousands of scattered students taking the same online course, but instructional management systems persist in a use of discourse technology that limits possibilities for knowledge building discourse.

4 SCRIPTS: GOOD IDEA, WRONG CONTEXT

It would be unfair to say that educational ICT has not gone beyond threaded discourse. It has gone far beyond it, perhaps too far. It has gone beyond enhancing the kind of ideational discourse people normally carry on orally and replaced it with discourse carried out according to scripts (Fischer et al. [2013]). The term "script", as used in current instructional research, is derived from its use by Schank and Abelson ([1977]) in describing frequently experienced social routines such as dining in a restaurant. The principal elements are roles (e.g., head waiter, waiter, customer) and conventional behaviors associated with the roles (e.g., being shown to a table by the head waiter, asking the waiter for the bill at the end of the meal). These elements continue to dominate scripted instruction, in which assigned roles are common and the scripts prescribe behavioral sequences tied to roles. Such scripts stand in contrast to the emergent character of much human action, including practically everything that would come under the headings of meaningful learning and creative thinking. These often take place within a script framework (for instance, the academic colloquium, which has defined roles and ritualized behavior) but the essence of the activity (for instance, arriving at a theoretical explanation of puzzling data) is invariably emergent and unscripted. Thus the extension of the script concept not just to the outward forms of classroom life (which are often highly ritualized) but to the cognitive and socio-cognitive processes of work with concepts and ideas is an extraordinary leap. The power of the script idea as developed by Schank and Abelson lay in recognizing and describing the more ossified forms of social behavior, the ones where emergence is minimized and predictability is maximized. Scripts offer a good model when applied to a suitable objective, such as learning the etiquette of an unfamiliar culture, but a bad model likely to defeat the purpose when applied to constructive work with concepts and ideas, where emergence is maximized and unpredictability is inherent.

5 CONFUSING PERFORMANCE SUPPORTS WITH LEARNING SUPPORTS

Educational technologists are generally well aware of the difference between performance support and learning support and recognize that what is optimal for one is not necessarily optimal or even beneficial for the other. A spelling checker is an obvious and widely accepted performance support for writing, but what is its effect on learning to spell? It might promote it, interfere with it, or render it unnecessary. The three possibilities have been debated for years, with inconclusive evidence supporting each position. The same has happened with regard to hand-held calculators in elementary mathematics instruction. But with more complex technology, the performance-learning issue becomes less clear-cut. Scripts, suggesting and reminding systems, and the like are clearly performance supports, but their use in education carries with it the supposition that they also support learning. This is especially apparent in workplace training, and may be appropriate there, when there is a "right way" to do something and performance supports guide the learner through doing it the right way. But when the challenge is self-organizing systems for emergence of increasingly high-level knowledge, reliance on performance supports as learning supports is more questionable. Script researchers talk about "internal scripts" as the student's internalization of the "external script" used in instruction. The implicit assumption is that the scripts represent not only a type of performance support but also the procedural knowledge learners are supposed to acquire and take away from the scripted activity. Hesse ([2007]) has listed five reasons, which we paraphrase here, for questioning whether scripting the "right way" of carrying out a collaborative task is a sound way of managing learning:

The "right way" may be wrong.

The "right way" may be different for different persons and situations.

The "right way" may only be good advice at an early stage.

The "right way" may be demotivating.

The "right way" may increase cognitive load and so diminish attention to goals.

Research on a variety of academic skills indicates that strategy instruction improves performance, but seldom does the research investigate whether students actually use the taught strategies. Effects could be of a more global nature, for instance through fostering mindful engagement (Salomon & Globerson [1987]). The stronger the strategy guidance provided by the technology, the more critical it becomes that these strategies constitute the "right way" for everyone. Seldom if ever is this requirement seriously investigated. What we know from biographies of major writers and scientists suggests there is no best way of productive thinking that should be imposed on learners.

6 TECHNOLOGY THAT SUPPORTS WORKING WITH IDEAS IN "DESIGN MODE"

Working constructively with ideas involves building something out of ideas—an explanation, a model, an elaboration or improvement of an idea. It means treating conceptual work as knowledge creation rather than simply knowledge acquisition. This calls for a major reorientation of approach to ideas, a switch from what we have labeled "belief mode" to "design mode" (Bereiter & Scardamalia [2003]). The term "belief mode" is derived from the traditional definition of knowledge as "true and justified belief". It includes all the many ways of advancing and evaluating knowledge claims, from "it's true because the textbook says so" to "the weight of evidence indicates" and beyond that to "from this perspective...." Design mode, by contrast, is the mode of invention, theory building, solving real complex problems with no ready-made solutions, identifying and exploiting promising ideas. A related term is "design thinking", originally referring to kinds of thinking promoted in design schools and architecture schools, but subsequently expanded to a kind of thinking applicable to complex problems of all kinds (Buchanan [1992]). Design mode is more concerned with whether an idea has potential than whether it is "true and justified" in its present form, and so the preferred discourse form is not pro-con argumentation but collaborative problem solving.

Technology for work in belief mode is abundant, especially in the form of software for argumentation (Andriessen et al. [2003]). Work in belief mode lends itself to scripted procedures: There are accepted procedures for hypothesis testing (often presented as "the scientific method") and models of rational argument, an enduringly popular one being that of Toulmin ([1958]). The same is not true of work in design mode. There are not established forms and procedures for treating ideas in design mode, and efforts to establish them would be resisted for good reason. However, smart classrooms are evolving in ways that can support creative work with ideas. These include affordances for real-time interactivity, complex adaptive approaches, and ubiquitous learning (Huang et al. [2012]; Kinshuk et al. [2010]; Kinshuk & Graf [2012]; Norris & Soloway [2013]). The same affordances can also be used to strengthen centralized control and to promote activity in belief mode, however, so it is important for practitioners and designers to have a clear conception of creative knowledge work as an objective.

The one characteristic of design thinking that is widely accepted and applicable to all situations is that design is an iterative process of idea testing and improvement. "Improvable ideas" is a core concept of Knowledge Building (Scardamalia [2002]). As suggested by Hakkarainen's cyclical Progressive Inquiry model (Muukkonen et al. [1999]), Knowledge Building involves transformational changes not only in knowledge but also in problem definition. These in turn lead to "theory" changes and further design iterations.

From our earliest days of designing knowledge-building technology, our focus has been on enabling students to work effectively in design mode. Initially this consisted mainly of providing epistemic markers for design mode activities such as theory building: hence, providing phrases such as "My theory...," "This theory does not explain...," and "A better theory..." that users could click on to incorporate into their note texts. We encourage customization and actively discourage mandated use or set sequences. More recent technological enhancements facilitate the identification and discussion of promising ideas (Chen et al. [2012]) and metadiscourse—discourse about the progress and problems of the main knowledge-building discourse. Such metadiscourse is aided by a variety of feedback tools that, for instance, map the community's use of theory-building markers or compare the community's vocabulary usage on a particular topic with the vocabulary in a related "expert" corpus (Resendes [2013]). Developing ways to support sustained creative work with ideas is an ongoing effort, however. On the horizon are dynamic 3-D visualizations showing the self-organizing process of constructing higher-level complex ideas out of simpler lower-level ones (Tergan & Keller [in press]).

Further development of technology to support working with ideas in design mode would clearly be a boon to innovation-driven businesses, but it could have a revolutionary impact on education, where both traditional knowledge-transmission and modern inquiry-oriented approaches have focused almost exclusively on activity in belief mode. The emphasis needs to be not simply on creative thinking but on *sustained* creative thought. "Ideas are the easy part", says design group Fahrenheit 212 ([2009]). By this they mean initial bright ideas, of the kind often generated through brainstorming. Initial bright ideas are usually in ample supply both in innovation-minded companies and in classrooms. The hard part is developing initial bright ideas into something of value, be it a merchantable product or a contribution to knowledge. This is design. It is creative work, sometimes at a higher level than what produced the original idea, and it is the essence of Knowledge Building.

Because of their shared conceptual basis, there ought to be considerable cross-fertilization between technology for knowledge creation in industry and technology for knowledge building in education. Customarily, technology transfer works in only one direction—from business applications to educational ones. But in a knowledge creation/knowledge building context transfer could work both ways. The seven design challenges listed earlier (higher levels of agency, and so on) are vital when the goal is the educational one of developing students into productive thinkers. They are all relevant to the success of knowledge-creating and design teams in industry, but they do not typically receive technological support. The knowledge management literature suggests these sorts of socio-cognitive conditions are the responsibility of managers. But technology that provides the necessary support for novice knowledge creators has, in our experience, proved helpful for adult knowledge workers as well, especially those who are not yet at the point where collaborative knowledge creation comes naturally. Important for students and experienced knowledge workers alike is a context that encourages collective cognitive responsibility (Scardamalia [2002]). A well-designed digital community workspace can do that.

To support collective cognitive responsibility in work with ideas, digital tools need to function at two levels: (1) the creation of a rich, interconnected network of ideas in the community's knowledge space and (2) higher-level views of group processes and the resulting knowledge products so as to enable evaluation of progress and determination of future moves. At the first level, users create connections: referencing, annotating and keywording notes, adding epistemic markers, highlighting promising ideas. Activities at the second level may take a variety of forms, which might include viewing near- and far- conceptual neighbors, compiling promising ideas in a content area, judging rate of conceptual progress as indicated by the presence of new concepts, and recognizing outliers—both people and ideas. The result should be an ever-evolving conceptual space, providing feedback to ongoing creative discourse, enabling each member to be part of the collective achievement.

7 NURTURING THE EMERGENCE OF NEW COMPETENCIES

In the almost universal top-down approach to curriculum design and standards setting, experts and stakeholders determine the knowledge and skills to be acquired. These are translated into tests, instructional procedures, and learning activities. Teachers then implement them with students, who usually have no idea of the origins and rationale of the goals or the procedures nor any way to contribute to or refine them. This traditional curriculum approach continues to prevail even in such supposedly leading-edge initiatives as the "21st century skills" movement (Johnson [2009]). Business executives, psychometricians, and educationists get together and agree on a list of skills needed for the 21st century (which bear a striking resemblance to the "higher-order skills" promoted throughout the previous 50 years). Then tests are constructed and curriculum developers are enlisted to prescribe procedures for developing the listed skills. However, in a report prepared for one of these 21st century skill projects, Scardamalia et al. ([2012]) argued that in a project with such forward-looking aspirations the traditional working-backward-from-goals approach ought to be augmented by provisions for the discovery of new needed competencies, rather than supposing that these can all be identified in advance. In order to discover new competencies, however, there need to be educational environments in which new competencies have a chance to emerge. The authors proposed a systemic approach containing various feedback loops enabling qualitative and not just quantitative shifts at all levels of the policy-maker to practitioner to learner hierarchy. In the traditional top-down system, the task of learning technology is to help enact the decisions made at higher levels in the system. In a dynamic systems approach, the job of technology is multifarious but overall it should promote self-organizing evolutionary processes in all parts of the education system, processes that moreover interact with each other to achieve coherent progressive development.

Technology able to do this would have to be very smart indeed, but not smart in a controlling fashion. Feedback mechanisms are key, but the feedback itself must be able to evolve to deal not only with emerging problems but also with emerging opportunities. The latter is more challenging. Trouble-shooting—detecting when things are going wrong and finding out why—is common in all kinds of enterprises, including education systems, but detecting and exploring opportunities is much less common, is the province of adventurous artists, designers, and entrepreneurs, and is virtually unknown in education. We do not suggest that some monster application is required that integrates all aspects of the educational process. Learning analytics (Siemens & Long [2011]), a discipline still in its formative stages, appears to be relished by some as a way of creating such an application but by others as a means of decentralizing control, making information more usable by teachers and students. Technology for opportunity-finding and exploration needs to start at the level of the classroom (we use that term to refer to any social environment organized for an educational purpose, recognizing that the "classroom" might be an after-hours club, a dispersed group of online learners, a museum exhibit, and so forth). That is where the opportunities will first emerge for going beyond "best practice" and the goals established by policy-makers.

8 CONCLUSION: TOWARD 2025 IN EDUCATIONAL TECHNOLOGY

The year 2025 or thereabout has become the focus of much visionary talk in education, spurred on by several major foundations and education reform groups that have selected some target year a decade or two out by which their education reform goals are to be achieved. What the surrounding society and especially the technological infrastructure will be like by 2025 is of course very difficult to predict, given the rate of change. However, in broad strokes we can with some confidence paint a picture in which computers are considerably more intelligent than today and have automated a number of human activities, including mental ones, that they can do better or at least more economically than we can. This prospect has led many educators to conclude that education for the future must focus on cultivating creativity, believed to be the last bastion of human superiority over the machine. However, if by creativity we mean the sorts of things taught in creativity workshops, that last bastion will probably not hold either. Generating novel ideas meeting defined constraints is something computers of the future ought to be able to do with ease, generating more ideas that meet more constraints than human intelligence can match.

Much alarmist commentary on the web reflects a mindset occupied with Humpty Dumpty's question, "Which is to be master?" One of the most authoritative pronouncements on the subject (Hawking et al. [2014]) warns, "Whereas the short-term impact of AI depends on who controls it, the long-term impact depends on whether it can be controlled at all." If we adopt a systems view, however, the design task is not to ensure the continuance of human control or to find a safe niche for human talent. It is to facilitate human-machine collaboration.

In education, facilitating human-machine collaboration means designing technology and ways of using it that integrate it into a complex system in which the principal interacting elements are students, teachers, intelligent machines, and ideas. As we have proposed here, the principal medium for such interaction is dialogue. Smart phones are already demonstrating that dialogue between person and machine is possible within fairly generous limits, and those limits are likely to be extended greatly. In work reported by Miyake et al. ([2011]), children carry on discussion with each other and with a robot (voiced and controlled by an assistant in another room, preliminary to having a robot able to carry on scripted conversation). Latent semantic analysis (Landauer & Dumais [1997]) and explanatory coherence analysis (Thagard [2000]) demonstrate that ideas can interact computationally with ideas in ways that produce meaningful emergent structures. Learning analytics, which enable the computer to discover patterns in unstructured data that are beyond human capacity, are developing in a variety of ways. Some applications raise the spectre of increasing centralized control (Yuan [n.d].), but others such as diagnostic analyses and "recommender systems" that suggest resources students might find useful or interesting (Manouselis et al. [2012]) could play positive roles in a self-organizing educational process.

All of this inevitably raises question about the role of teachers. One answer lies in the importance of a classroom culture conducive to sustained creative work with ideas (Scardamalia & Bereiter [1996]). With any interacting group of students a social organization of some kind will emerge, but it will not necessarily or even very likely be organized around the pursuit of knowledge and understanding. It may be organized around assigned tasks, topical interests, or in the worst cases organized around combat—students against the teacher or students against each other. Teachers we have worked with over the years consistently report that creating a knowledge building culture takes time and effort and that it needs continuing attention. But it would be a mistake to view such community building as a task separate from actual work with ideas. A community organized around knowledge building can be compared to a community organized around agricultural production. Not everything that goes on in a farm community is actual farming but everything is in some manner tied to it and the community thrives or declines on the basis of its production of marketable food. In the same way, a knowledge building community thrives or declines on the basis of its production of valuable knowledge. For such a community to develop, knowledge building has to be at the center of the community's development from the beginning.

Organization for knowledge creation and new competencies related to it does not negate or lessen the demand for older well-recognized competencies in literacy, numeracy, and subject-matter knowledge. More likely newly identified competencies will add new dimensionality to the traditional ones, as has happened when print literacy was expanded to "multiliteracy" and recently to "transliteracy," which includes not only ability to utilize diverse information sources but to synthesize coherent knowledge from fragmentary information thus obtained (Liu [2012]; Scardamalia & Bereiter in press-a). A great deal of recent educational technology is in aid of learning with understanding. But the proliferation of simulations, instruments, games, construction tools, and the like will not necessarily result in self-organization of understanding for learners. In fact, it may make coherence harder to achieve. There needs to be some glue. The glue nature gave us is discourse. What future smart technology may be able to provide is attractive and effective ways for idea-centered discourse to self-organize around the production of understanding.

Instructional management systems are now being designed to facilitate the forming of collaborative groups. That is a worthwhile start, but such groups need to be infused with an ethos of sustained explanation building, problem deepening, idea improvement, and collective cognitive responsibility. Developing such an ethos is the essence of creating a knowledge building community. It is clearly a task for the human beings involved. Can technology help with this task, or is its value confined to the intellectual and administrative aspects of collaborative work with ideas? Both organization science and cognitive science have taken a decided turn toward including affect, empathy, and interest as components of the knowledge creation process, interacting constructively with the conceptual and logical components rather than working separately to bias and motivate the process (Kunda [1999]; Liedtka & Ogilvie [2011]). Thagard, in his theory of emotional coherence ([2006]), presents a computational model of thought in which ideas, facts, and emotions together form a dynamic network that generates realistic cognitive outcomes. Thus a scientific groundwork is being laid that by 2025 should enable technology that actively collaborates in both the socio-emotional and the intellectual aspects of creative work with ideas. Educational technology designers can begin working toward this end by building into software learning environments semantic tools (Rosé et al. [2008]), knowledge visualizations (Marchese & Banissi [2013]), network analyses (Freeman [2004]), and other resources that students and teachers can use to provide real-time feedback to their work with ideas. Out of such limited forms of assistance may arise clearer understanding of the competencies and obstacles that more powerful technology will need to address.

REFERENCES

1. Anderson JR: *Rules of the mind.* Lawrence Erlbaum Associates, Hillsdale, NJ; 1993.
2. Arguing to learn: Confronting cognitions in computer-supported collaborative learning environments. Kluwer, Dordrecht; 2003.
3. Bereiter C: **THEORY BUILDING AND EDUCATION FOR UNDERSTANDING** .In *Encyclopaedia of philosophy of education* Edited by: Peters MA, Ghiraldelli P, Zarnic B, Gibbons A. 2012. Web document: [http://eepat.net/ doku.php?id=theory_building_and_education_for_understanding] http://eepat.net/doku.php?id=theory_building_and_education_for_understanding Web document: http://eepat.net/doku.php?id=theory_building_an d_education _for_understanding
4. Bereiter C, Scardamalia M: **LEARNING TO WORK CREATIVELY WITH KNOWLEDGE.** In *Powerful learning environments. Unraveling basic components and dimensions (pp. 55–68). (Advances in Learning and Instruction Series).* Edited by: Corte E, Verschaffel L, Entwistle N, Merriënboer J. Elsevier Science, Oxford, UK; 2003.
5. Bereiter C, Scardamalia M: **SELF-ORGANIZATION IN CONCEPTUAL GROWTH: PRACTICAL IMPLICATIONS.** In *International handbook of research on conceptual*

change. 2nd edition. Edited by: Vosniadou S. Routledge, New York, NY; 2013:504–519.

6. Bereiter C, Scardamalia M: **KNOWLEDGE BUILDING AND KNOWLEDGE CREATION: ONE CONCEPT, TWO HILLS TO CLIMB.** In *Knowledge creation in education*. Edited by: Tan SC, So HJ, Yeo J. Springer, Singapore; 2014.
7. Buchanan R: **WICKED PROBLEMS IN DESIGN THINKING.** *Design. Issues.* 1992,**8**(2):5–21.
8. Chen B, Scardamalia M, Resendes M, Chuy M, Bereiter C: **STUDENTS' INTUITIVE UNDERSTANDING OF PROMISINGNESS AND PROMISINGNESS JUDGMENTS TO FACILITATE KNOWLEDGE ADVANCEMENT.** In *The future of learning: Proceedings of the 10th international conference of the learning sciences (ICLS 2012)* –. Edited by: Aalst J, Thompson K, Jacobson MJ, Reimann P. ISLS, Sydney, Australia; 2012:111–118.
9. Dawkins R: *The blind watchmaker: Why the evidence of evolution reveals a universe without design*. Norton, New York; 1987.
10. Dillenbourg P, Jermann P: **DESIGNING INTEGRATIVE SCRIPTS.** In *Scripting computer-supported communication of knowledge. Cognitive, computational, and educational perspectives*. Edited by: Fischer F, Kollar I, Mandl H, Haake J. Springer, New York; 2006:259–288.
11. White paper: Ideas are the easy part. 2009.
12. Fischer F, Kollar I, Stegmann K, Wecker C, Zottmann J: **COLLABORATION SCRIPTS IN COMPUTER-SUPPORTED COLLABORATIVE LEARNING.** In *The international handbook of collaborative learning*. Edited by: Hmelo-Silver CE, O'Donnell AM, Chinn CA, Chan C. Routledge, New York, NY; 2013:403–419.
13. Freeman LC: *The development of social network analysis: A study in the sociology of science*. Empirical Press, Vancouver, BC, Canada; 2004.
14. Hawking S, Tegmark M, Russell S, Wilczek F: *Transcending complacency on superintelligent machines*. 2014.
15. Hesse FW: **DISCUSSION: BEING TOLD TO DO SOMETHING OR JUST BEING AWARE OF SOMETHING? AN ALTERNATIVE APPROACH TO SCRIPTING IN CSCL.** In *Scripting computer-supported collaborative learning*. Edited by: Fischer F, Kollar I, Mandl H, HaakeJörg M. Springer, Boston, MA; 2007:91–98.
16. Huang R, Hu Y, Xiao G: **THE FUNCTIONS OF SMART CLASSROOM IN SMART LEARNING AGE.** In *Proceedings of the 20th International Conference on Computers in Education ICCE 2012 (pp. 413–417)*. Edited by: Biswas G, Wong LH, Hirashima T, Chen W. National Institute of Education, Nanyang Technological University, Singapore; 2012.
17. Johnson P: **THE 21ST CENTURY SKILLS MOVEMENT.** *Educ. Leadersh.* 2009,**67**(1):11–11.
18. Johnson-Laird PN: *Mental models: Towards a cognitive science of language, inference and consciousness*. Cambridge University Press, Cambridge, UK; 1983.
19. John-Steiner V, Mahn H: **SOCIOCULTURAL APPROACHES TO LEARNING AND DEVELOPMENT: A VYGOTSKIAN FRAMEWORK.** *Educ. Psychol.* 1996, **31:** 191–206.
20. Kauffman S: *At home in the universe: The search for laws of self-organization and complexity*. Oxford University Press, New York; 1995.
21. Kinshuk , Graf S: **UBIQUITOUS LEARNING.** In *Encyclopedia of the Sciences of Learning*. Edited by: Seel N. Springer, Berlin; 2012:3361–3363.
22. Kinshuk CM, Graf S, Yang G: **ADAPTIVITY AND PERSONALIZATION IN MOBILE LEARNING.** *Technol. Instr. Cogn. Learn.*2010,**8**(2):163–174.
23. Kunda Z: *Social cognition: Making sense of people*. MIT Press, Cambridge, MA; 1999.
24. Landauer TK, Dumais ST: **A SOLUTION TO PLATO'S PROBLEM: THE LATENT SEMANTIC ANALYSIS THEORY OF THE ACQUISITION, INDUCTION, AND REPRESENTATION OF KNOWLEDGE.** *Psychol. Rev.* 1997, **25:** 211–240. 528 528
25. Lave J, Wenger E: *Situated learning: Legitimate peripheral participation*. Cambridge University Press, Cambridge, England; 1991.

26. Liedtka J, Ogilvie T: *Designing for growth: A design thinking toolkit for managers*. Columbia University Press, New York; 2011.

27. A Liu, This is not a book: Transliteracies and long forms of digital attention (Paper presented at the Translittératies Conference, ENS Cachan, Paris, 2012). 7 Novementer 2012. Web: , [http://liu.english.ucsb.edu/this-is-not-a-book-long-forms -of-shared-attention-in-thedigital-age-unbound-book-conference-amsterdam -the-hague/] A Liu, This is not a book: Transliteracies and long forms of digital attention (Paper presented at the Translittératies Conference, ENS Cachan, Paris, 2012). 7 Novementer 2012. Web:

28. Manouselis N, Drachsler H, Verbert K, Duval E: *Recommender systems for learning*. Springer, Boston, MA; 2012.

29. Knowledge Visualization Currents: From Text to Art to Culture. Springer-Verlag, London; 2013.

30. Martin R: *The opposable mind: Winning through integrative thinking*. Harvard Business Press, Boston; 2009.

31. N Miyake, H Ishiguro, K Dautenhahn, T Nomura, Robots with children: Practices for human-robot symbiosis, in Proceedings of the 6thInternational Conference of Human Robot Interaction, HRI 2011, ed. by A Billard, PH Kahn Jr, JA Adams, G Trafton (Lausanne, Switzerland, 2011). , [http://doi.acm. org/ 10.1145 /1957656.1957659] N Miyake, H Ishiguro, K Dautenhahn, T Nomura, Robots with children: Practices for human-robot symbiosis, in Proceedings of the 6thInternational Conference of Human Robot Interaction, HRI 2011, ed. by A Billard PH Kahn Jr, JA Adams, G Trafton (Lausanne, Switzerland, 2011).

32. Molenaar PCM: **ON THE IMPOSSIBILITY OF ACQUIRING MORE POWERFUL STRUCTURES: A NEGLECTED ALTERNATIVE.** *Hum. Dev.* 1986, **29:** 245–251.

33. Muukkonen H, Hakkarainen K, Lipponen L, Leinonen T: *Computer support for knowledge building*. 1999.

34. Nonaka I, Takeuchi H: *The knowledge creating company*. Oxford University Press, New York; 1995.

35. Norris C, Soloway E: **SUBSTANTIVE EDUCATIONAL CHANGE IS IN THE PALM OF OUR CHILDREN'S HANDS.** In *Handbook of Mobile Learning*. Edited by: Berge Z, Muilenburg L. Routledge, New York, NY; 2013.

36. Oshima J, Oshima R, Matsuzawa Y: **KNOWLEDGE BUILDING DISCOURSE EXPLORER: A SOCIAL NETWORK ANALYSIS APPLICATION FOR KNOWLEDGE BUILDING DISCOURSE.** *Educ. Technol. Res. Dev.* 2012, **60:** 903–921.

37. Piaget J: *Psychology and epistemology: Towards a theory of knowledge*. Viking Press, New York, NY; 1971.

38. Resendes M: *Effect of formative feedback on enhancing ways of contributing to explanation-seeking dialogue in grade 2*. Paper presented at the Summer Institute on Knowledge Building, Puebla, Mexico; 2013.

39. Rosé CP, Wang YC, Cui Y, Arguello J, Stegmann K, Weinberger A, Fischer F: **ANALYZING COLLABORATIVE LEARNING PROCESSES AUTOMATICALLY: EXPLOITING THE ADVANCES OF COMPUTATIONAL LINGUISTICS IN COMPUTER-SUPPORTED COLLABORATIVE LEARNING.***Int. J. Comput. Supported. Collaborative. Learn.* 2008, **3:** 237–271.

40. Salomon G, Globerson T: **SKILL MAY NOT BE ENOUGH: THE ROLE OF MINDFULNESS IN LEARNING AND TRANSFER.** *Int. J. Educ. Res.*1987, **11:** 623–638.

41. Scardamalia M: **COLLECTIVE COGNITIVE RESPONSIBILITY FOR THE ADVANCEMENT OF KNOWLEDGE.** In *Liberal education in a knowledge society*. Edited by: Smith B. Open Court, Chicago; 2002:67–98.

42. Scardamalia M: **KNOWLEDGE BUILDING ENVIRONMENTS: EXTENDING THE LIMITS OF THE POSSIBLE IN EDUCATION AND KNOWLEDGE WORK.** In *Encyclopedia of distributed learning*. Edited by: DiStefano A, Rudestam KE, Silverman R. Sage Publications, Thousand Oaks, CA; 2003:269–272.

43. Scardamalia M, Bereiter C: **HIGHER LEVELS OF AGENCY FOR CHILDREN IN KNOWLEDGE BUILDING: A CHALLENGE FOR THE DESIGN OF NEW KNOWLEDGE MEDIA.** *J. Learn. Sci.* 1991,**1**(1):37–68.
44. Scardamalia M, Bereiter C: **ADAPTATION AND UNDERSTANDING: A CASE FOR NEW CULTURES OF SCHOOLING.** In *International perspectives on the design of technology-supported learning environments*. Edited by: Vosniadou S, DeCorte E, Glaser R, Mandl H. Lawrence Erlbaum Associates, Mahwah, NJ; 1996:149–163.
45. Scardamalia M, Bereiter C: **KNOWLEDGE BUILDING: THEORY, PEDAGOGY, AND TECHNOLOGY.** In *Cambridge handbook of the learning sciences*. Edited by: Sawyer K. Cambridge University Press, New York; 2006:97–118.
46. M Scardamalia, C Bereiter, Education in an open informational world, in Emerging trends in the social and behavioral sciences, ed. by R Scott, S Kosslyn (Wiley Online Library, in press-aa) M Scardamalia, C Bereiter, Education in an open informational world, in Emerging trends in the social and behavioral sciences, ed. by R Scott, S Kosslyn (Wiley Online Library, in press-aa)
47. M Scardamalia, C Bereiter, Knowledge building and knowledge creation: Theory, pedagogy, and technology, in Cambridge handbook of the learning sciences, ed. by K Sawyer, 2nd edn. (Cambridge University Press, New York, in press-bb) M Scardamalia, C Bereiter, Knowledge building and knowledge creation: Theory, pedagogy, and technology, in Cambridge handbook of the learning sciences, ed. by K Sawyer, 2nd edn. (Cambridge University Press, New York, in press-bb)
48. Scardamalia M, Bereiter C, McLean RS, Swallow J, Woodruff E: **COMPUTER-SUPPORTED INTENTIONAL LEARNING ENVIRONMENTS.***J. Educ. Comput. Res.* 1989, **5:** 51–68.
49. Scardamalia M, Bereiter C, Lamon M: **THE CSILE PROJECT: TRYING TO BRING THE CLASSROOM INTO WORLD 3.** In *Classroom lessons: Integrating cognitive theory and classroom practice*. Edited by: McGilley K. MIT Press, Cambridge, MA; 1994:201–228.
50. Scardamalia M, Bransford J, Kozma R, Quellmalz E: **NEW ASSESSMENTS AND ENVIRONMENTS FOR KNOWLEDGE BUILDING.** In *Assessment and Teaching of 21st Century Skills*. Edited by: Griffin P, McGaw B, Care E. Springer Science + Business Media B.V, New York; 2012:231–300.
51. Schank RC, Abelson RP: *Scripts, plans, goals, and understanding*. Lawrence Erlbaum Associates, Hillsdale, NJ; 1977.
52. G Siemens, P Long, Penetrating the fog: Analytics in learning and education. EDUCAUSE Review 46(4), (2011). Available at: , [http://net. educause.edu /ir/library/pdf/erm1151.pdf] G Siemens, P Long, Penetrating the fog: Analytics in learning and education. EDUCAUSE Review 46(4), (2011). Available at:
53. Stahl G: *Group cognition: Computer support for building collaborative knowledge*. MIT Press, Cambridge, MA; 2006.
54. SO Tergan, T Keller, Knowledge and information visualization: Searching for synergies (Springer Lecture Notes in Computer Science, Heidelberg /New York, in press) SO Tergan, T Keller, Knowledge and information visualization: Searching for synergies (Springer Lecture Notes in Computer Science, Heidelberg / New York, in press)
55. Thagard P: *Coherence in thought and action*. MIT Press, Cambridge, MA; 2000.
56. Thagard P: *Hot thought: Mechanisms and applications of emotional cognition*. MIT Press, Cambridge, MA; 2006.
57. Thelen E, Smith LB: *A dynamic systems approach to the development of cognition and action*. MIT Press, Cambridge, MA; 1994.
58. Toulmin S: *The uses of argument*. Cambridge University Press, Cambridge; 1958.
59. Tsoukas H: **A DIALOGICAL APPROACH TO THE CREATION OF NEW KNOWLEDGE IN ORGANIZATIONS.** *Organ. Sci.* 2009, **20:** 941–957.
60. von Krogh G, Ichijo K, Nonaka I: *Enabling knowledge creation: Unlocking the mystery of tacit knowledge*. Oxford University Press, New York; 2000.
61. Yuan L: *Will analytics transform education? A critical view on the data we gather about the learners*. n.d.

CHAPTER 15

Metalearning: A Survey of Trends and Technologies

Christiane Lemke[2]· Marcin Budka[1]· Bogdan Gabrys[1]

[1].Bournemouth UniversityPooleUK

[2].Unister GmbHLeipzigGermany

ABSTRACT

Metalearning attracted considerable interest in the machine learning community in the last years. Yet, some disagreement remains on what does or what does not constitute a metalearning problem and in which contexts the term is used in. This survey aims at giving an all-encompassing overview of the research directions pursued under the umbrella of metalearning, reconciling different definitions given in scientific literature, listing the choices involved when designing a metalearning system and identifying some of the future research challenges in this domain.

Keywords: Metalearning Metaknowledge extraction Life-long learning

1 INTRODUCTION

The term *metalearning* first occurred in the area of educational psychology. One of the most cited researchers in this field, John Biggs, described metalearning as *being aware of and taking control of one's own learning* (Biggs 1985). Hence, metalearning is viewed as an understanding and adaptation of learning itself on a higher level than merely acquiring subject knowledge. In that way, a person aware and capable of metalearning is able to assess his or her learning approach and adjust it according to the requirements of a specific task.

Metalearning as used in a machine learning context has many similarities to this description. Subject knowledge translates into base-learning, where experience is accumulated for one specific learning task. Metalearning starts at a higher level and is concerned with accumulating experience over several applications of a learning system according to Brazdil et al. (2009).

In the last 20 years, machine learning research was faced with an increasing number of available algorithms including a multitude of parametrisation, preprocessing and postprocessing approaches as well as a substantially extended range of applications due to increasing computing power and wider availability of computer-readable data sets. By promoting a better understanding of machine learning itself, metalearning can provide an invaluable help avoiding extensive trial and error procedures for algorithm selection, and brute force searches for suitable parametrisation. Looking at how to profit from past experience of a predictive model on certain tasks can enhance the performance of a learning algorithm and allow to better understand what makes a given algorithm perform well on a given problem.

The idea of metalearning is not new, one of the first and seminal contributions having been provided by Rice (1976). However, the literal term only started appearing in machine learning literature in the 1990s, yet still many publications deal with problems related to metalearning without using the actual word. This contribution tries to grasp every point of view metalearning has been investigated from, citing books, research and review papers of the last decade. We hope this survey will provide a useful resource for the data mining and machine learning community.

The remainder of this paper is organized as follows. In Sect. 2 we review definitions of metalearning given in scientific literature, focusing on common themes occurring in all of them. Section 3 describes different notions of metalearning, linking them to the definitions given in Sect. 2. In Sect. 4 practical considerations arising when designing a metalearning system are discussed, while open research directions are listed in Sect. 5.

2 DEFINITION

In the 1990s, the term metalearning started to appear in machine learning research, although the concept itself dates back to the mid-1970s (Rice 1976). A number of definitions of metalearning have been given, the following list cites the main review papers and books from the last decade:

1. Metalearning studies how learning systems can increase in efficiency through experience; the goal is to understand how learning itself can become flexible according to the domain or task under study (Vilalta and Drissi 2002a).

2. The primary goal of metalearning is the understanding of the interaction between the mechanism of learning and the concrete contexts in which that mechanism is applicable (Giraud-Carrier 2008).

3. Metalearning is the study of principled methods that exploit metaknowledge to obtain efficient models and solutions by adapting machine learning and data mining processes (Brazdil et al. 2009).

4. Metalearning monitors the automatic learning process itself, in the context of the learning problems it encounters, and tries to adapt its behaviour to perform better (Vanschoren 2010).

Learning systems that adapt and improve by experience are a key concept of definitions 1, 3 and 4. This in itself however does not suffice as a description, as it basically applies to all machine learning algorithms. Metalearning becomes metalearning by looking at different problems, domains, tasks or contexts or simply past experience. This aspect is inherent in all of the definitions, although somewhat disguised in definition 3 using the term *metaknowledge*instead. Metaknowledge as described by the authors stands for knowledge to be exploited from past learning tasks, which may both mean past learning tasks on the same data or using data of another problem domain. Definition 2 differs in emphasising a better comprehension of the interaction between domains and learning mechanisms, which does not necessarily imply the goal of improved learning systems, but the pursuit of a better understanding of for which tasks individual learners succeed or fail.

Rephrasing, the common ground the above definitions share, we propose to define a metalearning system as follows:

DEFINITION 1

1.A metalearning system must include a learning subsystem, which adapts with experience.

2.Experience is gained by exploiting metaknowledge extracted (a)...in a previous learning episode on a single dataset, and/or

(b)...from different domains or problems.

Furthermore, a concept often used in metalearning is that of a bias, which, in this context, refers to a set of assumptions influencing the choice of hypotheses for explaining the data. Brazdil et al. (2009) distinguishes *declarative bias* specifying the representation of the space of hypotheses (for example representing hypotheses using neural networks only) and *procedural bias*, which affects the ordering of the hypotheses (for example preferring hypothesis with smaller runtime). The bias in base-learning according to this theory is fixed, whereas metalearning tries to choose the right bias dynamically.

3 NOTIONS OF METALEARNING

Metalearning can be employed in a variety of settings, with a certain disagreement in literature about what exactly constitutes a metalearning problem. Different notions will be presented in this section while keeping an eye on the question if they can be called metalearning approaches according to Definition 1. Figure 1 groups general machine and metalearning approaches in relation to Definition 1. Each of the three circles presents a cornerstone of the definition (1: adapt with experience, 2a: meta-knowledge on same data set, 2b: meta-knowledge from different domains), the approaches are arranged into the circles and their overlapping sections depending on which parts of the definition applies to them. As an example, ensemble methods do generally work with experience gained with the same data set (definition 2a) and adapt with experience (definition 1), however, the only approach potentially applying all three parts of the definition is algorithm selection, which appears where all three circles overlap.

3.1 Ensemble methods and combinations of base-learners

Model combination is often used when several applicable algorithms for a problem are available. Instead of selecting a single algorithm for a problem, the risk of choosing the wrong one can be reduced by combining all or a subset of the available outcomes. In machine learning, advanced model combination can be facilitated by ensemble learning according to Dietterich (2000) and Yao and Islam (2008), which comprises strategies for training and combining outputs of a number of machine learning

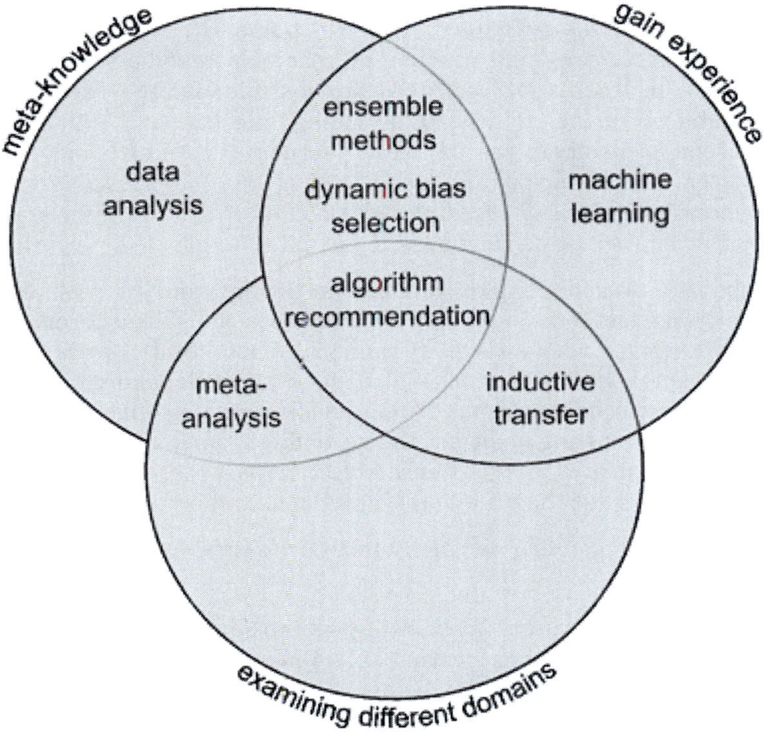

Figure 1. Notions of metalearning versus components of a metalearning system

algorithms. One often used approach of this type is resampling, leading to a number of ensemble generation techniques. Two very popular resampling-based ensemble building methods are:

- *Bagging* introduced in Breiman (1996), which denotes repeated random sampling with replacement to produce a dataset of the same size as the original training set. The dataset is subsequently used for training of a base model and the collection of models obtained in this way forms an ensemble with individual models' decisions combined typically using voting (in classification problems) or averaging (in regression problems).
- *Boosting* proposed in Freund and Schapire (1997), which manipulates the probability with which samples are drawn from the original training data, to sequentially train classifiers focusing on the 'difficult' parts of the training set. Hence each consecutive ensemble member focuses on the training examples that cannot be successfully handled

by the ensemble developed up to that point. The ensemble is usually built until a specified number of ensemble members is generated (although other stopping criteria are possible) and their decisions are combined using a weighted voting mechanism. Although the ensemble members can be 'weak' learners (i.e. models only slightly better than chance), this property must hold in the context of an increasingly difficult resampled dataset. As a result at some stage the 'weak' learner may in fact need to be quite complex and powerful.

The above approaches exploit variation in the data and are referred to as metalearning methods in Brazdil et al. (2009) and Vanschoren (2010). Bagging however does not satisfy point 2 of Definition 1, as consecutive random samples from the original dataset are independent from each other, so there is no experience from previous learning episodes involved. In the case of boosting however, the ensemble is built sequentially and it is the performance of previous ensemble members (i.e. experience gained while trying to solve the problem) that influences the sampling process.

More often, the following two approaches are considered as metalearning techniques:

- *Stacked generalisation* (or stacking) as introduced in Wolpert (1992), where a number of base learners is trained on the same dataset. Their outputs are subsequently being used for a higher level learning problem, building a model linking the outcomes of the base learners to the target value. The meta-model then produces the final target outcome.
- *Cascade generalisation* (Gama and Brazdil 2000), which works sequentially. When building a model, the output of the first base learner is appended to the original feature set and passed on to the next learner with the original target values. This process can then be repeated.

Although in these cases the information about base-learning is drawn in the sense of point 2a of Definition 1, these algorithms are limited to a single problem domain with a bias that is fixed a priori, so that they, using the definition above, do not undoubtedly qualify as metalearning methods.

3.2 Algorithm recommendation

A considerable amount of metalearning research has been devoted to the area of algorithm recommendation. In this special case of metalearning, the aspect of interest is the relationship between data characteristics[1] and algorithm performance, with the final goal of predicting an algorithm or a set of algorithms suitable for a specific problem under study. As a motivation, the fact that it is infeasible to examine all possible alternatives of algorithms in a trial and error procedure is often given along with the experts necessary if pre-selection of algorithms is to take place. This application of metalearning can thus be both useful for providing a recommendation to an end-user or automatically selecting or weighting algorithms that are most promising.

Vanschoren (2010) points out another aspect: it is not only the algorithms themselves, but different parameter settings that will naturally let performance of the same algorithm vary on different datasets. It would be possible to regard versions of the same algorithm with different parameter settings as different learning algorithms altogether, but the author advocates treating the subject and studying its effects differently. Such an approach has for example been taken in Gomes et al. (2012) and Miranda et al. (2012), where the authors discuss a hybrid metalearning and search based technique to facilitate the choice of optimal parameter values of a Support Vector Machine (SVM). In this approach, the candidate parameter settings recommended by a metalearning algorithm are used a starting point for further optimization using Tabu Search or Particle Swarm Optimization techniques, with great success. Reif et al. (2012b) investigate increasing the accuracy and decreasing runtime of a genetic algorithm for selecting learning parameters for a Support Vector Machine and a Random Forests classifier. Based on past experience on other datasets and corresponding dataset characteristics, metalearning is used to select a promising initial population for the genetic algorithm, reducing the number of iterations needed to find accurate solutions.

An interesting treatment of the above problem can also be found in Jankowski and Grabczewski (2009), where the authors propose to take into account not only the expected performance of the algorithm but also its estimated training time. In this way the algorithms can be ordered according to the estimated training complexity, which allows to produce relatively well-performing models very quickly and then look for better solutions, while the ones already trained are producing predictions. These ideas are further extended in Jankowski (2011), where some modifications of the complexity measures used are introduced.

The classic application area of algorithm selection in machine learning is classification. Smith-Miles (2008) however tries to generalise the concepts to other areas including regression, sorting, constraint satisfaction and optimisation. Metalearning for algorithm selection has also been investigated in the area of time series forecasting, where the term was first used in Prudencio and Ludermir (2004b). A comprehensive and recent treatment of the subject can be found in Wang et al. (2009) and Lemke and Gabrys (2010), where time series are clustered according to their characteristics and recommendation rules or combination weights derived with machine learning algorithms. In the area of data mining, algorithm recommendation was identified as an important research issue at the 2001 KDD conference and the 2006 KDD workshops according to Brazdil et al. (2009).

Several systems for algorithm recommendation have been implemented. Following a previous successful European commission funded project, a project named 'meta-learning assistant for providing user support in machine learning and data mining' (METAL 2002), investigated model selection and combination approaches. A tool resulting from this project is the data mining advisor (DMA), a web-based system providing rankings of classification algorithms for users as described in Giraud-Carrier (2005), which however is no longer accessible. The last updates on the METAL project webpage date back to 2004/2005, and the webpage is currently offline. There is however another project focussing on preprocessing for data mining with a metalearning approach, called MiningMart (Morik and Scholz 2004). Although the software tool is still available for download,[2] its most recent version is dated October 2006.

3.3 Dynamic bias selection

In classic algorithm recommendation, the bias depends on the available learning algorithm chosen and is not modified dynamically. Dynamic bias selection is often mentioned in relation to a continuous flow of training examples (data streams), where metalearning algorithms can be used for bias management and detecting concept drifts, as argued in Brazdil et al. (2009). In their metalearning review, Vilalta and Drissi (2002a) cite Bruha and Famili (2000) as the only example of dynamic bias selection apart from a few projects before 1992. In this contribution, a rule-based system which includes quality information about each rule, influencing the prediction process is used. The quality of a rule is updated continuously, which makes selection of the bias dynamic.

Very fast decision trees (VFDT) according to Domingos and Hulten (2000) dynamically adjust their biases with new incoming examples, with bias in this case referring to splitting tests in the tree nodes.

Another work qualifying as dynamic bias selection is the Learnt Topology Gating Artificial Neural Networks (LTGANN) by Kadlec and Gabrys (2008). In this contribution, neural networks are used for three different purposes: as base learners, as 'local experts' predicting the performance of one assigned base learner and as gating networks. The gating networks are used to discover relationships between different network topologies and their performance, influencing the topology of new networks added to the system.

3.4 Inductive transfer

A different flavour of metalearning runs under the name of 'inductive transfer', or 'learning to learn'. The emphasis here is not on investigating a preferably extensive set of problems as in algorithm selection; it is mostly used for a smaller selection of multiple related learning tasks. However, in the spirit of metalearning, knowledge from one problem domain is transferred across other domains or tasks. A learning mechanism thus accumulates experience that is supposed to improve performance through time. This notion puts a bigger focus on aspect 2 of Definition 1. Although aspect 1 still applies, most research in inductive transfer looks at a single learning mechanism and not a whole learning system.

Brazdil et al. (2009) distinguish two main forms of knowledge transfer using the example of neural networks. One is representational transfer where training of the base learner is carried out sequentially. Functional transfer refers to training several neural networks in parallel while sharing all or a part of their internal structure. A special case of functional transfer is multitask learning, where a neural network uses output nodes to accommodate for more than one task. Evgeniou et al. (2005) discusses inductive transfer in kernel methods using the example of Support Vector Machines and regularisation networks. Single-task kernel learning algorithms are extended to multi-task learning by forcing all hypotheses to share a common component along with the problem-specific deviations. Kernel learning from a different perspective is presented in Aiolli (2012): a suitable kernel matrix for a linear Hebbian classifier is learnt with improving a basic kernel by learning chains of kernel transforms. Based on the results on an initial problem set, the kernel can then be applied to related problems.

In a special issue on metalearning, Silver and Bennett (2008) present several contributions in the field of inductive transfer. Zhang et al. (2008) approaches the subject from a Bayesian perspective, using a framework including latent variables for modelling a shared structure among different learning scenarios. Silver et al. (2008) uses a neural network with extra contextual inputs for different tasks. The task hence shifts to finding a single learner for the domains, only distinguished ('indexed') by the additional inputs.

In a recent survey article Pan and Yang (2010), inductive transfer is presented as a special case of a wider category of 'transfer learning', alongside transductive and unsupervised transfer learning. Transfer learning has been defined as a mechanism ‘which aims to help improve the learning of the target predictive function in a new domain, using the knowledge gained in other domains’. Although this does not strictly adhere to Definition 1, the authors discuss relevant research issues of (1) what knowledge to transfer, (2) how to transfer it, and (3) in which situations to transfer the knowledge. This last point seems especially interesting as it can be equally well cast as in which situations not to transfer the knowledge, since it may happen that the source and destination domains are not related. In such a case the performance of the new model rather than benefiting, could suffer from the knowledge transfer (so called ‘negative transfer’) (Pan and Yang 2010).

3.5 Metalearning systems

The major usual steps of a modelling process consist of data analysis, data preprocessing, model building and a phase of interpretation and evaluation. Rather than applying metalearning in only a part of this process, latest research started taking a more holistic view by investigating metalearning frameworks and architectures.

While not yet mentioned in the seminal review of Vilalta and Drissi (2002a), Brazdil et al. (2009) give an overview of (semi-)automatic metalearning systems for data mining, only two of which target more than one aspect of the knowledge discovery process: Project CITRUS according to Wirth et al. (1997) seems to have been discontinued after a few publications in 1996 and 1997, however, it did target the complete modelling process. A bit more recently, Bernstein et al. (2005) propose the Intelligent Discovery Assistant (IDA), providing a template for ontology-driven assistants for knowledge discovery dealing with preprocessing, model building and post-processing. A realization of this idea has been materialized within the e-LICO project,[3] which investigated the concept of ‘meta-mining’—ontology and metaknowledge driven recommendation of data mining workflows as proposed in Nguyen et al. (2011) and evaluated in Nguyen et al. (2012). A somewhat related term, ‘domain-driven data mining’, also gained some recognition in the last years. The idea promotes a ubiquitous intelligence to be incorporated into the data mining process from a more methodological point of view, increasing reusability and understanding of algorithms. An overview of research done in this area and a discussion of future challenges and issues can be found in Cao (2010).

For continuous streams of data and the example of softsensors in process industry, Kadlec and Gabrys (2009) develop an architecture promoting life-long learning, where base-learners and pre- and post-processing methods can be plugged in and dynamically combined. A metalearning component optimises the system with regard to a global performance function. Jankowski and Grabczewski (2009) describe the implementation of an extensive metalearning architecture in detail, dealing with aspects like algorithm selection and parameter tuning, with the latter topic also addressed in Molina et al. (2012) for automatic tuning of parameters of decision trees.

METALA is an agent-based architecture with a metalearning component, which has been implemented as a J2EE based framework with details given in Hernansaez et al. (2004). It supports an arbitrary number of algorithms, which are managed by agents. Using metalearning on statistical and information-theoretic task properties, the best algorithm is dynamically selected, if the pool of algorithms and tasks is updated.

A distinct concept of lazy metalearning has been extensively studied in Bonissone (2012). The motivation for this work is the apparent lack of automation in model creation, which leads to bottlenecks in the models lifecycle and scalability (two other attempts at automation of model development methodology can also be found in Budka and Gabrys 2010; Budka et al. 2010). The main premise in lazy metalearning is that there is access to a large library of both local and global, pre-computed models together with their meta-information, which are perceived as commodity and which have been enabled by the recent expansion of cloud computing and crowdsourcing. The idea is to build dynamic on-demand ensembles using the models from the library as the building blocks, rather than optimizing and tuning of pre-computed models (Bonissone 2012). Since exhaustive enumeration of all possible combinations of models in a library would be intractable, a multi-step selection process based on metaknowledge, query information and correlation of errors of the ensemble members is employed. According to Bonissone (2012), a multi-criteria decision making process is followed in order to (1) create the model by pre-selecting the initial building blocks for the assembly and compiling their meta-information, which is an off-line phase, and (2) perform dynamic model assembly, where the best subset of models for a given query is selected on-line, i.e. during runtime. The process is also able to determine the weights of the ensemble models in the fusion schema, based on their local performance around the query. Some other recent approaches to development of metalearning frameworks can be found in Matijaš et al. (2013) for the problem of electricity load forecasting, Abbasi et al. (2012) for financial fraud detection or Tsai and Hsu (2013) for bankruptcy prediction.

4 CONSIDERATIONS FOR USING METALEARNING

Before applying metalearning to any problem, certain practical choices have to be made. This includes the choice of a metalearning algorithm, which can even constitute a meta-metalearning problem itself. Selection of appropriate metaknowledge and the problem of setting up and maintaining metadatabases have to be tackled, research efforts of which will be summarised in this section.

4.1 Prerequisites

As also elaborated on in Brazdil et al. (2009), metalearning can not be seen as a magic cure to machine learning problems for a variety of reasons. First of all, the extracted metafeatures need to be representative of their problem domain, otherwise, an algorithm will fail to identify similar domains. On the same note, if a problem has not been seen before, metalearning will be unable to exploit past knowledge to improve prediction performance. Performance estimation may be unreliable because of the natural limitations of estimating the true performance of the dataset. Different metafeatures might be applicable to each dataset. These issues emphasise the importance of being critical when designing a metalearning system.

4.2 Metalearning algorithms

Vanschoren (2010) gives a survey on efforts to describe properties of algorithms. The author distinguishes qualitative properties (for example type of data that can be handled, learning strategy, incrementality) and quantitative properties (bias-variance profile, runtime properties like scalability and resilience). In an effort to find an implementation and vendor-independent method for representing machine learning models, the XML-based standard PMML has been developed and gained some recognition in the last years. A detailed description of PMML can be found in Guazzelli et al. (2009).

The choice of a metalearning algorithm naturally depends on the problem and the task to be solved. Generally, traditional classification algorithms are very successful in metalearning algorithm selection and can include meta-decision trees (Todorovski and Dzeroski 2003), neural networks, Support Vector Machines or any other classification algorithms, with the *k*-Nearest Neighbours being another popular choice (Brazdil et al. 2009). Applying regression algorithms is less popular, even smaller is the number of available algorithms to learn rankings. One of the simplest ranking method involves dividing the problem space using clustering of available datasets according to a distance measure (usually k-Nearest Neighbour) of the metafeatures and using average performance ranks of the cluster into which a new problem falls (Brazdil et al. 2003). Brazdil and Soares (2000) also look at the magnitude and significance of the differences in performance. The NOEMON approach introduced by Kalousis and Theoharis (1999) builds classifiers for each pair of base forecasting methods with a ranking being generated using the classifiers' outputs. Todorovski et al. (2002) build decision trees using the positions in a ranking as target values.

4.3 Extracting metaknowledge

According to Brazdil et al. (2009), metaknowledge is derived in the course of employing a learning system. A very common form of metaknowledge is the performance of algorithms in certain problem domains, which is to be linked with characteristics of the task. Several possibilities for characterising a problem domain exist.

The most straightforward form of metaknowledge extracted from the data include statistical or information-theoretic features. For classification problems, Brazdil et al. (2009) mention the number of classes and features, ratio of examples to features, degree of correlation between features and target concept and average class entropy. For other application areas, features can look completely different, as for example summarised in Lemke et al. (2009) for the area of time series forecasting, where features can include, for example, length, seasonality, autocorrelation, standard deviation and trends of the series.

Vilalta and Drissi (2002b) propose measures for the difficulty of a classification problem that can be used as an input for metalearning. They include class variation, denoting the probability that, by means of a distance measure, any two neighbouring data records have a different class value and example cohesiveness, measuring the density of the example distribution in the training set. In a similar approach, Köpf and Iglezakis (2002) also suggest comparing observations with each other and extract 'case base properties', which assess the quality of a dataset using measures such as redundancy, for example induced by data records that are exactly the same, or incoherency, which, for example occurs if data records have the same features but different class labels.

Alternatively to looking at the data only, information of individual algorithms and how they solved the problem can be considered, for example their predicted confidence intervals. This can be achieved by using a model that is fast to build and train and investigating its properties. In this spirit, Bensusan et al. (2000) suggest building a decision tree for a classification problem and using properties of the tree such as nodes per feature, tree depth or shape to characterise it. Another approach is landmarking as proposed in Pfahringer et al. (2000), using the performance of simple algorithms to describe a problem and correlating this information with the performance of more advanced learning algorithms. A list of landmarking algorithms can be found in Vanschoren (2010). Landmarking algorithms can also be run on only a small sample of the data available, reducing the training time required. Performance information of different algorithms and learning curves generated when more data is added to the training set can then be used to select an algorithm according to Fürnkranz et al. (2002).

Empirical evaluation of different categories of metafeatures in the context of their suitability for predicting classification accuracies of a number of standard classifiers can be found in Reif et al. (2012c). The authors distinguish 5 such categories of features i.e. simple, statistical, information-theoretic, landmarking and model-based, which corresponds to the general categorization evident from the literature.

As with any learning problem, metalearning is subject to the 'curse of dimensionality' (Bishop 1995) and other issues, which can traditionally be solved by selecting a subset of relevant features. Although to the best of our knowledge, in the context of metalearning this issue has only been addressed in relatively few publications (e.g. Kalousis and Hilario 2001; Reif et al. 2012c; Todorovski et al. 2000), we assume that the reason for this is quite simple—meta-feature selection does not differ from feature selection at the base-level, and the machine learning literature is very rich in this regard (a comprehensive review of various feature selection techniques can be found in Guyon and Elisseeff 2003).

4.4 Metadatabases

As metalearning profits from knowledge obtained while looking at data from other problem domains, having sufficient datasets at one's disposal is important. Soares (2009) propose transforming existing datasets ('datasetoids') to obtain a larger number of them and show success of the approach on a metalearning post-processing problem. Vanschoren (2010) states that there is no lack of experiments being done, but datasets and information obtained often remain in 'people's heads and labs'. He proposes a framework to export experiments to specifically designed experiment databases based on an ontology for experimentation in machine learning. The resulting database can then, for example, give information on rankings of learning algorithms, the behaviour of ensemble methods, learning curve analyses and the bias-variance behaviour of algorithms. One example of such database can be The Open Experiment Database.[4] An analysis of this database together with a critical review can be found in Driessens et al. (2012).

An alternative approach to the problem of scarcity metadatabases has been presented in Reif et al. (2012a), where the authors describe a dataset generator able to produce synthetic datasets with specified values of some metafeatures (like kurtosis and skewness). Although the proposed generator appears to be at a very early stage of development, the idea is definitely very promising, also from the point of view of performing controlled experiments on datasets with specified properties. Similarly to feature selection, synthetic data generation has received a considerable attention in the recent generic machine learning and data mining literature, especially in the context of data streams and concept drift (please see Bifet et al. 2011 and references therein).

5 CONCLUSIONS AND RESEARCH CHALLENGES

Research in the area of metalearning is continuing in several directions. One area is the identification of metafeatures. As mentioned before, the vast majority of publications investigates extracting features from the dataset, mostly in the form of statistical or information theoretic measures. Landmarking is a different approach using simple base learning algorithms and their performance to describe the dataset at hand. However, Brazdil et al. (2009) argue that characteristics of learning algorithms and gaining a better understanding of their behaviour would be a valuable research avenue with very few publications, for example Vanschoren and Blockeel (2006), that exist in this area to date.

A lot of publications on metalearning focus on selecting the base-learning method that is most likely to perform well for a specific problem. Fewer publications like Brazdil et al. (2003) and Prudencio and Ludermir (2004a) consider ranking algorithms, which can be used to guide combination weights and to increase robustness of a metalearning system.

Regarding adaptivity and continuous monitoring, many approaches go further than the static traditional metalearning approaches, for example by using architectures that support life-long learning such as in Kadlec and Gabrys (2009). However, research in this area can still gò a long way further investigating continuous adjustment, rebuilding or discarding of base-learners with the help of metalearning approaches.

Users of predictive systems are faced with a difficult choice of an ever increasing number of models and techniques. Metalearning can help to reduce the amount of experimentation by providing dynamic advice in form of assistants, decrease the time that has to be spent on introducing, tuning and maintaining models and help to promote machine learning outside of an academic environment. In this context, architectures and frameworks using metalearning have been named in Sect. 3.2. However, many of these are work in progress, no longer maintained or tackle only one of the aspects in a modelling process, so this area would benefit from further research and implementations as well.

FOOTNOTES

1 In a more advanced form it is the relationship between data and algorithm characteristics, and algorithm performance.

2 http://www-ai.cs.uni-dortmund.de/MMWEB/downloads.

3 http://www.e-lico.eu/.

4 http://expdb.cs.kuleuven.be/.

ACKNOWLEDGMENTS

The research leading to these results has received funding from the European Union 7th Framework Programme (FP7/2007-2013) under grant agreement no. 251617.

REFERENCES

1. Abbasi A, Albrecht C, Vance AO, Hansen JV (2012) Metafraud: a meta-learning framework for detecting financial fraud. Manag Inf Syst Q 36(4):1293–1327
2. Aiolli F (2012) Transfer learning by kernel meta-learning. J Mach Learn Res Proc Trac 27:81–95
3. Bensusan H, Giraud-Carrier C, Kennedy C (2000) A higher-order approach to meta-learning. In: Proceedings of the ECML'2000 workshop on meta-learing: building automatic advice strategies for model selection and method combination
4. Bernstein A, Provost F, Hill S (2005) Toward intelligent assistance for a data mining process: an ontology-based approach for cost-sensitive classification. IEEE Trans Knowl Data Eng 17:503–518
5. Bifet A, Holmes G, Kirkby R, Pfahringer B (2011) Data stream mining a practical approach. Technical report. The Unibversity of Waikato
6. Biggs JB (1985) The role of meta-learning in study process. Br J Educ Psychol 55:185–212
7. Bishop C (1995) Neural networks for pattern recognition. Oxford University Press, New York

8. Bonissone PP (2012) Lazy meta-learning: creating customized model ensembles on demand. In: Advances in computational intelligence, Springer, Heidelberg pp 1–23
9. Brazdil P, Soares C, de Costa P (2003) Ranking learning algorithms: using IBL and meta-learning on accuracy and time results. Mach Learn 50(3):251–277
10. Brazdil P, Giraud-Carrier C, Soares C, Vilalta R (2009) Metalearning: applications to data mining. Springer, Berlin
11. Brazdil P, Soares C (2000) A comparison of ranking methods for classification algorithm selection. In: de Mantaras R, Plaza E (eds) Machine learning: proceedings of the 11th European conference on machine learning ECML2000, pp 63–74. Springer
12. Breiman L (1996) Bagging predictors. Mach Learn 24(2):123–140
13. Bruha I, Famili A (2000) Postprocessing in machine learning and data mining. ACM SIGKDD Explor Newslett 2:110–114
14. Budka M, Gabrys B (2010) Ridge regression ensemble for toxicity prediction. Procedia Computer Science 1(1):193–201.
15. Budka M, Gabrys B, Ravagnan E (2010) Robust predictive modelling of water pollution using biomarker data. Water Res 44(10):3294–3308.
16. Cao L (2010) Domain-driven data mining: challenges and prospects. IEEE Trans Knowle Data Eng 22:755–769
17. de Miranda P, Prudêncio R, de Carvalho A, Soares C (2012) An experimental study of the combination of meta-learning with particle swarm algorithms for svm parameter selection. In: Computational science and its applications-ICCSA, pp 562–575
18. Dietterich T (2000) Ensemble methods in machine learning. In: Proceedings of the first international workshop on multiple classifier systems, pp 1–15
19. Domingos P, Hulten G (2000) Mining high-speed data streams. In: Proceedings of the sixth ACM SIGKDD international conference on knowledge discovery and data mining, pp 71–80
20. Driessens K, Vanwinckelen G, Blockeel H (2012) Meta-learning from an experiment database. Proceedings of the Workshop on Teaching Machine Learning at the 29th International Conference on Machine Learning. Edinburgh, UK
21. Evgeniou T, Micchelli C, Pontil M (2005) Learning multiple tasks with kernel methods. J Mach Learn Res 6:615–637
22. Freund Y, Schapire RE (1997) A decision-theoretic generalization of on-line learning and an application to boosting. J Comput Syst Sci 55(1):119–139.
23. Fürnkranz J, Petrak J, Brazdil P, Soares C (2002) On the use of fast subsampling estimates for algorithm recommendation. Technical report. sterreichisches Forschungsinstitut fr Artificial Intelligence
24. Gama J, Brazdil P (2000) Cascade generalisation. Mach Learn 41(3):315–343
25. Giraud-Carrier C (2005) The data mining advisor: meta-learning at the service of practitioners. In: Proceedings of the fourth international conference on machine learning and applications, ICMLA '05, pp 113–119. IEEE Computer Society, Washington, DC, USA
26. Giraud-Carrier C (2008) Metalearning—a tutorial. In: Tutorial at the 7th international conference on machine learning and applications (ICMLA), San Diego California, USA
27. Gomes TA, Prudêncio RB, Soares C, Rossi AL, Carvalho A (2012) Combining meta-learning and search techniques to select parameters for support vector machines. Neurocomputing 75(1):3–13
28. Guazzelli A, Zeller M, Lin WC, Williams G (2009) PMML: an open standard for sharing models. R J 1(1): 60–65
29. Guyon I, Elisseeff A (2003) An introduction to variable and feature selection. J Mach Learn Res 3:1157–1182
30. Hernansaez JM, Botia JA, Skarmeta AF (2004) METALA: a J2EE technology based framework for web mining. Revista Colombiana de Computación 5(1)

31. Jankowski N (2011) Complexity measures for meta-learning and their optimality. In: Solomonoff 85th memorial. Lecture notes in computer science. Springer
32. Jankowski N, Grabczewski K (2009) Universal meta-learning architecture and algorithms. In: Duch W, Grabczewski K, Jankowski N (eds) Meta-learning in computational intelligence. Springer, Berlin
33. Kadlec P, Gabrys B (2009) Architecture for development of adaptive on-line prediction models. Memet Comput 4(1):241–269
34. Kadlec P, Gabrys B (2008) Learnt topology gating artificial neural networks. In: Proceedings of the international joint conference on neural networks (IJCNN 2008) as part of the 2008 IEEE World Congress on Computational Intelligence (WCCI'2008), pp 2605–2612
35. Kalousis A, Theoharis T (1999) NOEMON: design, implementaion and performance results of an intelligent assistant for classifier selection. Intell Data Anal 5(3):319–337
36. Kalousis A, Hilario M (2001) Feature selection for meta-learning. In: Cheung D, Williams G, Li Q (eds) Advances in knowledge discovery and data mining, pp 222–233. Springer
37. Köpf C, Iglezakis I (2002) Combination of task description strategies and case base properties for meta-learning. In: Proceedings of the 2nd international workshop on integration and collaboration aspects of data mining, decision support and meta-learning, pp 65–76
38. Lemke C, Gabrys B (2010) Meta-learning for time series forecasting and forecast combination. Neurocomputing 73(10):2006–2016
39. Lemke C, Riedel S, Gabrys B (2009) Dynamic combination of forecasts generated by diversification procedures applied to forecasting of airline cancellations. In: Proceedings of the IEEE symposium series on computational intelligence, pp 85–91
40. Matijaš M, Suykens JA, Krajcar S (2013) Load forecasting using a multivariate meta-learning system. Expert Syst Appl 40(11):4427–4437
41. Metal: meta-learning assistant for providing user support in machine learning and data mining. http://www.metal-kdd.org/ (2002)
42. Molina MDM, Romero C, Ventura S, Luna JM (2012) Meta-learning approach for automatic parameter tuning: a case study with educational datasets. In EDM, pp 180–183
43. Morik K, Scholz M (2004) The miningmart approach to knowledge discovery in databases. In: Intelligent technologies for information analysis. Springer, Heidelberg, pp 47–65
44. Nguyen P, Kalousis A, Hilario M (2011) A meta-mining infrastructure to support kd workflow optimization. In: eCML PKDD 2011, p 1
45. Nguyen P, Kalousis A, Hilario M (2012) Experimental evaluation of the e-lico meta-miner. In: 5th planning to learn workshop WS28 at ECAI 2012, p 18
46. Pan S, Yang Q (2010) A survey on transfer learning. IEEE Trans Knowl Data Eng 22(10):1345–1359
47. Pfahringer B, Bensusan H, Giraud-Carrier C (2000) Meta-learning by landmarking various learning algorithms. In: Proceedings of the seventeenth international conference on machine learning. Morgan Kaufmann, pp 743–750
48. Prudencio RB, Ludermir TB (2004a) Meta-learning approaches to selecting time series models. Neurocomputing 61:121–137
49. Prudencio R, Ludermir T (2004b) Using machine learning techniques to combine forecasting methods. In: Proceedings of the 17th Australian joint conference on artificial intelligence, pp 1122–1127
50. Reif M, Shafait F, Dengel A (2012a) Dataset generation for meta-learning. In KI-2012: Poster and Demo Track, pp 69–73
51. Reif M, Shafait F, Dengel A (2012b) Meta-learning for evolutionary parameter optimization of classifiers. Mach Learn 87:357–380.
52. Reif M, Shafait F, Goldstein M, Breuel T, Dengel A (2012c) Automatic classifier selection for non-experts. Pattern Anal Appl 1–14.

53. Rice J (1976) The algorithm selection problem. In: Rubinov M, Yovits MC (eds) Advances in computers, vol 15. Academic Press, Inc, London
54. Silver D, Bennett K (2008) Guest editor's introduction: special issue on inductive transfer learning. Mach Learn 73:215–220
55. Silver D, Poirier R, Currie D (2008) Inductive transfer with context-sensitive neural networks. Mach Learn 73(3):313–336
56. Smith-Miles KA (2008) Cross-disciplinary perspectives on meta-learning for algorithm selection. ACM Comput Surv 41(1):1–25
57. Soares C (2009) Uci++: improved support for algorithm selection using datasetoids. In: Theeramunkong T, Kijsirikul B, Cercone N, Ho T-B (eds) Advances in knowledge discovery and data mining. Springer, Berlin
58. Todorovski L, Blockeel H, Dzeroski S (2002) Ranking with predictive clustering trees. In: Elomaa T, Mannila H, Toivonen H (eds) Proceedings of the 13th European conference on machine learning. Springer, pp 444–455
59. Todorovski L, Brazdil P, Soares C (2000) Report on the experiments with feature selection in meta-level learning. In: Proceedings of the PKDD-00 workshop on data mining, decision support, meta-learning and ILP: Forum for Practical Problem Presentation and Prospective Solutions. Citeseer
60. Todorovski L, Džeroski S (2003) Combining classifiers with meta decision trees. Mach Learn 50(3):223–249
61. Tsai CF, Hsu YF (2013) A meta-learning framework for bankruptcy prediction. J Forecast 32(2):167–179
62. Vanschoren J (2010) Understanding machine learning performance with experiment databases. PhD thesis, Arenberg Doctoral School of Science, Engineering & Technology, Katholieke Universiteit Leuven
63. Vanschoren J, Blockeel H (2006) Towards understanding learning behavior. In: Proceedings of the annual machine learning conference of Belgium and the Netherlands, pp 89–96
64. Vilalta R, Drissi Y (2002a) A perspective view and survey of meta-learning. Artif Intell Rev 18:77–95
65. Vilalta R, Drissi Y (2002b) A characterization of difficult problems in classification. In: Proceedings of the 6th European conference on principles and practice of knowledge discovery in databases, Helsinki, Finland
66. Wang X, Smith-Miles K, Hyndman R (2009) Rule induction for forecasting method selection: meta-learning the characteristics of univariate time series. Neurocomputing 72:2581–2594
67. Wirth R, Shearer C, Grimmer U, Reinartz T, Schloesser J, Breitner C, Engels R, Lindner G (1997) Towards process-oriented tool support for kdd. In: Proceedings of the 1st European symposium on principles of data mining and knowledge discovery, Trondheim, Norway
68. Wolpert D (1992) Stacked generalization. Neural Netw 5:241–259
69. Yao X, Islam M (2008) Evolving artificial neural network ensembles. IEEE Comput Intell Mag 3:31–42
70. Zhang J, Ghahramani Z, Yang Y (2008) Flexible latent variable models for multi-task learning. Mach Learn 73(3):221–242

Index